ROYAL FAMILY

ROYAL FAMILY

Years of Transition

THEO ARONSON

John Murray

To the memory of
PRINCESS ALICE
Countess of Athlone
who lived through most of it

© Theo Aronson 1983

First published 1983
by John Murray (Publishers) Ltd.
50 Albemarle Street, London WIX 4BD

First published in the USA by
John Murray through Salem House 1984

This paperback edition
first published by Salem House, 1986

Printed in Great Britain
by Butler & Tanner, Frome

British Library Cataloguing in Publication Data
Aronson, Theo
Royal family.
1. Windsor, House of   2. Great Britain —
Kings and rulers
I. Title
941.082′092′2   DA28.1
ISBN 0-88162-251-6

Contents

Illustrations

ACKNOWLEDGEMENTS

Nos. 1, 2, 3, 4, 5, 6, 8, 11, 12, 16, 19, 22, 25 Reproduced by gracious
permission of Her Majesty The Queen; Nos. 7, 15, 17 from *George V* by
John Gore published by John Murray; Nos. 9, 14, 29 Central Press
Photos; No. 10 Sir Hill Child; No. 13 from a snapshot by the Duke of
York; No. 17 Vandyk Studios; Nos. 18, 32 Camera Press; Nos. 20, 24,
31, 33, 36 Popperfoto; No. 21 from *Our Princesses* by Lisa Sheridan
published by John Murray; No. 23 *Cape Times*, Cape Town; No. 26
from *The Queen and her Children* by Lisa Sheridan published by John
Murray; No. 27 from *Playtime at Royal Lodge* by Lisa Sheridan pub-
lished by John Murray; No. 28 from *The Queen and Princess Anne* by
Lisa Sheridan published by John Murray; Nos. 30, 34, 35 BBC
Copyright Photographs

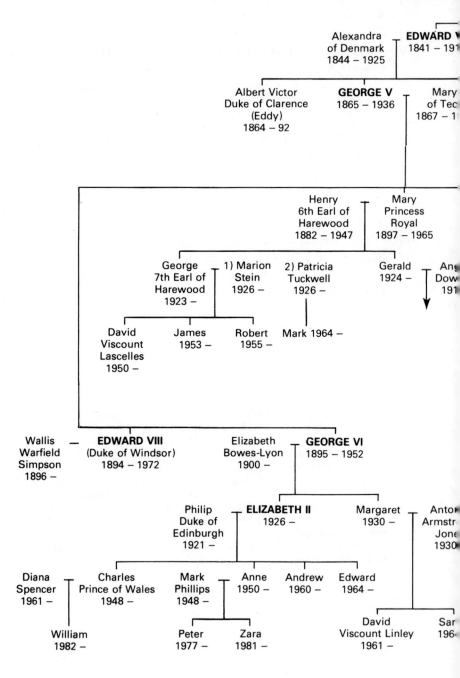

VICTORIA
1819 – 190

Alexandra
of Denmark
1844 – 1925

EDWARD V
1841 – 191

Albert Victor
Duke of Clarence
(Eddy)
1864 – 92

GEORGE V
1865 – 1936

Mary
of Tec
1867 – 1

Henry
6th Earl of
Harewood
1882 – 1947

Mary
Princess
Royal
1897 – 1965

George
7th Earl of
Harewood
1923 –

1) Marion
Stein
1926 –

2) Patricia
Tuckwell
1926 –

Gerald
1924 –

An
Dow
191

David
Viscount
Lascelles
1950 –

James
1953 –

Robert
1955 –

Mark 1964 –

Wallis
Warfield
Simpson
1896 –

EDWARD VIII
(Duke of Windsor)
1894 – 1972

Elizabeth
Bowes-Lyon
1900 –

GEORGE VI
1895 – 1952

Philip
Duke of
Edinburgh
1921 –

ELIZABETH II
1926 –

Margaret
1930 –

Anto
Armstr
Jone
1930

Diana
Spencer
1961 –

Charles
Prince of Wales
1948 –

Mark
Phillips
1948 –

Anne
1950 –

Andrew
1960 –

Edward
1964 –

William
1982 –

Peter
1977 –

Zara
1981 –

David
Viscount Linley
1961 –

Sar
196

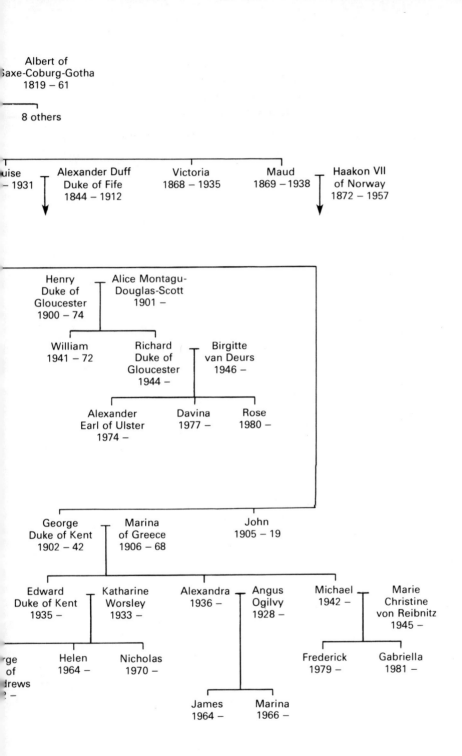

'A family on the throne is an interesting idea also. It brings down the pride of sovereignty to the level of petty life.'

WALTER BAGEHOT, *The English Constitution*

Author's Note

THE TITLE of this book indicates its scope. It is a family saga: the story of the British royal family from the death of Queen Victoria to the present day. Rather than an account of the reigns of the five monarchs during the twentieth century, this is a study of their dynasty. The focus, throughout, is on the family; on both its major and its minor members. The great political, economic and military events of the period are dealt with only where they affect directly the lives of the various members of the reigning House. It is a book which deals with personalities first, politics second. It is biography rather than history.

At the same time – and although the book is not a study of the institution of monarchy – it traces the way in which the royal family has adjusted to changing times in order, not only to survive, but to enhance its position in national life. It is an account of a royal House in a state of continuous transition.

This book has been inspired, to a certain extent, by my many conversations with the late Princess Alice, Countess of Athlone. Last surviving grand-daughter of Queen Victoria and great-aunt of Queen Elizabeth II, Princess Alice (1883–1981) lived through almost all of the period covered by this book. I am deeply indebted to the many memories that she shared with me. I am also fortunate in having been granted audiences by members of three more generations of the royal family. They are, in order of birth rather than precedence, HM Queen Elizabeth The Queen Mother, HRH The Princess Margaret, and HRH The Prince of Wales. I am very grateful for their help and interest; the information which they have so kindly given me has proved invaluable. I must also thank HRH Princess Alice, Duchess of Gloucester, for allowing members of the staff of HRH the late Duke of Gloucester to speak to me.

I am indebted to the various members of the royal households who have generously answered my questions, supplied me with information, checked certain passages or assisted me in other ways. However, the book is in no sense authorised and none of the household members is responsible for any errors that I might have made or any opinions that I have expressed. Their names, together with the names of those many others who, to a greater or lesser extent, have given me assistance, are listed here in alphabetical order.

They are Captain Alastair Aird, Comptroller to Queen Elizabeth The Queen Mother; Lieutenant-Colonel Sir Simon Bland, Private Secretary to the Duke of Gloucester; Mr André Bothner; Mr Victor Chapman, Assistant Press Secretary to the Queen; Miss Frances Dimond, Curator of the Royal Photographic Collection; Miss Mary Goldie, Secretary to the late Princess Alice, Countess of Athlone; Mr John Haslam, Assistant Press Secretary to the Queen; the Rt Hon. the Earl of Harewood; Lieutenant-Colonel Sir John Johnston, Comptroller the Lord Chamberlain's Office; Miss Joan Lascelles, Lady-in-waiting to the late Princess Alice, Countess of Athlone; the Countess of Longford; Sir Robin Mackworth-Young, the Queen's Librarian; Major The Lord Napier and Ettrick, Private Secretary to Princess Margaret; Mr Anthony Sampson; Mr Michael Shea, Press Secretary to the Queen; Mr William Tallon; Group Captain Peter Townsend; Mr Hugo Vickers; Mr Christopher Warwick; Mr Robert R. Webb; Mr R.I.B. Webster.

As always, Mr Brian Roberts has given me expert advice and assistance.

I am grateful to the staffs of the British Library, the Newspaper Library at Colindale, the Bath Reference Library and the Bristol Reference Library. I should also like to give a special word of thanks to Mrs S. Bane and the staff of the Frome Library for their always cheerful and efficient service.

I must acknowledge the gracious permission of Her Majesty The Queen to republish certain material of which she owns the copyright. Although I have listed all books consulted in the Bibliography, I am particularly indebted to the following books: *King George the Fifth* by Harold Nicolson, *Queen Mary* by James Pope-Hennessy, *Edward VIII* by Frances Donaldson, *King George VI* by Sir John Wheeler-Bennett, *Queen Alexandra* by Georgina Battiscombe, *A King's Story* by the Duke of Windsor, *The Royal House of Windsor* by Elizabeth Longford and *The British Monarchy in the Twentieth Century* by Philip Howard.

Prologue

The Queen is Dead

QUEEN VICTORIA, who knew her own mind on most subjects, certainly knew it on the subject of dying. She once described as 'very dreadful' the convention of having a host of relations crowded around a death-bed. 'That,' she wrote emphatically, 'I shall insist is never the case if I am dying. It is awful.'[1]

It was just as well then, that the eighty-one-year-old Queen was barely conscious during the last hours of her life. For not only her little bedroom but all the rooms of Osborne House on the Isle of Wight, in which she lay dying, were packed. 'The whole house,' wrote one despairing equerry, 'was crammed, and even all the houses in the vicinity were full.'[2] The fact that the Queen gradually weakened over a period of six days, from 17 January 1901, meant that there had been time to summon most of the members of her immediate family. Even her ebullient grandson, Kaiser Wilhelm II, had felt compelled to abandon the Berlin celebrations marking the 200th anniversary of his dynasty to invite himself to her bedside.

So it was under the anxious gaze, not only of her many relations but of assorted clergymen, doctors and nurses that Queen Victoria approached death. Her dying, as one of her sons-in-law so graphically put it, was 'like a great three-decker ship sinking. She kept on rallying and then sinking.'[3] Towards four o'clock on 22 January, with the short winter's day drawing to a close, a bulletin was finally issued to say that the Queen was dying. And it was just after half-past-six, noted another of the Queen's grandsons, the Duke of York, afterwards King George V, when 'our beloved Queen and Grand-mama, one of the greatest women that ever lived, passed peacefully away.'[4]

The announcement of Queen Victoria's death to the crowd outside the gates finally shattered the silence which had characterised Osborne House, not only during the Queen's final illness but throughout her long widow-hood. Scrambling into their carriages or flinging themselves across their bicycles, a mob of journalists went racing down the hill towards the post office in East Cowes, yelling as they went, 'The Queen is dead!' The scene, noted one tight-lipped equerry, was 'disgraceful'.[5]

Queen Victoria, who dearly loved a funeral, had given precise instructions regarding hers. Two detailed memoranda left her successor in no doubt as to how she wished to be buried. Among its myriad directions were two somewhat unusual ones: there were to be no undertakers and her funeral was to be a white, not a black, one. What cause was there for gloom? Was the Queen not about to be reunited with her adored Prince Albert?

For it was, of course, beside her long-dead husband that the Queen was to be buried. Side by side, for all eternity, Victoria and Albert were to lie beneath the golden-starred dome of the flamboyant mausoleum which she had built at Frogmore, in Windsor Home Park. In the course of the two weeks following her death, the new monarch, King Edward VII, was obliged to dedicate himself to the carrying out of his Mama's last wishes.

With undertakers forbidden, the Kaiser measured the Queen for her coffin. Only extreme firmness on the part of the Queen's sons, the new King and Prince Arthur, Duke of Connaught, prevented the officious Kaiser from lifting her into it. This, her sons maintained stoutly, was their duty. Prince Arthur was amazed to find that his formidable mother weighed so little. Before closing the coffin, they scattered her white dress with flowers and covered her face with her wedding veil.

For ten days the body lay in state in Osborne House. Not until 1 February did Queen Victoria set out on her final journey. Her coffin was to be taken from the Isle of Wight to London, where it would be borne in procession through the streets, and then to Windsor, for final burial in the Mausoleum. In all, the funeral was to be spread over four days.

Those four days in the winter of 1901 provided one of the great climactic spectacles of the age. In years to come children, who had watched the Queen's coffin pass by, could tell their children, and grandchildren, that they had seen Queen Victoria's funeral. A blend of family and national mourning, of grief and *bravura*, of solemnity and splendour, the funeral was one of the great set-pieces in the saga of the British Empire.

Friday the first day of February was one of brilliant winter sunshine: 'Queen's Weather' indeed. In deference to Queen Victoria's wishes, a white pall – fringed with gold and decorated with a cloth-of-gold cross – covered the coffin. White, or rather cream-coloured, horses were to draw the gun carriage. As the coffin was trundled down the hill from Osborne House to Trinity Pier, it was followed by a galaxy of royal mourners: the bearded men brilliantly uniformed, the women in black, heavily veiled.

At Trinity Pier, the remains were placed on the quarter-deck of the smallest of the royal yachts, *Alberta*. Often, on hot summer days, the Queen had crossed from the mainland or gone cruising in the *Alberta*. Now, as far as the eye could see, lay a vast fleet of battleships and cruisers, waiting to salute the little yacht as it carried Queen Victoria on her last voyage. Preceded by a flotilla of destroyers and trailing a convoy of other yachts, including the *Victoria and Albert* in which sailed King Edward and Queen Alexandra, the *Alberta* steamed for ten miles between two lines of towering battleships. With the guns of each ship thudding out as she passed slowly by, the air was loud with the thunder of these salutes and dense with drifting smoke. In the blaze of an early winter sunset, the *Alberta* reached Portsmouth.

On the following morning, a special funeral train carried the coffin to London. One of the Queen's ladies, peeping through the drawn blinds of her carriage, noticed that people were kneeling in homage beside the track, and railway officials reported that for the entire, eighty-mile journey, the train appeared to be travelling 'through an endless line of black-clad, bareheaded people.'[6]

The procession through the streets of London, from Victoria to Paddington stations, marked the climax of this momentous royal progress. The capital, which the Queen had come to dislike so much, was crowded. Every rooftop, every balcony, every pavement along the funeral route was packed with silent, soberly-dressed mourners. According to the Queen's wishes, buildings and lamp standards were draped in purple and white, and Handel's Funeral March was replaced by the less melancholy sounds of Beethoven and Chopin. Whenever there was a pause in the music, one could hear the tramp of feet and the scrunching of wheels.

Amidst a sea of brilliantly uniformed troops and drawn by eight cream-coloured horses rolled the gun-carriage. On it lay the coffin, its white pall half hidden by a Royal Standard, and the Crown, Sceptre and Garter insignia gleaming in the pale winter light. Behind came a cavalcade of emperors, kings and princes, superbly uniformed in tunics of red and blue and green and purple. On and on they came, plumes fluttering, orders flashing, gold braid glinting, top-boots gleaming, the jingle of accoutrements enlivening the steady clip–clop of their horses' hooves. Behind them came the state carriages in which drove the new Queen and a bevy of princesses, their faces smudgy behind their mourning veils. It took over two-and-a-half hours for the cortège to reach Paddington.

At Windsor station there occurred the one serious hitch of the day. When the coffin was placed on the gun-carriage for its journey up the hill to Windsor Castle, the horses began to plunge so violently that they broke part of the harness. When the head of the procession, unaware of the problem behind, moved forward, the gun-carriage remained where it was. Here was a dilemma. 'I had contemplated all sorts of things going wrong,' moaned Frederick Ponsonby, the late Queen's assistant private secretary, in charge of all arrangements at Windsor, 'but such a mishap had never occurred to me.'[7]

While frantic artillery officers tried to organise some sort of makeshift solution, Ponsonby reported to the King. If the traces could not be repaired, suggested Prince Louis of Battenberg, perhaps the Naval Guard of Honour could drag the gun-carriage through the streets? Although the King was agreeable to this, the artillery team was not. In fact, they were furious. After a hissed exchange, one of them hurried off to complain to the King about Ponsonby's plan.

'Right or wrong,' snapped the notoriously impatient King Edward, 'let him manage everything; we shall never get on if there are two people giving contradictory orders.'[8]

So, while the artillery officers looked on sullenly, the sailors prepared to pull the gun-carriage along the route. The delay had lasted for fifteen minutes; to poor Ponsonby, it seemed like two hours. But, in the end, the sight of a team of straw-hatted sailors manhandling the gun-carriage up to St George's Chapel added yet another highly memorable feature to the Queen's funeral.

What with the delay at the station and the intense cold in St George's Chapel, it was as well that the funeral service was short. When it was over, the body was taken to the adjoining Albert Memorial Chapel where it was to lie over Sunday.

It was not until the afternoon of Monday 4 February 1901 that Queen Victoria was finally buried in the Mausoleum. On this occasion all was perfection. The final service was brief, with the congregation confined to the members of the various royal families and their suites. Only after the last mourner had trailed home was the Queen's coffin sealed finally into the granite sarcophagus, and her white marble statue by Marochetti, which had been kept in readiness for decades, placed beside that of the Prince Consort.

To the members of Queen Victoria's family, driving back to Windsor Castle in the wintry gloom, it must have seemed as though they had left more than just the Queen's body among the Italianate splendours of the Mausoleum. For them, no less than for the rest of her subjects, Queen Victoria's death marked the end of an era. Few could remember a time when that small, plump, imperious figure in the white widow's cap had not presided over their destinies. The future, for their country and their dynasty, suddenly seemed uncertain, almost menacing.

'What a calamity!' wrote Queen Victoria's cousin, the British-born Grand Duchess of Mecklenburg-Strelitz, 'anxiety terrible as to what poor England will have to go through *now*! God have mercy on us all!'[9] And in her diary, the Queen's eldest daughter, the German Empress Frederick, wrote of the world's desolation without 'sweet darling beloved Mama; the best of mothers and the greatest of Queens, our centre and help and support – all seems a blank, a terrible awful dream.'[10]

'The thought of England without the Queen is dreadful, even to think of,' lamented Princess May, the future Queen Mary. 'God help us all!'[11]

However, there was one member of the royal family who did not share the general sense of despair and foreboding. And this was the most important member of all – King Edward VII. On at least one occasion during the four-day-long pageant of Queen Victoria's funeral he had given unmistakable proof of his faith in his own, and his country's, future.

In the course of that dramatic crossing of the Solent on 1 February, the King, aboard his yacht *Victoria and Albert*, had noticed that the Royal Standard was flying at half-mast. Sending for the captain, he demanded an explanation.

'The Queen is dead, Sir,' was the captain's bemused reply.

'The King of England lives,'[12] countered His Majesty.

With that, the Standard was hoisted to the top of the mainmast.

Part One

KING EDWARD VII
1901 – 1910

1

The Inheritance

ON THE DEATH of Queen Victoria, King Edward VII inherited what his mother used to call, with sublime self-confidence, 'the greatest position there is'.[1] And so, in a way, it was. Queen Victoria had been far and away the world's most important monarch: the Doyenne of Sovereigns, the Grandmama of Europe, the Great White Queen. Not only had she been related to almost every royal family on the Continent but her direct descendants occupied, or would one day occupy, ten European thrones. As Queen Victoria had been Europe's Grandmama, so King Edward VII became Europe's Uncle.

Enhancing this position of dynastic pre-eminence was the fact that the British monarch reigned over the world's most powerful nation. The nineteenth century had been very much Britain's century: Queen Victoria's reign had coincided with, indeed it had come to symbolise, a period of unparalleled national magnificence. Vigorous, wealthy, assured, uninhibitedly expansionist and unashamedly imperialistic, Britain ruled, not only the waves, but the greatest Empire that the world had ever known. Its monarch, in addition to being Europe's leading sovereign, was the world's greatest imperial figure, holding sway over something like a quarter of the earth's population and a quarter of the earth's land mass. London, that vast metropolis, was looked upon as the heart of the world. To many an Eastern or African subject, the British monarch, enthroned in this fabled, far-away capital, seemed more like a deity than a mortal. Queen Victoria, a Burmese official once explained to a member of King Edward's household, had been the embodiment of the 'Great Idea'. His countrymen believed that at 'a great solemn religious ceremony the sacred Attributes of the Great White Queen would be transferred to her son, the King, and received by him in the most solemn religious rite which his country can provide.'[2]

Even Kaiser Wilhelm II, no mean potentate himself and not much given to praising rival monarchs, felt compelled to express his sense of wonder at Queen Victoria's legacy. 'What a magnificent realm she has left you,' he exclaimed to his Uncle Bertie, 'and what a fine position in the world!'[3]

But this realm, in the century that lay ahead, was to become increasingly less magnificent. The twentieth century has seen a steady decline in British power and prestige. Abroad, the country has divested itself of its great empire; at home it has suffered economic decline. From a position of world dominance, it has shrunk to the status of just another European country. Yet, paradoxically, the 'fine position' of the British Sovereign has remained almost intact. Queen Elizabeth II, in the last quarter of the twentieth century, is as familiar an image in today's world as her great-great-grandmother Queen Victoria was in hers. Pictured in crown and ermine-trimmed robes, the Queen is arguably the most recognisable figure on earth. In some ways, hers remains 'the greatest position there is'.

Through all the years of industrial and imperial decline, through all the political and social upheaval, the British monarchy, and the British royal family, has retained, not only its position but its romantic appeal. Its popularity has remained almost constant. The royal family – with its triumphs and its heartbreaks, its brilliance and its mediocrity, its strengths and its vulnerabilities, all manifesting themselves in generation after generation – is still a glittering centre of national life.

'It is a family,' writes Anthony Sampson in *The Changing Anatomy of Britain*, 'that has become more expert than any other institution in one critical art – the art of survival. In spite of the magic and sentimentality that surrounds it, the family has to be more realistic and less fooled by its mystique than its admirers; the view from the palace is like looking at Britain from backstage, where sets, floodlights and props are seen as part of the illusion. While most other monarchies have been toppled or cut down, the British royal family have developed skills which have enabled them so far to survive each new republican threat. And the more Britain worries about her own survival and future, the more her other institutions become discredited, the more interesting and reassuring is the continuity of the institution that pre-dates them all.'[4]

Industrious, resilient and adaptable, the royal family has weathered many political and domestic storms. From them, it has emerged as firmly entrenched as ever. It has been, all in all, an extraordinary success story.

King Edward VII, the first of this line of twentieth-century monarchs, certainly looked like a king. He was in his sixtieth year at the time of his accession, and he gave off an unmistakable air of majesty. Impressively corpulent, imposingly bearded, and always impeccably dressed, King Edward never, even in the most brilliant company, looked like anything other than the most important person present. His carriage was erect, his bearing dignified, and his manners perfect. On state occasions he wore his robes or one of his many uniforms with great authority; in private, in his superbly cut suits and stylishly tilted hats he looked no less regal. His pale, bulbous eyes could become steely if confronted with some lapse of taste in dress or behaviour. His whole demeanour was one of self-assurance, of natural command.

Yet Edward VII was a far from forbidding personality. There was nothing ponderous or unapproachable about him. On the contrary, his manner was relaxed and charming. It would be impossible, claims Arthur Ponsonby, brother of Queen Victoria's assistant private secretary, to overestimate the King's charm: it 'amounted to genius'. 'It is not too much to say that . . . it *made* him. With a dignified presence, a fine profile and a courtly manner, he never missed saying a word to the humblest visitor, attendant or obscure official . . . no one was left out. The appropriate remark, the telling serious phrase and the amusing joke, accompanied by a gurgling laugh to a close friend, made all delighted even to watch him.'[5]

Nor was the King's charm affected or synthetic, part of the royal stock-in-trade. It sprang from a genuine desire to please, a genuine goodness of heart. 'Warm human kindness,' wrote one Foreign Secretary, 'was the very substance of the man.'[6] His politeness towards servants, his kindness towards strangers, his loyalty and generosity towards his friends, made him universally popular and greatly loved.

Perhaps most important of all, Edward VII had a taste for kingship. Or, at least, for its showier aspects. He loved all forms of public ceremonial – the pageantry of openings of parliament, the swagger of military parades, the braggadocio of state visits, the flash and glitter of receptions, balls and banquets. His manner, on these public occasions, could not be faulted. 'He was not a lover of the stage to no purpose,' wrote one observer, 'and like a highly trained actor, he studied and learnt the importance of mien and deportment, of entrance and exit, of clear and regulated diction and other details . . .'[7] With the beautiful, elegant and apparently ageless Queen Alexandra by his side, King Edward VII seemed the very quintessence of majesty.

That was one side of the coin. There was another, distinctly less satisfactory side. 'We shall not pretend,' lectured *The Times* on King Edward's accession, 'that there is nothing in his long career which those who respect and admire him would not wish otherwise.'[8] There was, in truth, a great deal. Edward VII, for all the stateliness of his appearance and manner, ascended the throne with a reputation for being little more than a self-indulgent roué. 'It was all *façade*, the most engaging, decorative but quite misleading *façade*,' wrote Arthur Ponsonby. 'There was practically nothing behind it.'[9]

To appreciate Ponsonby's harsh judgement, one has to go back to Edward VII's years as Prince of Wales. From babyhood, almost, he was the victim of his parents' high-minded ambitions. Queen Victoria and Prince Albert had decided that if the monarchy was to keep afloat on the rising tide of

democracy, the future King would have to be moulded into a model constitutional monarch. He would have to be a man who, by his breadth of vision,
unimpeachable morals and high sense of duty, would win the love and
respect of his people. His character would have to be an amalgam of all the
virtues; he would have to be fashioned into what the approving Bishop of
Oxford describes as 'the most perfect man'.[10]

How was this to be achieved? How best, in short, was the heir to the throne
to be educated? It was a question that was to reassert itself throughout the
coming century; in fact, not until the children of Queen Elizabeth II were sent
away to public schools was it solved satisfactorily. Any notion of sending
their son away would have horrified Queen Victoria and her husband. For
one thing, the Prince's rank would not have allowed for such relatively
egalitarian mixing; for another, it would have meant fraternisation with the
sons of the aristocracy – a class whom the Queen, and still more Prince
Albert, generally regarded as shockingly dissolute.

So the Prince was kept at home and subjected to a rigorous course of
training. He was isolated from boys of his own age, surrounded by a team of
upright, well-educated and serious-minded tutors, kept at his lessons from
morning to night and bombarded with information and advice – usually in
the form of ponderous memoranda – from his well-meaning father. Even his
periods of relaxation were watched over by a keen and usually disapproving
eye. These circumscribed years in the schoolroom were followed by hardly
less circumscribed spells at first Oxford and then Cambridge, where he lived
out of College, carefully cocooned from the more rakish elements of undergraduate life.

These years of educational force-feeding had no beneficial effects whatsoever. The Prince of Wales simply did not have the ability or application to
cope with so intensive a course of instruction. He emerged from it as an
affectionate, amiable, fun-loving but far from intellectual young man whose
main interest, sighed his disappointed father, was clothes. But the failure of
his parents' grandiose scheme did have one useful long-term effect: never
again have royal children been subjected to such a joyless, concentrated,
self-consciously elevating pattern of education. The schooling of Edward
VII's descendants might sometimes have been unimaginative but it has never
again been so serious-minded. If the experiment did not solve the problem of
how the heir to the throne should be educated, it at least demonstrated how he
should not be educated.

His nightmarish education behind him, the Prince of Wales set about
enjoying himself. During the long period between the Prince Consort's death
in 1861 and his own accession forty years later, the Prince established himself
as the most fashionable figure in European society. He established himself,
though, as very little else. Having no intellectual curiosity and distrusting
clever people, he confined his circle to the beautiful, the amusing, the worldly

and the rich. He seldom read a book and merely skimmed through news-papers. His taste, if not exactly vulgar, was philistine: he knew very little, and cared even less, about art and music. His interests were racing, yachting, shooting, gambling, eating out and fornicating. Every so often he would be involved in yet another scandal or would embark on yet another liaison. Equally at home in London, Paris, the South of France or some Continental spa, he was renowned for his zest, his gregariousness and his hedonism. As his disapproving mother used only too often to point out, the Prince of Wales lived purely for pleasure.

Nor was the Prince simply an easy-going and warm-hearted *bon viveur*. To those who knew him more intimately, he was not nearly as resolved a personality as he seemed. Away from the café table or the roulette wheel, he was moody, restless and quickly bored. Lacking in application, nothing could hold his interest long; without mental resources, he could not bear to be alone; very conscious of his royal dignity, he was easily affronted. It needed very little to make him lose his temper. For the most part he would lose it over trivia: a decoration incorrectly worn, a hitch in an arrangement, a delay in some ceremony. This quickly-flaring temper was to be passed on to his descendants.

The main trouble, of course, was that he did not have enough to do. His problem was the problem of all heirs apparent, or at least of those whose sovereign-parent lives an average, or longer than average, life-span. This problem, claimed his private secretary, Sir Francis Knollys, was inherent in the very nature of sovereignty. 'It has been the same thing with Heirs Apparent from time immemorial,' he commented, 'and I fear will continue to be so as long as there are monarchies.'[11] Knollys's prediction was to be borne out during the century which lay ahead. It remains relevant today.

What, in fact, is the position of an heir-apparent? The question has never been satisfactorily answered. 'There is no set-out role for me,' Edward VII's great-great-grandson, Prince Charles, was to complain over a century later. 'It depends entirely on what I make of it . . . I'm really rather an awkward problem.'[12] The carrying out of public engagements is not enough to engage the mind and fill the days of a man of even average intelligence; yet it is not really practical for him to be involved in the day-to-day business of the monarch – the meetings with ministers, the reading of Cabinet papers, despatches and telegrams, and the signing of documents.

Edward VII's heir, the future George V, was happy enough playing a fairly negative role. In turn, George V tried to solve the problem by sending his son, the far more mercurial Prince of Wales and future Edward VIII, on a series of world tours, as a sort of roving royal ambassador. George VI, called un-expectedly to the throne on the abdication of his brother, Edward VIII, had no training in the constitutional process whatsoever, and his early death meant that his daughter, Elizabeth II, did not experience the usual problems of an heir-in-waiting. In Queen Elizabeth's son, Prince Charles, the question seems to have been resolved as satisfactorily as is possible. As well as applying himself, with hitherto unknown diligence, to various national concerns, the Prince of Wales has been allowed – if not actually to work side-by-side with his mother – to have access to certain Cabinet papers and to talk to politicians of all persuasions.

Yet even he has complained of 'the limitations of his position, as a man with little formal authority of his own, the junior member of the "family firm" while important decisions are all taken by his mother the monarch.'[13]

This perennial problem, as it affected Queen Victoria's heir, was certainly intensified by her own intransigent attitude. That the Prince of Wales was denied any worthwhile occupation was entirely the Queen's doing. In the first place, she had a very poor opinion of her son's abilities; in the second, she was determined that no one should play the political role that her husband had once done. Considering the Prince to be irresponsible, immature and indiscreet, the Queen refused to involve him in the workings of the monarchy. She neither confided in him nor consulted him. He must see nothing, she would warn her ministers, of a confidential nature. Not until the Prince of Wales was over fifty was he allowed access to state papers. Only the social and ceremonial duties of the monarchy – the laying of foundation stones, the opening of schools, the presentation of awards, the inauguration of exhibitions, the making of speeches, the welcoming of foreign dignitaries – would she entrust to him. These he carried out with great aplomb. But about the more serious business of government the Queen endeavoured to keep him in complete ignorance.

The first to claim that the Devil would find work for idle hands, Queen Victoria resolutely kept her son's hands idle.

All in all, it was an impossible situation. Because the Queen considered her heir to be so frivolous, she refused to give him any employment: because he was given no employment, he became more frivolous still. A man of sound common sense, considerable diplomatic gifts, exceptional vitality and great panache, the Prince of Wales might have been of real service to his mother and his country.

There are several ways in which his talents could have been put to use. After all, the Queen had agreed to Disraeli's scheme whereby her youngest son, Prince Leopold, became her assistant and adviser in her dealings with foreign affairs. The Prince of Wales, with his knowledge of Europe, would have done the job equally well. The responsibility might have accustomed him to concentrated desk work, a skill which he never acquired. On the other hand, Gladstone's suggestion – that the Prince of Wales become Viceroy of Ireland – she turned down flat. To her prime minister's argument that such a post would give the Prince some employment, the monarchy a boost and Ireland a treat, the Queen made the crushing reply that this was a 'family' matter. In short, it was none of Gladstone's business.

The Prince's own suggestion, that he be 'successively attached' to each Office in Whitehall 'where he would learn the habits of business in general, and the work of the Department in particular',[14] was given equally short shrift by the Queen. She would not hear of it.

'As it was,' wrote one member of his household, 'the best years of a man's life, say from forty to sixty were to a great extent wasted, and King Edward came to the throne with a vitality already debilitated by the years of waiting.'[15]

It was no wonder then, that there was such widespread doubt, in court and government circles, as to the new King's ability to fulfil his great destiny. The King himself seems to have had momentary misgivings. On the night before he travelled to Osborne and Queen Victoria's death-bed, he spent a quiet evening in the home of Agnes Keyser, one of those undemanding middle-aged women friends in whose company he always found great solace. As the two of them sat in front of the blazing fire after supper, the Prince admitted to Agnes Keyser how 'utterly unworthy he felt to succeed the Queen.'[16]

He need not have worried. Queen Victoria, whenever faced with yet another proposal by some well-intentioned politican for the granting to the Prince of Wales some meaningful employment, had always maintained that no artificially created position could imbue her heir with the necessary sense of responsibility. Only when he was forced to assume full responsibility – when, in other words, he became King – would he tackle the job seriously.

In this, as in so much else, Queen Victoria was right. The Prince of Wales was to be an admirable King. But he was to be one in his own way.

How much better a king he would have been had his mother allowed him to play a more active part in the constitutional process, one does not know. But at least his years of waiting would have been more fulfilled and a pattern would have been set for the involvement of future Princes of Wales in the workings of the Crown. Who knows how different the career of Edward VII's grandson, the future Edward VIII, might have been had he been drawn into the business of the monarchy?

Be that as it may, King Edward VII was not one to waste time on vain regrets. He had far too much to do. During the last forty years of her life, Queen Victoria had become a remote, almost mythical figure, passing only occasionally through the streets of the capital like some precious ikon or rare madonna. Edward VII was determined to change this. If the monarchy hoped to maintain its relevance, it would have to become more accessible. So with characteristic gusto, the new King set about transforming the monarchy: bringing it out of the long twilight of Queen Victoria's widowhood into the glare and clamour of the twentieth century.

*

What, precisely, were the position and powers of the monarchy at the time of King Edward VII's accession?

Resoundingly proclaimed as the 'Most High, Most Mighty, and Most Excellent Monarch, Edward VII, by the Grace of God, of the United Kingdom of Great Britain and Ireland and of the British Dominions beyond the Seas, King, Defender of the Faith, Emperor of India', the new King appeared all-powerful. And so, on the face of it, he was. A hereditary monarch was, and remains, the supreme national figure – the personification of the state, the symbol of continuity, the emblem of permanence, the fount of all honours, the magnet of all loyalties, the embodiment of both the past history and the present identity of the nation. The sovereign is impartial, standing high above class or party political factions. While governments come and go, and statesmen rise and fall, the Crown remains, transcending the hurly-burly of everyday political life.

Nor does a hereditary monarch need to justify his or her existence as Head of State, as a president or a dictator might have to do. 'It is the happiness of a King of England,' explained *The Times* some years before Edward VII's accession, 'that we require from him no brilliant military achievement, no extraordinary diplomatic legerdemain, no startling effects, no scenic pomp, no histrionic dexterity. He may be great without the possession of extra-ordinary talents, and famous without dazzling exploits . . .'[17] What was wanted from the monarchy was a sense of stability.

Yet the status of the monarch was nothing like as masterful as it might have appeared to the uninformed observer. By the time of Edward VII's accession, the British Sovereign had no personal power. Nor had the monarchy had any for something like two centuries. Political power was vested in parliament: the king was a constitutional monarch, bound to follow the advice of his ministers. In theory he could summon, prorogue and dissolve parliament, dismiss or appoint prime ministers, confer titles and honours, grant pardons, and withhold his assent from bills passed by parliament. In practice, he could do none of these things. A monarch could not flout the advice tendered to him by his Cabinet no matter how personally unpalatable that advice might be. In short, a monarch reigned but did not rule.

The only time that the 'Royal Prerogative' – that is, the monarch's personal power – can be exercised is in the choosing of a successor to a prime minister who has died or resigned. Even then the sovereign must be certain that the choice of prime minister will command the support of his or her party. Most twentieth-century sovereigns, from Edward VII to Elizabeth II, have had occasion to exercise this function. If, at some stage in the future, the two-party system is replaced by coalition governments, the Queen and her successors may well have to exercise this right more frequently.

But if the monarch has no effective powers, he has considerable influence. Not only is he the representative of a revered and much-loved institution but, in the course of a long reign, a monarch is bound to gain considerable knowledge and expertise. 'It is impossible,' wrote Sir William Anson in his study of the British constitution, 'to be constantly consulted and concerned for years together in matters of great moment without acquiring experience if not wisdom.'[18] A sovereign such as Queen Elizabeth II, who has reigned for over thirty years, not unnaturally develops into a person of unquestioned influence and authority.

That other great analyst of the constitution, Walter Bagehot, once defined the monarchy's three rights as the right to be consulted, the right to encourage and the right to warn. His classic definition remains valid to this day.

But such constitutional niceties in the art of kingship are appreciated by a relatively limited circle. The man in the street is far more concerned with the public and domestic, as opposed to the constitutional, role of the monarch. And not only of the monarch, but of his family. 'A family on the throne . . .' as Bagehot put it, brings down 'the pride of sovereignty'[19] to the level of everyday life. Women are fifty times more interested, he maintained, in a royal marriage than a royal ministry. And so are a great many men. The royal family makes the state more intelligible and more interesting; it sets standards of social and moral behaviour; it invests the Crown with a reassuringly normal image. For as, during Queen Victoria's long reign, the middle classes became progressively more powerful, so did they begin to look to the royal family as the mirror of middle-class propriety. 'Let him set his people an example of domestic life,'[20] begged *The Times*, a shade wistfully, of the future King Edward VII; and, more and more, as the twentieth century progressed, did the public come to expect the monarch and his family to be dignified, hard-working and well-behaved. They had to be exemplars of all the virtues.

But at the same time as regarding the royal family as a somewhat grander, more romantic version of the average British family, the public remains attracted by the monarchy's more mystical element. Long after the theory of the Divine Right of Kings had been discredited, the idea of a hereditary monarchy, of a dynasty of kings stretching back for a thousand years, retained its hold on the imagination of the people. 'A powerful, magnetic appeal exudes from the monarch,' wrote one analyst as late as 1948, 'to which men are somehow peacefully and affectionately drawn.'[21] The monarchy fulfilled some atavistic need to worship. It would continue to flourish, claimed Bagehot, because it appealed to 'diffuse feeling'[22] rather than to reason. That was why it was important that its mystique be upheld. 'Its mystery,' he continued, 'is its life. We must not let daylight upon magic.'[23]

It is with the continuous adjustment of this finely tuned balance between daylight and magic that the British royal family has been very largely concerned during the course of the twentieth century.

*

King Edward VII lost very little time in making his mark. On the morning
after Queen Victoria's death, he travelled up to London from Osborne to
attend a meeting of the Privy Council at St James's Palace. After the Archbishop of Canterbury had administered the traditional oath of Sovereignty,
the King said a few words. Speaking without notes (itself an innovation) he
announced that he wanted to be known as Edward VII.

There was more to this simple announcement than met the eye or, in this
case, the ear. At one stroke the King was making a threefold bid for independence: he was flouting one of his parents' dearest wishes, he was
playing down his German ancestry, and he was establishing himself as an
unequivocally British king.

The Prince of Wales had been christened Albert Edward and it was as King
Albert Edward that Queen Victoria had intended him to be crowned. She had
made this abundantly clear. If it had been a matter of a choice between the two
names, she would have plumped for Albert. The Queen, whose mother had
been Princess Victoria of Saxe-Coburg and whose husband had been Prince
Albert of Saxe-Coburg, had expressed the wish that after her death the
British royal House be known as 'the *Coburg* line, like formerly the Plan-
tagenet, the Tudor . . . the Stuart and the Brunswicks.'[24] Her dream was of a
Coburg dynasty of British kings, bearing the name Albert, as they had once
borne the names Henry, Charles and George.

But it was her son, the first Coburg King of England, who shattered that
dream. After an obligatory reference to his late father's greatness, goodness
and wisdom, the new King made it clear to the Privy Council that he had no
intention of perpetuating his name. The name Edward, said the King, had
been borne by six of his ancestors. It was, as Lord Melbourne had claimed at
the time of the Prince's christening, 'a good English appellation.'[25] And it was
as a good English king that Edward VII wanted to be thought of.

In truth, there was hardly a drop of English blood in his veins. He was
almost all German. His father's ancestry was wholly German. His mother's
ancestry was hardly less so. Her mother, Princess Victoria of Saxe-Coburg,
had been German: her father, the Duke of Kent, had been the son of the
Hanoverian King George III of England and of his equally German queen,
Charlotte of Mecklenburg-Strelitz. All six sponsors at the Prince's christening had been either German-born or of German descent. 'The German
element,' declared Queen Victoria at one stage, should be 'cherished and kept
up in our beloved home.'[26]

It was Edward VII who first began to dilute the dynasty's 'German
element'. For one thing, he had married a Danish, instead of the customary
German, bride. For another, he felt no real affinity for his German relations or
the German people. And, perhaps most important of all, he seemed the very
personification of Englishness. King Edward VII was undoubtedly the most
English monarch since the Tudors.

If the King's rejection of the name Albert had been a symbolic gesture, his changes in the style of monarchy were far more tangible. He had, says Sir Lionel Cust, whom the King had appointed to the post of Gentleman Usher, 'a great idea of the importance attached to Court ceremonial and was glad of any opportunity of renewing some great ceremony which had been allowed to fall into desuetude during the long years of Queen Victoria's reign.'[27] These revived ceremonies were planned, says Cust, with extraordinary precision. 'He loved detail, no matter how small.'[28]

The Queen's sedate afternoon 'Drawing Rooms' were replaced by sumptuous evening 'Presentation Courts'. The State Concerts were discontinued and a special military band brought in to play at balls and banquets. The levées, the investitures, the Garter ceremony, the Opening of Parliament were all conducted with hitherto undreamed-of splendour. 'I shall never forget the first sight of the House of Lords on this occasion,' wrote one spectator at the King's first Opening of Parliament, 'with the mass of peers in scarlet robes, the bench of Bishops in their lawn sleeves, the Diplomatic Corps in their uniforms and decorations, and the lines of ladies in Court dress and jewels in the gallery above. I remember being much moved by the beauty of Queen Alexandra's slim figure . . . The King was also truly majestic in his attitude.'[29]

Unlike Queen Victoria, who had confined herself to her more remote houses for the greater part of the year, King Edward kept himself in the public eye. He was forever on the move; he was permanently on show. It was clearly his belief that if the monarchy was to survive in a more democratic age, its members must be seen to be playing their part in national life. That such activity happened to suit his temperament was all to the good.

The Times admitted that, as Prince of Wales, the King had 'never failed in his duty to the throne and the nation,'[30] and he certainly did not fail now. His public appearances were not confined to the great state ceremonies. King Edward VII carried out – admittedly in a more formal and stately fashion – the public tasks which are still being carried out today: receiving state visitors, opening or visiting hospitals, schools, museums and art galleries, attending garden parties, receiving deputations, awarding prizes, inaugurating here, commemorating there, inspecting somewhere else. He cut ribbons, he planted trees, he shook hands, he made speeches. So familiar was he with the form of greeting and response appropriate to each civic function that on one occasion, when a petrified public official forgot his lines, the King gave him – one line at a time – a speech of official welcome which the poor man repeated 'in the fashion of one taking an oath'.[31]

From the very start the King established an unvarying annual routine. The New Year found him playing host to a stream of guests at his country house, Sandringham, in Norfolk. At the end of January he moved to Buckingham Palace for the Opening of Parliament. Every night in February was given over to dinner parties or after-theatre supper parties. March and April he spent abroad: in Paris, at Biarritz or cruising the Mediterranean. In May he returned to London for the Season. This entailed an unending succession of dinners, balls, receptions and presentation parties. In June he moved to Windsor Castle for the racing at Epsom and Ascot. In July he spent a few days in some provincial centre, and throughout the summer he would be the star attraction at those mammoth, cripplingly expensive weekend house parties. The end of July found him at the Goodwood races; the beginning of August at Cowes. There followed a month at Marienbad for a much-needed cure. By September he was back in England for the Doncaster races; in October he was at Balmoral. During November and December he moved between Buckingham Palace, Windsor and Sandringham, always spending Christmas and New Year – again among a throng of guests – at Sandringham.

With the exception of his various Continental jaunts, the pattern set by Edward VII was to be followed by the royal family during the coming century.

Another of the King's changes was in the composition of the court. His effect 'upon the remains of the Victorians was . . .' claims one of his grandsons, 'much as if a Viennese hussar had suddenly burst into an English vicarage.'[32] All traces of his mother's dowdy regime were swept away. Those ladies-in-waiting in half-mourning were pensioned off; the Indian servants were shipped back home; all the household departments were systematically reorganised. Instead of simply taking over Queen Victoria's staff, the new King filled the main posts in his new household with long-standing associates.

Chief of these was his private secretary, Sir Francis Knollys, who had already served him for over thirty years. The value of a good private secretary to a monarch can hardly be overestimated and Queen Victoria and her descendants have been singularly fortunate in the men who have served them in this capacity. Without exception, they have been men of tact, sagacity and authority. To help Knollys there were two assistant private secretaries. These three men arranged engagements, attended to correspondence, wrote speeches and, most important of all, formed a direct link between the monarch and the government.

Another of the King's main appointees was his Keeper of the Privy Purse or Treasurer. As well as organising the King's finances, the Keeper of the Privy Purse was responsible for administering the running costs of the various royal homes. Equally important was the Master of the Royal Household. As supreme major-domo of all the palaces, his manifold duties included control of the army of stewards, housekeepers, pages, footmen and housemaids.

Two more important posts were the Comptroller in the Lord Chamberlain's department, responsible, among many other things, for most court

1 'The quintessence of majesty': Edward VII and Queen Alexandra at the Opening of Parliament, 1910

2 Edward VII with his son Prince George and his grandson Prince Edward (David)
aboard the royal yacht, 1908

ceremonial; and the Crown or Chief Equerry whose duty it was to organise all royal transport: coachmen, grooms, horses, carriages and motor cars.

For all practical, as opposed to purely ceremonial, purposes, these five posts or departments were the most important in the royal household. Around them swirled a sea of lesser functionaries: lords-in-waiting, gentlemen ushers, equerries, extra equerries and, for the Queen, a mistress of the robes, ladies of the bedchamber and women of the bedchamber. Chosen for their efficiency, amiability and urbanity, these people surrounding the royal family could always be relied upon to act with the utmost discretion. Their loyalty to the sovereign, and his trust in them, was absolute. By their vigilance and adroitness, they could give an air of assurance and importance to the most timid and lack-lustre of princes.

This was why members of the same family tended to serve the monarchy for generation after generation. Through different reigns, the same names crop up. Lord Stamfordham, for instance, was in turn assistant private secretary and secretary to Queen Victoria, then private secretary to her grandson the Duke of York, remaining with him throughout his years as Prince of Wales and as King. His grandson, now Lord Adeane, was assistant private secretary to George VI and later private secretary to Queen Elizabeth II. His son, the Hon. Edward Adeane, is private secretary to Prince Charles.

Standing, in some ways, even closer to the sovereign, were the personal servants: those valets or footmen or ladies' maids in whose company the monarch can relax completely. Edward VII's valet, Chandler, acted as a sort of whipping boy, uncomplainingly bearing the brunt of his master's explosive temper, knowing that, once the storm had passed, the King would be his usual genial self. The present Queen enjoys a less turbulent relationship with her long-serving dresser, Miss Margaret ('Bobo') MacDonald. Miss MacDonald is said to be one of the Queen's most trusted confidantes.

As King Edward VII moved from palace to palace, or even from country to country, so was he attended by a team of secretaries, equerries, police officers and personal servants. Each royal home had, of course, its own resident staff.

Except for the fact that the staff, in every department throughout the royal homes, has been drastically reduced, and that press secretaries are now essential members of the organisation, the structure of Queen Elizabeth's household remains very similar to that of Edward VII's.

Where Edward VII differed from the sovereigns who came after him was in his establishment of an inner court of half-a-dozen close friends. All were typical of the sort of worldly person he preferred; each could advise him on, and help him with, a different facet of his public and private lives, whether political, diplomatic, military, financial or amatory.

All in all, the King's circle differed radically from that of his mother. Wealth and wit were more important to him than birth. He ignored, says one of his biographers, 'the subtle gradations in rank in a manner singularly distressing to those anxious to maintain them.'[33] His circle was made up of financiers, actors, men-about-town, Americans and Jews; he was particularly fond of rich, self-made men.

Not all his guests approved of this social mixture. The young Tsarevich, afterwards Tsar Nicholas II, visiting Sandringham, wrote home to St Petersburg to complain about the composition of the houseparty. 'Most of them were horse dealers, among others a Baron Hirsch . . . I tried to keep away as much as I could, and not to talk.'[34]

Had Tsar Nicholas II talked a little more and so developed some of his Uncle Bertie's tolerant attitudes, he might well have helped bridge the chasm between the Crown and the Russian people.

The King's tolerance extended far beyond court circles. Just as he was prepared to befriend people regardless of their backgrounds or beliefs, so did he feel that it was a sovereign's duty to transcend sectional interests and to represent all his subjects. Once, after he had sent a concerned message to the ailing socialist, Keir Hardie, someone congratulated the King on his astuteness. He was furious. 'You don't understand me!' thundered His Majesty, 'I am the King of ALL the people!'[35]

The atmosphere at court was relaxed. In spite of his punctiliousness, Edward VII liked to see people enjoying themselves. On the very day of Queen Victoria's final interment, Frederick Ponsonby was astonished to find Kaiser Wilhelm II, King Leopold II of the Belgians and King Carlos of Portugal, all smoking cigarettes in the corridor at Windsor. This, he says, 'shocked me as, of course, no one had ever smoked there before.'[36] And Marie Mallet, at one time lady-in-waiting to Queen Victoria, found that she was the only member of the company assembled after dinner at Windsor who was not smoking. Even the late Queen's daughter, Princess Louise, was merrily puffing away.

The royal dinner table at which, in Queen Victoria's day, no one had ever spoken above a whisper, was completely transformed. The company was more brilliantly dressed, the talk more animated. 'The White Drawing Room where for the last two years of her life the Queen sat after dinner,' laments Marie Mallet, 'is now used as a card room, one table being for whist and the other for bridge, the King delights in the last-named game and plays every evening, Sundays included, till between 1 and 2 in the morning.'[37]

The King adopted any new invention with the greatest possible enthusiasm. Whereas Queen Victoria had dismissed motor cars as 'horrible machines',[38] King Edward was a dedicated motorist. The faster he was driven, the better he liked it. His fleet of claret-coloured cars was one of his greatest joys. 'A very good run, Stamper, a very good run indeed!'[39] he would say to his 'motor engineer' after some trouble-free drive. And he was just as ready to embrace all other modern conveniences and amusements: electric light, the telephone, the electophone (whereby one could be connected by headphone to any major London theatre) and the cinematograph. The King was to have the satisfaction of seeing the film of his Coronation procession.

Yet ensuring Edward VII's popularity even more than his frequent public appearances or his enlightened social attitudes was the fact that, in his person, there seemed symbolised the 'Merrie England' of so many of his subjects' imaginings. With his love of sport – of hunting, shooting and especially racing – he fulfilled admirably the public conception of an English country gentleman. For in spite of his cosmopolitanism, Edward VII was firmly rooted in the country. Sandringham, with its pigs, its horses, its crops and its game, was his favourite home. And it was to be the favourite home of the kings who came after him. To this day, the royal family are country people. With very few exceptions, they would all have echoed Queen Elizabeth II's admission that she would have been happiest living her life in the country, among her dogs and her horses.

And, of course, King Edward VII was interested in sport of another kind: his transformation from Prince of Wales to King made not a scrap of difference to his licentiousness. 'He was never happier,' claims Frederick Ponsonby, 'than in the company of pretty women.'[40] And the pretty woman in whose company he now spent most of his time was the warm-hearted and voluptuous Mrs George Keppel. Having first met her in 1898, when she was twenty-nine, the King remained devoted to her for the rest of his life. As the Pompadour of the Edwardian court, Alice Keppel became a figure of considerable importance. So sensible, so good-natured, so discreet, she could always be relied upon to exercise a good influence on the King.

The King might have been devoted to Alice Keppel but he could not be faithful to her. The casual affairs – in private supper rooms, in secluded arbours, in country house bedrooms – continued. And it is said that on one occasion a ship's officer, passing the porthole of the royal cabin, heard his Sovereign's guttural voice saying, 'Stop calling me Sir and put another cushion under your back.'[41]

Nor was the King's interest in women purely sexual. He was one of those men to whom feminine company, in or out of bed, was essential. 'What tiresome evenings we shall have,'[42] he sighed when Queen Alexandra's mourning for the death of her father obliged him to hold a series of men-only dinner parties. He hated sitting with the men over the port at the end of a meal; he would far rather be talking to some well-dressed, sharp-witted beauty. 'That he had many "affairs" is indisputable,' says Margot Asquith, 'but there were a great many other women in his life from whom all he sought was diverting companionship.'[43]

Although the general public were well aware of their monarch's convivial lifestyle, detailed knowledge of his sexual escapades was largely confined to the upper classes. And, by their unwritten code of conduct, they never gossiped about it to those whom they considered their inferiors. The press, who did know, remained reverentially silent on the subject. As Prince of Wales, the King had often been attacked and lampooned in the popular press for his hedonism but once he became King such criticism ceased. It is true, however, that on his accession *Reynolds Newspaper* went so far as to complain that the life of the new Sovereign had not been 'altogether edifying',[44] and that *The Times* imagined that there must have been occasions when the King had prayed 'Lead us not into temptation' with 'a feeling akin to hopelessness'.[45]

But even *Reynolds*, who had criticised him so mercilessly in the past, was soon admitting that 'he has made himself exceedingly popular during the brief time he has been sovereign; and we have no hesitation in expressing our belief that it is his desire to do his best to please all ranks in the community.'[46] There were certainly no press revelations about the Sovereign's libertine habits; nor was he ever hounded by reporters or photographers. He was able to enjoy those after-theatre suppers and outings *à deux* with a lack of publicity that would be unthinkable today.

'I recall with wonder and appreciation,' wrote the King's grandson, the future King Edward VIII, of his Edwardian youth, 'the ease with which we were able to move about in public places. The thought occurs to me that one of the most inconvenient developments since the days of my boyhood has been the disappearance of privacy. I grew up before the age of the flash camera, when newspapers still employed large staffs of artists to depict the daily events with pen sketches. This artistic form of illustration seldom achieved the harsh or cruel accuracy of the camera lens, nor could it match the volume and mobility of the present-day photographer dogging his often unsuspecting victim or waiting in ambush for a candid shot. Because our likenesses seldom appeared in the press, we were not often recognised in the street; when we were, the salutation would be a friendly wave of the hand or, in the case of a courtier or family friend, a polite lifting of the hat.'[47]

Even as late as the mid-1930s, it was possible for Edward VIII to come to an agreement with Fleet Street whereby the press promised to keep silent on the subject of his love affair with Wallis Simpson. The concluding of such an agreement is impossible to imagine in present-day Fleet Street. Even the Palace's most impassioned pleas for some measure of privacy are largely ignored. Indeed, the gradual invasion of privacy by an ever more relentless and inventive press is arguably the most trying development with which the royal family has had to contend during the course of the twentieth century.

Who, these days, can blame Prince Philip for his heartfelt exclamation when a photographer, having scrambled up a pole to get a better picture, crashed down onto the crowd below. 'I hope to God,' said the Prince, 'that he breaks his bloody neck.'[48]

*

Queen Alexandra, too, was setting quite a different style from her pre-decessor. Indeed, few women could have been less like the old Queen than the new. Where Queen Victoria was plump, plain, dowdy, serious-minded and awe-inspiring, Queen Alexandra was slender, stylish, warm-hearted and feather-brained. Where the Widow of Windsor had spent almost forty years in gloomy seclusion, the Queen of Hearts was the most glittering figure in the Edwardian cavalcade.

At fifty-six, Queen Alexandra still looked astonishingly young. A member of the late Queen Victoria's household, seeing her for the first time as Queen, referred to her as 'the lovely young Queen – for beautiful and young she looks beyond comprehension.'[49] Another described her as looking 'too pretty – about thirty-five apparently.'[50]

In some ways, Queen Alexandra was like a wax flower: ageless, unruffled, exquisite. She had all the bandbox elegance of a dressmaker's dummy. Always fashionably dressed, the Queen had by now perfected the style which best suited her: her high-dressed hair would be crowned by an elaborate toque; her slender neck encircled by a boned collar or row of pearls; her waist laced to its narrowest. It is she who first popularised those hydrangea shades which, for three generations, were to be almost obligatory summer fashion for British queens and princesses. In the winter she wore violet or cherry red lavishly trimmed with fur; at night she appeared in shimmering creations of white or silver or gold. Although no subsequent British queen has been as elegantly dressed as Queen Alexandra, they have all followed her example of perfecting, and remaining faithful to, a personal style.

To her position, Queen Alexandra brought all the grace, charm and vivacity that had for so long been missing from court and national life. She brought also a reputation for boundless sympathy with those in suffering. Decorative, dignified, socially accomplished and immensely popular, Queen Alexandra made the perfect Edwardian Queen.

Yet her lot was never an easy one. Born on 1 December 1844, the eldest daughter of the unpretentious prince who had become King Christian IX of Denmark, Princess Alexandra found herself married to one of the most difficult of husbands. Once the first flush of marriage had worn off, the Prince and Princess of Wales found that they had very few interests in common. Granted that they were both unintellectual, immature, fond of clothes and free with money, each preferred a very different way of life. He revelled in the glamour and bustle of society; she lived for her home and her family. He was a man of the world; she, for all her social talents and matchless chic, was an artless creature. He was a notorious philanderer; she was virtuous. Indeed, in some ways, Princess Alexandra never really outgrew the cosy, simple, clannish atmosphere of her Danish childhood.

But the shortcomings were not all on the husband's side. The Princess of Wales, despite the sweetness of her nature, had serious defects of character;

defects which she could ill afford as the wife of a man like the Prince of Wales. Where he was methodical, she was haphazard, unpunctual and badly organised. She had the sort of scatter-brained charm which can be maddening to live with. And whereas a clever, or at least a sharp-witted woman might have held his interest, her lack of brain made her boring. On public occasions she gave an impression of radiance: in private conversation she never shone.

To the Princess's various mental and temperamental failings was added a physical one. She had inherited a disease known as otosclerosis, which made her increasingly deaf. With each passing year she was less able to follow conversation. As a result, she tended to avoid people whose voices she found difficult to hear. This cut her off, more and more, not only from the company in which her husband delighted, but from her husband himself. He found it easier not to talk than to shout. It cut her off, too, from any opportunity of hearing others' opinions. The Princess of Wales had never been much of a reader; now she could no longer learn by listening to intelligent conversation. Her deafness strengthened considerably that barrier between herself and the realities of life.

And just as the Prince of Wales's lack of meaningful activity encouraged him to lead an ever more frenetic social life, so did Princess Alexandra's deafness force her away from that life towards those things which she anyway liked best: her children, her horses, her dogs and her homes. It was within the family circle that she was happiest; here her emotions were most deeply involved. Her five children – two sons and three daughters – were raised in the most indulgent fashion. So childlike herself, she was determined that they should have as carefree and extended a childhood as possible. To her children, Princess Alexandra was 'darling Motherdear', a gay, spontaneous, impractical and warm-hearted companion, hardly more grown-up than themselves.

It was Princess Alexandra who brought into the royal family many of the traits that are there still: a taste for domesticity, a brand of knock-about humour, a penchant for parlour games. She also introduced an engaging naturalness; a naturalness that was to be augmented by later brides such as Lady Elizabeth Bowes-Lyon, consort of King George VI, and Lady Diana Spencer, now Princess of Wales.

But not even the possessive Princess Alexandra could ensure that her children remained under the parental roof forever. By the time that she became Queen, only one of them – her second daughter, Princess Victoria – was still by her side. The eldest son, the strangely apathetic Prince Albert Victor, had died in 1892 at the age of twenty-eight. On his death the second son, Prince George, not only took his dead brother's place as Heir Presumptive but also became engaged to his fiancée, Princess May of Teck. They were married the following year. Of the three daughters – known, irreverently, as 'the Whispering Wales girls' – the eldest, Princess Louise, married the Duke of Fife, and the youngest, Princess Maud, married her cousin, Prince Charles of Denmark. This left only Princess Victoria at home. And this was how Queen Alexandra meant to keep it.

Another of Queen Alexandra's failings was her unpunctuality. It drove her impatient and punctilious husband to near distraction. 'Keep him waiting: it will do him good,'[51] she would exclaim airily as the King sat drumming his fat fingers in the next room. She was invariably twenty or thirty minutes late for dinner. In fact, on the sole occasion that she was five minutes early, astonished pages and footmen had to go scurrying all over the palace to assemble the guests and members of the household. The Opening of Parliament was once delayed because the Queen had broken a string of pearls. On another occasion, five deputations were kept waiting for almost two-and-a-half hours because the Queen, in spite of repeated messages, simply did not appear. 'Finally,' says one witness, 'at ten minutes to one the Queen came down looking lovely and quite unconcerned. All she said was, "Am I late?" The King swallowed and walked gravely out of the room.'[52]

Not until the reign of King George VI would punctuality, that 'prerogative of princes', again become an issue in the royal family. His Queen – now Queen Elizabeth the Queen Mother – is celebrated for her unpunctuality. It is said to be her only fault. Her unpunctuality stems, not from a lack of concern but from too much concern: a determination to give pleasure by spending more time than allowed for in chatting to members of the public.

Edward VII's attitude towards his distrait Queen was that of 'a Christian martyr'.[53] By now he knew that it was useless to remonstrate with her. With the passing years Queen Alexandra had become not only more unpunctual but more obstinate and self-centred. She would not 'even in a small matter like this,' the King once grumbled to his secretary when the Queen refused to keep an appointment to visit the Royal Academy, 'sacrifice the pleasure it gives her to remain at Sandringham twenty-four hours longer. I am powerless to do anything.'[54]

The King's almost saintly forbearance with his Queen's capriciousness might well have been in appreciation of her no less saintly tolerance of his marital infidelities. Reckoning that jealousy was a worse sin than licentiousness, Queen Alexandra usually turned a blind eye to his many affairs. She always behaved graciously towards his mistresses. Indeed, she had every reason to be gracious towards his latest mistress, Alice Keppel. For Mrs Keppel never flaunted herself nor took advantage of her favoured position. Indeed, she and her friends were entertained by Queen Alexandra.

The Queen was confident that no one could usurp her position; or even her place in her husband's heart. 'After all,' she is reported to have said after the King's death, 'he always loved me the best.'[55]

*

All King Edward VII's changes to the style, tone and presentation of the monarchy were there for everyone to see. What remained to be seen was how well the King was applying himself to the less public aspects of his job. A sovereign, even a constitutional sovereign, remains very much part of the executive machinery of government. Retaining those rights to be consulted, to encourage and to warn, the monarch must be in a position to do so; in other words, he or she must be kept fully informed on every aspect of national political life.

Copies of all important government papers arrive, throughout the day, in red despatch boxes for the sovereign's attention. No matter where the sovereign may be – at a desk in Buckingham Palace, in a study at Sandringham or Windsor or Balmoral, aboard the royal yacht – the 'boxes' must be attended to. They contain Cabinet minutes, memoranda, despatches and reports; departmental statements, letters from ministers, ambassadors and governors-general; documents for signature, programmes of forthcoming functions, suggestions for engagements, petitions, appeals, messages and protests. All these have to be read and digested; many of them demand written replies; some of them must be commented on and discussed with the sovereign's secretaries or responsible ministers. With the exception of Edward VIII, all twentieth-century British monarchs have applied themselves assiduously to the 'boxes'; the present Queen is said to spend at least three hours every day on them.

There are then those audiences to be granted to distinguished visitors – churchmen, military figures, holders of various offices at home and abroad, foreign ambassadors. There are Privy Council meetings – short, formal meetings of Privy Councillors (usually cabinet ministers) at which formal effect is given to proclamations issued by the Crown. There are regular meetings, usually with the prime minister but sometimes with other political figures, or with any individual minister with whom the sovereign might like to discuss some subject. It is in the course of these meetings that a monarch is able to bring his or her influence to bear.

The extent of this influence varies from sovereign to sovereign and from minister to minister. Quite naturally, some monarchs feel more at ease with one or other of their prime ministers and, in turn, some prime ministers feel more receptive to their sovereign's opinions. Towards the end of his reign, with twenty-five years of experience behind him, George V was apt to assume that his opinion was the only one that mattered. On one occasion he received the Foreign Secretary, Anthony Eden, in an unfamiliar room in the Palace, close to a bandstand outside. The King assured Eden that the band would not start playing until he gave the word. He then launched into a catalogue of subjects which he wished the Foreign Secretary to discuss at a forthcoming conference in Geneva. Just as Eden, in the few minutes that remained, opened his mouth to express his own opinion, the King rang a small handbell. 'Tell the bandmaster that he can start playing now,' he instructed the page. 'You were saying . . .'[56]

Those who doubted Edward VII's ability to apply himself to this more routine business of kingship were soon proved wrong. At his first Privy Council, the King announced that he was 'fully determined to be a constitutional sovereign in the strictest sense of the word.'[57] But he made it clear that he was not prepared to be anything less. The King was very conscious of his remaining rights: any minister who ignored those rights soon earned the rough edge of his Sovereign's tongue. He insisted on being kept fully informed on every matter, great or small. He was not going to be a 'mere signing machine'.[58]

It was true that the King had very little experience of, or taste for, desk work; that he was irked by formal meetings and bored by routine discussion. But such was his sense of duty that he always forced himself to do whatever was necessary. And when he was particularly interested in a subject, such as the strengthening of the armed services, he gave it his undivided attention. His relationship with his prime ministers, too, depended on how interesting or sympathetic he found them rather than on their politics. With his first two Conservative prime ministers, Lord Salisbury and Arthur Balfour, the King never felt especially at ease; with Sir Henry Campbell-Bannerman, whose Liberal party gained power in 1905, he was much more relaxed. But his relationship with Campbell-Bannerman's Liberal successor, Henry Herbert Asquith, was less happy. Their formal meetings could be unproductive.

In any case, Edward VII always preferred meeting his prime ministers socially; much more could be achieved, he reckoned, over a balloon of after-dinner brandy. Another method of doing business was through his own 'cabinet' – that small circle of friends, including Mrs Keppel, whom he knew well and could trust implicitly. Ministers, in turn, would consult the members of this little court if they needed to gain the Sovereign's ear.

So before very long, the King established himself as a monarch of considerable stature. His years as Prince of Wales had not been entirely devoted, it was now revealed, to pleasure. He had developed a string of valuable political contacts both in Britain and on the Continent. As a result he had been better informed, and far more discreet, than his mother had imagined. That *éminence grise* and leading member of the King's circle, Lord Esher, claimed that 'from 1864 the Prince knew everything that was going on, and very often more than the Queen herself.'[59] Denied the opportunity of putting this knowledge to use at the time, the King was now able to put it to very good use indeed. Those who had been ready to dismiss Edward VII as little more than a good showman with a strong personal magnetism and a certain talent for diplomacy, were to find themselves greatly impressed by his grasp of affairs.

Asquith, despite his lack of rapport with his Sovereign, once paid handsome tribute to the King's sense of royal responsibility. 'His duty to the State always came first. There was no better man of business; no man by whom the humdrum obligations – punctuality, method, preciseness and economy of time and speech – were more keenly recognised and more severely practised . . . Wherever he was, whatever may have been his pre-occupations, in the transactions of the State there were never any arrears, never any trace of confusion, and never a moment of avoidable delay.'[60]

And Sir Henry Campbell-Bannerman was surprised to find that the King was 'a wise and excellent' monarch, confounding 'in the most amazing way all those who doubted his qualities as a ruler and his capacity as a statesman.'[61]

2

The Dynasty

OF ALL ROYAL CEREMONIAL, the Coronation of a monarch is far and away
the most significant. For not only does this solemn, thousand-year-old,
four-part ritual – The Recognition, The Oath, The Anointing and The
Homage of the Lords Spiritual and Temporal – officially confirm the
accession, it invokes divine sanction on the new Sovereign. Its significance is
as much sacred and mystical as ceremonial and political. In the face of this
long-established, complicated and sumptuously-staged rite, even the most
cynical mind can be struck by a sense of wonder. 'I had a sudden feeling . . .'
admitted a *New Statesman* correspondent at the Coronation of Queen
Elizabeth II in 1953, 'a sensation that was like something spoken aloud:
"There is a secret here." What that secret was I could not say. No doubt it was
the primitive and magical feeling which ancient and beautiful ceremonials
still invoke, no matter how rational the breast.'[1]

A Coronation emphasises the often vaguely-held view of the monarchy as
'something distinct from ordinary life, as something more ancient and
durable than any political or family institution, as something sacramental,
mystic and ordained.'[2] It sets out to confirm a link between God and
Sovereign. Even as late as 1956, over a third of the British people questioned
in a national poll believed that, at her crowning, Queen Elizabeth II had been
somehow sanctioned by God to rule over them.

And a Coronation has further significance. Each Coronation serves as a
reaffirmation that the Sovereign – in effect the State, or government – will
rule according to Christian principles. It is, as one pair of sociologists somewhat extravagantly put it, 'an act of national communion' affirming the
moral values of 'generosity, charity, loyalty, justice in the distribution of
opportunities and rewards, reasonable respect for authority, the dignity of
the individual and his right to freedom.'[3] On a less exalted level, it is also an
affirmation that the Sovereign, and the Sovereign's family, will do their best
to live by those exacting Christian principles.

How deeply King Edward VII pondered the mysteries and obligations of his forthcoming Coronation one does not know. A man of simple religious faith, he was not given to analytical or metaphysical thought. There can be no doubt, though, that with his sense of majesty and love of pageantry, the King was greatly looking forward to his Coronation, set for 26 June 1902. And so was everyone else. By the middle of June the streets of London were bright with bunting, banners, garlands and Venetian masts; almost every boat-train was delivering yet another foreign prince or Indian maharajah or colonial deputation. Throngs of visitors from the provinces watched in open-mouthed wonder as the carriage processions went clattering to and from the railway stations.

But all was not quite as good as it looked. The King was unwell. For some time he had seemed listless, depressed and irritable; he appeared more bloated than ever. On the night of 14 June, while he and the Queen were at Aldershot for a huge military review, he was seized with the most violent pains. His hastily summoned doctors diagnosed appendicitis; but they announced that he had lumbago. Hoping to avoid both a postponement of the Coronation and what was, in those days, an extremely dangerous operation, they advised him to rest as much as possible.

But the King was a very difficult patient. As restless as ever, and suspecting that he had cancer of the stomach (both his brother, Prince Alfred, and his sister, the Empress Frederick, had recently died of cancer) he grew increasingly unmanageable. When the doctors tentatively suggested that the Coronation might have to be postponed after all, he would not hear of it. He would go to Westminster Abbey for his crowning if it killed him. By now it looked very much as though it might.

On 23 June, three days before the Coronation, he returned from Windsor to London and insisted on driving in state from Paddington Station to Buckingham Palace. In agonising pain but smiling bravely, he passed along the gaily decorated and wildly acclaiming streets. But that evening he was too ill to attend a banquet and reception. The Queen had to deputise for him.

By now his doctors had decided that an operation could be delayed no longer. In the face of their monarch's outraged protestations the doctors held firm. The Coronation was postponed. On 24 June the King was operated on at Buckingham Palace. That he would survive the ordeal seemed doubtful. The surgeon afterwards told Princess Victoria that 'his firm conviction was that His Majesty would die during the operation.'[4]

It was a complete success. And the King's first words, on coming round, were not, as the newspapers so gallantly claimed, 'Will my people ever forgive me?' but, more prosaically, 'Where's George?'[5] Prince George, his son and heir, was not only to hand but in a state of profound relief. 'I found him,' reported the Prince on the day after his father's operation, 'smoking a cigar and reading a paper. The doctors and the nurses say they never saw such a wonderful man.'[6]

The postponed Coronation took place on 9 August 1902, less than seven weeks after the operation. In spite of the fact that the majority of foreign royals had already left for home, the occasion was one of great splendour. King Edward, having spent several weeks convalescing aboard his yacht off Cowes, looked bronzed, healthy and eight inches slimmer round the waist. 'Good morning children,' he said, displaying himself in his robes to his assembled grandchildren before setting out for the Abbey. 'Am I not a funny-looking old man?'[7]

One of these grandchildren, the future Edward VIII, claims that his grandmother, Queen Alexandra, was late for this, as for every other, occasion. Watch in hand, the exasperated King burst into his wife's room exclaiming, 'My dear Alix, if you don't come immediately you won't be crowned Queen.'[8]

The story might or might not be true but there was no doubting the truth about the magnificence of Queen Alexandra's appearance on Coronation Day. Blithely ignoring tradition or even fashion, she chose what she knew would suit her. 'I know better than all the milliners and antiquaries,' she announced breezily, 'I shall wear exactly what I like and so will all my ladies – *Basta!*'[9] And she was right. In her dress of golden Indian gauze, her train of richly embroidered violet velvet and with row upon row of diamonds and pearls cascading to her waist, she achieved exactly the right blend of majesty and theatricality.

As her own hair was augmented by a toupee she asked the Archbishop of York (the Archbishop of Canterbury was too frail to crown both the King and the Queen) to make certain that, on anointing her, some of the holy oil touch her forehead and not merely her false coiffure.

The King played his part with great dignity and obvious enjoyment. He had felt, he assured someone afterwards, not the slightest fatigue. Among the varied congregation was one particularly notable group: this was a bevy of the monarch's specially invited women friends, including Alice Keppel. Their pew was irreverently referred to as 'the King's loose box'.[10] But it was the King's obvious affection for a member of his own family that left one of the day's deepest impressions: the warmth with which he kissed his heir, Prince George, after he had sworn allegiance, was plain for all to see.

Amid scenes of gratifying acclamation, the newly crowned Sovereigns drove back to Buckingham Palace in their golden coach. Lord Esher's claim that Queen Alexandra's chief attraction lay in her 'mixture of ragging and real feeling'[11] was admirably borne out on her arrival back at the Palace. On the one hand she refused, because of the deep religious significance of her anointing, to wipe the holy oil from her forehead; on the other, she delighted the children present by allowing them to try on her crown.

*

That so regal-looking a couple as King Edward and Queen Alexandra should wish to be seen in a correspondingly regal setting was only to be expected. 'I do not know much about Arrt,' King Edward used to say with his richly rolling 'r's, 'but I think I know something about Arr-r-angement.'[12]

So the 'Arr-r-angement' to which he applied himself with particular zeal was the renovation of the various royal residences. On his accession, the King had found himself with something like a dozen homes at his disposal. The majority of them were in a sadly neglected state. During her long widowhood, Queen Victoria had confined herself to three homes: Windsor Castle, Balmoral Castle and Osborne House. Of these, she had preferred Balmoral and Osborne. Not only had they been conceived and built by the Prince Consort but they were relatively remote from the hurly-burly of everyday political and social life.

As the political and social hurly-burly was precisely what Edward VII delighted in, he lost little time in ensuring that he had the right background against which to indulge this delight. With characteristic self-confidence, he set about converting his various castles, palaces and houses into settings 'worthy of the Sovereign and his Court at the beginning of the twentieth century.'[13]

Of the many royal residences, the one which best symbolises the British monarchy is Windsor Castle. For almost nine hundred years it has been associated with the kings and queens of England. Rising high above the Thames, it is a massive, complex and highly romantic fortress palace, its vast central keep dominating a confusion of walls, towers, battlements, gates, courts and residences. Surrounded by its great park, it looks assured, immutable, majestic.

Although the King had decided that Windsor Castle did not need much structural alteration (that extravagant royal builder, King George IV, had already carried out extensive renovations) he demanded 'complete reorganisation and decoration everywhere.'[14] A clean sweep was made of all the accumulated memorabilia of Queen Victoria's long reign. The famous Corridor, so imbued with the spirit of the old Queen, was rearranged. Farm houses on the estate were scoured for the magnificent furniture acquired by George IV a century before; the drawing-rooms became 'treasure troves'[15] of these elegant Regency pieces. Electric light, central heating and new bathrooms were installed; the 'almost medieval'[16] lavatories were replaced.

'I do not think even the Rothschilds could boast of anything better or more valuable,'[17] wrote the Queen with charming naïvety of the new decorations at Windsor.

But it was on his London home, Buckingham Palace, that the King lavished most attention. Since the death of Prince Albert, Buckingham Palace had hardly been touched. Queen Victoria had hated it: only for the most pressing reasons could she be induced to spend a night or two there. But

Edward VII, in his determination to re-establish the monarchy at the very centre of national life, decided to make this his principal home. A king, he had clearly decided, must live in the heart of his capital. Although he was not particularly fond of Buckingham Palace, King Edward was resolved that it should become an impressive royal seat. (None of the King's successors have liked the Palace any better than he did; Winston Churchill wisely talked Queen Elizabeth II out of a plan to use Buckingham Palace as an 'office' while she continued to live in her first married home, Clarence House.)

In Edward VII's day, Buckingham Palace was not much to look at. Known, originally, as Buckingham House, the property had first come into royal ownership when it was bought by the young King George III in 1762. The house had been virtually rebuilt by John Nash on the orders of the indefatigable George IV. Nash's not inelegant design, in the shape of an open square, had been completely blotted out by the erection, in 1850, of the east front, thus converting the plan of the palace into a hollow square. What the public now saw from the Mall was a dark, dreary, undistinguished block, whose façade of Caen stone was already crumbling in London's sooty atmosphere. Not until 1913, after the erection of the Victoria Memorial, was it given its present-day façade of Portland Stone.

If there was very little that Edward VII could do about the outside of Buckingham Palace (other than to widen the Mall into a more triumphant way) there was a great deal that he could do about the inside. Together with Queen Alexandra, he inspected the palace 'from end to end'.[18] The Queen was concerned only with the redecoration of her own apartments; with those, and with the accommodation for her faithful Woman of the Bedchamber, Charlotte Knollys, 'the inevitable Charlotte',[19] sister of the King's private secretary. In fact, it was with the utmost difficulty that the Queen was persuaded to move into the palace at all. Her London home for forty years had been nearby Marlborough House. To move from there, the Queen assured her son Prince George, would finish her. 'I feel as if by taking me away from it, a cord will be torn in my heart which *can* never be mended again,'[20] she lamented. (It was to be with as much reluctance that the wayward Queen, on the death of the King, moved out of the palace and back into Marlborough House.)

But Edward VII suffered no such pangs. Sitting in the middle of a roomful of palace workmen, growling instructions, gave him immense pleasure. 'Offer it up,'[21] he would command when someone suggested the placing of a cabinet here or the hanging of a picture there, and he would make an immediate decision. Under his sharp eye the state rooms were subjected to a thorough process of transformation: repainted, regilded, recurtained, re-carpeted, refurnished, centrally heated and electrified. On special occasions the enormous new looking glasses reflected great pyramids of hydrangeas, roses and carnations.

'I have no words to describe *how magnificent* it all is,' reported the Dowager Empress of Russia to her son, Tsar Nicholas II. 'Everything is so tastefully and artistically arranged – it makes one's mouth water to see all this magnificence.'[22] From a Russian Empress, this was praise indeed.

The third of the official royal residences was St James's Palace. This ancient, rambling, red-brick palace, built by Henry VIII, remains the titular seat of the Sovereign: ambassadors are accredited to the Court of St James. Until Edward VII's accession, his heir, Prince George, had occupied most of this Tudor palace; now that he had taken over Marlborough House, the King decided that his son's apartments, known as York House, should be adapted for the use of state visitors. Among the building's confusion of dark hallways, narrow passages and unexpected flights of stairs, were several spacious state rooms, including the Throne Room; in these the King held Levées and Investitures.

Other London homes under his control included Kensington Palace, Clarence House and, of course, Marlborough House.

Whereas all these properties belonged to the Crown, there were three others which belonged to the Sovereign personally. They were Osborne House, Balmoral Castle and Sandringham House. Queen Victoria had bequeathed the first two to her successor; the third was Edward VII's own country place.

As he could not afford to maintain all three houses, the King decided to leave Osborne House. He had never, as an adult, been closely associated with it. With his heir declining to take it on, the King handed the property over to the Admiralty. A naval training college was to be built in the grounds and part of the house converted into a convalescent home for naval officers. The rooms in which Queen Victoria had lived, and the room in which she had died, were to be kept as a permanent memorial to his mother.

Balmoral Castle was a different matter. It was essential that the King had a permanent home in Scotland and, together with such neighbouring houses as Abergeldie and Birkhall, Balmoral was the ideal centre for the King's various sporting activities.

Prince Albert, reminded of his native Thuringia by this wild Highland landscape, had organised the building of the royal Deeside retreat in the early 1850s. With its pale granite walls, its pepper-pot turrets, its battlements and its stepped gables, Balmoral was a mixture of German schloss and Scottish baronial hall. Inside it was a riot of tartan: tartan wallpaper, tartan curtains, tartan carpets, tartan upholstery. Whatever woodwork managed to evade this tartan tide was covered in dark, marmalade coloured paint and such antlers as did not adorn the walls were fashioned into chairs and settles. Lord Rosebery once said that he had imagined the drawing-room at Osborne to be the ugliest in the world until he had seen the one at Balmoral.

It is not surprising then, that among the many changes made by the King at

3 The apathetic Prince Albert
  Victor (Eddy) and the lively
  Prince George, as
  midshipmen, 1881

4 'Poor old Granny with little
  Georgie': Queen Alexandra
  with her grandson Prince
  George, afterwards Duke of
  Kent, 1905

6 The Prince of Wales, in his 'preposterous rig', for the Investiture at Caernarvon Castle in 1911

5 Prince George and Princess May, holding Prince John, at Abergeldie in 1906. The other children, from the left, are Princess Mary, Prince

Balmoral, the drawing-room was stripped of its tartan and made to look, according to one observer, 'like a room in one of the Gordon hotels.'[23]

But it was at Sandringham that Edward VII was to be seen at his most typical. No home better mirrored his particular lifestyle. The shooting estate of Sandringham, situated in the flat Norfolk countryside, had been bought in the early 1860s. Some seven years later, the original home having burnt down, the Prince had built another: a hideous, rambling pile of dark orange brick, looking more like a station hotel than the country seat of a future monarch. With the years it had become more hideous still, with expensive additions merely compounding its architectural crudities. But Sandringham had its compensations: the gardens were pretty, the estate was efficiently run and the game was plentiful. Edward VII was seldom happier than when taking part in some mammoth shooting party on his Norfolk property.

Within its cluttered rooms, the King and Queen led as informal a life as possible. Guests – and there were always dozens of guests – found themselves being treated like members of the family. Indeed, the house was so designed that visitors were often ushered straight into the presence of the royal family, all sitting down to tea in the entrance hall. The royal hosts even conducted the guests to their rooms.

Practical jokes were a great feature of life at Sandringham. Few people, noted Lady Angela Forbes, had more *joie de vivre* than King Edward VII. 'He enjoyed himself with the infectious gaiety of a schoolboy. That indefinable, but undeniable, gift of youth remained with him all his life.'[24] As it remained, even more markedly, with Queen Alexandra, the two of them indulged in all sorts of unsophisticated pranks. Their guests were spared nothing: applepie beds, pockets stuffed with sticky sweets, water squirted from bicycle pumps, pies made of mustard. One was quite likely to find the Queen of England sliding down the stairs on a silver tray. 'If anyone caught his foot in a mat, or nearly fell into the fire or out of the window,' sighs one long-suffering observer, 'the mirth of the Royal Family knew no bounds.'[25] A witty remark might raise a smile; a finger nipped in the door brought forth gales of laughter.

Yet, when all was said and done, the royal couple's chief concern was to give pleasure. There are numberless examples of their warmth and generosity. One Christmas the Queen came across a visiting footman gazing mournfully out of the window. 'You look lonely,' she said, 'and I cannot bear anyone to be lonely in my house at Christmastime.' After a long talk with him she disappeared, to come back with a pair of gold cuff-links in a leather case. 'Now these are my personal present to you,' she explained, 'you will get your ordinary present at the Tree tonight.'[26]

In fact, Christmas at Sandringham always saw the King and Queen at their most engaging. They turned the festival, says one of their grandsons, into 'Dickens in a Cartier setting'.[27] The couple would go to endless trouble.

Having chosen the presents themselves, they would spend hours in the ballroom arranging them on trestle tables surrounding the Christmas tree. Before dinner on Christmas Eve, the household and guests would assemble in the corridor outside the ballroom. One by one they would be called in to receive their gifts from the royal couple. 'It was all so beautifully done,' enthuses one member of the household, 'and the pleasure of giving seemed never to leave their Majesties, as it so often does with rich people.'[28]

There they would stand – this genial, portly, cigar-puffing monarch and his glittering Queen – radiating charm and goodwill. Their tradition, of Christmas at Sandringham, continued in the royal family for many decades. And although the present Queen now celebrates Christmas at Windsor, the season remains the one at which the entire royal family gathers together.

It has been mainly against the backgrounds favoured and revitalised by King Edward VII – Windsor Castle, Buckingham Palace, Balmoral Castle and Sandringham House – that the scenes, not only of his own life but of those of his descendants, have been played out.

To maintain his sumptuous lifestyle, King Edward VII was obliged to spend a great deal of money. 'Gentlemen,' his private secretary announced to a parliamentary commission appointed to organise the new King's finances, 'it is my happy duty to inform you that, for the first time in English history, the heir-apparent comes forward to claim his right to the throne unencumbered by a single penny of debt.'[29]

But if Edward VII had no debts, neither did he have any capital. He had never been able to save from either his parliamentary or his private income. So with Queen Victoria having bequeathed her large and carefully hoarded private fortune to her younger children, the King's personal wealth consisted solely of an annual, untaxed £60,000 a year income. This came from the Duchy of Lancaster. The Duchy, together with the Duchy of Cornwall, was all that was left of the extensive Crown Lands that had once belonged to the British Sovereign. But whereas the income from the Duchy of Lancaster always went to the monarch, the income from the Duchy of Cornwall (also, at that time, an untaxed £60,000 a year) went to the heir-apparent.

The remaining Crown Lands had long since been surrendered to parliament in return for a regular annual sum. This sum was known as the Civil List.

On his accession, Edward VII was granted an annual Civil List of £470,000, an increase of £85,000 on Queen Victoria's. Various provisions went to make up the Civil List: a joint Privy Purse of £110,000 for the King and Queen to cover their private expenses as sovereigns, the salaries and running expenses of the royal households, and several other minor provisions. Additional sums were voted for pensions, repairs to palaces and the upkeep of the royal yachts.

The cost of entertaining state visitors would in future be met out of public funds. Queen Alexandra would receive £70,000 a year in the event of her widowhood.

The heir-apparent, Prince George, Duke of York, who was created Prince of Wales in the year of his father's accession, was granted £30,000 which, together with his £60,000 from the Duchy of Cornwall, brought his annual untaxed income up to £90,000.

Whereas Buckingham Palace and Windsor Castle were maintained, for the most part, by the state, the sovereign was responsible – and remains re-sponsible – for the upkeep of Balmoral Castle and Sandringham House. But the royal family's claim to Sandringham as their own private property is said to be somewhat shakily based, as it was acquired and rebuilt with money from the tax-free revenues of the Duchy of Cornwall. Had the sovereign ever been faced with the sort of death duties that crippled other great families in later years, neither Sandringham nor Balmoral would have passed on intact to Queen Elizabeth II.

The Civil List is fixed at the start of each reign. During the first half of the twentieth century, the Civil List could be fixed in the happy certainty that it would prove adequate throughout the reign, no matter how long that reign might be. Indeed, the Civil List granted to Queen Elizabeth II on her accession in 1952 was £475,000 – just £5000 more than that granted to King Edward VII over fifty years before. Even allowing for the fact that some of the Crown expenses had by then been taken over by various government departments and that the Queen's husband was granted a separate allowance, the comparison is a remarkable one. Not until 1962 did the Queen's official expenditure begin to exceed her income; by the end of the decade inflation put the royal finances into, as Prince Philip called it, 'the red'.

The business of the Civil List settled, Edward VII turned his attention to the building up of his private fortune. This he entrusted to yet another member of his personal court, that astute German Jewish financier and self-made millionaire, Sir Ernest Cassel. (Another link between Cassel and the British royal family was later forged by the marriage between the financier's grand-daughter and Lord Louis Mountbatten in 1922.) Assisted by other members of the King's entourage and household, Cassel laid the foundation of that considerable fortune which has passed, untaxed, from one sovereign to another, with the result that the present Queen is now in possession of private funds said to be worth many millions of pounds.

At the time of Edward VII's accession, his son and heir, Prince George, at that stage Duke of Cornwall and York, was thirty-five years old. Both in looks and in personality, Prince George was a very different man from his father. Small and slim, with candid blue eyes and a neatly-trimmed beard and moustache, he was a handsome but altogether less imposing looking figure. He had almost nothing of his father's grandiose air. Where the father was expansive, self-confident and worldly, the son tended to be inarticulate, diffident and unsophisticated. In public he always appeared shy and un-smiling; his conversation was bluff but halting.

None of this is to say that Prince George was a weak or unresolved personality. On the contrary, he had a highly organised mind, a fully integrated nature. What he lacked in self-possession, he more than made up for in self-discipline. That this should have been so was due both to an innate strength of character and to his fifteen years in the Royal Navy.

It was certainly not due to any firmness on the part of his parents. Since his birth on 3 June 1865, Prince George had been thoroughly spoiled. His father, then Prince of Wales, had been determined that his two sons, Prince Albert Victor (always known as Eddy) and Prince George, should not have to endure the sort of joyless childhood which he had been forced to endure; while his mother, the impulsive Princess Alexandra, would have been temperamentally incapable of subjecting them to any such rigorous course of training. So the princes had been raised in a relatively informal and indulgent fashion.

At the ages of seven and six, Prince Eddy and Prince George had been placed in the hands of a thirty-two-year-old tutor, the Reverend John Dalton. Unlike those high-minded men who had been put in charge of the young Prince of Wales's education, the fair-minded Mr Dalton always put the interests of his pupils before those of their parents: he was greatly loved by his two charges and remained tutor to one or other of them for fourteen years. Mr Dalton was assisted by a French teacher and a drawing master. To counteract the parents' lax and erratic methods, the tutor kept his pupils to a rigid timetable. The mornings were devoted to lessons; the afternoons to cricket or riding. After tea they had more lessons and did their homework. They were in bed by eight.

Whereas this eminently sensible regime did very little for the lethargic Prince Eddy, it was of undoubted benefit to the bright, energetic and good-natured Prince George.

In 1877, when Prince Eddy was thirteen and Prince George just twelve, both boys were enrolled as naval cadets on the training ship *Britannia*. It was hoped that by keeping the princes together, some of Prince George's liveli-ness would rub off on Prince Eddy. It did not. After two years at naval college, Prince Eddy remained as backward as he had ever been. The only remedy that their tutor could suggest was more of the same: the two princes must remain together in the navy. So in 1879 they joined HMS *Bacchante* for three long cruises. Altogether, they spent almost three years on the *Bacchante*.

It was during the course of these first five years in the navy, claims one of

Prince George's biographers, that his character was shaped. 'His temperament, his prejudices and affections, his habits of thought and conduct, his whole outlook on life,' writes Harold Nicolson, 'were formed and moulded during the years between 1877 and 1882.'[30] This was largely due to the fact that Prince George's mind was simple, straightforward and consistent. Unimaginative and unintellectual, he was incapable of abstract or philosophic thought. As he matured, so did he mature along the lines already drawn in young manhood. The discipline learned in the navy remained with him all his life: it inculcated him with one extremely valuable characteristic – an unswerving sense of duty. Prince George might not have been clever, he might never have had an original thought, but he was always steady, dependable and conscientious.

The following ten or so years of naval life merely strengthened these traits. They also underlined the difference between his brother and himself. As Prince George became steadily more diligent, Prince Eddy became steadily more apathetic. His air remained that of a sleepwalker. Nothing – not a spell at Cambridge, nor a stint in the army, nor a tour of India – could give any shape to Prince Eddy's amorphous personality. He lived an utterly worthless existence, indulging in every sort of dissipation (there was even talk of a *male* brothel) and falling in and out of love like a schoolboy. The only answer seemed to be the conventional one: Prince Eddy must marry and settle down.

But even this plan was doomed to failure. Just a month after becoming engaged to the eminently suitable Princess May of Teck, Prince Eddy fell ill. On 14 January 1892, he died.

Prince George, at the age of twenty-six, found himself catapulted into the role of Heir Presumptive. Of the various frantic efforts made to equip him for his great destiny – he was created Duke of York, provided with an equerry and a comptroller, given his own apartments in St James's Palace and a cottage at Sandringham, packed off to Heidelberg to improve his German, encouraged to attend parliamentary debates – the most valuable was undoubtedly his marriage. For the royal family, considering Princess May of Teck too valuable a jewel to let slip through the monarchy's fingers, suggested that Prince George take over his dead brother's fiancée. After a decent interval, the couple became engaged. On 6 July 1893, when Prince George was twenty-eight and Princess May twenty-six, they were married.

Prince George's sudden shift to the position of future monarch was to set a strange precedent. For just as he, as the future King George V, had not been born to succeed to the throne, nor had King George VI or Queen Elizabeth II.

In the seven-and-a-half years between the Duke of York's marriage and his father's accession, the couple lived a relatively uneventful life. And this was how Prince George preferred it. For the unpretentious Prince, there was nothing to equal the joys of life as a country gentleman. Although he carried out his official duties – a state visit here, a public function there – with a certain professionalism, he had very little taste for the pomp of his position. York Cottage at Sandringham was the centre of his world. He loved it better, he would say, than anywhere else on earth. He spent his days pasting in his stamps, shooting vast quantities of birds, inspecting the estate, reading aloud to his wife and writing up his terse diary entries. And every eighteen months or so Princess May presented him with yet another child. In time, they were to have six.

Except for an occasional political discussion or some coaching in consti- tutional law, Prince George lived the life of any other Norfolk squire. Unlike his father in a similar situation, he never chaffed nor reacted against the lack of meaningful employment. Inclined to be self-doubting when it came to affairs of state, he was only too pleased to be left in the political dark. Feeling ill-at-ease among his father's smart friends, he much preferred his own quiet hearth.

Queen Victoria's death interrupted this enviably serene life. Whereas until then Prince George had lived very much 'in the shadow of the shadow of the Throne',[31] Edward VII saw to it that his heir was fully illumined by the light which beat so fiercely on his own throne. The new King was anxious for his son to be as closely involved in the workings of the monarchy as was practicable. He appointed the industrious Sir Arthur Bigge, who had been Queen Victoria's private secretary, as the Duke of York's private secretary. ('He taught me,' Prince George was to say of Sir Arthur, later Lord Stam- fordham, 'how to be a King.'[32]) He gave instructions that the heir be sent all important Cabinet papers and Foreign Office despatches. It was more than Queen Victoria had ever done for her heir.

And not only did the King initiate him politically, he encouraged him, sympathised with him and drew him out. That Edward VII was genuinely fond of his son there can be no doubt. The King used to say that he and Prince George were more like brothers than father and son. And Lord Esher claims that King Edward *'always'* spoke of Prince George 'with that peculiar look which he had – half-smile and half pathos – and that softening of the voice, when he spoke of those he loved. He used to say the words "my son" in quite a different tone from any which were familiar to me in the many tones of his voice.'[33]

It was greatly to the King's credit that his son's less confident personality was not permanently undermined by the contrast between them. Prince George, who had always revered his father (despite his disapproval of his rampant sexuality) could so easily have become more self-effacing than he was. Instead, the King's warm and tactful handling brought out the best in him. In later years whenever he was talking about his late father, George V's eyes were quite liable to fill with tears.

'My room opens out of Papa's and is on the ground floor,' wrote Prince George proudly from Windsor to Princess May in 1901, 'then I have got a writing table next to his in his sitting room, he wished it so . . . Fancy that being possible in dear Grandmama's time; anyhow it shows that Papa and I are on good terms with each other.'[34]

In fact, far from emulating dear Grandmama by keeping his heir at arm's length, King Edward told the Duke of York that he could show the highly confidential contents of the 'boxes' to his wife, Princess May.

'But Mama does not see them,' protested the Prince.

'No,' answered the King, 'but that is a very different matter.'[35]

It was indeed.

The Duchess of York had been born on 26 May 1867. Although the first two of the eight names with which she had been saddled were Victoria Mary, she was always known – after the month of her birth – as May. She had been the only daughter and the eldest of the four children of the Duke and Duchess of Teck. The Tecks had been a colourful couple. The Duke had been the son, by a morganatic marriage, of Duke Alexander of Württemberg; the Duchess, born Princess Mary Adelaide of Cambridge, had been a grand-daughter of King George III. This had made her a first cousin to Queen Victoria. The Tecks had thus been fringe members of the British royal family. And whereas the Duke and Duchess might not have been above criticism – he was moody, irascible and obsessed by the morganatic 'taint' in his blood, while she was extravagant, irresponsible and enormously fat – Princess May was generally regarded as being as irreproachably behaved a princess as one could hope to find.

She was very good-looking. Thirty-three at the time of Queen Victoria's death, she had a great refinement of feature: a tip-tilted nose, a 'wild-rose' complexion and clear blue eyes. Her pale golden-brown hair was dressed in the high-piled, tightly curled, frizzily-fringed fashion of the day. Because of her towering coiffure and erect carriage, she always appeared taller than she was; Princess May was actually an inch shorter than her five-foot-six-inch husband. Indeed, until the introduction of Queen Elizabeth II's husband, Prince Philip, into the royal family, its members have been exceptionally small people. Even Prince Charles is shorter than is generally imagined.

For Princess May, life with her cantankerous father and ebullient mother had brought out all the stability of her own nature. She was calm, even-tempered and unemotional. Her manner was reserved, even shy, but when one penetrated this façade, she revealed considerable depth of character, surprising self-confidence and a fund of common sense. Well educated and well bred, Princess May of Teck was a young woman of cultural interests and industrious habits.

It was small wonder then, that she had been considered so suitable a bride for the feckless Prince Eddy. Or that, on his death, she had been encouraged to marry his brother, Prince George. As it turned out, she ended up with the better husband and he with a wife of exceptional qualities.

But Princess May's early married life had not been particularly smooth going. In the first place, she had found herself installed in two far from convenient homes: York House in St James's Palace and York Cottage at Sandringham. The former was a rabbit warren of sunless rooms; the latter was more like an ugly suburban villa than a country house. Yet Prince George, whose years in the navy had given him a taste for cabin-like rooms, could see nothing wrong with this cramped and haphazardly designed little house. It was to be his country home – as Duke of York, Prince of Wales and King George V – for thirty-three years.

Worse still, from Princess May's point of view, was the fact that both houses had been fully furnished before her marriage. Her husband, with the help of his mother and a sister and the man from Maple's furniture emporium, had done it all. And whenever the Princess tried to rearrange the rooms, her mother-in-law, the Princess of Wales, was quite likely to put everything back.

Indeed, the presence of the light-hearted Princess Alexandra was a constant source of irritation to the serious-minded Princess May. The Princess of Wales had always been devoted to her son, and he to her. Even in adulthood, Prince George had been treated like a child by his doting mother. 'There is a bond of love between us,' she had written to him on his engagement, 'that of mother and child, which nothing can ever diminish or render less binding – and nobody can, or ever shall, come between me and my darling Georgie boy.'[36] So the Princess of Wales could see no reason why she could not see as much of her darling Georgie boy after his marriage as before. Trailing a tribe of her high-spirited Danish relations or a party of her husband's fashionable friends or, at very least, a daughter and a pack of yapping dogs, she would breeze into York Cottage at all hours of the day. On one occasion she and her daughters even joined the couple for breakfast.

That Princess May, with her intellectual curiosity, artistic tastes and forward-looking attitudes, should have resented the all-pervading presence of the Wales family is not surprising. What is surprising is that she managed, in the face of their frivolity and philistinism, to keep her composure.

Nor did the reserve of Princess May's public manner show to advantage against the vivacity of her mother-in-law. 'The Duchess of York,' wrote one equerry, 'could take a few lessons from [the Princess of Wales] and get rid of that *shy nod* which offends so much.'[37] In general company, Princess May often appeared gauche, stiff, tongue-tied. This shyness extended to her personal relations as well. 'She has something very cold and stiff and distant in her manner,' noted her husband's aunt, the Empress Frederick, 'each time one sees her again one has to break the ice afresh.'[38]

Even with Prince George she could never be completely at ease. 'It is so stupid to be so stiff together . . .'[39] she once sighed. The trouble was that they were both inarticulate and undemonstrative people. He hid his true feelings behind a quarter-deck bluster; she hers behind an almost unnatural imperturbability. Their legacy of shyness, passed on to their children, manifests itself in the royal family to this day.

But that their true feelings for each other were warm and loving there is no doubt. Their marriage might have been arranged but it soon developed into a love match.

'I have tried to understand you and to know you,' wrote Prince George a few weeks after their wedding, 'and with the happy result that I know now that I do *love* you darling girl with all my *heart*, and am simply *devoted* to you . . . *I adore you sweet May*, and I can't say more than that . . .'[40]

In fact, he could not *say* it at all; he was obliged to write it.

The couple's first child was born on 23 June 1894. It was a boy. In spite of Queen Victoria's strongly expressed wish that the child's first name be Albert, he was christened Edward. To his family and friends, he was always known as David. To the world, he was to be known, successively, as the Prince of Wales, King Edward VIII and the Duke of Windsor.

Some eighteen months later, on 14 December 1895, their second son was born. This time there was to be no haggling about a name. The baby was given the first name of Albert. Like his grandfather, the Prince of Wales, he became known as Bertie. In time, he succeeded to the throne – not as King Albert I, but as King George VI.

The couple's only daughter, Princess Mary, was born on 25 April 1897 and their third son, Prince Henry, was born three years later, on 31 March 1900. Two more sons were born after the accession of Edward VII: Prince George on 20 December 1902 and Prince John on 12 July 1905.

As might have been expected, Princess May was as reserved about the whole subject of child bearing as she was about almost everything else. The inactivity of pregnancy depressed her and its conspicuousness embarrassed her. Still, there could be no doubt that she had fulfilled one of her chief obligations. The succession, which had been held by so slender a thread at the time of Prince Eddy's death – with Prince George as the only male in direct line and his eldest sister woefully lacking in the qualities of a future queen regnant – was now assured. In the year of Edward VII's Coronation, there were four princes in the royal nursery. 'I shall soon have a regiment, not a family,'[41] quipped the gratified Prince George.

Princess May was fulfilling her obligations in a less obvious way as well. Gradually and tactfully, she was steering her husband out of the shallows of his mother's influence into deeper and wider waters. She helped him write his speeches; she encouraged him to read up about the places they were due to visit. 'In spite of her early diffidence and self-effacement,' claims one of Prince George's biographers, Princess May 'was a woman of distinctive personality and one whose range of interests, intellectual standards and refinement of perception would be bound in the end to enlarge, deepen and enrich her husband's mind and tastes.'[42]

Not only did the future Queen Mary prove to be of inestimable value to her husband but, in the course of almost sixty years, she gave her loyalty to no less than six successive British monarchs. Queen Mary's contribution to the British royal family is incalculable.

The first great public task to be undertaken by this modestly-mannered but conscientious couple was an eight-month-long tour of the Empire. The tour had been the brainchild of Lord Salisbury's government. Although, in their day, the Prince of Wales and his brothers had toured various countries, this was to be the first time that a royal couple had undertaken so extended a journey. It was to be the prototype of those mammoth royal progresses that became such a feature of the Empire and Commonwealth in the years to follow.

Although the highlight of the tour was to be the opening, in Melbourne, of the first parliament of the Commonwealth of Australia, it had been decided to extend the journey to include visits to New Zealand, the British South African colonies and Canada. A royal visit would be one way of showing the Mother Country's appreciation of her colonies' contribution towards the winning of the Boer War.

Only with difficulty had King Edward VII been convinced of the desirability of the tour. He hated the idea of being parted from his son so soon after his accession. But, as always, he took his ministers' advice and steeled himself for the long separation. The scenes of farewell, aboard the *Ophir* at Portsmouth, were extremely harrowing. At a luncheon the King could hardly propose the toast for sobbing; Prince George could hardly reply for waves of emotion; the Queen and Princess Victoria were in floods of tears.

'It was horrible . . .' wrote Prince George to his mother the following day. 'May and I came down to our cabins and had a good cry and tried to comfort each other.'[43] Making things still more 'horrible' was the prospect of an eight-month-long separation from their children. They were being left in the care of the King and Queen. These separations of parents and children came to be a feature of all future royal tours until, in 1983, the Princess of Wales insisted that her infant son, Prince William, accompany his parents on a tour of Australia.

Leaving Portsmouth on 16 March 1901, the royal couple visited Gibraltar, Malta, Port Said, Colombo, Singapore, Australia, New Zealand, Mauritius, South Africa and Canada. At the conclusion of the voyage Prince George, in his methodical fashion, noted that they had travelled 45,000 miles (33,000 by sea and 12,000 by land), laid 21 foundation stones, received 544 addresses, reviewed 62,000 troops, presented 4,329 medals and shaken hands, officially, with 24,855 people. They returned home on 1 November 1901.

On Prince George, and his conception of the role of the monarchy in relation to the Empire, this great royal tour had a profound effect. The voyage was undertaken at a time of tremendous change in the structure and ideals of the British Empire. Whereas his grandmother, Queen Victoria, had reigned over a collection of haphazardly acquired British dependencies, of colonies of British people who looked to Britain as home, Prince George – as King George V – reigned over a commonwealth of separate nations.

Gradually, the peoples of these various states were beginning to regard themselves, not simply as Britishers living abroad but as citizens of their new countries: as Australians or New Zealanders or Canadians or South Africans. These rapidly expanding nations were evolving a dual loyalty – to their own country first and to the mother country second.

With each year that passed, these ex-colonists came to care less and less about British domestic politics. Colonial governments managed their own affairs; men born in the colonies ran their own countries; colonial troops were just as disciplined and effective as their British counterparts; in almost every sphere of national life, these states were becoming increasingly self-sufficient.

The most important thing that still bound these nations together – more important than trade or defence or shared traditions – was their joint allegiance to a common sovereign. The Crown remained the most powerful link between them and the country from which they had sprung. The British monarch, as the Prime Minister Arthur Balfour put it to King Edward VII, 'is now the greatest constitutional bond uniting together in a single Empire communities of free men separated by half the circumference of the globe. All the patriotic sentiment which makes such an Empire possible centres in him . . .'[44]

Anything, he went on to say, which emphasised or made manifest the Sovereign's presence to these far-flung subjects was of the utmost import-ance. This was why this great journey of the heir to the throne, at a time when royal tours were a rarity, was so valuable. The voyage of the *Ophir* seemed to crystallise a still fluid situation; to prove and underline the fact that the Crown was indeed the bond that linked these countries, not only to Britain but to each other.

But it was not merely on Prince George's concept of Empire that this tour had made an impact. His contact with the colonists, who showed such affection for and deference to the Crown, brought home to him the fact that what they chiefly expected from the monarchy was worthiness. The Crown must be aureoled, not only in magnificence, but in respectability. It was for her high standards of morality and industry that Queen Victoria had been so greatly revered. The lesson was not lost on her grandson. It left him with a lasting conviction that the public and private lives of those who succeeded her should be above reproach. His conviction remains one of the tenets of the monarchy.

In a more immediate way too, the Prince had benefited from the tour. It had given him an increased self-confidence. Away from the somewhat over-powering presence of his father, and obliged to play the central role at every function, Prince George had gained in assurance.

The same was true of Princess May. Having been forced to make an effort, to hold always the centre of the stage, she had proved that she was quite capable of doing so. 'She is at last coming out of her shell,' reported one of her ladies, 'and will electrify them at home as she has everyone here.'[45]

The reasons for this emergence of Princess May were twofold: she was a passionate sightseer, deeply interested in all the strange, new places that she was visiting; and she was imbued with a strong sense of royal obligation. The British monarchy, to her, was a sacrosanct institution; therefore, to add to its lustre, Princess May was prepared to bring her capacities into full play. Although she could not entirely conquer her shyness, her sense of vocation during this tour could not be faulted.

'Only give me the chance and I will do the things as well as anybody,' she once remarked, 'after all why shouldn't I?'[46]

3

'A Regiment of Princes'

Just as Prince George and Princess May had pioneered a new sort of Empire tour, so had King Edward VII embarked on a new style of royal diplomacy.

In the course of her long reign, Queen Victoria had very rarely discussed politics with her fellow sovereigns; even more rarely had she discussed them with foreign statesmen or diplomats. She had made only one official journey to a foreign capital: this was her visit to Napoleon III's Paris in 1855. Only under extreme pressure would she agree to spending even half-an-hour with a fellow monarch in the private drawing-room of a British Embassy or in a hastily refurbished station waiting-room. In a way, Queen Victoria's attitude had reflected that of her country. During the second half of the nineteenth century, Britain had withdrawn into a position of 'splendid isolation'. Protected by her powerful navy, sustained by her mighty Empire, Britain had kept studiously aloof from any European entanglements and alliances. Rich, strong and self-assured, the country had stood firmly on its own two feet.

But Edward VII's accession coincided with a change in national attitude. The protracted Boer War of 1899–1902 had shaken the country out of its complacency. European sympathy with the Boers had opened the eyes of British statesmen to the fact that their country was without friends or allies. Nor, with the various nations of Europe becoming increasingly powerful, could Britain any longer depend exclusively on the supremacy of her navy. The moment had come, it was now decided, to turn to Europe.

At the same time, there had been a gradual shift in the European balance of power. The old Three Emperors' Alliance – an agreement between the autocratic rulers of Russia, Germany and Austria – had fallen away, and Tsarist Russia was now allied to Republican France. In this changed but still fluid situation, Britain could see the chance of making some European friends.

The claim that King Edward VII was 'the right man in the right place'[1] was never more valid than in connection with the newly-born British interest in

Europe. The King was a European to his fingertips. He was never greatly interested in the Empire. He once told Richard Haldane, his War Minister, that 'there was far too much talk of Empire nowadays.'² Throughout his life, as Prince of Wales and as King, Edward VII had a passionate interest in Continental Europe: in its politics, its diplomacy and its richly varied way of life. France, and particularly Paris, was like a second home to him. If any one person could symbolise Britain's abandonment of its posture of splendid isolation and its new commitment to Europe, that man was King Edward VII.

Throughout his nine-and-a-half-year reign, Edward VII involved himself deeply in European affairs. He never spent less than a quarter of each year on the Continent or cruising in its waters. A great deal of this time was devoted to political discussions: with fellow sovereigns, statesmen, ministers and diplomats. The King's knowledge of Continental affairs was considerable, and more often than not his talks took place without any responsible British minister in attendance. And the fact that he was related to almost every European sovereign gave his political contacts an added significance. He had family connections in Berlin, St Petersburg, Vienna, Madrid, Brussels, The Hague, Stockholm, Oslo, Copenhagen, Bucharest, Sofia, Athens and Lisbon. It was no wonder that he was known as the Uncle of Europe or that he was regarded as so influential a figure on the European stage.

Never, indeed, had the myth that the destinies of Europe were being controlled by a family of kings been given more substance than during these years that Edward VII was riding the royal carousel. There were his meetings with the aged Emperor Franz Josef under the linden trees at Bad Ischl; his negotiations with the debonair King Alfonso XIII aboard the tilting decks of the *Victoria and Albert*; his talks with the vainglorious Kaiser Wilhelm II amid the splendours of Schloss Friedrichshof; his conversations with the gentle Tsar Nicholas II under the weird northern light of the Baltic Sea. King Edward VII passed in spectacular cavalcades through the streets of Paris or Lisbon or Rome.

By these meetings – both formal and informal – with various Continental heads of state, Edward VII made manifest his country's new policy towards Europe: the *entente cordiale* with France, the agreement with Spain, the convention with Russia. Indeed the Triple Entente, by which Britain became allied to France and Russia, was generally regarded as 'the triumph of King Edward's policy';³ no one could deny that he was presiding over a momentous shift in the European balance of power. And even when he was not actively promoting some aspect of British foreign policy, he was creating a more harmonious atmosphere between his own and other countries.

All these royal junketings were being watched, with an increasingly suspicious eye, by Germany. Edward VII might have been a peacemaker to some but to the Germans he was 'the Encircler': a satanic schemer intent on ringing Germany with enemies. To each of his Continental visits, the German press was quick to attribute some sinister, Machiavellian motive. That the King's diplomatic manoeuvres were simply a reaction to the threat of the burgeoning Second Reich, they refused to allow. His main purpose, it was claimed, was the isolating of Germany in a hostile Europe.

With his countrymen's suspicions of King Edward VII, Kaiser Wilhelm II was in full accord. 'He is a devil,' he once announced at a public banquet in Berlin. 'You can hardly believe what a devil he is.'[4] And Edward VII – in private at any rate – was hardly more complimentary about the Kaiser. To the King, the German Emperor was a brash, unpredictable, mischief-making megalomaniac.

This mutual antipathy led many to assume that the hostility between King Edward VII and Kaiser Wilhelm II was a contributory factor in the outbreak of the First World War. The assumption is groundless. Their rivalry merely happened to coincide with, indeed epitomise, the rivalry between their two countries. Edward VII's dislike of his nephew was no more a cause of the First World War than his love of Paris had been responsible for the *entente cordiale*. Much more important than their antagonism was the fact that the countries in which they reigned were rival power blocs. When set against this potentially explosive situation, the quality of the relationship between the British and German reigning houses counted for little.

Because of his tireless political activity, the King earned his reputation as a supreme royal diplomat: 'The Peacemaker of Europe'. Who could doubt that the British monarch – so lavishly uniformed, so self-confidently mannered, so surrounded by pomp and deference – was not the manipulator of Europe's affairs, the 'arbiter of Europe's destiny'?[5]

How valid were these titles? Not very; and to his credit, the King himself never claimed them. Admittedly, there were times when his enthusiasm for foreign affairs caused him to take too much into his own hands; or when Continental statesmen, impressed by his enormous prestige, sound judgement and obvious interest, approached him before approaching his government. But the King was not nearly as indispensible as he appeared. He could initiate nothing. The most that he could do was to ease the way for his ministers. They found him extremely useful when it came to making an initial advance or creating a sympathetic atmosphere. He could prepare public opinion, he could encourage negotiations, he could set the seal on agreements.

And this he did superbly. Any clerk at the Foreign Office could draw up a treaty, claimed the French ambassador in London after the King's celebrated visit to Paris in 1903 had paved the way for the establishment of the *entente cordiale*, 'but there was no one else who could have succeeded in producing the right atmosphere for a *rapprochement* with France.'[6]

'His Majesty did what no minister, no cabinet, no ambassadors, neither treaty, nor protocols, nor understandings, no debates, no banquets, and no speeches were able to perform,' claimed Arthur Balfour, Leader of the Opposition, after the King's death. 'He by his personality, and by his personality alone, brought home to the minds of millions on the Continent the friendly feeling of the country.'[7]

Edward VII's particular brand of royal diplomacy was to die with him. Never again was the British Crown to play so active a part in Continental affairs. The various state visits paid by his successors might have been – and still are – politically motivated, but a sovereign such as the present Queen is in no way involved in political discussions.

Even in King Edward VII's day there was a distinct contrast between the myth of his reputation and the reality of his power. Seldom has this been more pointedly illustrated than in the matter of a certain photograph, published in a newspaper during one of the King's annual sojourns at Marienbad. It showed the King in earnest conversation with a leading statesman. 'Is it Peace or War?' ran the dramatic caption to the picture. What the two men had actually been discussing, it was later revealed, was whether halibut tasted better boiled or baked.

Although Prince George and Princess May, who had been created Prince and Princess of Wales towards the end of 1901, were in no way involved in the King's Continental journeys, their annual ritual was a pale carbon copy of his British routine. As he moved, so did they. When the King was in residence at Sandringham House, they were at York Cottage. When he was at Windsor Castle, they were at Frogmore House, a cream-coloured, collonaded building in Windsor Home Park. When he was at Balmoral, they were at the little fortress of Abergeldie. When he was at Buckingham Palace, they were at Marlborough House.

Yet the two couples – King Edward and Queen Alexandra, and Prince George and Princess May – lived somewhat disparate lives. Prince George might have shared his father's enthusiasm for shooting, yachting and racing, but he was an altogether less cosmopolitan, less urban figure. By nature he was more conservative, more conventional and more insular. Prince George was as much an Englishman as his father was a European. He would have been quite happy never to have set foot outside the British Isles.

For her part, Princess May found the King too restless, too jocular, too innovatory. He was too keen on change for change's sake. Although the King always treated the couple with great kindness, they could never feel entirely at ease with him. Prince George's replies to his father's affectionate letters are curiously stilted and colourless, and Princess May always felt tongue-tied in his presence. The truth was that they were intimidated by him as a man and in awe of him as a monarch.

With Queen Alexandra, the relationship was outwardly friendly. Prince George was still devoted to his 'darling Motherdear' while he was not blind to her faults. And although Queen Alexandra judged her daughter-in-law to be rather dull and – because of her morganatic blood – not quite royal enough, she appreciated at least some of her qualities. She particularly appreciated Princess May's sympathetic attitude towards her deafness.

'You my sweet May,' wrote the Queen on one occasion, 'are always so dear and nice to me and whenever I am not quite *au fait* on account of my *beastly ears*, you always by a *word* or even a turn towards me make me understand – for which I am *most grateful* as nobody can know what I often have to go through.'[8]

But both Prince George and Princess May found themselves becoming increasingly irritated by the Queen's selfishness, immaturity and unpunctuality. Twice a year Queen Alexandra spent several weeks in her native Denmark. To her it was incomprehensible that her son and daughter-in-law did not share her enthusiasm for these family holidays. Around the aged King Christian IX would gather all the members of his widely scattered, judiciously married and high-spirited clan; for weeks on end this collection of emperors, kings and princes, with their wives and children, would give themselves over to a feast of family gossip and childish amusements.

To the conscientious Prince George who, under his wife's influence, had outgrown his taste for the sort of pranks in which his mother's family delighted, these Danish jamborees were now 'a dawdle and a waste of time'.[9] For Princess May, they were worse. So organised, so industrious, so reserved, she was exasperated by the idleness and gregariousness of the Danish family. Queen Alexandra found their attitude almost sacrilegious. With all the audacity of the pot calling the kettle black, she castigated the couple for their selfishness. They were '*so* spoilt,' she exclaimed, 'that they think everything *dull* where there is no shooting!! Or where they can't do exactly as they can at home *voilà tout*!!!'[10]

As far as Prince George was concerned, there was more than a grain of truth in his mother's accusations. The Prince did resent anything that interfered with his well-ordered home life, and shooting had by now become a passion with him. He was certainly a highly skilled shot, ranking among the dozen best in the country. Long-sighted, sharp-eared, slightly built and quick on his feet, the Prince could happily spend all day shooting on the Norfolk marshes.

Princess May, on the other hand, was not the sort of wife who was content to spend her day following the guns. What she enjoyed most were new sights and foreign travel. Often, while her husband accompanied the King to Goodwood for the racing or Cowes for the yachting, Princess May would go abroad. In the course of Edward VII's reign the couple were obliged to carry out several state and private journeys. These Princess May enjoyed enormously. In 1904 they visited the Emperor Franz Josef in Vienna. Here the atmosphere was so stultified that by comparison even the naturally with-drawn Princess May appeared relaxed and informal. In the following year they spent several months in India. The marvels of this vast sub-continent fired her imagination as no other had done or would ever do. In 1906 they were in Madrid for the wedding of Prince George's cousin, Princess Ena of Battenberg to King Alfonso XIII of Spain. A week after their return they were in Norway for the Coronation of Prince George's sister Maud and her husband, the former Prince Charles of Denmark, who had recently been invited to ascend the newly-created throne of Norway as King Haakon VII.

Everywhere she went, Princess May tried to cram in as much sightseeing as her schedule would allow. She particularly enjoyed visiting palaces. Her passion for historic buildings was not shared by her husband. 'With all my love of history you can imagine what a pleasure all this has been to me,' she once wrote during a visit to France, 'alas for my poor George all these things are a sealed book, such a pity and so deplorable in his position! And he misses so much that is interesting in one's life.'[11]

Not until 1903, when Prince George was almost forty, did he see Hampton Court; and then only because he happened to be driven there in a new-fangled motor-car. His comment, on accompanying his wife to an exhibition of paintings in a Paris salon, was that he had seen 'some ghastly pictures'.[12] And he pronounced *A Midsummer Night's Dream* to be 'very dull and tiresome'.[13]

One can appreciate why, many years later, King George V's biographer confided to his diary that his subject's years as Duke of York and Prince of Wales were proving to be singularly unexciting. 'For seventeen years,' com-plained Harold Nicolson, 'he did nothing at all but kill animals and stick in stamps.'[14]

It was during Edward VII's reign that Princess May developed two other passions: one, for collecting and cataloguing various *objets d'art*, particularly those to do with the history of the royal family; the other, for the theatre. It must be admitted, though, that her knowledge of the first was never as deep or infallible as was generally supposed: her interest was in family history rather than in art. And she went to the theatre to be entertained rather than to be mentally stimulated. But when set against the philistinism of the rest of the royal family, Princess May's interests seemed positively erudite.

It was no wonder then, that she should be so anxious to arouse in her children a taste for cultural matters. This was the one area where she did not want them to emulate their father. Each evening before dinner the Princess would have the children brought into her boudoir and, as she lay on the sofa with the youngsters seated in little chairs all round her, she would read and talk to them.

'Looking back upon this scene,' remembers her eldest son, 'I am sure that my cultural interests began at my mother's knee. The years that she had lived abroad as a young girl had equipped her with a prodigious knowledge of Royal history. Her soft voice, her cultured mind, the cosy room overflowing with personal treasures are all inseparable ingredients of the happiness associated with this last hour of a child's day.'[15]

It makes, on the face of it, a charming picture: the quiet, lamplit room, the golden-haired mother in her elaborately frilled negligee, the freshly scrubbed faces of her children bright with interest as they listen to her stories of long-dead kings and queens.

But the appearance was deceptive. Everything in the royal nursery was not as lovely as it seemed. For if Prince George and Princess May were succeeding in some spheres of their life, they were failing as parents.

Princess May, noted the Empress Frederick on one occasion, 'does not seem to have the passionate tenderness for her little ones which seems so natural to me.'[16] She considered the Princess to be very cold, stiff and unmaternal. And although the Empress Frederick's attitude towards young children might have been a shade too effusive, there can be no doubt that Princess May was a singularly undemonstrative mother. It was not that she disliked her children; it was simply that her natural reserve, allied to the fact that she had very little understanding of a child's mind, made her appear detached and unemotional.

Nor did the conventions of her time and class give her the opportunity of getting to know her children better. Like all members of the Victorian and Edwardian upper classes, the parents lived quite separate lives from their children. The youngsters grew up in the care of nurses, footmen and other servants. Only at set periods – usually for an hour or so in the late afternoon – were they brought in to see their father and mother. These somewhat awesome occasions were rendered more awesome still for the children of Prince George and Princess May. For one thing, they were very conscious of the fact that their parents, being royal, were somehow special. For another, their elders were never alone with them; even on the most informal occasions, their father would be accompanied by an equerry and their mother by a lady-in-waiting. The whole atmosphere surrounding their parents was mannered, unnatural, impersonal.

'I have always to remember,' Princess May was to say at a later stage, 'that their father is also their King.'[17] She might have had to remember it; her children never forgot it.

In a way, it was as if the parents were reverting to Queen Victoria's day, when the children had been kept firmly in their place. Prince George's own boyhood, in spite of all Mr Dalton's attempts to adhere to a rigid timetable, had been singularly free of parental constraints. The periods which he had spent in the company of his jovial father and feathery mother had always been devoted to what the parents had called 'romps'. His father had always been wanting to whisk him away for treats and his mother had been forever invading the nursery.

Princess May, on the other hand, was so out of touch with life in the nursery that it was years before she realised why her eldest son, Prince Edward, burst into tears the minute he was brought in for his daily tea-time inspection. It appears that his nurse, out of some sort of perverted love for him, used to pinch him or twist his arm before ushering him into his parents' presence. This meant that the bawling Prince Edward would promptly be returned to her sole care.

And if Prince Edward suffered from too much of his nurse's attention, the second son, Prince Albert, suffered from too little. The nurse neglected him shamefully. Through her haphazard method of feeding him, Prince Albert developed chronic stomach trouble. Only after this incompetent nurse had suffered a nervous breakdown did Princess May discover that she had not had a single day off work in three years.

Yet within her limitations – of personality and convention – Princess May did her best for her children. With the birth of each of the six of them, she would start an album in which she would record the stages of their childhood: the first tooth cut, the first step taken, the first word spoken. During those late afternoon sessions, when she would read or chat to them, she also taught them to keep their hands busy, by knitting or crocheting. Throughout their lives, her sons would happily ply the crochet hook or the tapestry needle. (Mrs Simpson was astonished, years later, to discover the Prince of Wales working away at the tapestry frame on the occasion of her first visit to his country home.) And although Princess May was a strict disciplinarian, she could always be relied upon to take the children's side when she felt that her husband was being too harsh with them.

For Prince George could be harsh. No more than his wife did he really understand children. He might take them fishing or play cricket with them or teach them to shoot but he could never be relaxed with them. He treated them rather as a captain might treat his crew: firmly, fairly and at one stage removed. Indeed, seldom was Prince George's naval training more in evidence than in his dealings with his children. He retained, says Sir John Wheeler-Bennett, 'the temperament of the naval officer, with its rigidity of outlook, its categorical sense of duty, its expectation of immediate obedience, impeccable conduct and extreme orderliness, and, in addition, its cheery gusto.'[18] To these traits he brought his own quick, violent temper.

So although Prince George was a kind, genial, well-intentioned man, he was neither a patient nor an imaginative one. As such, he made a bad father. With all six children having inherited their parents' shyness, Prince George's handling of them merely intensified this affliction. His chaffing, bantering tone embarrassed them; his blunt interrogations unnerved them; his dressing-downs terrified them. No words that he was ever to hear, admitted

Prince Edward in later life, were so alarming as the summons, delivered by a footman: 'His Royal Highness wishes to see you in the Library.' The Library – with guns rather than books ranged behind the glass-fronted cabinets – 'became for us the seat of parental authority, the place of admonition and reproof.'[19]

It was during these early years then, that the foundations were laid for a relationship between parents and sons that was to be little short of deplorable and, in the case of the eldest son, disastrous.

Prince George approached the question of his sons' education in much the same fashion as had his father. Indeed, Prince George was determined that their upbringing should mirror his. The two eldest boys, Prince Edward and Prince Albert, were to follow the pattern laid down by Edward VII thirty years before for Prince Eddy and Prince George. They would be taught at home by tutors until they were old enough to join the Royal Navy as cadets.

So, at the end of the nursery stage of their lives (the neurotic nurse had been replaced by the altogether more satisfactory Mrs 'Lalla' Bill) the two princes were handed over to a kindly valet, Frederick Finch, and to an equally kindly but entirely unsuitable tutor, Henry Hansell.

Chosen chiefly for his prowess as a sportsman, Mr Hansell was upright, humourless and unimaginative. The only sensible suggestion he seems ever to have made was his first one: that his pupils would be far better off at a preparatory school. But as Prince George would not hear of it, the princes were subjected to several years of Mr Hansell's uninspired regime. Determined to create the atmosphere of a school, he converted a first floor room into a classroom, complete with desks, blackboards, bookshelves and cupboards. Lessons were at regular hours and Prince Edward was made head-boy or 'captain'. With Prince George having stipulated that his sons must learn whatever was necessary for them to pass into the Royal Navy, the princes were taught neither Latin nor Greek. Their lessons – English, French, German, History, Geography and Bible Study – were augmented by outings to churches and famous historical buildings. As Mathematics were not Mr Hansell's forte (Prince George was shocked to find that his sons could not strike the average weight of stags) outside tutors were brought in to teach Algebra and Geometry. Homework was done either before breakfast or after tea and quite often consisted of memorising long passages from Shakespeare or Tennyson.

'Looking back . . .' remembered one of them in later years, 'I am appalled to discover how little I really learned.'[20] If Queen Victoria had paid too much attention to the education of her heir, the future King George V was paying too little to the education of his.

Of the two princes, the elder, Prince Edward, or David, was emerging as the more satisfactory. Although by no means bookish, he was alert, intelligent, very conscious of his position, both as the eldest child and as a future monarch. He had a certain engaging, wistful quality. His charm was exceptional. Prince Albert, or Bertie, was more highly-strung. His moods swung between deep depression and almost hysterical excitement. He had an explosive temper. Making life still more difficult for this sensitive boy were two physical defects: he had knock knees and a bad stammer. The first was remedied by the wearing of painful splints; the second was not to be remedied until after his marriage. This speech defect, manifesting itself between the ages of seven and eight (the fact that this naturally left-handed boy was forced to use his right hand is said to have contributed to his stammer) ensured that he became more shy, more inarticulate, more inhibited and more cut off from his fellows than ever.

But all was not unrelieved gloom. Away from the intimidating presence of their parents and tutors, the royal children led happy enough lives. The three eldest – Prince Edward, Prince Albert and Princess Mary, born in the four years between 1894 and 1897 – formed a closely united trio. With a three-year gap between Princess Mary and the fourth child, Prince Henry, she quite naturally fell in with her two older brothers. Blonde and high-spirited, Princess Mary served as a challenge to them. She rode better than they did, she spoke French better than they did, she was bolder than they were. 'Supported by her formidable "mademoiselle" [Mlle Josè Dussau] she wielded a sweet tyranny over our lives,'[21] remembered Prince Edward.

Only rarely were these three fair, slight, good-looking royal children allowed to come into contact with others of their own age. There was the occasional embarrassed game of football with boys on the Sandringham estate, or the even more decorous dancing classes at Marlborough House. Such contacts released them, if only briefly, from their strange 'walled-in'[22] life.

Given the status of the royal family, this isolation was inevitable. But it was not entirely without design. 'You are so many among yourselves,' Queen Victoria once wrote to one of her many grandchildren, 'that you *want no one else*.'[23] In other words, the Queen was warning her grandchild not to befriend anyone from outside the family. The warning holds good today. Although the royal children now mix far more freely with others and, as a result, are far better adjusted and more articulate, it remains inadvisable for them to make outside friends. For one thing, it tends to dissolve some of the necessary mystique of being royal; for another, so few people can be trusted.

'The children soon discover that it's much safer to unburden yourself to a member of the family than just to a friend . . .' Prince Philip said years later. 'You see, you're never quite sure . . . a small indiscretion can lead to all sorts of difficulties.'[24]

And even when princes grow up and go out into the world – as all of them, from Prince Eddy and Prince George to Prince Charles and his brothers, have done – they tend to make no close friends. Their intimate companions remain their brothers or sisters or cousins at various removes. The closest friends of that most social of princes, the future Edward VIII, were his brother, the Duke of Kent, and his cousin, Lord Louis Mountbatten.

Nor do members of the family ever talk about each other. Even so gregarious and loquacious a member as Queen Victoria's last surviving granddaughter, Princess Alice, Countess of Athlone, would never gossip about living members of the immediate royal family.

'There are very few people I know,' said Princess Anne recently, 'whom I would speak to with any degree of freedom about the family or what one does at home, because that's just the sort of thing people tend to remember most and chat about.'[25]

'We learned a lot about the Prince,' said one of Prince Charles's brother officers in the navy, 'but nothing about the rest of the family.'[26]

The price to be paid for this remoteness is a certain air of unreality, a certain obsession with self. Someone like Prince Charles feels this lack of contact with everyday life very keenly. Yet his isolation is as nothing compared with that of a couple of generations ago. The writer James Pope-Hennessy, visiting Sandringham while researching his biography of Queen Mary, was very forcibly struck by this aspect of royal life. 'It was like a visit to a morgue,' he writes, 'and everywhere were their faces, painted, drawn or photographed; few pictures not directly relating to themselves: most curiously *borné* their horizon seems to have been, ringed in by their own family and their own likenesses . . .'[27]

Although Prince George's children regarded York Cottage as their principal home, they rotated with their parents between Marlborough House, Frogmore and Abergeldie. Of the three, Abergeldie was far and away the favourite. Their annual holidays among the rugged scenery of the Deeside left them all – and particularly Prince Albert – with an undying love of the Scottish Highlands.

But there can be little doubt that the most exciting time was that spent in the company of their grandparents, King Edward VII and Queen Alexandra. For two long periods, when Prince George and Princess May were aboard the *Ophir* in 1901 and when they toured India in 1905, the children were left in the care of their grandparents. It need hardly be said that they were thoroughly spoiled. 'If children are too strictly or perhaps too severely treated,' ran the King's theory, 'they only fear those whom they ought to love.'[28] As a result, their lapses went unreprimanded; their boisterousness went unchecked; their every whim was acceded to. Any governess or tutor, daring to suggest that it was time for their lessons, would be waved airily away by Queen Alexandra. 'It's all right,' King Edward would growl, puffing away at his cigar, 'let the children stay with us a little longer. We shall send them upstairs presently.'[29]

And even when their parents were home, the children would be shame-lessly indulged by their doting grandparents. They were certainly much less in awe of the King than they were of their own father. Once, when a tailor's assistant arrived to fit Prince Edward for a suit, she hesitated to enter his room. 'Come in . . . there's nobody here,' exclaimed the Prince. 'Nobody that matters, only Grandpapa!'[30]

Sometimes after tea, if they had done their homework, Prince Edward and Prince Albert would be allowed to run up to the big house at Sandringham to say goodnight to their grandparents. 'It was like being given an open-sesame to a totally different world, and excitement never failed to possess me as the gaily lighted house materialised out of the dusk,'[31] remembered Prince Edward. Here, in the huge hall, decorated in the red, blue and gold of the royal racing colours, would be assembled that colourful and richly assorted company in whom Edward VII took such delight. To the strains of Gottlieb's German Orchestra playing selections from Strauss operettas, the guests would be talking, laughing, drinking, smoking, eating or playing cards. One could have imagined oneself in the home of some rich Midlands industrialist rather than that of the King of England.

On young Prince Edward, this kaleidoscopic scene was to make an indelible impression. 'This brilliantly varied company – statesmen, diplo-mats, bankers, luminaries of the arts and international society, *bons vivants* – gave me,' he claims, 'my first tantalising glimpse of another life.'[32]

On the last night of the year 1909, the usual New Year's Eve 'first footing' ritual was being observed at Sandringham. So that King Edward and Queen Alexandra could be the first to open the front door after the stroke of midnight, the house was emptied of guests and servants. On this occasion, however, the customary ceremonial went awry. All unwittingly, one of the royal grandchildren had entered the empty house by another door and now, just as the King and Queen were approaching the front door, he flung it triumphantly open. The superstitious King was very put out. 'We shall have some bad luck this year,'[33] he announced gravely.

He was right. The year 1910 was to be one of the unluckiest – and the last – of Edward VII's reign. But even before the end of the old year, the King had found himself enmeshed in a web of troubles. His health was not good. His bronchial attacks were becoming more and more frightening. He smoked too much; he ate too much; there was always the danger that his violent bouts of coughing or bursts of temper could lead to a haemorrhage. An old sixty-eight, the King often felt tired and depressed.

He was increasingly troubled by the political situation. In spite of all his peacemaking efforts, Europe was tottering from one diplomatic crisis to the next. Each year seemed to bring the possibility of war closer. In Britain, too, the political scene was far from reassuring. Although the King concurred with Lord Esher's dictum that 'the functions of a Monarch are those of influence and of criticism, a restraining rather than an impelling power',[34] he resented an increasing tendency on the part of his ministers to ignore him altogether. Time and again he complained of being 'completely left in the dark'; of being fobbed off with perfunctory reports of Cabinet meetings. He insisted that it was his 'constitutional right to have all the despatches of any importance, especially those initiating or relating to a change of policy, laid before him prior to their being decided upon.'[35]

As a natural conservative, the King was alarmed by what he considered to be the radicalism of the Liberal Government which, in 1905, had replaced the Conservatives. He felt that its policies of social reform were undermining the whole structure of society. He was constantly having to complain to the Liberal Prime Minister, Herbert Asquith, about the inflammatory behaviour of two of his ministers, David Lloyd George and Winston Churchill.

But what worried Edward VII most of all was the conflict developing between the House of Commons and the House of Lords. It was a conflict in which the Sovereign was directly involved. For with the Liberals determined to curtail the powers of the House of Lords and the Lords just as determined to reject any such legislation, the King was being forced into a difficult situation. There was a strong possibility that he would have to use his Royal Prerogative to create new peers to ensure the passing of the projected legislation. The King was loath to do any such thing. Might not the weakening of the House of Lords lead, in time, to the weakening of that other hereditary institution, the monarchy? Hating the idea of the Crown being drawn into the controversy, the King tried hard to find a compromise solution. He even talked, in moments of despair, of abdicating.

'The Monarchy,' he predicted dolefully at this time, 'will not last much longer. I believe my son will stay on the throne, as the people are fond of him, but certainly not my grandson.'[36]

His prediction was to be proved right. But the reason for the future Edward VIII's abdication of the throne – in order to marry the woman he loved – would have astonished him.

Yet Edward VII's nature was such that in spite of failing health and political worries, he insisted on keeping to his usual time-table. In March 1910 he crossed to France. In Paris he caught a cold. By the time he reached Biarritz, he was so ill that he was advised to go to bed. This he refused to do. Queen Alexandra, about to set out on a Mediterranean cruise, begged him to leave 'that horrid Biarritz'[37] (rendered still more horrid by the presence of Mrs Keppel) and accompany her. He would not hear of it. With the constitutional crisis about the future of the House of Lords still unresolved, he had to be ready to return at any moment. This proved unnecessary and it was not until 27 April 1910 that the King arrived back at Buckingham Palace.

During the following nine days, in spite of increasing tiredness, he insisted on carrying on as usual. Nothing could undermine that ingrained sense of duty. He granted audiences, he worked at his papers, he supervised various alterations at Sandringham. To his pleasures, too, he applied himself with no less dedication. He went to the opera, he played bridge, he dined with friends, he entertained Mrs Keppel.

But by now he was so grey-faced, so short of breath, so racked by coughing that his doctors decided that the Queen should be sent for. She and her daughter, Princess Victoria, came hurrying back from Corfu. They arrived home on the evening of 5 May, to be met, at Victoria station, by Prince George, Princess May and their two eldest sons. Characteristically, the King had given orders that the Queen was to be welcomed home in the Grand Entrance by all the great officers of state and the household, but Prince George arranged for her to arrive quietly, by the garden entrance. Only on seeing her shrunken husband did the Queen realise how ill he was.

By the following morning he was worse. Yet the King insisted on being dressed in formal clothes to receive various callers. Most of the day he spent in an armchair, fighting for breath. In the afternoon, he suffered a series of heart attacks. Still he refused to go to bed. 'No, I shall not give in,' he protested. 'I shall go on: I shall work to the end.'[38]

Quite clearly, he did not have much longer to live. With typical generosity, Queen Alexandra included Mrs Keppel among those whom she allowed in to take leave of the King. And it was no less typical that the last coherent words the King spoke concerned his horse, 'Witch of the Air', which had won the 4.15 race at Kempton Park. When Prince George told him the news, the King, who had already been telegraphed about it, whispered, 'Yes. I have heard of it. I am very glad.'[39]

Just before midnight on 6 May 1910, King Edward VII died. He was in his sixty-ninth year.

'A terrible day for us all . . .' wrote Prince George, now King George V, in his diary that night. 'I have lost my best friend and the best of fathers. I never had a word with him all my life. I am heartbroken and overwhelmed with grief, but God will help me in my great responsibilities and darling May will be my comfort as she has always been. May God give me strength and guidance in the heavy task which has fallen on me.'[40]

Part Two

KING GEORGE V
1910–1936

4

King-Emperor

'A WEEK of intimate talks with the King and Queen,' recorded Lord Esher at Balmoral in August 1910. 'He is brave and frank. He told me very sincerely his aims and ideals. He means to do for the Empire what King Edward did for the peace of Europe.'[1]

The new King, in other words, was intending to take a different line from the old. It was an eminently sensible decision. Neither by taste, temperament nor experience was King George V fitted to emulate King Edward VII. He could never hope to play the sort of swashbuckling Continental role that his father had done. He had no talent for diplomacy, he had very little interest in European affairs, he disliked foreigners. George V was to be, above all, a British king. His political interests lay with Great Britain and with its Empire. His years in the navy and his subsequent journeys to various British dominions, colonies and dependencies had made him very conscious of his country's imperial role: the new King felt able to identify himself far more readily with Britons living abroad than he could with those Continentals so beloved of his father.

At the time of his accession, George V was still very much a King-Emperor. The sovereignty of the British Crown – and, of course, the British government – over the Empire was still absolute. In theory, the final say in colonial affairs still remained with the monarch. And the new King saw the retaining and strengthening of the ties between the United Kingdom and its Empire as one of his chief obligations. He was not to know how fundamentally this relationship was to change during the course of his reign.

But this was not, by any means, the only way in which the tenor of the new reign was to differ from the old. George V's predeliction for his own country affected every aspect of his public and private life. Where Edward VII had seen to it that the dynasty became less German, George V saw to it that it became more British. The royal family – much to the satisfaction of the old aristocracy and the general public – came to symbolise what were chauvinistically regarded as the essential British virtues. They seemed to stand for everything that was decent and sober and honest. The lessons learned on the King's overseas tours – that Queen Victoria had been so greatly revered because of her high standards of morality and industry – were now to be put into effect. The new King saw, as his main duty, the upholding of the dignity and integrity of the Crown. By and large, his concept of a respectable, hard-working representative monarchy remains unaltered, and remarkably successful, to this day.

As a result, the atmosphere at court was changed fundamentally. It became more domestic, less cosmopolitan. Although the monarchy lost none of its magnificence, the home life of the monarch appeared almost middle class when compared with the glitter of the Edwardian court.

'You have no idea,' wrote Lord Esher from Windsor, 'of the change that has come over this place . . . Everything is so peaceful and domestic.'[2] 'The King's domesticity and simple life are charming,' he wrote on another occasion. 'The King allows people to sit after dinner, whether he is sitting or not. There is no pomp . . . There is not a card in the house.'[3]

Nothing better typified this new unpretentiousness than the fact that the King and Queen continued to live in York Cottage. In his will, Edward VII had left the big house to Queen Alexandra. This meant that while she and Princess Victoria occupied an enormous country house, the King and Queen, their six children, their equerries, ladies, secretaries, their children's tutor, governess, and their servants, were all crammed into something hardly bigger than a suburban villa. One of the King's assistant private secretaries, having been driven first from the schoolroom and then the billiard room, was finally obliged to use his little bedroom as an office. Official telephone calls had to be made in a passageway.

Yet it would never have occurred to George V to complain. York Cottage had been good enough before; it was good enough now. The moves from Marlborough House to Buckingham Palace, from Frogmore to Windsor Castle, from Abergeldie to Balmoral had meant sufficient upheaval. Nothing was going to shift him out of York Cottage, the one house which the King regarded as home. Ill-at-ease in grandiose surroundings and disliking entertaining, he had every reason to be satisfied with the tiny rooms and inconvenient layout of York Cottage.

This same honest-to-goodness quality marked his dealings with those who worked with him. Everyone – ministers, secretaries, equerries, servants – found him straight-forward, sensible, conscientious and orderly. His honesty, particularly about the gaps in his education, could be disarming. 'Sandringham-cum-Appleton, Sandringham-cum . . .' he once read out loud from a report. 'What's this "cum"; what does "cum" mean?' On being given the explanation by a member of the household, he exclaimed, 'Oh, it means "with". Then why can't they say so? They never taught me Latin.'[4]

And on another occasion he rejected the draft of a speech. 'That is too high-faluting,' he grumbled, 'everyone would know those were not my words.'⁵

Yet for all the simplicity and decorum of his lifestyle, the new King did not escape criticism. A certain section of society, for whom the sun had shone so brightly during his father's reign, found the new court intolerably lack-lustre. It was all too *bourgeois* by half, they sighed. They resented the fact that the King preferred to dine at home, that his idea of an evening's fun was reading aloud to the Queen, that he strongly disapproved of marital infidelity. There was even a rumour that the King disliked racing. This was nonsense. George V had inherited all his father's interest in the Sport of Kings, and was to pass it on to his successors.

At the same time, he was having to deny another rumour accusing him of far from puritanical behaviour. He was said to be a heavy drinker. The rumour sprang from the fact that the King had a loud voice, a hearty laugh, a salty turn of phrase and a blotchy complexion. This gossip, long current and revived on his accession, did not bother him unduly; the King was an abstemious man and, in time, the story died a natural death.

The new Queen was also having troubles. Queen Mary (as neither 'May' nor her first name 'Victoria' seemed suitable, she had plumped for her second name 'Mary') was finding that her position was 'no bed of roses'.⁶ There were suddenly so many things to do, so many people to see, so many decisions to be taken. Quite literally overnight, and not without some friction, Queen Mary was obliged to replace Queen Alexandra at centre stage. Nor did she always shine by comparison. There were some who found the new Queen stiff, cold, intimidating. Because, in her elaborate hats, she looked taller than her husband, it was rumoured that she dominated him. 'King George the Fifth and Queen Mary four-fifths' ran a current quip. A contradictory rumour had it that it was he who dominated her. She was said to be afraid to speak up for herself. The truth was that neither dominated the other but that the Queen, with her reverence for the Crown, was from now on to sublimate herself to the husband who had become her monarch.

Drawing the couple together quite as much as their shared responsibilities and their shared sense of royal vocation was their shared apprehension about the coming Coronation. They were dreading it. Not only did the King and Queen suffer from an inhibiting shyness in public (although in later life Queen Mary protested that she had never been '*stutteringly* shy'⁷) but the King was highly strung and prone to tears. Both looked upon the Coronation, in which they were to be the centre of attention in an elaborate, moving, complicated and deeply significant ceremony, as 'a terrible ordeal'⁸ to be got through.

But it all went beautifully. The crowds were gratifyingly enthusiastic, the press was laudatory, the royal guests were suitably impressive, the ceremonial was magnificent. 'Today was indeed a great and memorable day in our lives and one we can never forget . . .' wrote the King in his diary on 22 June 1911. 'The service in the Abbey . . . was grand, yet simple and most dignified and went without a hitch. I nearly broke down when dear David came to do homage to me, and it reminded me so much when I did the same thing to beloved Papa, he did it so well. Darling May looked lovely and it was indeed a comfort to have her by my side . . .'[9]

'Dear David' – the King's eldest son Prince Edward – had been equally moved by his act of homage to his father. Kneeling at the feet of the newly-crowned King, the sixteen-year-old boy had sworn: 'I, Edward, Prince of Wales, do become your liege man of life and limb, and of earthly worship; and faith and truth I will bear unto you, to live and die, against all manner of folks. So help me God.' When the King kissed his cheeks, noted the Prince, 'his emotion was great, as was mine.'[10]

By now, Prince Edward's position had changed considerably. His father's accession had meant that not only was he Heir Apparent but also Duke of Cornwall – a title that brought with it vast estates and properties in London and the West of England. In addition to this he had been created Prince of Wales on his sixteenth birthday, 23 June 1910, and was subsequently invested with the Order of the Garter. This had allowed him, in spite of being under age, to take precedence over the other peers of the realm at the Coronation.

His father's accession had brought changes in his day-to-day life as well. Much to the Prince's disappointment, it had meant the end of his naval career. For, during the last four or so years, Prince Edward had been a cadet at the naval colleges of first Osborne and then Dartmouth. 'The Navy,' his father had proclaimed when his son's tutor, the earnest Mr Hansell, had once again dared to suggest that Prince Edward be sent to a proper public school, 'the Navy will teach David all that he needs to know.'[11] In February 1907, when he was twelve-and-a-half years old, Prince Edward entered Osborne.

His father's faith in the advantages of a naval education for his heir was a clear example of his conservatism. It could hardly have been anything else. The navy might have helped shape George V's character but it had taught him precious little. In any case, he had not, at that stage of his life, been heir to the throne. Acutely conscious of the gaps in his knowledge (at his accession, admits his biographer, the forty-four-year-old George V had not yet attained 'the normal educational standard of the average public schoolboy at leaving age'[12]) the King was still trying to repair these gaps. Why, then, he considered an identical education as being suitable for his own heir is difficult to understand. One would have thought that some schooling in languages, history and geography would have been more valuable than mathematics, engineering and navigation; and certainly more valuable than learning to tie knots, splice rope, read signals and box the compass.

7 Nine sovereigns at Windsor for the funeral of Edward VII, May 1910. Standing, from the left: Haakon VII of Norway, Ferdinand of Bulgaria, Manoel of Portugal, Wilhelm II of Germany, George I of Greece, Albert I of Belgium. Seated: Alfonso XIII of Spain, George V, Frederick VII of Denmark

8 George V and Queen Mary caught in a moment of informality at the Delhi Durbar of 1911

9 'My name is George, too', says a
urchin to George V during one c
the King's celebrated industrial t

10 Supreme Commander on a
kitchen chair: George V in France
during the First World War

In later years the Prince of Wales, looking back at his time at naval college, admitted that 'it is small wonder that our characters and outlook tended to develop along narrower, more prescribed, and more stereotyped lines than those of our contemporaries at public schools.'[13]

The contrast between the cloistered, artificial, privileged life led in the various royal homes and the rough-and-tumble of naval college was profound. Cadet Prince Edward ('Just Edward' he answered on being asked 'Edward what?'[14]) was subjected to all the customary rigours: the 6 a.m. reveille, the ice-cold baths, the iron discipline, the barked orders, the ragging, the bullying, the punishments. Because he was so small and as an antithesis to 'Wales' he was known as 'Sardine'. As a pupil he hardly shone and this meant, of course, further dreaded summonses to his father's library whenever his report cards arrived. Yet the King was not always unsympathetic; there were times when he proved surprisingly understanding about his son's poor academic record.

During Prince Edward's last term at Osborne, and just before going on to Dartmouth, he was joined by his brother, the thirteen-year-old Prince Albert. As the school's rigid system did not allow for contact between seniors and first-termers, the boys could not re-establish their old close companionship. They could occasionally meet, in secret, and then Prince Albert could pour out his heart to his older brother.

For there was no doubt that he needed to pour it out. Life at naval college was infinitely more difficult for Prince Albert than it was for Prince Edward. He had to cope, not only with the harsh regime and the unfamiliar communal living, but with homesickness, shyness, slowness and his embarrassing stammer. And although Prince Albert was an attractive, warm-hearted personality, he did not make friends easily. When set beside his charming, good-looking, articulate elder brother, Prince Albert appeared gauche and tongue-tied.

Academically, his record at Osborne was even worse than Prince Edward's. By no means clever, Prince Albert's stammer made him appear more stupid still. Not unnaturally, he hesitated to speak up in class. As a result he, too, was subjected to his father's pained letters and to those frightening sessions in the library. It was all to no avail. In his final examinations at Osborne, in December 1910, the fourteen-year-old Prince Albert was placed 68 out of 68.

Yet to those who took the trouble to get to know him better, Prince Albert was not quite as hopeless a case as he seemed. When relaxed, he could be friendly, easy-going, even mischievous. And he had one very pronounced and valuable characteristic: an unflagging tenacity. 'He shows the grit and "never say I'm beaten" spirit which is strong in him,' noted the Captain of the College; 'It's a grand trait in anybody's character.'[15]

On going on to Dartmouth early in 1911, Prince Albert had again been preceded by his older brother, who was by now in his second year at the naval college. But the brothers were not together long. Their father's accession to the throne had meant that Prince Edward, as Prince of Wales, had to cut short his naval career. King George and Queen Mary had other plans for their eldest son. He was to spend periods in France and Germany studying the languages, and to go to Oxford.

This latter decision astounded the Prince of Wales. He knew – and in fact shared – his father's suspicion of scholars and intellectuals, but in the face of his protestations, his father held firm. It appears that the persistent Mr Hansell had finally got his way: the Prince of Wales was to go to his tutor's old college, Magdalen.

Unlike his grandfather, Edward VII (who had been the first Prince of Wales to go to Oxford), Prince Edward was allowed to live in College and mix freely with the other undergraduates. This was hailed by the press as evidence of the democratisation of the monarchy. It was hardly that. Not surprisingly, with his poor academic background, the Prince was spared having to pass University entrance examinations; he was accompanied by his tutor, an equerry and a valet; his especially redecorated rooms boasted the first undergraduate bathroom.

But at least he entered fully into most university activities, particularly extra-mural activities. The painstaking efforts of the University's most brilliant minds seemed to make less impression than the examples of 'carousing' set by the other undergraduates. The Prince did not risk taking a degree. Yet he impressed both the dons and his fellows by his naturalness and his approachability.

'Bookish he will never be; not a "Beauclerk", still less a "British Solomon",' was to be the College President's summing-up of the Prince's stay at Oxford. 'Kings, perhaps fortunately, seldom are the last. That is not to be desired . . .' But at least the Prince was 'getting to know what Englishmen are like, both individually and still more in the mass.'[16]

It was at about this time, remembered the Prince of Wales in later years, that he first made a disconcerting discovery about himself: although he was prepared to play his part in all the pomp and ceremony in which he, as heir apparent, found himself so suddenly enveloped, he recoiled from the accompanying homage. He wanted to be treated like any other youngster. For any member of a royal family this was, and is, an unsettling realisation. The most resolved royal personalities are those who – like the present Queen Mother – simply accept public homage as their due. For a future king, this aversion presented a serious dilemma.

And the pull – between his public and private selves – was making the Prince of Wales feel increasingly uneasy. Those about him noticed that he seemed diffident, almost ashamed of his status; for one so young, he was oddly grave. 'I have had two walks alone with the Prince of Wales,' wrote the always observant Lord Esher. 'He is a most captivating, strange, intelligent boy . . . He is sad – with the sadness of the world's burdens.'[17]

Be that as it may, the most unnerving and adulatory of the Prince's public appearances had to be got through in the course of Coronation Year. This was his formal investiture as Prince of Wales at Caernarvon Castle. The idea of reviving this ancient ceremony had come from that attacker of inherited privilege, Lloyd George, who had seen it as a way of providing his fellow countrymen with a spectacular Welsh pageant. So the Prince duly prepared himself for the ceremony to be enacted within the ruined battlements.

Unlike his great-nephew, Prince Charles, who was to undergo a similar ceremony over half a century later, Prince Edward was not expected to identify himself with the Welsh people in any meaningful fashion before the Investiture. Whereas Prince Charles attended a Welsh university to learn the language, Prince Edward merely practised his moves, studied his speech and memorised a few words of Welsh.

He was far more concerned about the costume he was expected to wear. This was to be a 'fantastic' creation of 'white satin breeches and a mantle and surcoat of purple velvet edged with ermine'. His refusal to appear in this 'preposterous rig'[18] led to a full-scale family row. What, he demanded, would his fellow naval cadets say? In the end, it was the Queen who smoothed things over. He should not take a mere ceremony so seriously, she said; his friends would understand that princes are obliged to do things which might look silly; it was only for this once.

In the end, the Prince of Wales gave in. And it was in his period costume that he appeared before some ten thousand people at Caernarvon on a sweltering July day in 1911. With his titles having been 'mellifluously'[19] proclaimed by the Home Secretary, Winston Churchill, the Prince was formally invested by his father. Almost sick with heat and nerves, he was led out to be presented to the people and to speak those few words in Welsh.

The scene has been captured for posterity in numberless photographs. There, under the old walls of Caernarvon Castle stands the little family group: the neatly-bearded King George V in his admiral's uniform, the statuesque Queen Mary in her white, ostrich feather laden hat and, between them, their small, slight, wistful-eyed son, his fair hair trapped by a glittering gold circlet.

Making King George V's adjustment to his new role more difficult were the various political crises which beset the early years of his reign. 'In their significance, intensity and scope,' claims one observer, these political problems were 'incomparably more intricate and alarming than any which had faced [King George's] immediate predecessors.'[20]

The difficulties surrounding the bill to limit the powers of the House of

Lords, which had so bedevilled the last months of Edward VII's reign, had yet to be resolved. Until they were, with the passing of the Parliament Bill in August 1911, the King was deeply involved. For the Liberal government had talked the monarch into giving secret guarantees that he would create new peers if the bill were vetoed by the House of Lords. For someone of King George's uncomplicated nature, the secrecy and complexity of these manoeuvres were extremely distasteful. The secrecy, particularly, distressed him. 'I have never in my life done anything I was ashamed to confess,' he afterwards grumbled. 'And I have never been accustomed to concealing things.'[21]

Equally worrying were those other burning questions of the day: widespread industrial unrest, the growth of the Labour Party, the excesses of the Suffragette Movement, the bitter, long-simmering problem of Home Rule for Ireland, with its threat of civil war.

The King, for all his political inexperience, took a great interest in these various issues. Essentially a conciliator, he was particularly alarmed by the strikes and riots that seemed to be spreading throughout many mining and industrial areas. In order both to see conditions for himself and to show royal sympathy for these working class people, he undertook a series of tours to the troubled areas.

This, at the time, was something quite new. Whereas King Edward VII and Queen Alexandra had been ready enough to show themselves to the crowds as they drove by to perform some public function, King George and Queen Mary were the first British monarchs to make direct contact with the great industrial populations of the country. As with their Empire tour in the *Ophir*, the couple were pioneering a style of royal visit; one that became common practice for their successors. Tentative and limited as their efforts were when compared with later royal tours of inspection, they represented an important advance in the gradual transition of the monarchy during the twentieth century.

'We must endeavour,' the King's private secretary Lord Stamfordham once said, 'to induce the thinking working classes, Socialist and others, to regard the Crown, not as a mere figure-head which, as they put it "don't count", but as a living power for good, with receptive faculties welcoming information affecting the interests and social well-being of all classes, and ready, not only to sympathise with these questions, but anxious to further their solution.'[22] By these pioneering tours, King George V went a long way towards realising his secretary's ambitions: this royal identification with ordinary people, as opposed to only the aristocratic and middle classes, became a source of real strength for the monarchy during the years ahead.

'He was a very wonderful King,' remembered one old-age pensioner many years later. 'He changed life completely from Edward VII's way.'[23]

From now on, in visit after visit, King George and Queen Mary would move among the members of the proletariat. Always somewhat ill-at-ease with the fashionable and the intellectual, the couple felt relaxed and confident among these grimy-faced workers at the pit-head or these neatly-aproned housewives on the doorstep. There are numberless stories about the royal couple's interest in and concern for those in suffering.

Numberless, also, were stories about the tours' lighter moments. Much to the consternation of attendant officials, Queen Mary would insist on drinking cups of tea in the kitchens of miners' cottages. 'My name is George, too,' announced one grinning, raggedly-dressed urchin to his brilliantly uniformed and highly amused Sovereign.

'Is the father very dark?' asked the Queen of a fair-haired mother, whose dark-haired baby she was inspecting in a maternity ward.

'Sure Ma'am, I don't know,' answered the mother unblinkingly, 'he never took his hat off.'[24]

King George V's industrial tours had been one way of making his mark; another, infinitely more spectacular way, was the Delhi Durbar of 1911. The Durbar had been entirely the King's own idea. Not long after his accession he had announced his intention of holding a Coronation Durbar. Brushing aside all opposition on the part of the government, the King went ahead with his plans. In his politically naïve way, King George imagined that his personal appearance at Delhi would counteract growing Indian nationalism and strengthen what he regarded as the beneficial rule of the hereditary princes. He was convinced that their paternalistic methods were in tune with the traditions of the broad mass of the Indians. What better way, then, of rekindling the loyalty of the Indian subject peoples than the appearance, in their midst, of their mighty King-Emperor?

The Delhi Durbar, held on 12 December 1911, was every bit as magnificent as the King had hoped. Everything – the fifty thousand troops, the massed bands, the golden-domed pavilion, the two solid silver, gold-inlaid thrones, the King-Emperor wearing his new £60,000 Imperial Crown, the Queen-Empress wearing her flashing diadem, both in their purple velvet, ermine-lined Coronation robes, the long file of glitteringly dressed rajahs paying homage to the royal couple – all this was guaranteed to impress the vast crowds gathered in the sunlit amphitheatre.

The sovereigns themselves were hardly less impressed. 'The Durbar yesterday was the most wonderful and beautiful sight I have ever seen and one I shall remember all my life,'[25] wrote the King to Queen Alexandra. When the royal couple had left, the crowd surged forward to the golden pavilion and, flinging themselves to the ground, pressed their foreheads against the marble steps.

In Britain, the Durbar was generally regarded as an unqualified success; it was a reaffirmation of Empire, a superb pageant that was to set a precedent for future Emperors of India. Even in India there appeared to be very little evidence of dissenting voices. 'There was no interruption in the crescendo wave of popular enthusiasm,'[26] trumpeted the *Times of India*. Indeed, one would have had to have been very perspicacious to appreciate that this was not, in fact, the high noon of the Indian Empire, but its sunset. King George V would have been astounded to know that his son, King George VI, was to be the last Emperor of India.

If the effect of the Durbar on the Indian question was transitory, its effect on King George was profound. 'Those who best knew him,' wrote John Gore, 'are generally agreed that the Indian Durbar greatly influenced the King's character. They consider that that tremendous experience, the magnificent ceremonial among those millions of his subjects, many of whom felt for him and hailed him almost as a god, convinced him finally and for his life of the majesty of his office and of the magnitude of his responsibilities . . . the dizzy and lonely heights of his position as King-Emperor were brought home to him.'[27]

For King George and Queen Mary, this avalanche of duties and responsibilities meant that they could devote even less time to their children. With the two eldest, the Prince of Wales and Prince Albert, at Oxford and Dartmouth respectively, there were still, in the year 1913, four below the age of sixteen. These were Princess Mary, Prince Henry, Prince George and Prince John.

At sixteen, Princess Mary was very good-looking. '*La belle rose anglaise*'[28] exclaimed Madame Poincaré, the wife of the French President, on first seeing her. Princess Mary was everyone's idea of an English rose: blue-eyed, fair-haired, fresh-complexioned. She was very much an outdoor girl and, like so many girls brought up among a family of brothers, something of a tomboy. She rode, she cycled, she fished, she was an ardent gymnast. Shy in public, in private she was the least inhibited of the children. Unlike her brothers, Princess Mary was able to apply herself to her lessons – languages, literature, geography and history – with enthusiasm. In the capable hands of her governess and in the occasional company of the daughters of the Duke of Devonshire, Princess Mary enjoyed and benefited from a sound education. She was probably the best educated of King George V's children.

'The trouble is,' the Prince of Wales once complained good-naturedly to Lady Airlie, one of his mother's ladies-in-waiting, 'that she is far too unselfish and conscientious. That is why she was so overworked at her lessons. When my brothers and I wanted her to play tennis she used to refuse because she had her French translation to do, or she hadn't read *The Times* for the day. Is that normal for a girl?'[29]

'What a pity it's not Mary,' the Prince once observed on being reminded of his destiny, 'she is far cleverer than I am . . .'[30]

Early in 1913, Princess Mary was confirmed. From that time on she was to be seen, more and more, walking a couple of paces behind the King and Queen at public ceremonies. In private, too, the Princess became more closely associated with her parents. The King and Queen were able to establish a better *rapport* with their only daughter than with their sons. In fact, Princess Mary was the King's favourite child. She might have been reduced to crimson blushes by his jokes at her expense but she was very rarely scolded by him. And although the relationship between parents and daughter was never a particularly demonstrative one, there is no doubt that they felt more at ease with this bright and well-behaved girl than they did with the boys. Until Princess Mary's marriage, she remained her parents' closest, most constant companion.

With their third son, Prince Henry, the King and Queen were less pleased. Any hopes that they might have harboured of third-time-lucky when it came to their son's academic achievements were soon dashed. On the contrary, it was the same old story. From the uninspiring Mr Hansell's mock classroom, Prince Henry emerged with the same ungovernable temper, the same lack of enthusiasm, and the same volatile temperament as his brother, Prince Albert. He, too, suffered from knock knees and was forced to wear painful splints. His even poorer health, however, was responsible for his being set along a different course. A weak chest resulted in his being packed off to Broadstairs, first in the care of a governess and then as a pupil to St Peter's Court preparatory school. In this, Prince Henry was making history: he was the first member of the royal family to go away to school. The King had finally been talked round. St Peter's Court, he now proclaimed, would give his son 'the best training mentally, physically and morally.'[31] To the general public, it was fresh proof of the way in which the monarchy was becoming more closely identified with the lives of ordinary people.

In his new-found belief in the virtues of a school education for his son, the King was being too optimistic by half. In the main, Prince Henry's school-room achievements were well below average; his main interest was sport. 'All you write about is your everlasting football of which I am terribly sick . . .'[32] wrote his exasperated mother on one occasion. Still, he passed his final examinations at St Peter's Court quite well and in September 1913 – and here was another innovation – the thirteen-year-old Prince Henry entered Eton College. As he was destined for a career in the army and would be going on to Sandhurst, he began drilling with the Eton OTC.

All in all, Prince Henry was an unremarkable youngster. On the credit side he was natural, simple and modest but he lacked self-confidence, he lacked application and he lacked system. He was not even, despite his enthusiasm, a particularly good sportsman. Only for shooting did he show any real talent:

in time, he became an excellent shot. In this, at least, Prince Henry did not disappoint his father.

Prince George, the fourth son, was very different. Nearly three years younger than Prince Henry, he far outstripped him. In fact, of all the brothers, Prince George was cleverest. Intellectually and culturally, he stood head and shoulders above the rest. His charm and good looks were exceptional. Unlike Prince Henry, whom he followed to St Peter's Court, Prince George made good progress. At the end of each term he would return to Buckingham Palace 'quite a little hero'.[33] With his mother, he was to establish a relatively warm relationship. He shared her artistic interests; he had inherited her flair for decorating and her enthusiasm for collecting. The two of them would sit happily knitting together or working at their tapestry frames. Yet like his two eldest brothers, Prince George was destined to become a naval cadet.

Prince George was especially friendly with the Prince of Wales. Although separated by more than eight years, the two princes were drawn to each other. Just before going up to Oxford, the Prince of Wales spent several weeks in the company of his young brother. 'I found in his character qualities that were akin to my own;' he writes, 'we laughed at the same things. That winter we became more than brothers – we became close friends.'[34] Both – in their different ways – engaging, wayward and unconventional, the Prince of Wales and Prince George became very closely associated in the turbulent years ahead.

About the youngest son, Prince John, there was an air of mystery. He was seldom seen and even less talked about. It was generally assumed that he was the customary skeleton in the royal cupboard. The truth was that since the age of four, Prince John had been subject to epileptic attacks. Mentally, he was sub-normal. In the fashion of the time, the boy was kept apart from his brothers and sister. When he was eleven, the Prince was entrusted to the care of Mrs 'Lalla' Bill, the nurse who had cared for all the royal children, and installed in a house on the Sandringham estate. He was to die, suddenly, at the age of thirteen on 18 January 1919.

'The news gave me a great shock,' Queen Mary wrote in her diary that evening, 'though for the poor little boy's restless soul, death came as a great release.'[35]

The outbreak of the First World War, on 2 August 1914, placed King George V – as the Second World War was to place his son King George VI – in a curious position. The King was the Supreme Commander of his country's fighting forces yet not since George II had fought the French at Dettingen in 1743 had a British monarch led his armies into battle. This, for a constitutional monarch, was no longer practical nor advisable. And although the King remained, more than ever, the all-transcending national symbol, he was less than ever involved in the major decisions of the day – the military decisions. For whereas every parliamentary bill was debated with his knowledge and passed with his assent, the military decisions could be taken without reference to him at all. His cousins, the Tsar of Russia and the German Kaiser, appeared to be playing significant military roles; King, George, as a constitutional monarch, was militarily negligible.

It was just as well. Monarchs who were too closely involved with the conduct of war tended to be blamed, and indeed to lose their thrones, when things went wrong.

Yet King George V was keenly interested in the conduct of the war. He was always ready to voice his opinions and to champion his favourites. He saw to it that he was kept fully informed – not only by the Cabinet and the War Councils but by the various commanders and private friends serving in the forces – of every aspect of the struggle. 'The King's knowledge of all the details of what goes on is remarkable,' wrote Lord Esher, 'and he never seems to forget anything that he is told.'[36]

On no less than five occasions the King crossed to France to spend several days with the army. On one of these occasions he suffered a serious accident. While he was reviewing some troops, the King's mare suddenly reared and fell backwards, pinning him down. Shocked and in terrible pain, the King was carried away. It was afterwards discovered that he had fractured his pelvis in two places. Those close to the King claim that he was never again the same man; it could almost be said that he had returned from France a war casualty.

The war had a considerable effect on his day-to-day life. His annual routine was drastically changed. Holidays were cut down to a minimum, he never saw Balmoral, he rarely left Buckingham Palace. To his normal constitutional duties and his work on the 'boxes' were now added those seemingly endless wartime tasks. Besides his visits to the army in France and to the fleet, he reviewed troops, inspected naval bases, conferred decorations, toured industrial areas, tramped through munitions factories, visited hospitals. Day in, day out, year in, year out, the King and Queen performed their depressing and often gruelling duties.

The couple were particularly upset by their hospital visits. Far from being the sort of man who gloried in war, King George was humane and compassionate. The sight of the maimed and the wounded, the enormous casualty lists, the deaths of friends on active service, wrung his heart. Yet the King and Queen forced themselves to wave, to smile, to look interested, to ask questions, to speak cheerful, encouraging, hopeful words. To the new recruits, the hideously wounded, the workers in the munitions factories or the helpers in the soup kitchens, the presence of the royal couple brought immense comfort. 'No previous monarch,' claims his official biographer, 'had entered into such close personal relations with so many of his subjects.'[37] The visits forged yet another link between Crown and people.

Added to the couple's general anxieties were family ones. Their two eldest sons, the Prince of Wales and Prince Albert, were both on active service: the one in the army, the other in the navy.

The decision that the princes should go to war was another step forward for the monarchy. Queen Victoria had never allowed her sons to see active service. And on one occasion when there was a likelihood that her two grandsons, Prince Eddy and Prince George, would become embroiled in some colonial campaign, she forbade it in the strongest possible terms. But King George V's slight reservations about the matter collapsed in the face of the Prince of Wales's entreaties; while to Prince Albert the King could only say that he felt sure that his son would not like to be treated differently from anyone else.

As far as the heir was concerned, the War Office was not quite so amenable. On being gazetted to the Grenadier Guards (despite the fact that he was only five feet, seven inches tall) the Prince of Wales came up against official resistance to his being sent to France. 'What does it matter if I am killed?' he asked the disapproving Lord Kitchener. 'I have four brothers.'[38] His possible death, answered Lord Kitchener bluntly, was not really the problem; it would not do for the heir to the throne to be taken prisoner. But the persistent Prince got his way. He was sent to France, not as a combatant, but as a member of the staff of Field-Marshal Sir John French. In the course of the next four years, he spent a great deal of his time trying to get into the firing line.

These war-time years saw the Prince at his best: modest, friendly, un-complaining, courageous and enthusiastic. There was no doubt about his eagerness to share all dangers and discomforts. That he was seldom allowed to do so was not his fault. The men understood that and, in time, the Prince won immense popularity. More even than his parents, was the Prince of Wales able, and willing, to make contact with ordinary people. For the monarchy, this was to prove invaluable. 'I tried to make her see,' wrote Lord Esher of a wartime visit to Queen Mary, 'that after the war thrones might be at a discount, and that the Prince of Wales's popularity might be a great asset.'[39]

Prince Albert's career in the navy was somewhat more chequered. In September 1913, with his training at Dartmouth completed, the Prince had joined HMS *Collingwood* of the First Battle Squadron as an ordinary mid-shipman. For the next four years, Prince Albert served in the navy as plain 'Mr Johnson'. But a duodenal ulcer rendered his time in the navy as anything but plain sailing. For several long periods he was obliged to absent himself from his duties. These forced spells of inactivity depressed him considerably. No less anxious than the Prince of Wales to be in the thick of the fighting, Prince Albert felt guilty about not playing his part.

His opportunity came at the Battle of Jutland. The twenty-two-year-old

Prince had not long rejoined HMS *Collingwood* as a sub-lieutenant, after one of his spells of illness, than the First Battle Squadron was involved in the attack on the German Fleet in the North Sea. The engagement, on 31 May 1916, was the greatest naval battle of the war. All through that long misty afternoon Prince Albert remained at his post in the turret while the desperate fighting raged all round him.

'I never felt any fear of shells or anything else,' he confided to the Prince of Wales afterwards. 'It seems curious but all sense of danger and everything else goes except the one longing of dealing death in every possible way to the enemy.'[40] King George, on hearing of his son's bravery under fire, felt very proud. The fact that a monarch's son had been involved in so potentially hazardous a situation was exceptional. Not until Queen Elizabeth II's second son, Prince Andrew, fought in the Falklands War of 1982, was a British prince again exposed to such real danger.

Not long after Prince Albert's moment of glory his naval career came to an end. Once again his ulcer caused him long periods of discomfort and in-activity. By the time he was successfully operated on, in November 1917, he had agreed regretfully to leave the navy. He left it with a reputation for reliability, zeal and good sense. Although not blessed with his older brother's powers of attraction, Prince Albert was an unaffected and likeable young man, and one who had borne those long periods of pain and frustration with remarkable fortitude.

Although there was never any doubt about King George V's patriotism, he was never as rabidly anti-German as a great many of his subjects. Of German descent and as a member of the great international family of kings, he had a much more balanced view of the situation. In the early days of the war he had resisted several hysterical suggestions for the purging of all things German from the national scene; such changes as he felt necessary to make had been made without fanfare. Princess Mary's beloved German maid had been sent quietly home; the Kaiser and his eldest son had been deprived of their honorary British commands and their names had been dropped from the Army List; in the face of considerable public agitation, the King had reluc-tantly agreed to a private removal, from St George's Chapel, Windsor, of the banners of various enemy Knights of the Garter and to the striking of their names off the roll of the Order. He had refused, though, to have the brass plates bearing their names taken down above the Garter stalls. 'They are historical records,' wrote his secretary firmly, 'and His Majesty does not intend to have any of them removed.'[41]

Against his better judgement, the King had also been obliged to accept the forced resignation of his close relation, Prince Louis of Battenberg, as First Sea Lord. Prince Louis's undoubted abilities had apparently counted for nothing when set against his undoubtedly German name.

By the year 1917, with the longed-for victory against Germany as seemingly remote as ever, civilian frustration gave rise to a new jingoistic clamour. This time it was directed against the royal family itself. What hope was there of a British victory, it was asked, when Britain's reigning family was German? Certain Socialists took the argument a step further. What need was there of a reigning family at all? With Russia having just got rid of its Tsar, why should Britain not get rid of its King? There was no reason, argued H.G. Wells publicly, why Britain should suffer 'an alien and uninspiring court'.

To this King George gave a characteristically robust answer. 'I may be uninspiring,' he growled, 'but I'll be damned if I'm alien.'[42]

Yet there was no denying that the name of his House was alien. Not that anyone was exactly sure what that name was. Was it 'Saxe-Coburg and Gotha'? No, thought the College of Heralds, it was probably 'Wettin' or, even more outlandish, 'Wipper'. Well, whatever it was, the Prime Minister, Lloyd George, was all for changing it. What was needed was an uncompromisingly British name.

Various suggestions were made and rejected. It was Lord Stamfordham, the King's secretary, who came up with the answer – 'Windsor'. Nothing could have been more suitable. Windsor Castle – so old, so assured, so enduring – had always been regarded as the monarchy's spiritual home. The House of Windsor had a resoundingly British ring to it.

The new name was proclaimed in London on 17 July 1917. That process of Anglicisation of the British royal family, begun by King Edward VII, was given a considerable boost by King George V's changing of the family name. In the years ahead, and through the marriages of the King's sons, it became less German still.

The change of name was not confined to the King's immediate family. Other branches of the royal family to be affected by the ruling were the Tecks and the Battenbergs. The King's two brothers-in-law, the Duke of Teck and Prince Alexander of Teck, became respectively the Marquess of Cambridge and the Earl of Athlone, taking their late mother's family name of Cambridge. And the King's two cousins, the recently dismissed Prince Louis of Battenberg and Prince Alexander of Battenberg, became respectively Marquess of Milford Haven and Marquess of Carisbrook, with the family name Anglicised to Mountbatten.

In time, the new names of Windsor and Mountbatten became interestingly juxtaposed. When George V's grand-daughter, the future Queen Elizabeth II, married Prince Louis of Battenberg's grandson, Lieutenant Philip Mountbatten, in 1947, it was assumed that their children would bear the surname Mountbatten. This meant, in effect, that their eldest son, Prince Charles, would found a new reigning dynasty, with the name Mountbatten replacing Windsor as the name of the royal House. But two months after her accession in 1952, Queen Elizabeth II issued a proclamation to the effect that this would not be the case: she and her children would be 'styled and known as the House and Family of Windsor.' Eight years later she issued a further, if less precise, statement: although the name of her House was to remain Windsor, her husband's surname would from now on be part of the royal surname. Her descendants were to be known as 'Mountbatten-Windsor'.

At the same time as changing the name of his House, King George V made provision for the titles to be borne by members of the royal family in the future. The King was anxious to avoid that embarrassing proliferation of princes, characteristic of so many Continental royal families. His provisions affected the male line only, as the children of sovereign's daughters inherit no titles through the mother. Today, for instance, Princess Anne's son is simply Peter Phillips. But the sovereign's sons, born princes and styled Royal Highness, become royal dukes in adult life. In turn, their children are also princes and princesses but only the eldest son succeeds to the ducal title. *His* children are not princes and princesses but, because their father is a duke, they are lords and ladies. In this way, by restricting the use of the title Royal Highness to two generations only, King George V was able to limit the number of future princes to the immediate royal family.

The Kent family illustrates perfectly the process. George V's youngest surviving son, Prince George, became HRH Duke of Kent. His three children were Prince Edward, Princess Alexandra and Prince Michael. On the Duke of Kent's death in 1942, his elder son became HRH Duke of Kent. *His* eldest son – as the eldest son of a duke – has the courtesy title of the Earl of St Andrews. As Princess Alexandra's husband has no title, her eldest son is merely Mr James Ogilvy. But HRH Prince Michael's eldest son – despite the fact that Prince Michael is not a duke – is Lord Frederick Windsor. This is because George V, not wishing the change from prince to commoner to be too sudden, decreed that the younger sons in the third generation should rank as the younger sons of dukes.

It was as the first sovereign of the House of Windsor then, that King George V appeared on the balcony of Buckingham Palace on 11 November 1918 to face the vast, hysterically applauding multitude below. For in spite of those four long, heartbreaking, disillusioning years, in spite of the carping about the King's German ancestry, in spite of the collapse of monarchies all over Europe, it was to Buckingham Palace that the crowds surged to celebrate the coming of peace. Deep into the night the crowd cheered the figures of the King and Queen as time and again they appeared on the red and gold draped balcony, smiling their slightly shy smiles, nodding their slightly stiff nods, waving their slightly self-conscious waves. Yet, no less than those of the uninhibited crowds below, were the hearts of the King and Queen stirred by this momentous occasion.

'Another wonderful scene,' wrote Queen Mary of their final balcony

King George V

appearance that night, 'a day full of emotion and thankfulness – tinged with regret at the many lives who have fallen in this ghastly war.'[43]

Father and Sons

'IN SPITE OF the unceasing labours and devotion to public duties of the King and Queen during the last three years,' wrote Lord Cromer towards the end of the war, 'the fact remains that the position of the Monarchy is not so stable now, in 1918, as it was at the beginning of the War. It seems therefore imperative that in the critical times with which the country is now faced, no stone should be left unturned in the endeavour to consolidate the position of the Crown.'[1]

The ubiquitous Lord Esher put it even more bluntly. In a letter to the King's secretary, he declared that the monarchy now stood at 'the parting of the ways'. The Crown and its cost 'will have to be justified in the future in the eyes of a war-torn and hungry proletariat, endowed with a huge preponderance of voting power.'[2]

Their lordships had every reason to be apprehensive. The end of the war had seen a wholesale collapse of European monarchies. The three mightiest thrones of Continental Europe – those of Austria, Germany and Russia – had fallen; King Constantine had been driven out of Greece; all the reigning kings, princes, grand dukes and dukes of imperial Germany had been stripped of their positions and powers; even in the Netherlands the royal House was under threat. The Spanish throne had always been unsteady and in just over a decade it, too, was toppled. The only major European throne still standing was the British.

Republicanism, which had by now spread over most of the Continent, had an ardent champion in that hero of the hour, the American President, Woodrow Wilson. He saw republicanism as the New World's cure for the Old World's ills. He felt confident that it alone could meet the aspirations of the common man. 'The strength of Republicanism,' warned Lord Esher, 'lies in the *personality* of Wilson . . . He has made the "fashion" of a Republic. We can "go one better" if we try.'[3]

But how? The British working class, in those years after the First World War, was hardly less discontented that their Continental brothers. Ex-servicemen were suffering from an inevitable disillusionment, unemployment was high, wages were low, pensions were inadequate, houses were scarce. In turn, this industrial distress affected the popularity of the throne. At one review of ex-servicemen, the King was faced by a defiant, banner-waving crowd. There was even some talk, at political meetings, of the possibility of the Red Flag one day flying over Buckingham Palace.

That the Royal Standard continued to fly over the Palace was due to many things: victory in battle, a national sense of continuity, a dislike of violent change, a reverence and affection for the throne, an awareness of the way in which the monarchy had become identified with all the people rather than (as was so often the case on the Continent) with the aristocracy alone, and, not least of all, an appreciation of the personalities of King George and Queen Mary. Not even the most dedicated republican could deny that they were an upright, hard-working and well-intentioned couple. Both by their tireless public appearances and by their no less tireless work behind the scenes, the King and Queen were proving their worth.

'I went to a football match at which there were 73,000 people,' reported a delighted King George to his mother, 'at the end they sang the National Anthem and cheered tremendously. There were no bolsheviks there!'[4]

And as for the not unfair criticism that the King and Queen might, in the post-war world, appear somewhat out of date, the monarchy had an answer: the modern trend towards republicanism could be counteracted by the no less modern figure of the Prince of Wales. In order to popularise the Crown, to keep the monarchy moving with the times, the undoubted talents and energies of the Prince of Wales must be put to good use.

What chance was there for President Wilson's theories, however alluring, when set against the aura of romance which enveloped the young heir to the throne?

And the potency of the Prince's personal magnetism was needed as much abroad as at home. Since the end of the war, the bonds of Empire had shown signs of slackening; the link between the mother country and the colonies could no longer be taken for granted. These countries were becoming increasingly restive. There was considerable resentment at being tied, in a fashion, to Britain's apron strings. As yet, the various countries making up the Empire were not really autonomous. The idea of a free association of equal partners, united by a common allegiance to the Crown in a British commonwealth of nations, had still to be formulated. But during the 1920s the relationship between Britain and her colonies was changing. What was important was that the most significant link between these countries – the Crown – be kept intact. Whatever else changed, that must remain.

What better way of ensuring this than by sending a representative of the monarch to visit these far-flung dominions? And what better representative than the Prince of Wales? Here was no staid, old-fashioned, puppet-like

11 The royal family on the occasion of the Duke of York's wedding in 1923.
Standing, from the left: the Prince of Wales, Prince Henry, George V, the Duke
of York, Prince George. Seated: Princess Mary and Queen Mary

12 An unusually relaxed and intimate study of George V and Queen Mary
chatting to Colonel Calley in April 1924

Balmoral 1928.

George R.I.

13 George V and his grand-daughter, Princess Elizabeth (the future Queen
Elizabeth II) photographed by the Duke of York at Balmoral in 1928

14 George V at the helm of the royal yacht

princeling, but an informal and engaging young man, very much in tune with the changing world. As Prime Minister Lloyd George, with whom the idea originated, once explained, 'the appearance of the popular Prince of Wales in far corners of the Empire might do more to calm the discord than half-a-dozen solemn imperial conferences.'[5]

The Prince was all for it. But as usual, he felt uncertain about his role as heir apparent. 'Who exactly was I?'[6] he asked of himself. On the one hand, his experiences at naval college, Oxford and on the battlefields of France had taught him that he was really no better than anyone else: on the other, his father was constantly reminding him that he could not act like other people, that he must remember who he was. 'The Monarchy,' warned that long-serving courtier, Sir Frederick Ponsonby, 'must always retain an element of mystery. A Prince should not show himself too much. The Monarchy must remain on a pedestal.'

When the Prince protested that he saw one of his chief tasks as the bringing of the Crown nearer to the people, Ponsonby disagreed. 'If you bring it down to the people,' he argued, 'it will lose its mystery and influence.'[7]

It was a vital question. How close should the Crown be brought, not down, but to the people? The Prince of Wales, by the exercise of his considerable charm and talent, seemed intent on bringing it very close indeed. Yet after his abdication as Edward VIII in 1936, it was thought, in palace circles, that he had rather forced the pace, that he had somehow got the balance wrong, that the process of democratisation should be slowed down. Not until his successor, King George VI, had been on the throne for some years was the balance restored. That the Prince of Wales had helped popularise the monarchy there can be no doubt but there was a nagging feeling that he had somehow diminished it.

At the same time the Prince faced that other perennial dilemma. What exactly was a Prince of Wales expected to do? It was during this period that he one day called on his mother's lady-in-waiting, Lady Airlie.

'He sat for over an hour on a stool in front of the fire smoking one cigarette after another and talking his heart out,' she wrote in her diary. 'He was nervous and frustrated, pulled this way and that. The Queen had told him that she was urging the King to keep him in England – "to learn to govern" as she put it, and to make up for the gap in his constitutional experience caused by the war. Mr Lloyd George on the other hand had evolved a plan for a series of Empire tours for the heir to the throne, to strengthen relations with the people of the Commonwealth. The King was inclining to this idea, and the Prince himself preferred it . . .'

'I shall have to work to keep my job,' said the Prince to Lady Airlie. 'I don't mind that, but the trouble is, they won't let me have a free hand.'[8]

*

And so, for six years, from the age of twenty-five in 1919 until the age of thirty-one in 1925, the Prince of Wales travelled the world. In the course of four mammoth official tours, he visited fifty-five countries and covered 150,000 miles. It was an exhilarating and an exhausting business. Travel suited his mercurial temperament but the strain on this ever-smiling 'Salesman of the Empire' was tremendous. So much of what he had to do was dull routine, yet he was expected to do it with every indication of enjoyment. His experiences were the experiences of all members of the royal family, then and now, who undertake tours abroad.

'I had come to comprehend as never before,' he afterwards wrote, 'the varied burdens of duty that lie upon a Prince of Wales, imposing far greater mental and physical strains than were generally appreciated at the time. Lonely drives through tumultuous crowds, the almost daily inspections of serried ranks of veterans, the inexhaustible supply of cornerstones to be laid, the commemorative trees to be planted, deputations to be met, and everywhere the sad visits to hospital wards, every step bringing me face to face with some inconsolable tragedy calling for a heartening word from me, and always more hands to shake than a dozen Princes could have coped with – such was the substance of my official days.'[9]

No wonder that he could quote the advice of an old courtier as being the soundest he had ever been given: 'Only two rules really count. Never miss an opportunity to relieve yourself; never miss a chance to sit down and rest your feet.'[10]

It was during the 1920s that the Prince of Wales developed, both at home and abroad, into the most popular figure of the age. Slight, slim, good-looking, with an enduring boyishness that belied his years, he was the prototype Prince Charming, the darling of the Empire. No international personality was as well known, no country boasted a better roving ambassador, no bachelor in the world was more eligible. Heir to the greatest throne on earth, the Prince of Wales nevertheless seemed to epitomise his times: he appeared casual, unconventional, impatient of protocol, and determined to enjoy every minute of the day. Not even at his most engaging has the Prince of Wales's grand-nephew, Prince Charles, been able to match his predecessor's allure.

Yet to those who knew him well, the Prince of Wales was not quite the golden boy of popular imagination. He had some grave defects of character. He lacked serious-mindedness. He seldom read, he was not really interested in politics, he avoided anyone who was too scholarly or informed. He was impulsive, restless, unreliable. Lacking inner resources, he gave himself over to the pursuit of pleasure. He loved parties, practical jokes, fancy dress, the whole frenetic round of the Jazz Age. In many ways he was not unlike King Edward VII during his years as Prince of Wales.

But, at the same time, this Prince of Wales had a strong streak of melancholia; during his ever more frequent black moods he could be petulant and inconsiderate. He was not even as democratic or progressive as he was imagined to be. His apparent enlightenment was merely a reaction to what he regarded as his father's stuffiness. His public diffidence, that dislike of homage, led many to believe that he was less concerned with his position than was actually the case.

With the passing years, those who were close to the Prince found themselves becoming more and more irritated by his free-and-easy behaviour. 'He could be *very* naughty,'[11] claimed his Aunt, Princess Alice, Countess of Athlone. Less mature, less disciplined, less conscientious and less dignified than his father had been at his age, and lacking the anchor of a wife, the Prince of Wales was always ready to kick over the traces. The longer he toured the Empire, the more frequent were the complaints about his frivolity, his unpunctuality, his rudeness and his lack of consideration.

But, on the whole, such grumblings were rare. For most of the time, the blonde, blue-eyed and wistful-looking Prince moved in an aura of adulation. The world was his oyster and wherever he went, he was fêted, acclaimed and fawned upon. Few could deny that in the course of these highly publicised global junketings, the Prince of Wales had fulfilled his main task superlatively. His presence had aroused emotions of intense loyalty towards the Crown. He had proved that in the post-war world it could still spread its indefinable, unifying magic.

The final victory over 'those beastly Germans'[12] had brought the ageing Queen Alexandra immense satisfaction. Throughout the war she had flung herself, with characteristic impetuosity, into any activity which she imagined would help defeat the enemy. Unlike Queen Mary, whose powers of organisation had contributed to the setting up of various wartime institutions, Queen Alexandra simply followed the promptings of her generous heart. She gave away vast sums to wartime charities, she lent her name to various fund-raising schemes, she spent hours visiting hospitals. For these hospital visits, she became especially celebrated. Her obvious concern, as she moved gracefully through the wards, brought great comfort to the wounded. Once, on being told that a patient was feeling particularly depressed because he had just heard that his wounded knee would be permanently useless, the Queen hurried to his side. As she had suffered from a stiff leg for years, she could sympathise with the man's despair.

'My dear, dear man,' she said. 'I hear you have a stiff leg; so have I. Now just watch what I can do with it.'[13] With that, the Queen lifted her skirt and swung her lame leg over the seat of a nearby chair.

One really could not imagine Queen Mary doing that.

Ready enough to give money away, Queen Alexandra stubbornly refused to make any financial sacrifices. She would not hear of running Marlborough House or the big house at Sandringham along even slightly more economic lines. She could never understand that, as a King's widow and not his consort, her parliamentary allowance was now taxed. Nor could she comprehend that increases in taxation meant that, by the end of the war, her income was less than half of what it had been before it. To any talk of cutting down expenses, Queen Alexandra remained conveniently deaf.

'I don't care,' she would exclaim blithely. 'I shall do as I please; if I get into debt *they* can pay.'

'*Who* will pay, Ma'am?' insisted one bold member of her household. 'Certainly not the nation for they won't pay a penny. It will all fall on King George or Princess Victoria and it isn't right or fair on them.'[14]

To this, the Queen proved more deaf than ever. She had not heard a word, she protested.

King George V's forebearance with his erratic mother was little less than saintly. Not only did he help her out financially but he visited her and wrote to her as often as his crowded schedule would allow. Another source of comfort to the Queen were her grandchildren. On them she could lavish all the love and attention denied them by their less demonstrative parents. The Prince of Wales, who had inherited what he called her 'wonderful way with people'[15] was devoted to her. The two of them would often sit playing cards or doing jigsaw puzzles. She, in turn, adored him. 'May God grant him a perfect wife!'[16] she would exclaim.

But, on the whole, the passing years had brought Queen Alexandra few consolations. Seventy-three at the end of the First World War, she simply could not adjust to growing old. In this, she was proving quite different from the widowed queens who followed her: Queen Mary and the Queen Mother. What she minded losing, most of all, was her marvellous beauty. Year after year, decade after decade, it had seemed as though time would never touch her. When it did, it took everything. Queen Alexandra's beauty had depended on youth, or at least the illusion of youth. Unlike some women, she could not look both old and beautiful. And, with her looks went her elegance. From having been so transcendently smart, she suddenly appeared quaintly old-fashioned, even bizarre. In the post-war period of rapidly changing fashions, she clung to the styles of her heyday: the towering toques, the spotted veils, the feather boas, the nipped-in waists and the floor-length skirts.

Nor was Queen Alexandra equipped for the changing tempo of old age. Without mental resources, she could find few ways of amusing or interesting herself. Her pleasures, like her beauty, had depended on youth. Her talk, these days, was all of the past. She would bemoan her lost looks, her failing sight, her poor memory, her total deafness. Always rather distrait, her weakening faculties made her more so. Unabashed, she would suddenly ask some startled guest if her wig were on straight, and a visitor to Marlborough House once discovered her walking about the room chanting *God Save the King* over and over to herself.

For the last half-dozen or so years of her life, Queen Alexandra lived away from the public gaze, preferring the company of her devoted household. To them, she remained the 'Beloved Lady', a mistress of exceptional qualities.

And so, in a way, she was. Despite all the contrariness of her nature, Queen Alexandra had made a considerable contribution to the British monarchy. For she brought more than just her decorativeness, gaiety and grace into the reigning House. She increased immeasurably its popularity and its accessibility. By creating a harmonious family circle, by introducing a simplicity and a domesticity into its daily life, Queen Alexandra ensured that the royal family was able to adjust more easily to changing circumstances. She helped keep the British court free of much of the pomposity, formality and intransigence that had been the downfall of many Continental courts. The unpretentiousness which Queen Alexandra introduced into the British royal family – which seemed so exceptional at the time – is the royal rule today.

Queen Alexandra died, at the age of eighty, on 20 November 1925.

In the year 1922 King George V turned fifty-seven, Queen Mary fifty-five. By now the couple had developed fully the appearance, attitudes and lifestyles that remained constant for the rest of the King's reign. Although they carried out their public duties conscientiously and with great dignity, they were happiest in the comparative peace and privacy of their own homes. With the passing years, the King had come to value simplicity and seclusion more and more, and the Queen, who had never had any taste for society, was only too ready to fall in with her husband's wishes. Except when attending official functions, the couple lunched and dined at home; they entertained only when strictly necessary; they were usually in bed by ten-thirty. The King was happiest shooting at Sandringham or Balmoral; the Queen was content to carry on with her hobby of reorganising and cataloguing the royal collection of paintings, furniture and china. In the sixteen years between the end of the First World War and the King's death, the couple spent only seven weeks out of Britain; and five of these were spent cruising the Mediterranean for the sake of the King's health. Surrounded by all the turbulence of the 1920s, the royal couple lived a tranquil, well-ordered, highly respectable life. The palaces might have been magnificent, the pomp unequalled and the organisation faultless but the atmosphere remained curiously domestic.

One significant result of the King's distaste for dinner parties and country house visiting (a distaste which became even more marked in his son, George VI) was a gradual distancing of the Crown from the great families and from the aristocracy generally. As the reign progressed, so did the King become

less a leader of society and more a national *paterfamilias*. 'The important thing
to remember,' said one grandee without too much exaggeration, 'is that in
the eyes of the royal family we're all glorified footmen and ladies' maids.'[17]

Queen Mary, who had long since dedicated herself to the smoothing of her
husband's path, was quite happy to defer to him in everything. 'She had more
originality of mind than he,' writes Lady Airlie, 'and their views on current
topics often differed widely, but when he contradicted her she never argued
with him, or tried to press the point as most women would.'[18] Repressing her
own 'naturally gay and sociable temperament'[19] the Queen adapted herself to
his staid, rigidly conservative outlook. Only very rarely did she try, un-
successfully, to follow some current fad or fashion. When the King once
discovered her trying out a new dance step with one of the courtiers, he was
so incensed that she never repeated the experiment. Nor did he leave her in
any doubt about what he thought of her attempt to shorten her skirts. The
Queen, claims Lady Airlie, had very shapely legs, but because of the King's
firmly held conviction that a woman's legs should not be seen in public, his
wife's were destined to remain forever unappreciated.

In fact, Queen Mary's unchanging, instantly recognisable appearance was
entirely due to the King's prejudices in the matter of dress. Just as he, who
always looked immaculate, stuck to the frock coats and top hats of his youth,
so did he expect the Queen to adhere to the styles of her youth. In that era of
boyish fashions, Queen Mary remained faithful to the pre-war opulence
approved of by her husband.

In the long run, her unvarying style was to prove a distinct advantage: it
helped, in that time of flux and dissolution, towards giving the monarchy its
stable, dependable, traditional air. Whatever else might change, one could
always be sure of Queen Mary's toques, pearl chokers, pastel colours, fur
trimmings, lavish fabrics, parasols, ankle-length skirts and long, pointed
shoes.

In the same way that she deferred to her husband's tastes and never
questioned his opinions, so did Queen Mary put up with his violent temper
and his occasionally coarse talk. Examples of his explosive comments and
bawdy observations are legion. 'That's right; break up the whole bloody
place!'[20] he bawled at a nervous footman who dropped a tray. Sir Samuel
Hoare, on being forced to resign as Foreign Secretary because of the regrettable Hoare-Laval Treaty – decided upon in Paris – was not at all amused by
the King's little joke: 'no more coals to Newcastle, no more Hoares to
Paris.'[21] And the monarch's disconcertingly frank question to Charles Lind-
bergh, newly arrived from his trans-Atlantic flight, was 'What do you do
about peeing?'[22]

Queen Mary's way of coping with his ribald remarks was to behave as
though she had not heard them. And whenever his vehemently expressed
opinions came flooding out of the audience room for all to hear, the Queen,

with her twitching smile, would simply cross to the door and close it.

The royal couple remained devoted to each other. 'King George's rough manner and his rather oriental views on wifehood and womanhood sometimes combined to hide the very real love and admiration he had for his wife,' claims Lady Airlie. 'But how often when I was sitting reading to her before dinner, while she rested on her sofa, wrapped in a kimono of a lovely pale shade, embroidered cushions behind her beautifully coiffured head, would he come in with some letter about which he wanted to consult her. There was no mistaking the pleasure with which his eyes would light on her . . .'[23]

'It is delightful to think we shall meet I hope in three days,' wrote the Queen to her husband during one of their rare separations. 'Three weeks is a long time to be parted for a Darby and Joan such as we are!'[24]

Unfortunately, this domestic idyll did not embrace the whole royal family. Far from it. Relations between the King and his sons were worse than ever. By 1922 the ages of these four young men – the Prince of Wales (David), Prince Albert (Bertie), Prince Henry (Harry) and Prince George – ranged from twenty-eight to twenty. It was an age-span with which the King felt particularly ill at ease. So hidebound, so disciplined, so unimaginative, so obsessed with duty and responsibility, the King simply could not appreciate the fact that his sons wanted to lead different sorts of lives. Not only did he feel unable to communicate with the younger generation, he disapproved violently of almost everything they did. He subjected them either to his embarrassingly hearty brand of banter or to his strongly worded censure.

Having enjoyed so satisfactory a relationship with his own father, it was odd that George V should have been incapable of establishing a more sympathetic rapport with his own sons.

Yet, for all the King's complaining, these four princes played their public roles to the best of their abilities. Their responsibilities were the responsibilities of all members of a royal family, then and now. They were representatives of the Crown, minor versions of the Sovereign, planets to the Sovereign's sun. In times of the monarch's absence or illness, they were expected to deputise for him. They acted as Counsellors of State, empowered to hold investitures, receive delegations, accept ambassadors' credentials and sign documents.

Their official duties were considerable. They accompanied their parents on state occasions such as the Opening of Parliament or Trooping the Colour; and on social occasions such as garden parties or race meetings. They undertook tours and missions abroad; they visited industrial areas at home. They became presidents of hospitals, institutes, societies and associations. They received the freedom of cities. They inspected troops and talked to ex-servicemen. They attended dinners and receptions. They laid foundation stones, they planted trees, they made speeches, they shook thousands upon thousands of hands. Quite often, their duties reflected, and still reflect, their particular interests; so that nowadays Princess Margaret is associated with the world of theatre, her cousin the Duke of Gloucester with architecture and the Princess of Wales with children.

A difference in King George V's time was that his sons had far more leisure than is the case today. Not only was a prince not expected to earn his own living but no prince was as meaningfully employed as is, say, the present Prince of Wales. But even if they had been, it is doubtful whether they would have met George V's exacting standards.

The King was especially critical of his eldest son: of his clothes, his friends, his amusements, his conduct both at home and abroad. 'You dress like a cad. You act like a cad. You *are* a cad. Get out!' a palace official once heard the King roaring in his 'best storm at sea voice'.[25] He was only too ready to believe every highly coloured report, in American newspapers particularly, detailing the heir's apparently outrageous behaviour. Father and son seemed to speak a different language. Once, at Sandringham, the Prince congratulated the King on doing something which he described as 'good propaganda'. The King was furious. 'I told him never to say anything like that again. I do things because they're my duty; not as propaganda.'[26] Indeed the King, who saw his main task as upholding the dignity of the Crown by setting high standards of industry and morality, would never have dreamed of consciously courting popularity or seeking praise.

By this stage of his life, the Prince of Wales had managed to get away from home: he had established himself, with his own staff, at York House, his parents' old home in St James's Palace. 'I don't want to marry for a long time,' he admitted to a friend. 'But at twenty-five I can't live under the same roof as my parents. I must be free to lead my own life.'[27] From York House, whenever he was home from those long Empire tours, the Prince of Wales would apply himself, both to his manifold duties and to his no less manifold pleasures.

But even here he could not escape his father's censure. 'At times,' wrote a friend, 'his parents humiliated him to the point where he actually burst into tears. I tried to put some stuffing into him. After one really angry row with his father, he came to my house and flung himself into a chair and shouted "I'm fed up! I've taken all I can stand."

'I told him, "You don't *have* to take any more! Stand up for yourself!"

'He went on, "I want no more of this princing! I want to be an ordinary person. I *must* have a life of my own!"

'I said, "Ah, that's different! You *can't* be an ordinary person . . ."'[28]

Nor could he be. For the Prince of Wales was suffering, more than most, from that recurring royal problem: the reconciling of one's public and personal lives.

Almost ceaselessly cheered, applauded, photographed, stared at, deferred to and fawned upon, the members of the family could never think of themselves as anything other than royal. They could never hope to enjoy, to the full, the advantages of a private life. The dichotomy holds good to this day. Even the most emancipated member of the royal family feels the weight of royal birth, the pull of royal responsibilities. The Prince of Wales, as King Edward VIII, was to break under the strain; others, such as Princess Margaret, have never wholly resolved the problem.

'I don't know what it's like *not* to be royal,' Princess Anne said recently. 'How can you answer that question unless you've got a comparison? I don't have one . . .' There was, she sighed, 'a constant battle'[29] between priorities – between one's public obligations and one's private inclinations.

And another member of the family, Prince William of Gloucester, who was to be killed in an aeroplane accident in 1972, once claimed that it was 'almost impossible to describe what it is like being a member of the Royal Family. I suppose in essence what it boils down to is this: you can never be your real self. Just to know you are Royal inhibits you. It wasn't that anyone ever said to me, you are a Royal Prince and you must act like one. I simply knew that whether I liked it or not, I was automatically separated by my heritage from the rest of the world.'[30]

Any such reservations about one's royal status would have been all but incomprehensible to King George V. Except that public appearances were always a challenge to his innate shyness, he had no difficulty whatsoever in reconciling his public and private lives, and he could see no reason why his sons' lives should not be carbon copies of his.

His second son, Prince Albert, who had been created Duke of York in 1920, was finding it almost as difficult as the Prince of Wales to please his demanding father. It was noticed that his stammer was always worse in the King's presence. Faced by his father's steely gaze, his small stock of self-confidence deserted him. Yet left alone, Prince Albert acquitted himself very well. When, for instance, the Prince travelled to Romania to represent the King at the Coronation of King Ferdinand and Queen Marie, he was said to have made an 'unqualified success' of his mission.

But the King refused to believe it. It was left to Lord Stamfordham to impress upon the sceptical monarch that once Prince Albert 'got away on his own he was a different being and never failed to "rise to the occasion".'[31]

King George remained sceptical. He once sent Prince Albert, then away on tour, a press photograph. 'I send you a picture of you inspecting Gd of Honour (I don't think much of their dressing) with yr Equerry walking on yr right side next to the Gd, & ignoring the officer entirely. Yr Equerry should be outside and behind, it certainly does not look well.'[32]

Resignedly, the Prince wrote back to explain that the photograph had been taken after and not during the inspection.

Even though Prince Albert was nothing like as sociable as his elder brother, he found the court intolerably dull. 'No new blood is ever introduced,' he once complained during Ascot Week, 'and as the members of the party grow older every year there's no spring in it, and no originality in the talk – nothing but dreary acquiescence is the order of the day. No one has the exciting feeling that if they shine they will be asked again next summer – they know they will be automatically, as long as they are alive. Traditionalism is all very well, but too much of it leads to dry rot.'[33]

The third son, Prince Henry, by now an officer in the 10th Royal Hussars, won his father's grudging approval only for his sporting prowess. Diffident, insecure, accident-prone, Prince Henry devoted a great deal of his time to vigorous physical exercise. His passions were confined to hunting, shooting, riding and polo. To Prince Henry, no less than to the other sons, the King adopted his brusque, quarter-deck manner. Once, on returning from an overseas tour, the Prince found that the family had already gone in to luncheon. 'Late as usual!'[34] barked his father by way of greeting.

The family table was again the scene for another confrontation between the King and his third son. This time it was at breakfast. Prince Henry, having been caught creeping into the palace at five in the morning after a night's dancing, had been reported to his father. It was a cast-iron rule that the princes came down to breakfast at five to nine, then stood waiting for the arrival, as Big Ben struck nine, of their parents. On this particular morning Prince Henry compounded his crime by being a minute or two late. As he hurried in, his father fixed him with his fierce, unblinking gaze. Prince Henry promptly fainted.

'The strange part,' says one observer, 'is that instead of being sympathetic, the other boys were delighted.'

'I can well believe it,' commented a member of the household. 'The brothers were all jealous of one another. The only time they were happy was when one of them got into trouble with their father. He considered them dolts, the lot of them . . .'[35]

And of all four sons, the youngest, Prince George, probably suffered most from his father's blustering talk and unyielding attitudes. His emotional, artistic, unconventional nature was something that the King would never have been able to appreciate. Like his two eldest brothers, Prince George had been sent to the naval colleges of Osborne and Dartmouth; since then he had served in the Royal Navy. He hated it. Sitting beside Lady Airlie at dinner one evening, Prince George admitted that he was 'dreading' his next voyage. He was 'very unhappy' in the navy and longed to break new royal ground by entering the Civil Service or the Foreign Office. But his father would not hear of it.

'His only reason for refusing is that it has never been done before,' complained the Prince. 'I've tried to make him see that I'm not cut out for the

Navy, but it's no use. What can I do?'[36]

With their mother, Queen Mary, the relationship of these four princes was somewhat better. She could sometimes be relied upon to put in a good word for them or to act as a buffer between them and their father. Yet they did not really feel at ease with her, or she with them. Her first loyalty, reckoned the Queen, lay with her husband and, in any case, she remained strangely inhibited with her sons. 'They were strangers to her emotionally,' says Lady Airlie, 'a nest of wild birds already spreading their wings and soaring beyond her horizon.'[37] The Queen could never bring herself to discuss anything really serious or intimate with them. 'David dined with me in the evening,' reads a typical report from the Queen to the King, 'we talked a lot but of nothing very intimate.'[38]

'She really is far too reserved,' commented Prince Albert to the Prince of Wales on one occasion, 'she keeps too much locked up inside herself.'[39]

The royal family, noted one member of the household, 'were not given to talking things out together, even *en famille*. If anything was wrong, the subject was carefully avoided. They would talk about shooting, the weather, a friend's marriage, the shocking behaviour of the French – but never a word about the subject gnawing their souls.'[40]

With their only daughter, Princess Mary, the King and Queen were on quite different terms. They doted on her. For year after year this shy and attractive princess had lived very close to her parents. During the war she had done her share of public duties: launching appeals, visiting hospitals, presenting awards, inspecting canteens, working for various charitable organisations. She had even crossed to France in her capacity as a commandant of the British Red Cross Society, to tour various camps and hospitals.

After the war, Princess Mary blazed yet another royal trail: she spent two years working as a nurse in the Hospital for Sick Children in Great Ormond Street. At the time, Princess Mary's decision seemed daring in the extreme. 'Is she a *real* Princess?'[41] was the inevitable question asked by the children of this capable and cheerfully smiling nurse as she went about her everyday tasks. Simultaneously, Princess Mary was involved in a more conventional royal activity: she was a girl guide and in 1920 became President of the girl guides. It is reassuring to read that even in this repressed royal household, the Princess was subjected to the usual brotherly ragging.

'You see,' she once explained on arriving uncharacteristically late for some guide rally, 'I had to change *after* luncheon. My brothers always tease me so much when I am in uniform, that I simply couldn't face them in it!'[42]

But her brothers had more serious concerns about her than this. In the year 1921, Princess Mary turned twenty-four. By the standards, particularly royal standards, of the time, this was late for a girl to be unmarried. The Prince of

Wales was especially worried by his sister's continuing spinsterhood. The truth was that King George was very loath to lose his favourite child; the Prince of Wales was afraid that his father was planning to keep her permanently by his side, as Queen Alexandra had kept Princess Victoria.

But his fears proved groundless. On 22 November 1921, the King and Queen announced their daughter's engagement. She was to marry Henry, Viscount Lascelles, the eldest son of the Earl of Harewood.

On the face of it, the choice was an odd one. Viscount Lascelles seemed hardly of the stuff that young girls dream of: almost fifteen years older than his bride-to-be, he was thin, gaunt, unattractive. He was not, it was approvingly claimed, 'a ladies' man'; nor did he care for 'modern girls'.[43] But he was not without certain advantages. The son of a Yorkshire magnate and landowner, Viscount Lascelles was very rich and would, one day, be richer still. He was heir to the palatial Harewood House near Leeds, to Portumna Castle in Ireland, and owner of the grandiose Chesterfield House in London. His interests showed an unusual versatility: for besides his passion for the conventionally aristocratic pastimes of riding, hunting and horse-racing, Viscount Lascelles was a celebrated collector of art treasures, pictures, furniture and china.

Even so, it was not every day that a commoner, no matter how rich, could marry a King's daughter. 'I get commoner and commoner,' quipped the Prince of Wales at the time, 'while Lascelles gets more and more royal.'[44]

The couple were married, in great state, in Westminster Abbey on 28 February 1922. For the younger generation of the royal family, the extent of public enthusiasm came as something of a surprise. There was nothing like a royal wedding, they were discovering, to dispel any air of boredom or dissatisfaction with the monarchy.

'The actual ceremony in the Abbey was beautiful and everything was arranged wonderfully well,' reported a gratified Prince Albert to the Prince of Wales who was touring India at the time. 'Mary looked lovely in her wedding dress and was perfectly calm all through the ceremony.'[45]

Prince Albert had an additional involvement in his sister's wedding. For among Princess Mary's eight bridesmaids was one in whom he was particularly interested: this was the twenty-one-year-old daughter of the Earl of Strathmore, the bewitching Lady Elizabeth Bowes-Lyon.

With the Prince of Wales so often away on his Empire tours, the public spotlight tended to fall, more and more, on Prince Albert, by now Duke of York. It was a position in which he did not feel at all comfortable. Natural, friendly and willing to learn, the Duke of York none the less suffered from some cramping defects of temperament: he was introspective, self-pitying, easily cast down by minor difficulties. His shyness, combined with his stammer, made public speaking a form of torture. He had a poor control of his temper; he took himself, and his troubles, deadly seriously. To some extent, these failings were compensated for by his tenacity. For the Duke of York was determined to do whatever had to be done to the best of his ability.

Ill health having forced him out of the navy, the Duke of York had joined the Royal Naval Air Service and, in spite of a strong dislike of flying, had won his pilot's licence. He was to be the first British monarch to be a fully qualified pilot, thus starting a family tradition of flying. There are few princes these days who are not fully licensed pilots. The Air Force had been followed by a few terms at Trinity College, Cambridge where again he proved himself to be, if not clever, at least painstaking. What he did excel at was individual sports: he was a good shot, a good golfer and a tennis player of championship class. In time, he was to play at Wimbledon. On his various official duties, both at home and abroad, he acquitted himself surprisingly well.

But it was in an area not hitherto associated with the monarchy that the Duke of York was making his mark. He was a royal pioneer in the field of industrial relations. Just as the Prince of Wales was bringing the Crown nearer to the people in the dominions, so was the Duke of York bringing it into closer contact with the working classes at home. He agreed to become President of the Boys' Welfare Association, afterwards renamed the Industrial Welfare Society: an organisation responsible for the development of better working conditions.

Determined to be more than a royal figurehead, the Duke of York took his position as President very seriously. He attended council meetings, he toured factories, he went down coal mines, he tramped through construction yards, he climbed scaffolding, he drove locomotives. And wherever he went, he impressed both officials and workers by the intelligence of his questions and the acuteness of his comments.

For this interest in the workers and this knowledge of their jobs, the Duke of York earned the title of 'the Industrial Prince'. His brothers referred to him, less reverently, as 'the Foreman'.[46] By such things as the Duke's active involvement in industry, the monarchy started to break away from the largely ceremonial, charitable and social activities of Edward VII's day and to establish the present climate in which Prince Philip or Prince Charles are able to speak out authoritatively on economic and industrial matters.

Out of Prince Albert's activities grew the celebrated Duke of York's Camp. From 1921 and for almost two decades, these summer camps – to which, in the interests of inter-class contact, working boys and public school boys were brought together – became an institution. Year after year the slight figure of the Duke of York, in his open-necked shirt, baggy shorts and long socks, would be seen sitting happily among a crowd of youngsters, all bellowing the famous Camp song, 'Under the Spreading Chestnut Tree'. To later generations, the concept of these summer camps might seem naïve; at the time, this experiment in social integration, presided over by the King's son, was both bold and valuable. And it had been, from first to last, the Duke's own inspiration.

That the Duke of York derived some measure of satisfaction, even self-confidence, from these activities there can be no question, but, for all that, he remained a tense, hesitant and unresolved young man. The two things which his nature most ardently craved, affection and encouragement, were conspicuously lacking in his home circle. The King and Queen were proud of, and pleased enough with, his efforts but both found it difficult to express this pride and pleasure. Now and then they might write him an appreciative letter but, in the main, he was left with his feelings of self-doubt and isolation.

But all this was about to undergo a change. In the summer of 1920, when the Duke of York was twenty-five, he met the twenty-year-old Lady Elizabeth Bowes-Lyon.

Lady Elizabeth was the youngest-but-one of the ten children of the fourteenth Earl of Strathmore. Her mother had been a Cavendish-Bentinck. Born on 2 August 1900, Lady Elizabeth had been raised in an atmosphere quite different from that of the royal family. Her childhood, divided between the ancient Scottish castle of Glamis and the elegant Queen Anne mansion of St Paul's Walden Bury in Hertfordshire, had been spent in the midst of a merry, united and loving family. From this warm and secure background, Lady Elizabeth had emerged as a gay, vital, unaffected and kind-hearted young woman; and one who was already showing signs, both of a remarkable inner serenity and of an exceptional strength of character. She was also a beauty. Small and graceful (she was five feet, two inches tall) Lady Elizabeth was blessed with typically Celtic looks: black hair, blue eyes and a skin like cream.

It did not take long for the Duke of York to fall in love with this enchanting young woman. But when, in the spring of 1921, he asked her to marry him, she refused. She was reluctant to exchange her free-and-easy life for the restrictions of life as a member of the royal family. She was also rather shy and, contrary to general belief, was to remain so throughout her life. 'I'm a very shy person,' she recently admitted. 'I thought that I would become less shy with the passing years but it hasn't happened. I *dread* making speeches.'[47] This shyness was a superficial trait only: it did not denote any want of self-confidence. She knew how to master it. Yet it probably contributed to her reluctance to accept the Duke of York's offer. But he, whose chief characteristic was perseverance, persevered. In this venture, at least, the young man had his parents' unqualified support. The King, in his oblique fashion, conceded that his son would be 'a lucky fellow'[48] if Lady Elizabeth accepted him; while Queen Mary claimed that she was 'the one girl who could make Bertie happy.'[49]

The Duke's persistence was rewarded on 13 January 1923. 'All right. Bertie' read the pre-arranged wording of his telegram announcing the glad news to his parents. 'We are delighted and he looks beaming,'[50] recorded the Queen two days later. And the King, who had been thoroughly disarmed by the fact that the young woman, far from being afraid of him, treated him with great directness, pronounced her to be 'charming, so pretty and engaging and natural.'[51]

Why, in the end, had Lady Elizabeth Bowes-Lyon agreed to marry the Duke of York? One may be sure that the better she came to know him, the better she came to appreciate his hidden qualities: his kindness, his sincerity, his dependability. He was also very good-looking. And she, with her innate self-confidence, may well have been drawn to his very lack of it. Always so ready to help, to encourage and to give pleasure, Lady Elizabeth might not have been able to resist the opportunity of being the one to provide what was so badly needed; needed, moreover, by so highly placed a figure in national, and international, life. Not every young woman gets a chance of marrying the King of England's son. Lady Elizabeth cannot, as Frances Donaldson in her shrewd analysis of her probable motives has put it, 'have been entirely cold to her opportunity.'[52]

The couple were married in Westminster Abbey on 26 April 1923. There was much public approval of the fact that the bride was British and a commoner; it all seemed part of the Anglicanisation of the monarchy, of the bringing of it closer to the people, of keeping it in tune with changing times. The couple themselves, as they drove through the acclaiming streets in the fitful spring sunshine, appeared so strikingly good-looking, so touchingly young, so charmingly fresh. 'I am very, very happy,' admitted the normally inarticulate Duke of York to his mother, 'and I can only hope that Elizabeth feels the same as I do. I know I am very lucky to have won her over at last.'[53]

He had every reason to be pleased with himself. For in Lady Elizabeth Bowes-Lyon, the Duke of York had gained a wife of inestimable value, while the dynasty and the country had gained a person of outstanding qualities of heart and mind and spirit.

'Today twenty-three years ago dear Grandmama died,' wrote King George in his diary on 22 January 1924. 'I wonder what she would have thought of a Labour Government!'[54]

For on that day Stanley Baldwin resigned as Prime Minister of the Conservative administration and the King asked Ramsay MacDonald to form the country's first Labour Government.

The new Labour ministers were equally conscious of the great significance of the occasion. 'As we stood waiting for His Majesty, amid the gold and crimson magnificence of the Palace,' wrote one of them, 'I could not help marvelling at the strange turn of Fortune's wheel which had brought [us] . . . to this pinnacle beside the man whose forebears had been Kings for so many splendid generations. We were making history. We were, perhaps, somewhat embarrassed, but the little, quiet man whom we addressed as "Your Majesty" swiftly put us at our ease.'[55]

His Majesty, despite being a natural conservative, took it all in his stride. He was quite ready, not only to work with the Socialist administration but to help his inexperienced ministers as much as he could. His attitude towards them was impeccable. With a penchant for honest-to-goodness personalities, the King was anxious for contact between court and ministers to be as free from embarrassment as possible. He even – this most sartorially meticulous of men – relaxed the rules regarding the hitherto obligatory wearing of full dress uniform in his presence.

Although this Labour government lasted a few months only, its term greatly enhanced the King's reputation as a constitutional monarch. For whether working with a Labour, Liberal, Conservative or, after 1931, National government, George V always behaved with commendable impartiality. Even in the midst of the passions aroused by the General Strike of 1926, he kept his neutral position. When one wealthy coal owner called the striking miners 'a damned lot of revolutionaries'[56] the King suggested that *he* try living on their wages before judging them. And when someone advised him to play a more active role in the dispute, the King wisely declined 'to entertain the idea of intervention except, of course, at the request of the Prime Minister.'[57]

More and more, as the years went by, did King George V reveal himself as a conciliator. For all his outspokenness and bluster, he was a man of peace. Time and again he would urge his ministers to refrain from provocative public statements, to hold private discussions with their opponents, to seek moderate solutions. Although his ministers were sometimes astonished by the frankness, verbosity and strength of his opinions, they could always rely on the ultimate restraint and soundness of his decisions. In fact, his common sense was the King's most outstanding characteristic. In the end, he came to personify 'the ordinary British citizen's dislike of passionate doctrines and preference for compromise and toleration'.[58] He came to be regarded, not only as the nation's head, but as its father-figure.

This was why, when the King fell dangerously ill towards the end of 1928, and was out of the public eye for the best part of a year, there was such widespread concern and alarm. Faced with the possibility of his death, the nation had suddenly come to realise how much it loved and respected him. The thanksgiving service held in Westminster Abbey to mark – prematurely as it turned out – the King's full recovery, was an occasion of great national rejoicing.

Of considerable comfort to the King during his long convalescence was the

15 The annual Christmas broadcast: George V in 1934

16 Queen Mary, the Duchess of York, Princess Margaret, Princess Elizabeth and the Duchess of Kent on their way to the Trooping the Colour ceremony, 1935

presence of his grand-daughter, Princess Elizabeth, the daughter of the Duke and Duchess of York. Born on 21 April 1926, 'sweet little Lilibet' was a great favourite with the King. When, in 1927, the Duke and Duchess of York had been absent on a six-month-long tour of Australia and New Zealand, the King and Queen had taken charge of the little Princess. 'I am glad to be able to give you the most excellent accounts of your sweet little daughter, who is growing daily,' King George had written to his son. 'She has four teeth now, which is quite good at eleven months old, and she is very happy and drives in a carriage every afternoon, which amuses her.'[59]

Now, with the King convalescing at Bognor on the south coast, the three-year-old Princess Elizabeth was sent along to cheer him up. His delight in her company, says Lady Airlie, was extremely touching. 'He is fond of his two grandsons, Princess Mary's sons [George and Gerald Lascelles] but Lilibet always came first in his affections. He used to play with her – a thing I never saw him do with his own children – and loved to have her by him . . . she made his convalescence at Bognor bearable to him.'[60]

And Archbishop Lang was once witness to the strong hold which the little Princess had on her grandfather's affections. Ushered into the Sovereign's presence, the Archbishop was astonished to see him playing 'horse' to Princess Elizabeth's 'groom'. The King-Emperor was shuffling about the carpet on all fours while his golden-haired little grand-daughter – the future Queen Elizabeth II – led him about the room by his beard.

'The Boy Will Ruin Himself'

'BERTIE,' asked King George V of the Duke of York at dinner one evening early in 1931, 'is David still in love with the lace-maker's daughter?'[1]

The 'lace-maker's daughter' in question was Mrs Dudley Ward, whose father, Colonel Charles Birkin, was a wealthy lace manufacturer. And the answer to the King's query was that the Prince of Wales was still very much in love with Freda Dudley Ward. They had first met in 1918 and since then, in spite of – or possibly because of – the fact that she was married with two children, she had been the great love of his life.

This is not to say that the Prince did not have other affairs. He was extremely attractive to women and was, in turn, attracted to them. But the Prince of Wales was far from being the great lover of popular imagination. He certainly took very little notice of the sort of pretty young girl whom he might be expected to marry. He had a decided taste for married women, particularly if they were of a motherly, somewhat domineering type. It has been suggested that he was always in search of the maternal love that had been denied him by his own mother. The three women with whom he was most closely associated before he met Mrs Ernest Simpson – Lady Coke, Mrs Dudley Ward and Lady Furness – were all married. Of the three, Freda Dudley Ward was undoubtedly the one whom he would have chosen for a wife. And as he could not marry her, he remained single.

In that more deferential period, it was still possible for the Prince of Wales to conduct the sort of love life that would now be impossible. The Prince's affairs were talked about among his own set and in society generally, but the Prince was never subjected to the relentless journalistic scrutiny that is commonplace today. The attitude of the press was more reverent and less intrusive. In later years the Prince of Wales was to complain about excessive publicity and, during the Abdication crisis, his every move was reported; but, in the ordinary way, he was never faced, as Prince Charles or his brothers might be today, by round-the-clock cameramen, hoping for some evidence of indiscretions.

The Prince's irregular love life, allied to his continuing bachelorhood (in 1931 he turned thirty-seven) were a source of deep concern to King George. That, combined with the Prince's taste for what Queen Mary described as 'rushing about'[2] made relations between father and son increasingly edgy. Making matters still worse was the perennial problem of the position of an heir to the throne. His years of touring the Empire over, the Prince of Wales had returned home to take up the thankless role of a king-in-waiting. That he should resent his equivocal position is understandable; that he should have to endure it was unavoidable. For there was almost no way in which King George V could involve his heir in the everyday business of the monarchy. As the Prince's biographer, Frances Donaldson, has pointed out, the work of government was much greater and more complex by the 1920s than it had been a generation or two before. In Queen Victoria's or King Edward VII's day, a word in the ear of some reigning monarch who happened to be one's first cousin twice removed could often get things started; by now the increased volume of work, the speed of communications and the complexity of national and international affairs had put paid to any such amateur activities. Politics could no longer be treated as 'a training ground for kings'.[3] A monarch, always acting on the advice of his ministers, could learn his trade only through practical experience; there was not much that he could share with or delegate to his heir.

On the other hand, there seems to have been no reason why King George V could not have discussed political or constitutional matters more fully with the Prince of Wales. Perhaps, like Queen Victoria, King George did not have much faith in his son's abilities; or perhaps – for all his later protestations – the Prince of Wales was not really interested in the often dull and routine day-to-day business of the monarch.

Whatever the reason, the Prince of Wales found himself in a position which, he complains, 'seemed to leave me dangling futilely in space between the ceremonial make-believe symbolising the power of high and mighty princes and the discouraging realities of a world that insisted upon relegating even a conscientious Prince to a figure-head role.'[4]

For, in his way, the Prince of Wales was conscientious. He worked every bit as hard as he played. By the zest, professionalism, naturalness and charm with which he carried out his many public duties, he made a considerable contribution to the evolution of the British monarchy in the twentieth century. His obvious distress at the poverty which he encountered on his tours of inspection led many to believe that he held progressive, even radical political views and that he identified himself with the sufferings of the common man. This belief was unfounded. The Prince of Wales was as conservative as the majority of young men of his class. But his reputation as a concerned, enlightened and forward-looking Prince, who was somehow being held in check by more reactionary forces, did the monarchy no harm.

Rightly or wrongly, the Prince had come to symbolise the hopes and aspirations of youth. Few doubted that his chief aim was the modernisation of the monarchy.

In yet another effort to distance himself from the stuffiness and predictability of his father's court, the Prince found himself a country retreat. This was Fort Belvedere, an odd, mock-Gothic, long-neglected house lying on the edge of Windsor Great Park. Into its restoration the Prince of Wales flung himself with all his customary enthusiasm.

Unsuspected at the time, the Fort was to be the setting of the most dramatic events in the Prince's life. For in 1930, the year in which he acquired it, the Prince of Wales met Wallis Simpson.

'It seemed unbelievable,' wrote the Duchess of Windsor of that intoxicating period before the Abdication crisis, 'that I, Wallis Warfield of Baltimore, Maryland, could be part of this enchanted world.'[5]

Unbelievable indeed. For here was an American woman, without beauty, youth, wealth or, by European aristocratic standards, birth, who had captured the heart of the foremost royal figure of the period. And, in spite of being twice divorced, she was one day to marry him.

Her background, in time, was to become very well known: her birth on 19 June 1896 into a world of genteel poverty; her first disastrous marriage to the unstable Earl Winfield Spencer; her daringly emancipated years of travel; her divorce and remarriage to the stolid Englishman, Ernest Simpson; the years in their flat at Bryanston Court during which she developed into a *soignée* and efficient hostess; and finally her meeting, through the American-born Lady Furness, with the Prince of Wales.

It would be tempting to claim that a great love was born at the moment that the Prince first met Wallis Simpson, at a weekend house-party in the autumn of 1930. Or at least that this self-assured American woman made an indelible impression on him. But the truth was that it was not until they had met several times – usually at parties given by his latest love, Lady Furness – that he began to pay her any attention. Gradually, during the following two years, the Prince saw more and more of Wallis Simpson: during weekend parties at the Fort, at dinner parties given by friends, in restaurants, in night clubs and finally in her flat at Bryanston Court.

At first the Prince was always accompanied by Lady Furness, while Wallis was always with her husband, Ernest Simpson. But, in time, the complaisant Simpson got into the habit of leaving his wife alone with the Prince and, in January 1934, Lady Furness left to spend a couple of months in America.

When Thelma Furness returned, it was to find the Prince of Wales behaving very coldly towards her. His other love, Freda Dudley Ward, was experiencing the same thing. Previously, the Prince had telephoned Mrs

Dudley Ward every day; now, when he failed to do so and she rang him instead, the puzzled Freda Dudley Ward was told that the telephonist had orders that she was not to be connected.

Lady Furness's suspicions – that the Prince had fallen in love with Wallis Simpson in her absence – were confirmed during one of those weekends at the Fort. She needed only to see Wallis Simpson playfully slapping the Prince's hand as he fingered a piece of lettuce to realise the truth.

'Wallis,' she thought. 'Wallis, of all people!'[6]

Of all people, Wallis Simpson had finally entered what she called her 'enchanted world', and the British monarchy had entered an extremely precarious phase.

On his accession, King George V had declared his intention of making the affairs of the Empire his particular concern. His plan had been, not only to attend the Coronation Durbar in India but to visit all the British dominions. His ambition had never been realised. The Durbar had marked the beginning and end of his imperial journeying. The First World War, combined with the complete loss of his always poor appetite for foreign travel, put paid to his scheme. In any case, the politically troubled 1920s would not have allowed for any long absence of the monarch.

So the King was quite ready to leave all Empire tours to his sons. During the last fifteen or so years of his reign, one or other of the four handsome princes was constantly to be seen – brilliantly uniformed, gallantly smiling, tirelessly attentive – as the representative of the Crown in some distant corner of the globe.

This is not to say that the King had lost interest in imperial matters. On the contrary, he remained as deeply concerned as ever. No British monarch had been as well informed on Empire affairs as King George V. He had come to the throne with his imperial powers and status unimpaired; the Empire, at that time, had appeared to be as powerful as ever. In fact, during the course of his reign, it was to continue to expand until in 1933 it reached its geographical zenith, with an area of almost fourteen million square miles and a population of 493 million. It was therefore paradoxical that King George V, whose chief ambition had been to strengthen the ties of Empire, should be the one to preside over what looked like the beginnings of its dissolution.

For gradually, from the end of the First World War, the bonds of Empire began to slacken. In 1921, after years of bitter struggle, the Irish Free State had been set up and granted dominion status. With the four already largely self-governing dominions – Australia, New Zealand, Canada and South Africa – becoming increasingly self-sufficient, the old conception of Great Britain as the mother country withered away and the Empire evolved into a free association of equal partners. Definition of this new concept was arrived at by the Imperial Conference of 1926. The dominions, decided the Conference, were now 'autonomous communities within the British Empire, equal in status, in no way subordinate one to another in any aspect of their domestic or external affairs, though united by common allegiance to the Crown, and freely associated as members of the British Commonwealth of Nations.'[7]

This conception, of a British Commonwealth of equal and independent nations, was embodied in a bill, known as the Statute of Westminster, which became law in December 1931. Its passing symbolised the end of Britain's imperial mission.

Although it is unlikely that George V would have understood all the intricacies of the Statute of Westminster, he fully appreciated the fact that, hand in hand with this yielding up of British parliamentary sovereignty, went an enhancement of the status of the British Sovereign. For the Crown had now become the chief symbol, the supreme unifying factor in this association of free nations. This was a development which was fully understood and expanded by King George V's successors, King George VI and Queen Elizabeth II.

The effect of all this on the King's 'character and actions and thoughts during the last years of his life cannot be exaggerated,' claims John Gore. 'From then onwards all other considerations, public and private, were subordinated in his thoughts and actions to the one supreme task and duty of so maintaining the high conception of constitutional monarchy which he had established, that the sole remaining symbol and link which bound the Empire together as a Commonwealth of free nations should continue to grow in strength and reality and remain unaffected by his death.'[8]

But the King was equally conscious of another aspect concerning the Crown's newly exalted status. More than ever, he reckoned, should the demeanour of the wearer of the Crown be above reproach. In the course of the *Ophir* tour and again during his two visits to India, the King had come to appreciate how strong and searching a light played on the occupant of the British throne: in later reigns, with the development of radio, television and more aggressive journalism, the light became more searching still. So the character and conduct of the monarch was of the utmost importance in the affairs of the Commonwealth. More than ever now must the monarch, and the monarchy, be seen to be setting the standards.

But were the standards of his sons, and particularly of his eldest son, worthy of this great destiny?

It was not until he was twenty-six, in 1929, that the King's youngest son, Prince George, was allowed to leave the navy. Ill health was given as the reason for his early retirement; he was said to suffer from seasickness and a chronically weak digestion. From the navy he went on to set another royal precedent by entering, first the Foreign Office and then the Home Office. In neither of these posts could he have been said to have made much impression. Prince George shone far more brightly in the carrying out of his official duties. For to his strikingly good looks – he was tall and slim with dark blue eyes and a radiant smile – he brought a great charm of manner. Both at home and on his tours of Canada, South America and Southern Africa, Prince George won great popularity. After the Prince of Wales, Prince George was regarded as the most dashing of the King's sons.

He was also the odd-man-out. Where even the Prince of Wales shared the hunting, shooting, fishing tastes of his breed, Prince George's interests were more artistic, more cultural, more sophisticated. Ready enough to drive fast cars or fly planes, he was just as happy visiting art galleries, listening to records or playing Cole Porter on the piano. An excellent linguist and an avid newspaper reader, he was far better informed than his brothers. The cinema, the theatre and the ballet he loved; that glittering theatrical star of the period, Gertrude Lawrence, once discovered him sitting in front of her dressing-room mirror, trying on one of her wigs. While the other men of the family were shooting at Sandringham, he would be sunbathing on the Riviera. His rooms in St James's Palace were filled with his steadily growing collection of pictures and antiques.

But Prince George was more than just a sophisticated playboy. His nature had its darker side. Like all the sons of George V, Prince George had a quickly-flaring temper: he was mercurial, moody, easily irritated and notoriously impatient. The celebrated diarist, Sir Henry ('Chips') Channon, who knew him well, claims that he had 'drunk deeply from life'.[9] Just how deeply, few could say for certain. 'He was a scamp,' reports one equerry. 'He was always in trouble with girls. Scotland Yard chased so many of them out of the country that the Palace stopped counting.'[10] In later years, a well-known figure in London society, Michael Canfield, was claimed to be his son. There were rumours of hashish-smoking sessions with a decadent young South American, and one of Prince George's women friends is said to have 'seduced him into taking drugs and so corrupted him that he was led to the brink of suicide.'[11] He had to be packed off to the country for a cure.

Other rumours concerned the Prince's catholic sexual tastes. The young Prince Louis Ferdinand, a grandson of Kaiser Wilhelm II, told Sir Robert Bruce Lockhart that he liked Prince George because 'he was artistic and effeminate and used a strong perfume.'[12] And from Randolph Churchill, Lockhart heard that the Prince had been involved in a homosexual scandal: 'letters to a young man in Paris. A large sum had to be paid for their recovery.'[13]

True or not, the currency of such stories would hardly have endeared the debonair young Prince to his father. The King could only deplore the influence which the Prince of Wales was having on his youngest brother; their joint night-clubbing and party-going could reflect nothing but discredit on themselves and the monarchy. And as, by the year 1934, the thirty-one-year-old Prince George was still not married, King George must have feared that in this matter, too, Prince George was taking his lead from the Prince of Wales.

In fact, of the King's four surviving sons, only the Duke of York was married by 1934. King George, as a young married man with five sons in the nursery, had been able to boast that he was raising a regiment. Some thirty years later, this pride of princes had produced only two girls in the next generation: these were the little daughters of the Duke and Duchess of York – Princess Elizabeth and Princess Margaret Rose.

It was with a mixture of pleasure and relief, then, that the King and Queen heard the news, in August 1934, of Prince George's engagement. His choice of bride was what one might have expected. Not for Prince George some pretty little English debutante, but an elegant, cosmopolitan, twenty-seven-year-old member of one of Europe's royal families. She was Princess Marina of Greece and Denmark.

Into the by now thoroughly British royal family, the beautiful Princess Marina brought a breath of Continental air. Born on 30 November 1906, she was very much part of the complicated network of inter-related European royals. Her paternal grandfather had been the Danish prince (he was Queen Alexandra's brother) who had become King George I of the Hellenes. Her maternal grandfather had been the Grand Duke Vladimir, brother of Tsar Alexander III, and the grandest of Russian grand dukes. Princess Marina's youth had been divided between the relative simplicity of life in the Athenian palace of her parents, Prince and Princess Nicholas of Greece, and the over-whelming opulence of the Vladimir Palace in St Petersburg.

The First World War had put an end to this privileged and well-ordered way of life. The Russian Revolution had either killed off or scattered the Romanovs and by 1923 the maelstrom of Greek politics had finally deposited Prince and Princess Nicholas and their three daughters in Paris. Here they were obliged to live the uncertain, impecunious life of most royal emigrés. It was during these lean years in Paris that Princess Marina learnt the thrift that she was never to lose.

In the spring of 1934, with her two older sisters already married, the twenty-seven-year-old Princess Marina paid one of her periodic visits to London. She had met Prince George on previous occasions but in the course of this visit he began to pay her serious attention. If any young woman could win the interest of Prince George, then clearly the attractive, artistic, sweet-natured, well-dressed and lopsidedly-smiling Princess Marina was the one to do it. Nothing was said that spring but in August Prince George suddenly flew to Yugoslavia where the Princess was visiting her sister Princess Olga, by then the wife of Prince Paul of Yugoslavia. Within three days the couple were engaged.

King George and Queen Mary were delighted. The Queen, with her knowledge of the intricacies of royal dynastic relationships, was particularly pleased with the proposed alliance. And knowing something of her son's temperament, she was pleased that he had chosen a princess of the House of Greece and Denmark. 'The women of that Danish family make good wives,' she said. 'They have the art of marriage. Look at Queen Alexandra. Could any other wife have managed King Edward as well as she did?'[14]

The wedding, in Westminster Abbey on 29 November 1934, aroused extraordinary enthusiasm. Not since the marriage, over ten years before, of the Duke and Duchess of York, had London been treated to a piece of royal pageantry. And there was no doubt that the couple's exceptionally good looks had captured the public imagination. Prince George, whom the King had created Duke of Kent a few days before the ceremony, looked resplendent in the full dress uniform of the navy which he so disliked. Princess Marina, in a simple, silver, sheath-like dress by Molyneux (Prince George had talked her out of Jean Patou) looked like a fashion plate. It was the general public's first glimpse of an elegance that became renowned.

The Kent wedding allowed for yet another royal innovation. 'Never in history,' intoned the officiating Archbishop of Canterbury, 'has a marriage been attended by so vast a company of witnesses . . . The whole nation, nay the whole Empire, are the wedding guests.'[15] This was not simply a piece of ecclesiastical hyperbole: the wedding of the Duke and Duchess of Kent was the first royal ceremony to be broadcast, throughout the world, by radio.

And the occasion was marked by one of those apparently trivial incidents which, in time, assume considerable significance. On the night before the ceremony, the King and Queen held a glittering reception at Buckingham Palace. To it, the Prince of Wales had invited Wallis Simpson. On presenting her to his parents, the Prince had said, quite simply, 'I want to introduce you to a great friend of mine.' There had been a short exchange of pleasantries and the couple had moved on. It was the one and only time that the King and Queen spoke to Mrs Simpson.

'If I had only guessed then I might perhaps have been able to do something,' sighed Queen Mary a couple of years later, 'but now it's too late.'[16]

It was too late then.

For by now Wallis Warfield Simpson had come well and truly into her own. During the next few years Mrs Simpson was to be one of the most talked-about women in the world.

What was it, specifically, that attracted the Prince of Wales to Wallis Simpson? In later years, one of King George V's grandsons, the twice-

married Lord Harewood, claimed that he was sometimes accused of pur-
posely choosing his wives from unconventional backgrounds. True or not,
there must be, for members of the royal family, a strong attraction for people
who come from a completely different world. Whether it is necessarily wise
to marry out of prescribed circles is another matter, but that royals should be
drawn to unconventional and independent personalities is understandable.
Both the flamboyant Disraeli and the rough-hewn John Brown held great
charm for Queen Victoria; and in every generation since, members of the
family have been involved in what seemed like unsuitable attachments.

It is partly in this light that the Prince of Wales's obsession with Wallis
Simpson should be viewed. In all, she could hardly have been less like the sort
of aristocratic English rose whom he would have been expected to marry.
Thirty-eight in 1934, with a jaw that was too square and a nose that was too
big she was, she readily admits, no beauty. She had an elegance that was a
shade too metallic and a vivacity that was a shade too assertive. Mrs Simpson
looked what she was: a sophisticate, a *femme du monde*, a woman with – in that
favourite word of the period – glamour.

So surrounded by sycophants and conformers, the Prince found her particularly American characteristics – her breeziness and her directness –
irresistably refreshing. She was the only woman, he once told her, who had
ever been interested in his job. While she listened with flattering attention, he
would expound his somewhat woolly philosophy of modern kingship, of
how he planned to reshape the monarchy. Whether or not she was really
interested is neither here nor there. What was important was that he felt he
had found a confidante, a sympathiser, a supporter. Wallis Simpson had all
along been conscious of the fact that he was essentially a lonely man; not
necessarily in the physical sense, but emotionally. With her experience of
men, she would have known how to listen, how to draw him out, how to feel
that he had discovered a soul mate. She became what so many princes lack – a
friend.

More important though, in the Prince of Wales's case, was that in Wallis
Simpson he had found the dominant mother-figure for whom he had always
been searching. Where he was a submissive personality, she was a strong one.
Her attitude towards him, from the start almost, was anything but sub-
servient: it was bold, bantering, bossy. With the Prince, at forty, still looking
so incredibly boyish and with her always looking so immaculate, they could
almost have been taken, if not exactly for mother and son, certainly for a
governess and her charge.

To those who did not understand the Prince's complex personality, it was
assumed that his interest in Wallis Simpson was purely physical: that she had
some sort of sexual hold over him. This was impossible to prove but it seems
highly unlikely that he would have given up his throne for a woman with
whom he had no intellectual or spiritual rapport.

And Mrs Simpson, how did she feel about him? One cannot know her precise feelings – any more, possibly, than she did herself. She has been accused of being hard and calculating and ambitious, but she would have had to have been less than human not to have taken advantage of the opportunity that was opening up before her. And after all, was he not, besides being the Prince of Wales, an attractive and appealing man? Would she have encouraged him if he had been old and fat and boring?

'I was stimulated; I was excited,' runs her breathless account of those heady days, 'I felt as if I were borne upon a rising wave that seemed to be carrying me ever more rapidly and ever higher.'[17]

Just how high she imagined she was going to be carried is an open question. That the Prince of Wales intended marrying her was by now becoming obvious. Her marriage to Ernest Simpson was, not unnaturally, in ruins. A divorce would leave her free to marry again. Did she, in her heart of hearts, imagine that she would one day become Queen of England? She does not say. But then nor does she say that she knew that she could never possibly become Queen. Could she really have imagined that a woman with three husbands living could sit on the throne? That she would be the successor to Queen Alexandra and – more improbable still – Queen Mary? Did she understand that this was impossible?

Perhaps, coming from America (a country in which, the Prince had claimed, nothing was impossible) she imagined that she might indeed become Queen Wallis. Often enough, she had heard the Prince explaining his plans for the modernisation of the monarchy. Might not his first step towards this modernisation be the sweeping away of old prejudices by the setting up of the twice-divorced American commoner as his Queen?

One person only had the authority to convince the Prince of the utter impracticality of his plan. And this was the very person with whom he could not bring himself to discuss it – his father, King George V.

The Prince of Wales's emotional predicament was merely one of the many problems besetting George V towards the end of his reign. For the ageing monarch, the 1930s were particularly distressing years. The decade had started badly. The world-wide financial crisis and the collapse of the Labour government had forced the King into the most politically controversial act of his reign. Exercising his constitutional right, he persuaded the Labour Prime Minister, Ramsay Macdonald, to join with the Conservatives and Liberals in forming a National Government. The monarch's action split the Labour Party. That the King was within his rights to 'encourage' his ministers to sink party differences there was no question: what was in doubt was his wisdom in doing so.

He certainly felt that he had done the right thing. 'Please God,' he exclaimed after a general election had approved the National Government, 'I shall now have a little peace and less worries.'[18]

It was a vain hope. The King worried continuously: about his worsening health, about the radical social and political changes of the period, about the growing threat of fascism abroad, about economic distress at home. In an effort to make some sort of personal sacrifice during this period of financial stringency, he insisted that his Civil List be reduced by £50,000. (The Prince of Wales did not take at all kindly to his father's suggestion that he give up £10,000. 'The King and I are being had for a pair of mugs,'[19] announced the Prince to his companions in a night club in Bayonne.)

By now it would have needed more than failing health or political and social upheavals to disrupt King George's annual routine. It ran with the precision of a well-oiled clock. The pattern, laid down by his father, Edward VII, he adhered to with all the rigidity of his nature. 'My father's life was a masterpiece in the art of well-ordered, unostentatious, elegant living,' wrote the Duke of Windsor. 'No matter the place, no matter the occasion, per-fection pervaded every detail.'[20] King George might have been a simple man but he was also very conscious of the fact that, as a monarch, he was expected to maintain a certain standard of magnificence. All the public ceremonies – the Opening of Parliament, Trooping the Colour, the Ascot processions, the courts, the balls, the banquets, the investitures, the garden parties – were brilliantly stage-managed affairs. With the King always impressively dressed and the Queen never looking anything less than regal, the couple played their parts with apparently effortless ease.

But it was never effortless. For the sake of the monarchy, the King and Queen had mastered their natural shyness, their taste for privacy and their preference for a quiet, simple, countrified life, to emerge as two assured and unmistakable symbols of majesty.

Yet instead of the splendour of their position making them increasingly remote from the majority of their subjects, the royal couple had become gradually less so. Much of this was due to yet another of those monarchal adjustments to a changing world. On Christmas Day 1932, King George V inaugurated a new tradition: he broadcast a message to the people of Great Britain and the Commonwealth. From then on, each Christmas Day, the Monarch's deep, vibrant, natural-sounding voice was to be heard in living rooms all over the world. For the monarchy, the value of these annual Christmas talks was incalculable. They revealed the King, as nothing had ever done before, as a decent and concerned patriarch of his people. In George V, the nation saw epitomised all the features which had made the monarchy such a popular institution: its durability, its dignity, its high standards, its position above political and sectional interests.

Whereas King Edward VII and Queen Alexandra had brought the monarchy back into the mainstream of national life, King George V, with

Queen Mary, had identified it more closely with the mass of the people.

This was why, when on 6 May 1935, King George and Queen Mary went to St Paul's Cathedral to attend their Silver Jubilee Thanksgiving Service, there was such an outpouring of national enthusiasm. For the King was being hailed, not only as a monarch but as a person. He might not have been as romantic or as intelligent as some of his predecessors but there had been few with his unswerving sense of duty or his unquestioned integrity.

The King was being hailed, too, as a family man. The Thanksgiving Service was as much a family as an official occasion. The general public knew almost nothing about the various tensions within the royal family. To them, King George was the head of a close-knit, harmonious and attractive clan; an ageing man surrounded by his children and grandchildren. By now the royal family had come to be regarded as a grander, more colourful version of the average British household.

'Masses of troops,' wrote the watching 'Chips' Channon on Jubilee Day, 'magnificent and virile, resplendent in grand uniforms, with the sun glistening on their helmets. The thunderous applause for the royal carriages. The Yorks in a large landau with two tiny pink children [Princess Elizabeth and Princess Margaret]. The Duchess of York was charming and gracious, the baby princesses much interested in the proceedings and waving. The next landau carried the Kents, that dazzling pair; Princess Marina wore an enormous platter hat, chic but slightly unsuitable. She was much cheered . . . So it passed. Finally the Prince of Wales smiling his dentist smile and waving to his friends, but he still has his old spell for the crowd . . . then more troops and suddenly, the coach with Their Majesties. All eyes were on the Queen in her white and silvery splendour. Never has she looked so serene, so regally majestic, even so attractive. Suddenly she has become the best-dressed woman in the world.'[21]

Not only on the day of the Thanksgiving Service but every day for weeks afterwards, the celebrations continued. Wherever the King and Queen appeared, they were vociferously cheered; each night they were obliged to come out onto the central balcony of the palace to wave to the roaring crowds. The King was deeply touched and honestly surprised by the warmth and spontaneity of his reception.

'I'd no idea they felt like that about me,' he exclaimed wonderingly. 'I am beginning to think they must really like me for myself.'[22]

'I hope,' wrote Queen Mary from Balmoral in the autumn of 1934 to her third son, Prince Henry, at that stage touring Australia, 'now you my darling boy will think about marrying on your return.'[23] To help him make up his mind, she enclosed the names of a couple of likely princesses.

The Queen's concern was understandable. Prince Henry, whom the King had created Duke of Gloucester in 1928, would turn thirty-five next birthday. This was a relatively advanced age for a prince to be unmarried. Fortunately, the Duke of Gloucester had spared his parents the sort of anguish caused them by the Prince of Wales and Prince George. The Duke of Gloucester might have lacked his brothers' good looks, social graces and lively minds but he was an altogether more dependable and considerate young man.

His ruling passion, after sport, was his military career. Yet it was a sadly frustrated one. Although a competent enough officer in the 10th Royal Hussars, he was precluded, as a King's son, from taking part in any active service that was likely to prove politically controversial. And as most military action tended to be politically controversial, the Duke of Gloucester was always being prevented from joining his regiment abroad. It was another of the disadvantages of being born royal.

To his increasing despair, the Duke had to content himself with carrying out the customary princely duties. Yet among them were two especially exotic missions: in 1929 he went to Japan to confer the Garter on the Emperor; and a year later he represented the King at the Coronation of the Emperor of Ethiopia. It was on a more conventional royal visit, to Australia and New Zealand in 1934 (he was replacing, not for the last time, his brother Prince George who felt unable to face the strain of yet another tour in the same year) that one of the accompanying journalists wrote an acute summing-up of Prince Henry's qualities.

'His chief appeal is, perhaps, his very normality. In a nation of democrats he is unaffected and natural to a degree. In a nation of horse-lovers he is a dashing and fearless rider. In a nation which has never troubled much about pomp and panoply, he is essentially a lover of simplicity and would rather put on riding breeches and an open shirt and gallop over the hills than receive the curtseys of innumerable debutantes under the bright lights of society. The Duke has neither the sophistication of the Prince of Wales nor the seriousness of the Duke of York. He is a young man with a job he intends to do, but a young man who likes a joke and who can tell a good story with anyone.'[24] He was also a young man who liked a drink; for by now Prince Henry had discovered that there was nothing like a glass of whisky to ease the day's tensions.

Yet, such was the indefinable allure of the monarchy that even this far from remarkable young man could arouse on the faces of the Australian crowds, noted another observer, a look 'which amounts to something very near adoration.'[25]

Back from Australia, and invariably obedient to his parents' wishes, the Duke of Gloucester applied himself to the question of his marriage. 'I would like to get married,' he wrote solemnly to his father, 'if only I know that I would remain in the Army long enough to command my regiment when my turn comes.'[26] Bachelor commanding officers, he had noticed, were always preferred to married ones. On this point the King was reassuring. He saw no reason why the Duke should leave the 10th Hussars. Nor did he feel it necessary to coerce the somewhat reluctant Prince Henry into marrying either of the princesses suggested by Queen Mary. 'I am sure you could find someone who would make you a good wife and be a help to you in all your duties,'[27] he wrote.

The Duke of Gloucester did not need to look far. His closest friend was Lord William Scott, son of the seventh Duke of Buccleuch. Lord William had a thirty-four-year-old unmarried sister, the small, shy, pretty, piquant-faced Lady Alice Montagu-Douglas-Scott. The Duke of Gloucester spent a considerable time in her company during the summer of 1935 and in August she accepted his proposal of marriage.

He could hardly have chosen better. Lady Alice Montagu-Douglas-Scott, in spite of being a member of one of the most illustrious families in the land, was a modestly mannered, simply dressed, softly spoken, country-loving young woman. No more than her prospective husband did she have the taste for intellectual or sophisticated society. She was happiest on horseback, with her dogs or her paintbox. Yet, in common with the wives of all King George V's sons, Lady Alice was a woman of dedication and resilience. Behind that quiet façade lay great reserves of strength.

The King and Queen were delighted with their son's choice. Lady Alice was summoned to Balmoral, the engagement was announced, and she was duly photographed on the terrace among the members of the royal family. Why, asked one of her sons on looking at those engagement photographs many years later, was his mother's skirt shorter than the others? 'Because it wasn't my dress,' she explained briskly. 'It was Aunt Angela's. I hadn't anything smart enough to go to Balmoral in. I hadn't a silk dress.'[28]

Yet when Lady Alice did have a smart enough dress – her wedding dress of pale pink satin – there was a fear that she might be denied the opportunity of wearing it. Plans for the splendid ceremony to be held in Westminster Abbey on 6 November 1935 had to be scrapped because of the death, three weeks before the date, of her father, the Duke of Buccleuch. Much to Queen Mary's annoyance, the venue had to be changed from a public ceremony in the Abbey to a private one in the chapel of Buckingham Palace. 'Anyhow,' wrote the Queen to the Duke of Gloucester, 'Alice will wear her wedding dress and the bridesmaids theirs and we shall all wear the dresses we have chosen.'[29]

But the public were not cheated of all ceremonial. The service over, the newly-married couple made the customary appearance on the balcony: the Duke of Gloucester handsome in his frogged, braided and tasselled Hussar uniform, and the Duchess charming in her pink dress and tulle veil.

'Now,' wrote the King in his diary that evening, 'all the children are married but David.'[30]

*

David

G.R.I.
July 6th 1935.

Bertie

17 George V with his eldest sons, the Prince of Wales and the Duke of York

18 The Duke and Duchess of Windsor on their wedding day, 3 June 1937

And it was David, the Prince of Wales's future – and consequently the future of the monarchy – that chiefly preoccupied King George V during the few months of life that were left to him. 'After I am dead,' the King said to his new Prime Minister, Stanley Baldwin, 'the boy will ruin himself in twelve months.'[31] For the King knew all about Mrs Simpson. When it was suggested that the affair would blow over, he could not agree. He realised that this was more serious than the Prince's other love affairs had been. Yet neither the King nor the Queen ever mentioned the subject to their son. Not even when the very existence of the monarchy was at stake, could this inhibited couple bring themselves to discuss so intimate a matter. The price for that extra-ordinary lack of contact between parents and sons was now being extracted. On the other hand, it is unlikely that their opinions or warnings would have swayed the besotted Prince. The parents could only take comfort from the fact that their second son, the more serious-minded Duke of York, was so happily and suitably married.

'I pray to God,' the King once exclaimed to a friend, 'that my eldest son will never marry and have children, and that nothing will come between Bertie and Lilibet and the throne.'[32]

By the time that he said this, King George probably realised that he did not have much longer to live. He had recently suffered a recurrence of his old bronchial trouble and by the time that he arrived at Sandringham for Christmas 1935, he was feeling weak and listless. It was only fitting that it should be at his beloved Sandringham that the King should spend the last weeks of his life. On the death of his mother, Queen Alexandra, in 1925, King George had finally moved out of York Cottage into the big house, and it was from here that he made his last Christmas broadcast.

By New Year's Day, 1936, it was clear that he was seriously ill; and by 15 January that he was dying. For the following five days he did not leave his room. 'The King's life is moving peacefully to its close,'[33] ran the famous bulletin on the evening of 20 January 1936. Just before midnight, at the age of seventy and in the presence of his family, King George V died.

'*Am brokenhearted . . .*' wrote Queen Mary afterwards, 'at five to twelve my darling husband passed peacefully away – my children were angelic.'[34]

Queen Mary might have been brokenhearted but her composure, throughout her husband's illness and death, was exemplary. And never was her sense of royal obligation, of dynastic continuity, better illustrated than at the moment of his death. Turning from her husband, the dead King, to her eldest son, the living King, Queen Mary took his hand and, making a deep obeisance, kissed it. There was now a new monarch to be served.

All unwittingly, Queen Mary made another significant gesture that night. Not long after her husband had died, and demonstrating yet again what the household called her 'self-control and consideration for others', the Queen sent out 'to enquire after Ruth Fermoy's baby.'[35] Lady Fermoy was a

Sandringham neighbour: her newly-born baby, christened Frances, later became, as Viscountess Althorp, the mother of Diana, the present Princess of Wales and Britain's future Queen.

The new monarch, King Edward VIII, was equally capable of the dramatic gesture. With George V's coffin having been brought from Sandringham to London to lie in state, for five days, in Westminster Hall, an apparently endless stream of people passed by to pay their last respects. At each corner of the catafalque stood a motionless figure of an officer in the Brigade of Guards. At midnight on the last evening, on the new King's suggestion, these four guards were replaced by the late King's four sons: King Edward VIII, the Duke of York, the Duke of Gloucester and the Duke of Kent. There they stood, these four young men in the uniforms of their respective services, heads bowed, hands motionless on the hilts of their drawn swords. It was a splendidly romantic gesture and one which touched Queen Mary deeply.

But George V's funeral was marked by another, even more dramatic incident. As the gun-carriage bearing the coffin went trundling through the streets of the capital, followed by the slowly pacing King Edward VIII and his brothers, its jolting caused the jewelled Maltese Cross atop the Imperial Crown to work loose and go tumbling onto the road. A quick-thinking company sergeant major retrieved the cross and put it into his pocket. To those who had noticed it, it seemed like a bad omen.

'Christ!' King Edward VIII was heard to mutter. 'What will happen next?'

'A fitting motto,' remarked a watching member of parliament to his companion, 'for the coming reign.'[36]

Part Three

KING EDWARD VIII
1936

The Crown in Crisis

NEVER had the British monarchy seemed more resolutely set for a process of democratisation than on the accession of King Edward VIII. It was generally believed that the forty-one-year-old King epitomised everything that was fresh and modern and forward-looking. He held, wrote the Prime Minister, Stanley Baldwin, 'the secret of youth in the prime of age'.[1] Not that anyone thought of him as being in the prime of age. For together with Queen Alexandra's charm, her grandson seemed to have inherited her gift of perpetual youth. With his slight figure, his *retroussé* nose and his full head of neatly-combed blonde hair, Edward VIII looked, said one observer, 'like a boy of eighteen'.[2] Another, watching him at the Opening of Parliament, claimed that he appeared 'exactly as he did in 1911 at the investiture at Caernarvon. Not a day older, a young, happy Prince Charming . . .'[3] *The Times* spoke approvingly of his 'unerring eye between dignity and solemnity' and of his interest in all conditions of people 'which more "democrats" profess than feel.'[4]

Edward VIII was going to be King, it was fondly imagined, of the young and the progressive and the underprivileged.

The King saw himself in very much the same light. What he wanted to be, he claimed, was 'a King in a modern way'. He would have liked to have been known as 'Edward the Innovator': a democratic monarch free of the restraints, artificiality and ceremonial that had characterised his father's court. He was anxious to 'throw open the windows' of the monarchy, 'to let into the venerable institution some of the fresh air' which he had breathed as Prince of Wales. He planned to 'broaden its base', to make it more 'responsive to the changed circumstances'[5] of his times.

How successful, or indeed desirable, would Edward VIII's intended remodelling of the monarchy have been? In his study *Crown and People*, published in 1978 and based mainly on the Mass Observation Archive at the University of Sussex, Philip Ziegler claims that 'one very general conclusion does seem to emerge from the welter of miscellaneous evidence. There is as great a risk in reform as there is in standing still, perhaps even a greater risk. Change for the sake of change is not merely pointless but dangerous. The British people do not want any *fundamental* changes in the way the royal family conducts its life.'[6]

One of the great strengths of the British monarchy is its ability to adapt slowly. Even Edward VII, for all his sense of showmanship and enlightened social attitudes, remained very conscious of the dignity of the Crown; he was never anything less than majestic. And it was certainly not for his progressive qualities that George V was so greatly loved and respected. George VI's instinct, to revert to the decorum and relative remoteness of his father's day, was the right one. And it has been by a gradual, if continuous, adjustment to changing social realities that Queen Elizabeth II has strengthened and popularised the monarchy to such an extraordinary extent. Who can tell what damage a precipitate Edward VIII might have done to a structure which depends, ultimately, on commanding the admiration, affection and, not least, adulation of the people?

In any case, the new King seems to have had no very clear idea of how he was going to change things; or even of what exactly it was that he was planning to change. As he himself admitted, he was no radical. His views on most of the political issues of the day were distinctly conservative, even reactionary. One friend described him as being 'against too much slipshod democracy'.[7] He knew what he was against rather than what he was for: he was against state control, the League of Nations, disarmament, officialdom and what has since come to be known as the 'Establishment'. In his own circle, he was against what were regarded as 'George the Fifth men': that is anyone whom he considered stiff, stuffy, hidebound. And for reasons which were becoming increasingly obvious, he was against the prevailing 'hypocritical' attitude towards divorced persons.

The widespread belief that Edward VIII was a reforming monarch whose good intentions were thwarted by reactionary court, clerical and government circles is utterly without foundation. His cavalier attitudes might have rubbed some of them up the wrong way but there was never any suggestion of an Establishment 'plot' against him.

Such changes as the new King did make were trivial. He put the clocks back half-an-hour from the 'Sandringham time', so strictly adhered to by his father, to normal time. He created the 'King's Flight'. He dispensed with the regulation whereby the Yeomen of the Guard had to wear beards. He cut expenses in the royal households. He bypassed officials. He even, on one famous occasion, walked along the Mall instead of using the obligatory Daimler.

Harmless enough in itself, the King's informality extended into areas where it could be dangerous. It might give his public appearances a winning spontaneity but it was distinctly out of place when applied to official business.

His staff found him unpunctual, haphazard and inconsiderate. The 'boxes', to which his father had always attended so assiduously, were allowed to pile up at the Fort unopened. When they were opened, their confidential contents were often left scattered about, for any curious eyes to see.

The truth was that by now Edward VIII was interested in very little other than Wallis Simpson. 'It was scarcely realised at this early stage,' wrote Major Alexander Hardinge, his long-suffering private secretary, 'how overwhelming and inexorable was the influence exerted on the King by the lady of the moment. As time went on it became clearer that every decision, big or small, was subordinated to her will . . . It was she who filled his thoughts at all times, she alone who mattered, before her the affairs of state sank into insignificance.'[8]

On one point only was Hardinge mistaken: Mrs Simpson was not simply a 'lady of the moment'. She was there to stay. Those who imagined that all that was needed was to sit tight while the King's obsession with Mrs Simpson ran its course were to be proved wrong. Only gradually did it dawn on his entourage that the King intended marrying her.

By now this was his firm resolve. And not only did he intend marrying her but he intended making her his Queen. Coronation Day had been set for 12 May 1937; if the King hoped to have Mrs Simpson crowned as Queen Wallis beside him, he would have to have married her before then; and she would have to have been a free woman for a decent interval before that. So the first move would be for Wallis Simpson to divorce her husband. As, in those days, there was a wait of six months between the granting of a decree *nisi* and a decree absolute, her petition would have to be filed by the autumn of that year.

Conveniently, Ernest Simpson seems to have fallen in love with someone else, the woman whom he was to marry as his third wife. (As Wallis Simpson's first husband was to marry four times, her second husband three times and she three times – that is ten marriages between three people – her somewhat casual attitude towards divorce can be more readily understood.) When she told Ernest Simpson that she was about to start divorce proceedings, he obligingly moved out of their flat into the Guards Club. He was never one for scenes.

The King's next move was to get people, or at least official circles, used to the idea of Mrs Simpson. Far from wanting to keep her under cover, he was determined that she should be generally accepted. So he gave two formal dinner parties at St James's Palace. To one he invited Stanley Baldwin ('Sooner or later my Prime Minister must meet my future wife,'[9] he told her) and after both parties he published the list of guests, including Mrs Simpson, in the Court Circular. 'It did not pass unnoticed,' wrote Wallis Simpson, 'that Ernest was not present.'[10]

Nor did his next public exposure of Mrs Simpson pass unnoticed. Like his grandfather, Edward VII, and unlike his father, George V, the new King had a taste for Continental travel. Not for him that inflexible annual round of Newmarket and Cowes and the grouse moors on 12 August. He was far happier golfing at Biarritz, swimming off Eden Roc or stalking chamois in the Tyrol. So instead of spending that summer at Balmoral, as his father had done for the last quarter of a century, the King – again like Edward VII before him – took *his* Mrs Keppel across the Channel. From a Yugoslavian port, they set off on the famous cruise of the *Nahlin*.

If the world had not known about his love affair before then, it certainly came to know about it during the course of this well-publicised journey, by land and sea, through the Balkan countries. Their behaviour could hardly have been more indiscreet. But then discretion, as the King assured Wallis Simpson, was a quality which he had never much admired. The crowds who thronged about them were left in no doubt whatsoever that this small, skinny man dressed, on occasion, in nothing more than a pair of shorts, was passionately in love. Nor did his travelling companions have any doubt that his love was not only passionate but submissive. She was, to use the sort of Americanism in which he delighted, the boss.

But not quite the whole world knew about the King's obsession. The British press, demonstrating an astonishing discretion and loyalty, played down Mrs Simpson's role in this Balkan jamboree. It even went so far as to cut her out of photographs whenever she appeared beside the King. The result was that the general British public knew nothing whatsoever about the King's love affair. When, some months later, the news finally burst, they were amazed.

Back in England, Mrs Simpson prepared herself for the hearing of her divorce petition. The suit was to be heard in Ipswich in Suffolk and so, in order to establish residence, she took a house in nearby Felixstowe. Ernest Simpson having obligingly provided evidence of theoretical adultery with the engagingly named Miss Buttercup Kennedy at the equally engagingly named Café de Paris at Bray, the decree *nisi* was awarded on 27 October 1936. Only in six months' time, on 27 April, would the decree become absolute. 'However,' wrote the King, 'with my Coronation fixed for May 12, this seemed to allow ample time for me to work things out.'[11]

To ensure that the press continued to behave with discretion, the King had come to an arrangement with Lord Beaverbrook, Esmond Harmsworth and several other newspaper proprietors, whereby they all agreed to play down the Simpson divorce as well as 'limiting publicity after the event'.[12] Compared to the publicity that later accompanied the love affairs and divorce of someone like Princess Margaret, this press constraint seems almost unbelievable.

The American press suffered no such constraints. Already, on the day before the hearing, the *New York Journal* had boldly claimed that KING WILL

WED WALLY. Now, on reporting the divorce proceedings at Ipswich (in which town, some enterprising journalist had discovered, Cardinal Wolsey had been born) one newspaper ran the inimitable headline: KING'S MOLL RENO'D IN WOLSEY'S HOME TOWN.

People had to take him, Edward VIII once said in a disgruntled moment, as he was. If what they wanted was a carbon copy of his late father, there was always the Duke of York.

Although the Duke of York was not just a carbon copy of King George V, he was not unlike him in some ways. The Duke had inherited his father's iron sense of duty, his high moral standards, his preference for a familiar routine and his taste for domesticity. 'The pattern of their lives was much the same, with the steady swing of habit taking them both year after year to the same places at the same time and with the same associates,' wrote the Duke of Windsor many years later. 'Strongly rooted each in his own existence, they tended to be withdrawn from the hurly-burly of the life I relished.'[13]

For the last half-a-dozen or so years, the Duke of York had been more withdrawn from the hurly-burly than ever. Since the return from their successful tour of Australia and New Zealand in 1928, the Duke and Duchess of York had been enjoying a relatively quiet life. Confident that his older brother would one day marry and have children (and even if he did not, with only eighteen months dividing them, the King might outlive the Duke) the Duke of York never imagined that he might be called upon to ascend the throne. The possibility would have appalled him. He was quite content with playing a minor role; with carrying out his somewhat unspectacular round of public duties.

That he was able to do these with increasing self-confidence was due, mainly, to two factors. The first was his mastery of his stammer. Before setting out for Australia, the Duke of York had agreed wearily to see yet one more speech therapist in the hope that his impediment could be cured. From the time of his very first visit to the celebrated Lionel Logue, the Duke showed an improvement. Logue's method of treatment was both psychological and physical: he built up the patient's self-confidence and he taught him how to breathe correctly. The Duke was delighted with his progress. Although he never overcame his dislike of public speaking and always spoke slowly and hesitantly, he was largely cured of that humiliating and frustrating stutter.

Even more important in the building up of his self-confidence was the presence of his wife. The York marriage was extremely happy. It was quite obvious that the couple were devoted to each other. 'They reminded me of us,' wrote Duff Cooper to his wife after an evening at the theatre, 'sitting together in the box having private jokes, and in the interval when we were all sitting in the room behind the box they slipped out, and I found them standing together in a dark corner of the passage talking happily as we might. She affects no shadow of airs or graces.'[14]

And not only did the Duchess of York give her husband the love to which his insecure nature so readily responded but by her exceptional qualities she encouraged, inspired and supported him. Their characters were wonderfully complementary. Where he was hesitant, she was assured; where he was a worrier, she was serene; where he was introspective, she was outgoing; where he was short-tempered, she was long-suffering; where he shunned the limelight, she flowered in it. Like her brother-in-law, King Edward VIII, she knew how to handle crowds. She was always ready with the spontaneous gesture, the warm smile, the appropriate word.

Yet the Duchess of York was far from being assertive or domineering. On the contrary, she was tactful, softly spoken, sunny-natured, feminine. Her sense of dedication might have been as rigid as her husband's but she had a certain lightness of touch, an invincible *joie de vivre*, a sparkle. As one observer has astutely remarked she was – in the most decorous possible way – something of a flirt: her way was to bestow all her attention, to draw people out, to give pleasure.

And, in a strange fashion, the Duchess of York was able to transmit some of her own self-assurance to her husband. Many years later when he, as King George VI, was opening parliament in a Commonwealth country, he faltered in the course of his address. Although he could not have seen his wife's face as she sat beside him, shimmeringly dressed and smiling tranquilly, she gave a barely perceptible nod. On this, he took courage and continued.

The Duke of York was at his best in his home circle. Here he was kind, amusing, good-natured. He revelled in those purely family holidays at Sandringham or Balmoral. In the winter of 1924–25 the couple had spent several months in East Africa, a place beloved of so many members of the royal family. 'We walked for days; it was the most wonderful, wonderful time,'[15] the Queen Mother was to say wistfully in later years. The Duke was an excellent father. In this he was certainly no carbon copy of George V. His two daughters, Princess Elizabeth and Princess Margaret (born on 21 August 1930) were raised simply, naturally and with great affection. There was no artificial barrier between parents and children. The four of them were a closely-knit, demonstrative and loving family. In the year of Edward VIII's accession, Princess Elizabeth turned ten and Princess Margaret six. In temperament, the two princesses were very different. The elder daughter was quieter, more serious-minded, more responsible. The younger was livelier, prettier, more mercurial.

Never suspecting that their elder daughter would one day wear the crown, the Duke and Duchess of York had not been faced with the customary problem of how best to educate the heir. Indeed, the system they adopted could hardly have differed more from the one imposed on the future King Edward VII by Queen Victoria, or even the less exacting regime chosen by the future King George V for his children. Miss Marion Crawford, a sensible Scotswoman chosen as Princess Elizabeth's governess in 1932, expressed herself surprised and gratified at the lack of parental interference. Their requirements for their daughters' education were anything but demanding.

What girls needed, the Duchess of York maintained, was plenty of fresh country air, the ability to dance and draw and appreciate music, good manners, perfect deportment and feminine grace. So Miss Crawford – or 'Crawfie' as the princesses inevitably called her – drew up a six-day timetable, with the mornings devoted to half-hour lessons in the usual subjects, and the afternoons to singing, dancing, music and drawing. Queen Mary, on being consulted, suggested more history, more Bible reading and the study of genealogy.

The family had two homes. Their London home was 145 Piccadilly: an impressive mansion near Hyde Park Corner. Then, in 1931, King George V had given them The Royal Lodge in Windsor Great Park, a delapidated Regency house which they restored, altered and painted a delicate pink. The Duke was an enthusiastic and knowledgeable gardener and some of his happiest hours were spent landscaping the grounds of Royal Lodge. Rhododendrons were his special interest and in the early summer the gardens looked superb.

In the autumn the family would go to Birkhall, near Balmoral. Their 1936 holiday was made uncomfortable by the somewhat abrasive presence of Mrs Simpson at Balmoral. Not unnaturally, the Duchess resented the fact that Mrs Simpson took it upon herself to act as the King's hostess at the castle.

The Duke was equally put out by his brother's precipitate changes of personnel and arrangements at the castle. The Duke of York, like his late father, loved Balmoral and was deeply hurt by the fact that his brother had not even bothered to consult him about his proposed changes. 'David only told me what he had done after it was over, which I might say made me rather sad,' reported the Duke to Queen Mary. 'He arranged it all with the official people up here . . .'[16]

Queen Mary understood her son's resentment only too well. Thirty-five years before, as Duchess of York, she had bewailed King Edward VII's sweeping and insensitive innovations.

But even worse, from the Duke of York's point of view, was his brother's perfunctory attitude towards him. 'I never saw him alone for an instant,'[17] he complained to Queen Mary. Throughout the King's stay at Balmoral, the Duke of York felt 'shut off from his brother, neglected, ignored, unwanted'.[18] At no time did the King take him into his confidence about his future plans.

For not even at this late stage, apparently, was the Duke of York fully aware of the possible consequences of the King's feelings for Mrs Simpson. Like the other members of his family, he assumed that the affair would die a death; that she would disappear as Mrs Dudley Ward had disappeared. In any case, he refused to believe that, if faced with a choice between love and duty, the King would choose love; that he would actually go so far as to give up the crown in order to marry Mrs Simpson. It was unthinkable.

Only on returning to London from Scotland early in November 1936 did the Duke finally realise that this might be a possibility. He was visited by the King's private secretary, Major Alexander Hardinge. Hardinge had come to tell him that the Prime Minister, after much heart searching, had finally tackled the King on the question of Mrs Simpson. The discussions had been inconclusive but, for the first time, the implications of the King's obsession with Mrs Simpson could no longer be ignored. With her decree *nisi* having been granted, the King was quite clearly set on marrying her. And it was equally clear – to almost everyone, that is, other than the King himself – that if he did marry her, he would have to abdicate his throne. The crown would then pass to the Duke of York.

The Duke was appalled. 'A nightmare web,' as Sir John Wheeler-Bennett puts it, began 'slowly enmeshing him.'[19]

Among the surging and eddying floodwaters that followed the granting of Mrs Simpson's decree *nisi*, one thing stood firm as a rock: the King's determination to marry her. No pleas, arguments or calls to honour and duty could change his mind on this. There were times when he thought that he might, as he put it, 'get away with it'[20] – that is, marry her and hang on to his crown – but there was never a time when he considered giving her up.

In the course of several meetings with the King, the Prime Minister came to understand something of the monarch's feelings for Mrs Simpson. 'The King's face wore at times such a look of beauty,' reported the astonished Baldwin, 'as might have lighted the face of a young knight who had caught a glimpse of the Holy Grail.'[21] Deaf to all Baldwin's appeals, the King could only repeat that Wallis Simpson was 'the most wonderful woman in the world',[22] and that he could not live without her.

Eventually, the Prime Minister was obliged to make the position crystal clear. His Majesty, explained Baldwin, had three options. He could give up Mrs Simpson; he could marry her against the advice of his ministers and so force the government to resign; he could marry Mrs Simpson and abdicate. As the second option, for a constitutional monarch, was 'manifestly impossible', the King – if he wanted to remain King – had only one option: he must renounce Mrs Simpson.

This King Edward refused to consider. He would marry Mrs Simpson even if it meant abdication.

'I set it all before him,' Baldwin was afterwards to say. 'I appealed to one thing after another. Nothing made the least impression. It was almost uncanny; like talking to a child of ten years old. He did not seem to grasp the issues at stake. He seemed *bewitched* . . .'[23]

But even as he faced the bleak logic of his constitutional position, the King thrashed about for some other means by which he might be able to have his cake and eat it. For there is no doubt that he wished to remain King. Surely there was some way in which he could take advantage of his enormous popularity? In the midst of the maelstrom, the King carried out several public engagements. He opened parliament, he visited the Fleet at Southampton, he toured the distressed areas of Wales. On each occasion he acquitted himself superbly. The general public, who as yet knew nothing about their monarch's dilemma (the vast majority had not even heard of Mrs Simpson) were as charmed and enthusiastic a they had ever been.

One by one his sympathisers came up with ideas whereby this adored King might remain on his throne. Some favoured a morganatic marriage; others suggested that the whole matter rest for a year or two; Winston Churchill thought of forming a 'King's Party' that would somehow champion the monarch's cause; Wallis Simpson favoured a direct appeal to his subjects by a radio broadcast: something along the lines of the 'fireside chats' given by President Roosevelt.

Nothing came of these various suggestions. They were all swept away in the storm that broke on 2 December 1936. For on that day the British press finally broke its long silence. Both the King and Mrs Simpson were astonished by the sensationalism of its tone. Overnight, it seemed, the King's popularity had evaporated. Mrs Simpson was particularly upset. The sight of those black headlines staring at her from her breakfast tray (by now she was living permanently at the Fort) completely unnerved her. They convinced her that she must get out of England as soon as possible. Already she had discussed the possibility with the King and, on the morning of 3 December, they came to a decision. She would seek sanctuary with friends in the South of France. At seven that evening she left the Fort.

Mrs Simpson was not the only one to have been alarmed by the strident tone of that morning's press. At two-thirty that afternoon Queen Mary sat down to write a note to her eldest son.

'Darling David,' she wrote. 'This news in the papers is very upsetting, especially as I have not seen you for ten days. I would much like to see you, won't you look in some time today? I shall only be out from 3 to 5. Ever your loving Mama, Mary.'[24]

Queen Mary had written her letter from Marlborough House. She had moved there, from Buckingham Palace, almost exactly two months before.

At the time of King Edward VII's death in 1910, Queen Mary had been somewhat put out by the reluctance of her mother-in-law, Queen Alexandra, to move out of the Palace; now she found herself experiencing similar emotions. 'Sad to think that this is my last day in my old House of twenty-five years . . .' she wrote on 1 October 1936 when the last of her vast collection of *objets d'art* and family souvenirs had been moved out, 'but one must be content with the happy memories that remain.'[25]

The immediate prospects certainly did not look very happy. Not long after her husband's death, Queen Mary had overcome her natural reserve to speak to Lady Airlie about her eldest son. Had Lady Airlie ever been disappointed in her children? All children caused their parents some disappointment, answered the lady-in-waiting, but one had to remember that they had their own lives to lead. 'Yes,' countered Queen Mary, 'one can apply that to individuals but not to a Sovereign. He is not responsible to himself alone.'

'I have not liked to talk to David about this affair with Mrs Simpson,' she continued, 'in the first place because I don't want to give the impression of interfering in his private life, and also because he is the most obstinate of all my sons. To oppose him over doing anything is only to make him more determined to do it. At present he is utterly infatuated, but my great hope is that violent infatuations usually wear off.'

The King was giving Mrs Simpson, added the jewellery-loving Queen wistfully, 'the most beautiful jewels'.[26]

Nor, when her son visited her after his celebrated cruise on the *Nahlin* that summer, could Queen Mary bring herself to discuss anything but trivia with him. Although she knew that he had been accompanied by Mrs Simpson, she confined her conversation to the weather in the Adriatic and to the sort of questioning which reminded the King 'of how she used to talk to us when we returned from school.'[27]

Not until the evening of 16 November, after the King had first made clear to the Prime Minister his firm intention of marrying Mrs Simpson and, if necessary, of abdicating the throne in order to do so, did he pluck up the courage to speak to his mother. Changing into white tie and tails, he drove to Marlborough House for dinner. With Queen Mary was her daughter, the thirty-nine-year-old Princess Mary, Countess of Harewood, who had been created Princess Royal on the death of her aunt, Princess Louise, in 1931. Always close, mother and daughter had been drawn closer still since the death of King George V. During the tumultuous events that followed, the Princess Royal became Queen Mary's chief support.

The outcome of the talk between the three of them was as expected. When the Queen and the Princess Royal heard that the King was prepared to give up the throne to marry Mrs Simpson, they were astounded. 'To my mother,' writes the Duke of Windsor, 'the Monarchy was something sacred and the Sovereign a personage apart.'[28] Queen Mary could understand that her son was in love with Mrs Simpson. As a woman of experience, she would have been able to understand if he had wanted to have her as his mistress. What she could not understand was that he could contemplate marrying a divorced woman with, as she headshakingly put it, 'two husbands living'.[29] And as for such a woman becoming Queen of England, it was out of the question. His 'duty', insisted Queen Mary, was to give her up. This was a course of action which the King was not even prepared to consider. 'All that matters is our happiness,'[30] he repeated over and over again.

At the end of this inconclusive meeting, the King begged his mother to receive Mrs Simpson. He felt sure that she needed only to meet this paragon to understand why he was determined to marry her. 'For me the question is not whether she is acceptable but whether I am worthy of her,'[31] he said.

That the King of England should admit such abject sentiments would have been incomprehensible to Queen Mary. She refused to receive Mrs Simpson. When pressed for a reason, the Queen let slip her habitual control and exclaimed, 'Because she is an adventuress!'[32] Her son was never to forget that insult.

In fact, the Queen's overriding emotion, throughout the coming weeks, was one of anger. A visitor, expecting to find her in tears, describes her as 'furious and outraged'. Her cheeks, says Lady Airlie, would burn 'bright spots of crimson' at the mention of the King's possible renunciation of the throne for love. How *could* he desert his kingdom? Once, when Lady Airlie was criticising Catherine the Great, Queen Mary sprang to her defence. 'She loved her kingdom,' argued the Queen. 'She was prepared to make any sacrifices for it, to go to any lengths – even to commit terrible crimes for it.'

'I realised then,' says the lady-in-waiting, 'that her own nature, so gentle in private life, had a side which was as steel.'[33]

Yet on the following day the Queen wrote her son a conciliatory letter. 'As your mother, I must send you a line of true sympathy in the difficult position in which you are placed – I have been thinking of you all day, hoping you are making a wise decision for your future . . .'[34]

And to Lady Airlie the Queen said quietly, with a sigh, 'He's very, very much in love with her. Poor boy.'[35]

On that same day the Queen received the Prime Minister. Baldwin, who had always found Queen Mary's reserve unnerving, was astonished by her brisk welcome. 'For, instead of standing immobile in the middle distance, silent and majestic, she came trotting across the room *exactly like a puppy dog*; and before I had time to bow, she took hold of my hand in both of hers and held it tight.

' "Well, Prime Minister," she said, "here's a pretty kettle of fish!" '[36]

*

In the course of the following few days, the King finally confided in his three brothers. Because they had always been what he called 'a somewhat complicated quartet',[37] the King saw them separately. Most seriously affected was the Duke of York. For several weeks previously, and in mounting anxiety, the Duke had vainly been trying to see his brother. Now, on finally hearing from the King's own lips that he might abdicate, the Duke of York was aghast. He could find nothing to say. 'His genuine concern for me,' said the King later, 'was mixed with the dread of having to assume the responsibilities of kingship.'[38] To his private secretary, the Duke of York could only confess that he felt 'like the proverbial sheep being led to the slaughter.'[39]

The Duchess of York was equally apprehensive. She may have had more taste and talent for public life but she had no wish to become Queen. Nor did she want to see her highly-strung husband subjected to the strain of wearing the crown.

The Duke of Gloucester took the news more philosophically. The two brothers had never been close: 'apart from our mutual interests in horses and riding, we had little in common,'[40] wrote the King. With three lives – those of the Duke of York and his two daughters – between him and the throne, the Duke of Gloucester had no fear of being called upon to assume kingship. But he suspected that he might have to give up his beloved soldiering in order to devote more time to royal duties.

The Duke of Kent showed more emotion than either of his brothers. He was deeply upset; not only by the King's news but by the off-hand manner in which he broke it to him. 'The Duke of Kent unburdened his heart,' wrote 'Chips' Channon a few days later, 'said he loved the King more than anyone, how the King ignored him, how he had not even seen him since the Balmoral visit . . . The King had rung him up on the telephone before dinner that evening to say that he was going to marry Wallis, and the Duke of Kent had not known whether to congratulate him or not, hence his nervousness and irritability. And he only rang him because he knew he would meet him at our dinner . . .'[41]

'He is besotted on the woman,' the Duke of Kent exclaimed angrily to the Prime Minister, 'one can't get a word of sense out of him.'[42]

Having unburdened himself to his brothers, the King went back to ignoring them. At no stage did he have a serious discussion with the Duke of York on his brother's unwillingness or fitness to take up the duties which he was about to abdicate. He conducted all his negotiations without any reference to his brother whatsoever. The dramatic breaking of the press's long silence on the subject of the King's marriage took the Duke of York by complete surprise. He expressed himself 'horrified'.[43]

That night – it was 3 December, the day on which Mrs Simpson fled to France – the King answered his mother's urgent summons to Marlborough House. Here he found the Duke and Duchess of York and, once again, the

Princess Royal. Among the glittering *objets* of Queen Mary's sitting-room they sat, this family who had never been able to discuss anything other than generalities, discussing the most painful and important event of their lives. The King tried to explain away his cavalier treatment of his mother. 'I have no desire to bring you and the family into all this,' he said. 'This is something I must handle alone.'[44]

Having made this extraordinary statement, the King left them in no doubt whatsoever about his determination to marry Mrs Simpson, whether it cost him his crown or not. He asked the Duke of York to come and see him at the Fort the following morning.

But neither on the next morning nor on the two mornings after that could the King make time to see his brother. He did not even return his telephone calls. Finally, after repeated requests, the Duke of York was invited to the Fort on the evening of Monday 7 December 1936.

'The awful and ghastly suspense of waiting was over,' wrote the Duke. 'I found him pacing up and down the room, and he told me his decision that he would go.'[45]

King Edward VIII had made his decision two days before. On Sunday 5 December, the Prime Minister was formally told that the King would abdicate. One by one the various schemes for a way out of his dilemma had collapsed. Neither the British government nor the Dominion governments would hear of a morganatic marriage; the Cabinet turned down the King's request for a broadcast to the nation; wisely, King Edward would have no truck with the formation of a 'King's Party'; nor was he prepared to play for time. A suggestion that he postpone the marriage until after his Coronation, the King refused to consider. For all his unconventionality, Edward VIII was too conscious of the majesty of his position, and of the solemnity of a Coronation, to think of being crowned while the question of his marriage remained unresolved.

The Coronation, he argued, 'is essentially a religious service. The King is anointed with holy oil; he takes the Sacrament; as Defender of the Faith he swears an oath to uphold the doctrines of the Church of England, which does not approve of divorce. For me to have gone through the Coronation ceremony while harbouring in my heart a secret intention to marry contrary to the Church's tenets would have meant being crowned with a lie on my lips . . .'[46]

One thing only weakened his resolve to abdicate: Wallis Simpson's urgings for him not to do so. In the course of a helter-skelter, journalist-hounded drive through France, and from the home of her friends in Cannes, she was in constant touch with him. Time and again, over an appalling telephone line, she assured him that his popularity would carry the day; that he should fight for his rights. In this she showed a profound misunderstanding of the monarchy: she imagined that the man was more important than the institution.

When she could not change his mind about abdicating, she tried renouncing him. He would not hear of it. She next agreed to someone's suggestion that she withdraw her divorce petition. It was too late for that now, countered the King. She would flee, she threatened, to China. He cut her short. 'I can't seem to make you understand the position,' he bawled down the mouthpiece. 'It's all over. The Instrument of Abdication is already prepared.'[47] Only then was she convinced.

Just how seriously Wallis Simpson meant to give up King Edward VIII has since been questioned. There is a theory that her sacrifice was not as selfless as she pretended: that, between them, she and the King had decided that she would appear in a better light if it were to become known that she had made an offer to renounce him. It would help to dispel the widespread impression that she was simply a hard, scheming, self-seeking adventuress determined, at any cost, to land a king. It would make her look noble, tragic, self-sacrificing.

Be that as it may, it was too late for any such gesture. On the night of Tuesday 8 December the Duke of York was summoned to join the King, the Prime Minister and several others at the Fort for dinner. While the rest of them sat with doleful faces, the King, his decision made, was as lively as a cricket. By his charm, his assurance and his informed talk, he held the table spellbound.

'Look at him,' whispered the Duke to one of the other guests. 'We simply cannot let him go.'[48] More than ever was the Duke of York made to feel conscious of his own inadequacy.

On the following day Queen Mary and the Princess Royal drove down to the Duke of York's home, Royal Lodge, to meet the King. Here the Queen was told of her son's irrevocable decision to abdicate. She heard him out in silence. 'She still disapproved of and was bewildered by my action,' he afterwards wrote, 'but now that it was all over her heart went out to her hard-pressed son, prompting her to say with tenderness: "And to me, the worst thing is that you won't be able to see her for so long." '[49] For it had been decided that the lovers should not see each other until Mrs Simpson's divorce had become absolute, in five months' time.

'I do hope that she will make him happy,' Queen Mary was later to say to Lady Airlie. 'It is no ordinary love he has for her.'[50]

Throughout the Abdication crisis, Queen Mary's behaviour was an example and an inspiration to her family. 'Thank God,' wrote one of them at the time, 'we have all got you as a central point, because without that point [the family] might easily disintegrate.'[51]

And it was not only the royal family, but the institution of monarchy itself which seemed in danger of disintegrating. The Duke of York feared that 'the whole fabric [might] crumble under the shock and strain of it all.'[52] Queen Mary shared her son's apprehensions. Her duty, as she saw it at the time, was to reassure public opinion. The whole country was rife with rumours; therefore she must behave as though nothing were wrong. With every appearance of normality, the Queen carried out her various private and public engagements. She did her Christmas shopping, she visited museums and exhibitions, she went to see the birds in Dulwich Park. The Crystal Palace had burnt down at the end of November and in a studied gesture of re-assurance, the Queen paid a visit to the ruins on the very day that the press finally broke its silence. The sight of the dignified and indomitable Queen, still dressed in mourning for her late husband, had the intended effect on public opinion. Monarchs might come and go, but the monarchy lived on.

The fact that the British monarchy emerged from the Abdication relatively unscathed was, says James Pope-Hennessy, 'triumphant proof that the life-work of King George the Fifth and Queen Mary had not been in vain.' 'In any other country,' wrote the Queen when it was all over, 'there would have been riots, thank God people did not lose their heads.'[53] Not for many years, though, was the royal family able to shake off the traumatic effects of the King's abdication. To this day, the subject is either studiously avoided or mentioned with a perceptible shudder.

The full extent of what Queen Mary considered her son's shameful dereliction of duty was finally and vividly brought home to her on the night of 9 December when, together with the Duke of York, she studied the draft Instrument of Abdication. Scathingly, she referred to it as 'the paper drawn up for David's abdication of the Throne of this Empire because he wishes to marry Mrs Simpson!!!!!' It was, she continued, 'a terrible blow for us all and particularly poor Bertie.'[54]

Making it even worse for 'poor Bertie' was the fact that, at this time of terrible ordeal, he was deprived of the presence of his chief comfort and support. The Duchess of York was at home at 145 Piccadilly, ill with influenza. 'Dickie, this is absolutely terrible,' the Duke of York was to blurt out to his cousin, Lord Louis Mountbatten, in a couple of days' time. 'I never wanted this to happen; I'm quite unprepared for it. . . I've never even seen a State paper. I'm only a naval officer, it's the only thing I know about.'[55]

Now, in his mother's drawing-room at Marlborough House, the Duke of York felt suddenly overwhelmed by the situation. 'I broke down,' he writes, 'and sobbed like a child.'[56]

'The person who most needs sympathy,' snapped the indignant Queen Mary a day or two later to someone who spoke of her eldest son's 'sacrifice', 'is my second son. *He* is the one who is making the sacrifice.'[57]

On 10 December 1936, in the presence of his three brothers, King Edward VIII sat down at his desk at the Fort to sign the Instrument of Abdication. On the following day, with the Abdication Bill having been ratified by parliament, the Duke of York succeeded to the throne as King George VI.

Edward VIII's abdication served the monarchy as a supreme example of the impossibility of reconciling one's public role with a private life that is too much at variance with it. An occasional lapse is permissible, but for a monarch to hope to separate, permanently, his public obligations from his personal inclinations – to lead, in short, a double life – is unrealistic. The Abdication served also as a lesson in how far a constitutional monarch could exercise his personal will. For all his popularity, Edward VIII counted for very little against the forces of the constitution. And he appreciated this. Edward VIII might not have been the most exemplary of kings but he was king enough to know that if he wanted to save the monarchy, he would have to give way to the powers that were opposing the monarch.

There remained the question of the abdicated King's title. On the suggestion of the new King, he was in future to be styled His Royal Highness, Duke of Windsor. 'It shall be the first act of my reign,' said King George VI. 'I shall announce it at my Accession Council tomorrow morning.'[58]

One last scene had still to be played out: the ex-King's farewell broadcast to the nation. This had been in the nature of a last wish. As he was to leave England on the night of 11 December 1936, he arranged to make his farewell broadcast from Windsor Castle just before setting out. His family – his mother, his sister, his three brothers and Queen Mary's brother, the Earl of Athlone, and his wife Princess Alice – assembled for the final dinner. 'Queen Mary, ever magnificent, was mute and immovable and very royal,' reported 'Chips' Channon, 'and had thoughtfully left off her mourning black for the evening so as not to cast more gloom.'[59]

After dinner, the ex-King drove to Windsor Castle to deliver his broadcast. It was a moving and dignified address. 'And now we all have a new King,' ran the closing sentences. 'I wish him, and you, his people, happiness and prosperity with all my heart. God bless you all. God save the King.'[60]

He then returned to Royal Lodge to say his final farewells. The destroyer, *Fury*, was waiting at Portsmouth to take him across the Channel. 'It isn't possible! It isn't happening!' exclaimed the distraught Duke of Kent as his brother took his leave.

'When David and I said goodbye we kissed . . .' wrote the new monarch, 'and he bowed to me as his King.'[61]

Part Four

KING GEORGE VI
1936–1952

'Making Amends'

'BERTIE,' King George V had once said, 'has more guts than the rest of his brothers put together.'[1]

The new, forty-year-old King was going to need all the 'guts' he had. In both his own estimation and that of the public, he was woefully lacking in kingly qualities. How could he possibly take the place of the predecessors: of his widely revered father or his scintillating brother? He was even old enough to remember his grandfather, the assured and majestic King Edward VII. So self-depreciating, the new King felt that he had neither the presence, the personality nor the experience for his role. He was overwhelmed by the magnitude of the task that had so suddenly been thrust on him; he was oppressed by the relentless publicity, by the prospect of public speaking, by the volume of work in the 'boxes'. On his first public appearances he looked tense, drawn and uncertain.

Nor was he helped by knowing, or suspecting, that the majority of his subjects shared his uncertainties. 'There's a lot of prejudice against him,' confided Stanley Baldwin to a friend. 'He's had no chance to capture public imagination as his brother did. I'm afraid he won't find it easy going for the first year or two.'[2]

It was rumoured that Baldwin had at one stage considered superceding the Duke of York by his brother, the Duke of Kent. Not only was the Duke of Kent the father of a male heir (his first son, Prince Edward, had been born on 9 October 1935) but he was an altogether more imposing-looking figure and an accomplished public speaker. He was married, moreover, to a born princess: the sophisticated and elegant Princess Marina. When set against the more homely Yorks, the Kents certainly made, in 'Chips' Channon's phrase, 'a dazzling pair'.

It is an unlikely story. Neither the British constitution nor royal tradition allowed for any such cavalier treatment of the order of succession. The Abdication had been traumatic enough; this was not the time for tampering with the dynastic rights, not only of the Duke of York and his two daughters, but of the Duke of Gloucester. In any case, for all his apparent shortcomings, the Duke of York was a far worthier man than the light-weight Duke of Kent.

There were others who thought that this might be a good opportunity to do away with the monarchy altogether. One Conservative member of parliament estimated that, in a straight vote in the Commons, a hundred votes would have been cast in favour of a republic. And the popular Labour member, James Maxton, went so far as to move an amendment to the Abdication Bill calling for the abolition of the monarchy and the establishment of a 'completely democratic form of government'.[3] The amendment was defeated, but that it should have been moved at all was significant.

Rumours about the new King's physical disabilities were widespread. The Archbishop of Canterbury did not help matters by a well-intentioned reference, in his Abdication broadcast, to the King's speech impediment. The 'occasional and momentary hesitation . . .' in the Sovereign's speech, intoned His Grace, 'need cause no sort of embarrassment, for it causes none to him who speaks.'[4] The same could not have been said of the Archbishop's tactless remark.

There were reservations, too, about the thirty-six-year-old Queen Elizabeth's ability to fulfil her great destiny. She might have proved successful enough in a minor role but what sort of queen would she make? She had neither Queen Mary's commanding presence nor the stylishness of someone like Princess Marina, or, for that matter, Wallis Simpson. For years Queen Elizabeth had been known as 'the little Duchess'; might she not, with her small stature, her wispy fringe, her ready smile and her uncertain taste in clothes, prove to be rather too 'little', too lacking in majesty? She was the first commoner to become Queen since Tudor times; would not a princess, born and bred, have made a more suitable queen?

King George VI's redoubtable aunt, Princess Alice, Countess of Athlone, always maintained that only those who had been born royal, only those who had been trained from youth 'to such an ordeal' could sustain the role 'with amiability and composure'.[5] Would the new Queen's lack of a royal background tell against her?

'The press is trying to work up popularity for the new regime and perhaps in time it will succeed,' noted a sceptical 'Chips' Channon. After all, he went on to concede, 'George V and Queen Mary were actually unpopular when they began their reign, and they lived to see themselves adored.'[6]

But it is easy to exaggerate the extent of the private and public misgivings about the abilities of King George VI and Queen Elizabeth. There was one requirement – and this the chief one – which they were fulfilling superbly. They provided the sense of monarchal continuity and stability which was so badly needed after the upheaval of the Abdication. That, and a return to the respectability of George V's day. Once the first numbing shock of their sudden accession had worn off, the new sovereigns set about making, as the

King put it, 'amends for what has happened.'[7] King George VI had come to
the throne too unexpectedly for him to have worked out any theories about
the sort of reign he planned to inaugurate. All he could say, in his first
message to parliament, was that 'It will be my constant endeavour, with
God's help and supported by my wife, to uphold the Honour of the Realm
and promote the Happiness of my peoples.'[8]

In a private letter to the Archbishop of Canterbury, the Queen admitted,
'I can hardly now believe that we have been called to this tremendous
task and (I am writing to you quite intimately) the curious thing is that we are
not afraid. I feel that God has enabled us to face the situation calmly.'[9]

Within days the King was impressing those about him by his air of quiet
determination. It was with relief that they were able to recognise the traits
which had made George V such a successful King: his common sense, his
dedication, his integrity, his moral courage. The new King may not have
been particularly quick, clever or original but he had a comforting dependability. Even the fact that he had chosen to be known as George VI was
reassuring.

Before long, 'Chips' Channon reported that 'the King and Queen have
gained greatly in presence and dignity'[10] and that at their first Opening of
Parliament 'the King seemed quite at ease and so did the Queen.'[11]

Sustaining the royal couple throughout this period of adjustment was their
sincere and simple religious faith. It was this, too, which made their Coronation, on 12 May 1937, an additionally significant event. In the ordinary way,
a sovereign has a year or more in which to prepare himself for his crowning
but, for the sake of both convenience and continuity, it had been decided to
keep the date set for Edward VIII's Coronation. On the Sunday evening
before the ceremony, the Archbishop of Canterbury came to Buckingham
Palace to speak to the couple about the spiritual aspects of the Coronation. 'I
prayed for them and for their Realm and Empire and I gave them my personal
blessing,' recorded the Archbishop. 'I was much moved, and so were they.
Indeed, there were tears in their eyes when we rose from our knees. From that
moment I knew what would be in their minds and hearts when they came to
their anointing and crowning.'[12]

But that was not quite all that was in their minds. King George VI's own
account of his Coronation was full of telling observations and amusing
asides. The solemn ceremony was marked by countless minor mishaps,
culminating in the newly crowned, slowly pacing King being brought to an
abrupt halt by one of the bishops standing on his robe. 'I had to tell him to get
off it pretty sharply as I nearly fell down,'[13] noted the King.

Among all the splendours of the Coronation ceremony – the blaring
trumpets, the swelling anthems, the richly embroidered copes and vestments,
the costumed pages, the glittering crowns, the King in satin and velvet and
ermine, the Queen in white, all shimmering with gold thread – were two

notable innovations. Both concerned the royal family. One was the presence
of Queen Mary; the other the presence of the King's little daughters.

A Queen Dowager does not usually attend the Coronation of her husband's successor but the presence of Queen Mary was a reassuring sign of
family solidarity. No less reassuring was the sight of the two little princesses
– the eleven-year-old Princess Elizabeth and the six-year-old Princess
Margaret – both in white lace dresses, purple velvet robes and golden
coronets.

Nothing could have stressed more vividly the feature that became one of
the great advantages of George VI's reign: a family at the centre of national
life. At the time of Edward VIII's abdication, J.H. Thomas, the Socialist
politician and trade union leader, had spoken out bluntly on the subject. 'And
now 'ere we 'ave this obstinate little man with 'is Mrs Simpson,' he complained to Harold Nicolson. 'Hit won't do, 'Arold, I tell you that straight. I
know the people of this country. I *know* them. They 'ate 'aving no family life
at Court.'[14]

The 'obstinate little man' had known this. In his Abdication broadcast,
King Edward VIII had admitted that his brother had 'one matchless blessing,
enjoyed by so many of you and not bestowed on me – a happy home life with
his wife and children.'[15]

Once again, there was to be a family on the throne.

By few was the radio broadcast of George VI's Coronation listened to more
attentively than by his elder brother, the Duke of Windsor. Side by side the
Duke and his future wife sat through the long account of the ceremony. Her
mind, she tells us, was in a turmoil. What he was thinking, she did not know.
But when it was all over he assured her that he had no regrets. This was true.
He was as obsessed with her as ever. 'He sees through Wallis's eyes, hears
through her ears and speaks through her mouth,'[16] wrote one observer at the
time.

By then the couple were at the Château de Candé, near Tours, busy with
the preparations for their wedding. The date had been set for 3 June. Until
Wallis Simpson's divorce had become absolute, on 3 May, the couple had
lived apart: he in Austria, she in the South of France. Not until that Spring had
she come to the Château de Candé. On being consulted, King George VI had
favoured Candé as the most suitable of the houses offered them for their
wedding: he considered it a more dignified setting than some villa on the
frivolous Riviera.

He could hardly, though, have approved the date. For 3 June had been King
George V's birthday. To Queen Mary, especially, this was an almost sacred
date; hardly a suitable one for the marriage of a king who had betrayed his
trust in order to become the third husband of a woman whom Queen Mary

regarded as little more than an ambitious *intrigante*.

If the Duke of Windsor had imagined that, with the Coronation over, his family's attitude towards his marriage would soften, he was soon disillusioned. At one stage he had cheerfully assumed that members of the royal family would attend the wedding and that his two younger brothers, the Dukes of Gloucester and Kent, would be 'supporters' at the ceremony. He seemed never to appreciate the extent of his family's disapproval, even repugnance, at the whole business of his abdication and marriage. This was why he was so shocked on receiving, on the day before the wedding, a letter from George VI in which the monarch made clear that although, in future, his brother would be entitled to style himself a Royal Highness, his wife would not. She would be known simply as the Duchess of Windsor. Whereas the Duke's sisters-in-law, the Duchess of Gloucester and the Duchess of Kent, were always bowed and curtsied to, the Duchess of Windsor would not be entitled to any such royal homage. She would not be regarded as royal at all.

The Duke was enraged. 'This is a nice wedding present,'[17] he exclaimed bitterly.

The royal family had very good reasons for this apparently mean-minded act. As King George VI explained to Stanley Baldwin, a Royal Highness remains a Royal Highness for life; there is no means of depriving someone of the title. Knowing very little about Wallis Simpson, they probably assumed that this third marriage would last no longer than the others; that having failed in her plan to become Queen of England, she would drop her latest husband as airily as she had dropped her previous ones. Or perhaps the Duke, on finally realising what sort of woman she really was, would drop her; or simply tire of her, as he had tired of others, and marry someone else. This would mean that there might be, not only one but two embarrassing Royal Highnesses floating about the world.

The Duke of Windsor was never to forget this insult to himself and, even more important, to his wife. It rankled for the rest of his life.

So it was without the presence of a single member of his family that the Duke of Windsor married Wallis Simpson (or Wallis Warfield rather: she had had her name changed by deed poll, back to its unsullied origins, a few weeks before) at the Château de Candé. It was a day of glorious sunshine. A little altar had been arranged in a small salon and the setting transformed by Constance Spry's stylish flower arrangements. Both the bride and bridegroom behaved with admirable grace and dignity. Yet to the handful of guests, there was something indescribably sad about it all. The atmosphere was full of might-have-beens. When one thought of the sort of ceremony he should have been having, of all the theatrical pomp of a service in Westminster Abbey, this seemed so makeshift.

But that the Duke of Windsor was without any regrets was only too obvious. The tears that coursed down his cheeks after the ceremony were tears of pure happiness. In his morning suit and with his blonde hair neatly brushed, he looked as radiant as a schoolboy on holiday.

It is to the Duchess, though, that in those thousands of photographs that appeared throughout the world, the eye is always drawn. There she stands in her elegant, ice-blue, slim-fitting, floor-length dress, her hat a simple halo of tulle and feathers, a diamond and sapphire bracelet clasped to her wrist – looking so clear-eyed, so confident, so enigmatic.

'She is . . .' wrote Harold Nicolson fulsomely of Queen Elizabeth, 'one of the most amazing Queens since Cleopatra.'[18]

Be that as it may, the new Queen very quickly dispelled any reservations about her fitness for her role and established herself as a person of exceptional qualities. In looks, manner and attitudes she set very much her own style. Cecil Beaton once compared her to a fragrance from a past age, and it was as a graceful, feminine, pretty-as-a-picture Queen that she now presented herself.

To help create this effect, Norman Hartnell, the couturier, was invited to Buckingham Palace. In his quiet fashion, the King suggested that Hartnell accompany him on a tour of some of the Palace paintings. Cigarette in hand, the King drew his attention to the Winterhalter portraits of such nineteenth-century beauties as the Empress Eugenie of the French and the Empress Elizabeth of Austria. It was this 'picturesque grace',[19] indicated the King, that Hartnell should recreate in his dresses for the Queen. From this conversation evolved, not only those frothy, lavishly embroidered crinolines for which Queen Elizabeth became celebrated but her whole soft, sumptuous, distinctive way of dressing. Queen Elizabeth looked, enthused Lady Diana Cooper on one occasion, 'like a lily and a rose in one'.[20]

With this newly acquired aura of romance went a newly acquired majesty. In spite of her smallness and her tendency to plumpness, Queen Elizabeth looked undeniably regal: her carriage was erect, her manner assured, her gestures unhurried. She moved as though in slow motion. On so vastly increased a scale, her talent for public appearances seemed more remarkable than ever. A visiting foreigner was greatly impressed by the *éclat* with which the Queen laid yet another foundation stone: 'as though she had discovered a new and delightful way of spending an afternoon.'[21] And Harold Nicolson described her public manner as superb. 'She really does convey to each individual in the crowd that he or she has had a personal greeting.'[22] Those bright blue eyes seemed able to seek out, if only for one flattering second, every single face.

'The Queen then goes the rounds,' wrote Nicolson on the occasion of a dinner at Buckingham Palace. 'She wears upon her face a faint smile indicative of how much she would have liked her dinner party were it not for the fact that she was Queen of England. Nothing could exceed the charm or dignity which she displays and I cannot help feeling what a mess poor Mrs Simpson would have made of such an occasion.'[23]

Yet the Queen's most important contribution was a less obvious one: this was her support for and encouragement of her husband. The King's frequent public allusions to his wife's help in carrying out his duties were far from conventional tributes. They were in heartfelt appreciation of her constant inspiration. Never had her qualities of tranquillity, optimism and resilience been more valuable to her husband than during the first few years of his reign. They not only sustained him but brought out all his own latent strengths. 'That was the measure of her greatness as a woman,' said a close friend in later years. 'She drew him out and made him a man so strong that she could lean upon him.'[24]

Most valuable was Queen Elizabeth's creation of a harmonious family life. Even among the impersonal and overwhelming splendours of Buckingham Palace, she managed to spread a relaxed and cheerful atmosphere. As the two princesses were still being educated at home by 'Crawfie', the family remained very close. Amongst themselves, they behaved with the utmost naturalness. Unsophisticated in their own tastes, the parents encouraged simplicity and artlessness in their daughters. Providing one did one's duty, life should be the greatest possible fun. In a return, almost, to the 'romps' of Queen Alexandra's day, the princesses grew up in an atmosphere of family jokes, parlour games, sing-songs and charades.

King George VI and Queen Elizabeth were the first sovereigns to abolish the custom of royal children bowing or curtseying to their parents. The princesses greeted their mother and father as simply and effusively as did any other children. It was all a far cry from the old regime when, in the evenings, Queen Mary would rise to her feet when her husband left the room and remain standing while, one by one and in order of age, her four sons would go up to her, bow, and then withdraw.

'There was something unique about the King's home life,' claimed his aunt, Princess Alice, who had already experienced four reigns. 'Just a small, absolutely united circle of the King, the Queen and the princesses. They shared the same jokes and they shared each others' troubles.'[25] Whatever the strains of his official duties, George VI could always be sure of a warm, loving, understanding atmosphere at the very core of his daily life.

Because of Princess Elizabeth's sudden elevation to the position of Heir Presumptive (not Heir Apparent: the Queen could still have given birth to a son, who would automatically have become the undisputed future sovereign) she began, on turning thirteen, to take a course in British constitutional history with Sir Henry Marten, Vice-Provost of Eton. Like the lessons given to her father at Cambridge, and to her grandfather by Professor J.R. Tanner, Princess Elizabeth's lessons owed a great deal to the shrewd and sparkling pages of Walter Bagehot.

It was during these early years of the reign that the differences between Princess Elizabeth and Princess Margaret became even more apparent. As the elder, fully aware of her enhanced status and increased responsibilities, became ever more tidy, methodical and conscientious, the younger became less so. Adored by her parents, and particularly by her father, the pretty little Princess Margaret delighted them by her talents for music and mimicry. There was nothing like one of her pert imitations to bring a smile to King George VI's often careworn face. If Queen Elizabeth could see something of the King's earnestness in their elder daughter, she could see something of her own more sparkling personality in the younger.

Queen Elizabeth's first great public triumph came in the summer of 1938, when she accompanied the King on a state visit to Paris. The sudden death of the Queen's mother, Lady Strathmore, a few weeks before the visit was turned to brilliant advantage by the royal dressmaker, Norman Hartnell. Appreciating that the Queen would have to wear mourning, and that white was permissible for royal mourning, he hurriedly recreated the Queen's entire wardrobe of pastel-coloured dresses in white. The effect was dazzling. The Queen's unusual all-white trousseau, allied to her habitual charm of manner, turned the four-day state visit into a great personal success.

'We have taken the Queen to our hearts,' trumpeted one French newspaper. 'She rules over two nations.'[26]

But the French state visit was more than just an opportunity for Queen Elizabeth to display her social gifts and striking wardrobe. The King and Queen went to Paris – as King Edward VII had gone in 1903 and King George V and Queen Mary in 1914 – as instruments of their country's foreign policy. Edward VII's brand of personal diplomacy might have died with him but a state visit remained a gesture of considerable political significance. This Parisian visit by George VI was designed to symbolise, and strengthen, Anglo-French solidarity in the face of an increasingly menacing international situation.

For King George VI had succeeded, as his official biographer has put it, to 'a barren heritage'.[27] In the long term, the King was to preside over the gradual decline of British power and prestige; in the shorter term, he was to experience the growing aggression of the Axis Powers and the anguish of the Second World War.

George VI's Coronation had coincided with the resignation of Stanley Baldwin and the succession of Neville Chamberlain as Prime Minister. In his efforts to contain the Axis Powers by appeasing them, the new Prime Minister had the King's wholehearted support. A peace-loving man, who had lived through the horrors and heartbreaks of one World War and the hardships and disillusionments of the subsequent peace, King George VI was not alone in imagining that another war could be avoided. Having great confidence in Chamberlain, he gave him every encouragement. The Prime Minister's tireless, tortuous and demeaning negotiations with Hitler having ended in the ephemeral triumph of the Munich agreement, a relieved King George VI, with the Queen beside him, led the Prime Minister out onto the Palace balcony to receive the cheers of the no less relieved crowds below.

Nor was the King content to leave everything to Chamberlain. Throughout this agonising period and even after the hollowness of the Munich agreement had become apparent, the King was anxious to make some personal contribution towards peace. Time and again he suggested that he make a direct appeal to Hitler. His offers were refused. It would not do for the King to suffer a rebuff. In any case, the days had long since passed when the word of a monarch carried any weight in international affairs. Not even Edward VII, for all his celebrated diplomatic manoeuvrings, had been able to alter the tides of peace and war.

No, the King's prestige would be put to much better use in strengthening friendships than in conciliating enemies. This was why he had gone to Paris. And this was why it was decided that he should visit Canada and the United States in 1939.

The tour was a great success. Setting off on 5 May across the foggy, iceberg-infested Atlantic ('the poor Captain was nearly demented because some kind cheerful people kept on reminding him that it was about here that the Titanic was struck, and *just* about the same date . . .'[28] wrote the Queen blithely to Queen Mary), the King and Queen spent almost a month in Canada. It was the first visit of a reigning sovereign to the dominion, and the first of the sort of royal tour that has become commonplace during the reign of Queen Elizabeth II. Giving it an added significance – and underlining an anomaly of the British Commonwealth – was the fact that George VI was visiting Canada not as King of England but as King of Canada.

It was the first time, too, that a British King and Queen had moved so freely among the crowds. The Queen was responsible for this departure from normal procedure. Having just laid the foundation stone of a new building in Ottawa, and having been told that some of the masons were Scots, she insisted on breaking away from the official party in order to go and speak to them. Always oblivious of time, she spent ten minutes in happy Scottish reminiscence. Again, at the unveiling of a war memorial, she asked to go down among the thousands of veterans. Never, claimed the Governor-General, Lord Tweedsmuir, would he forget the agonised look on the faces of the detectives as Their Majesties moved unescorted and unprotected through the crowd.

It marked the beginning of that casual and spontaneous moving about among the people that was to become known by the Australian term 'walkabout' during the reign of Queen Elizabeth II. From this time on the Queen invariably suggested to the King that they cross to chat to the waiting crowds. The Queen, enthused Lord Tweedsmuir 'has a perfect genius for the right kind of publicity.'[29]

Today, the Queen Mother is modest about her role in such changes. 'It's just that life was getting more informal,' she protests. And on discussing the general relaxations that characterised King George VI's reign, the Queen Mother has an interesting comment to make. 'We never consciously set out to change things; we never said "Let's change this or introduce that." Things just evolved.'[30]

Lord Tweedsmuir had a word, too, for the King's less obvious but no less valuable qualities. He found him, he said, 'a wonderful mixture of shrewdness, kindliness and humour'.[31]

It was these unobtrusive qualities which made an equally good impression on President Roosevelt. On 9 June the royal couple crossed into the United States, thereby establishing themselves, once again, as the first British sovereigns to visit the country. Their reception in Washington and New York was tumultuous, with the Queen – looking so radiant beside the gaunt Eleanor Roosevelt – winning all hearts. But it was in his private talks with the President that the King was at his best.

In the course of two long political conversations, the King and the President were able to discuss the international situation and the relationship between their two countries in the event of a war. The King was greatly impressed by Roosevelt. 'Why don't my ministers talk to me as the President did tonight?' he afterwards demanded. 'I feel exactly as though a father were giving me his most careful and wise advice.'[32] The President was hardly less impressed by the King. Previously inclined to dismiss the royal couple as 'two nice young people',[33] he had soon come to appreciate that there was more to them than that.

From this meeting there developed a close friendship between the King and President Roosevelt. Throughout the war, the two men were to write regularly to each other. On the larger scale, the royal visit was of considerable benefit to Anglo-American relations. Just as in Canada all isolationist and neutralist talk had been drowned in the ecstatic reception of the royal couple, so in the United States did they arouse feelings of friendship towards Great Britain.

On the King the effect of this North American tour was as profound as the effect of the Delhi Durbar had been on his father. Time and again, he and the Queen were to say that it had 'made' them. The warmth of his reception by these open, friendly, honest-to-goodness people made the King appreciate that he was liked for himself, not merely as the wearer of the crown. He set out for home on 15 June 1939, feeling more assured, more confident, less overawed by the magnitude of his responsibilities.

He returned, too, with a new conception of his role. In a private letter, Lord

19 The new Sovereign and the new Heir: George VI and Princess Elizabeth

20 'That dazzling pair': the Duke and Duchess of Kent in the late 1930s

21 The devoted father, George VI, with his daughters Princess Elizabeth and Princess Margaret

Tweedsmuir had referred to him as 'a people's King'[34] and this was how King George VI now began to see himself. 'There must be no more high-hat business,' he explained to one of his entourage during the tour, 'the sort of thing that my father and those of his day regarded as essential as the correct attitude – the feeling that certain things could not be done.'[35] The King's first task, after the Abdication, had been to consolidate the monarchy; now he could go ahead and modernise it.

In the end, and by a very different road, King George VI and Queen Elizabeth were to arrive at Edward VIII's professed ideal of a progressive, adaptable and popular monarchy.

A Family in Uniform

'THIS WAR,' wrote Winston Churchill to King George VI early in 1941, 'has drawn the Throne and the people more closely together than was ever before recorded and Your Majesties are more beloved by all classes and conditions than any of the previous princes of the past.'[1]

Always allowing for a little rhetoric on Churchill's part, the sentiments were not far off the mark. For the Second World War did bring Crown and people closer together. Whereas, at the end of the First World War, the widespread collapse of various Continental thrones and the changing social order had made the future of the British throne look uncertain, the Second World War saw a consolidation of the monarch's position. That this should have been so was almost entirely due to the wartime conduct of the King and Queen. For them, no less than for their country, this was their finest hour.

Yet their achievement was not easily won. For one thing, the lack-lustre and still largely unknown King tended to be overshadowed by the colossal figure of Winston Churchill. The King had neither his Prime Minister's commanding presence nor his oratorical gifts. For another, his position as a constitutional monarch precluded him from playing any active part in the waging of the war. He might have been Supreme Commander but, like George V before him, George VI was militarily negligible. Indeed, in the eyes of some, there seemed to be no meaningful role for a King in wartime: the royal family were regarded as 'peacetime luxuries'.[2] And in those days of serious social inequalities, the contrast between the imagined comfort in which the King and Queen were living and the privations suffered by the bombed-out poor, seemed more marked than ever.

That the royal couple were able to overcome these obstacles and win such widespread admiration was no mean accomplishment. One point in their favour was that they, and the entire royal family, remained in the midst of the people. To a suggestion that the two princesses be sent away to the safety of Canada, the Queen had an unequivocal answer: 'The children could not go without me, I could not possibly leave the King, and the King would never go,'[3] he explained briskly. So determined, in fact, were the royal couple to remain among their subjects, come what may, that they both underwent a course of weapons training. 'I shall not go down like the others,'[4] announced the Queen.

Day after day the King and Queen carried out their gruelling round of self-imposed wartime duties: inspecting troops, touring munitions factories, visiting hospitals. It was, though, by their countless appearances in the badly bombed cities throughout the country that King George VI and Queen Elizabeth won such enormous popularity and did such immeasurable good. Picking their way through the splintered glass, smouldering wood and high-piled rubble, they would commiserate with the men and women who had lost everything in the previous night's raid. Their unfeigned concern went straight to the hearts of these suffering people. 'It was certainly very moving to see their faces light up as they recognised him,'[5] wrote a witness of the King's visit to one bomb-shattered city.

'I think they liked my coming to see them,'[6] wrote the King in his diary modestly after a visit to devastated Coventry. It was one of his main jobs, he noted on completing a tour of the still smoking ruins of Southampton, Birmingham and Bristol, to help and encourage others.

Queen Elizabeth was arousing feelings of near-adoration. So boundlessly sympathetic, she brought not only consolation but cheer. Very shrewdly, she refused to wear uniform. Morale would be strengthened and the mystique and glamour of monarchy much better served, she reckoned, by her looking as attractive and normal as possible. Of course she wore her best clothes when visiting the East End, she once exclaimed: 'If the poor people had come to see me *they* would have put on their best clothes.'[7] So it was in her off-the-face hats, suede gloves, pastel colours and high-heeled shoes that the Queen moved amongst the crowds of aproned housewives and raggedly-dressed children.

'Oh, ain't she lovely,' called out the admiring women, 'ain't she just *bloody* lovely!'[8]

Few appreciated the strain imposed by these visits of consolation. There was always a fear that the royal couple might appear condescending; that the fact that they lived in relative safety and comfort would be resented. And they were faced by such harrowing sights. 'I feel quite exhausted after seeing and hearing so much sadness, sorrow, heroism and magnificent spirit,' the Queen once wrote to Queen Mary, 'the destruction is so awful and the people so wonderful . . .'[9]

'We felt absolutely *whacked*,'[10] she admitted privately, when the war was over.

Nor did this sharing of the strains of war end when the King and Queen stepped back across their own threshold. On the contrary, they lived in conditions almost as bleak as those of a great many of their subjects. Eleanor

Roosevelt, spending a few days as their guest at Buckingham Palace, was astonished by the lack of comfort. The bomb-blasted windows had been replaced by isinglass, the freezing rooms were heated by only one small electric fire, the meals – although served on gold and silver plate – were as utilitarian as any in the land. 'If we ever went anywhere to stay,' remembered the Queen in later life, 'we always took our two pats of butter with us.'[11] The King and Queen, declared Mrs Roosevelt, 'are doing an extraordinarily outstanding job for their people in these most trying times.'[12]

The royal couple were able to identify themselves even more closely with the sufferings of their subjects when their own home was bombed. A daring enemy bomber-pilot flew straight up the Mall and, watched by the astonished King, dropped six bombs on Buckingham Palace.

'A magnificent piece of bombing, Ma'am, if you'll pardon my saying so,'[13] remarked one of the Palace policemen to the Queen when the couple came down to inspect the damage.

The Queen's comment was no less to the point. 'I'm glad we've been bombed,' she said. 'It makes me feel I can look the East End in the face.'[14]

Out of the public eye, George VI's wartime contribution was equally impressive. Steeling himself to face the microphone, which he hated, he made several broadcasts. That they were delivered in his slow, hesitant manner made them all the more moving. Always interested in medals and determined that civilian heroism, of which he saw so much, should be recognised and rewarded, the King announced the creation of the George Cross and Medal. It was on his insistence that the decoration was awarded to the beleaguered island of Malta when the morale of its hard-pressed defenders was at its lowest.

In his capacity as Head of State, the King proved extremely useful to the government. He made direct appeals to fellow sovereigns and other heads of state, he could be relied upon to smooth paths by personal intervention, he carried on – both formally and informally – a valuable correspondence with President Roosevelt. His relationship with Winston Churchill was excellent. After some initial reservations – for the King would have preferred Lord Halifax to succeed the discredited Neville Chamberlain – monarch and prime minister established a close rapport. 'I could not have had a better Prime Minister,'[15] wrote the King in his diary.

And Churchill, in the dark days of 1942, when everything seemed to be going wrong, paid handsome tribute to the contribution of King George VI and Queen Elizabeth. 'The whole British Empire, and most of all, the United Kingdom of Great Britain and Northern Ireland,' he said on receiving the Freedom of the City of Edinburgh in October 1942, 'owes an inestimable debt to our King and Queen. In these years of trial and storm they have shared to the full the perils, the labours, the sorrows, and the hopes of the British nation.'[16]

*

No less than the King and Queen was Queen Mary determined to share the dangers and privations of war. She would not hear of going to Canada to join her brother, Lord Athlone, who was about to become Governor-General. She was not even prepared to leave Marlborough House. For a member of the royal family to desert the capital in wartime would not be 'at all the thing',[17] she announced. Only on being told by the King that her presence in London would cause unnecessary trouble did she agree to go to the West Country for the duration of the war. On 4 September 1939, the seventy-two-year-old Queen Mary set out, with seventy pieces of personal luggage and a staff of sixty-three, for Badminton, the home of her niece, the Duchess of Beaufort. She remained there for almost six years.

For this essentially urban Queen, life in the country was an entirely new experience. She applied herself to it with all her customary zest. But her adaptation to rural living was not without its comic moments. 'So *that's* what rye looks like,'[18] she exclaimed on having her attention drawn to a particularly good crop. And once, in her zeal to collect scrap for the war effort, she arrived home in triumph, dragging a gratifyingly large iron contraption for her dump. It turned out to be a neighbour's plough.

The rural pursuit for which Queen Mary became most celebrated, however, was her well-intentioned clearing up of the Badminton estate; particularly the stripping of ivy from trees, walls and buildings. The Queen's relentless battle against ivy allowed full scope for her chief characteristics: her determination to keep busy, her passion for tidiness and her iron sense of achievement. With a toque anchored firmly on her rigidly-dressed hair and surrounded by her 'wooding squad' – an assortment of far less dedicated equerries, ladies-in-waiting, secretaries, soldiers and guests – the indefatigable Queen Mary threw herself heart and soul into her self-appointed task.

Occasionally, Queen Mary would motor up to Windsor to see the King and Queen. She found the Castle, with its dark passages, shrouded furniture and bare walls, most depressing. Of great interest, though, was the presence of her two grand-daughters, Princess Elizabeth and Princess Margaret, who were spending the war at Windsor. 'Lilibet much grown, very pretty eyes and complexion, pretty figure,' Queen Mary reported to Lord Athlone on one occasion. 'Margaret very short, intelligent face but not really pretty.'[19]

Like all mothers, and in spite of the fact that the King saw to it that she was sent confidential news summaries from the Foreign Office, Queen Mary complained that her son neglected her. She was kept 'quite in the dark', she protested, about national affairs. This was particularly annoying when she remembered how King George V had always kept *his* mother, Queen Alexandra, 'informed about everything.'[20]

She could not complain about neglect on the part of her other children. Her daughter, the Princess Royal, spent long periods at Badminton and whenever possible, her other sons, the Dukes of Gloucester and Kent, visited her. By way of a reprimand, perhaps, for the Duke of Gloucester's increasing fondness for a glass of whisky, she once wrote to the Duchess to suggest that the Duke bring his own whisky this time, 'as we have *not* got much left and it is so expensive.'[21]

Queen Mary's Badminton activities did not end with ivy-stripping. Besides her manifold private occupations – reading, letter-writing, cataloguing photographs, sorting through papers, filing information, embroidery – she carried out various public duties. She organised the collection of salvage, she toured bomb sites, she visited factories and hospitals, she served in canteens, she helped at fêtes. She never failed to give lifts, in her old green Daimler, to any serviceman whom she happened to pass on the road.

The Queen was particularly fond of giving lifts to American servicemen. She was very amused by their frankness, their lack of reverence and their colourful language. They were never dumb-struck, as British soldiers tended to be, by her presence. Through these encounters with young men from widely varying backgrounds, Queen Mary derived enormous benefit. For the first time since girlhood, almost, she was brought into contact with everyday people. The members of her household claimed that these contacts made her 'more democratic than ever before'.[22]

As though to prove it, Queen Mary once described an experience during a visit to Bath. 'Some Australian soldiers and airmen happened to be there,' she wrote to Lord Athlone, 'and asked me to be photographed "with the boys". I said yes and they crowded round me and I suddenly felt an arm pushed through mine and an arm placed round my waist in order to make more room, I suppose. It really was very comical and *unexpected* at my age.'[23]

Such good-natured informality Queen Mary could take in her stride: what she, with her ingrained sense of royal vocation, did mind was not being recognised or acknowledged. The present-day, and invariably unfulfilled, yearning for a measure of royal anonymity was not at all her style. On one occasion, when she was driving back from Bath, she passed a school out of which was pouring a crowd of uniformed girls. The Queen, as usual, was sitting erect in the small seat behind the chauffeur so as to be more visible. As the unmistakably regal figure in the hearse-like car drove slowly by, the schoolgirls merely stared in a 'desultory, adenoidal kind of way'. Even when she waved and smiled, they did not respond.

'*Cheer*, little idiots, can't you?'[24] exclaimed the Queen testily.

'We had two wars to deal with,' complains the Duchess of Windsor in her autobiography, 'the big war . . . in which everybody was caught up, and the little war with the Palace, in which no quarter was given.'[25]

And it was with the waging of this 'little' war that the Windsors' emotions seem to have been most intensely caught up. At one stage, the Duke of Windsor had blithely assumed that it would simply be a matter of time before he returned home to take up his royal duties. 'I would give Bertie a hand,' he once declared, 'just as he had given me a hand when I was King.'²⁶ Not even George VI's denial of a royal title for the Duchess of Windsor had opened the Duke's eyes to the true position. Sooner or later the family feud would be patched up and he and the Duchess would return to take their rightful place in the family circle. These, apparently, were the Duchess's views as well. 'I don't want to spend all my life in exile,'²⁷ she answered briskly when a friend asked her why they had not yet bought a house in France. Only gradually, and painfully, did the truth dawn on them.

With the outbreak of war in 1939 the Windsors returned briefly to England. They were neither met nor accommodated by any member of the royal family. The Duke had one short meeting with the King and that was all. King George VI professed himself astonished at his brother's cavalier attitude towards the Abdication: 'he was not a bit worried as to the effects he left on people's minds as to his behaviour in 1936. He has forgotten all about it.'²⁸

But the King had not. The Duke, anxious for some wartime duty, had expressed a preference for a post in Britain; this the King ignored and the Duke was sent back to France as liaison officer with the British Military Mission to General Gamelin. He remained there until the fall of France in 1940. During the course of his escape, through Spain to Portugal, the Duke became enmeshed in a secret Nazi plot to set him up as King, with the Duchess as Queen, after a successful German invasion of Britain. How deeply involved the Duke was in these machinations remains an open question, but his main preoccupation still seems to have been with his wife's status. He would take advantage of the two flying boats which had been sent to take him back to England only, he declared, if the Duchess were granted equality with the wives of his two youngest brothers.

Fortunately, his appointment as Governor of the Bahamas afforded the royal family a way out of the impasse. The Windsors sailed directly to the Bahamas and remained there throughout the war. 'It was now clear beyond all question,' claimed the Duchess at a later stage, 'that David's family were determined to keep him relegated to the farthermost marches of the Empire.'²⁹

But her battle for the royal family's acceptance raged on. Even the victories looked suspiciously like defeats. Once, from the Bahamas, and without the Duke's knowledge, the Duchess wrote to Queen Mary. The Bishop of Nassau was returning to England and as the Duchess felt sure that he would be received by Queen Mary, she gave him a letter to present to her mother-in-law. The letter could hardly have been more self-effacing or respectful. The Duchess mentioned her regret at being the cause of the coolness between mother and son; she assured the Queen that the Bishop would be able to give her news of the Duke; she said something about the importance of family ties in wartime.

In due course, the Bishop of Nassau presented the letter. Queen Mary asked several questions about her son but none about his wife. Nor did she reply to the letter. But several weeks later, in a letter to the Duke of Windsor, the Queen, for the first time, acknowledged the Duchess's existence. 'I send a kind message to your wife,' she wrote.

'Now what do you suppose,' asked the astonished Duke, 'has come over Mama?'[30]

Not a great deal, was the answer to that particular question. Queen Mary's message indicated no breach in the family's defences.

What was the reason for the royal family's unyielding attitude? As the years went by, so did one of the strongest original reasons for their refusal of a royal title for the Duchess – the assumption that the marriage would not last – fall away. But the Duke's refusal to return permanently to Britain unless his wife were awarded royal status could not have been entirely unwelcome to his family. Although George VI is said to have felt uneasy about his brother's continuing exile, the two most influential women in his life – his mother and his wife – did not. To Queen Mary, so conscious of the sanctity and mystery of the monarchy, the idea of this twice-divorced woman being received into the family remained as repugnant as ever. While to Queen Elizabeth, the possibility of the popular Duke outshining his less showy brother remained a serious threat.

Queen Elizabeth would have been less than human had she not shown a certain resentment of the fact that, because of King Edward's infatuation with Mrs Simpson, her husband was now being subjected to such intolerable strains. When someone once claimed that the Duchess was very good for the Duke and that the pouches under his eyes had quite disappeared, the Queen's answer was uncharacteristically sharp.

'Yes,' she said, 'who has the lines under his eyes now?'[31]

That it should have been Queen Elizabeth who had set her face so resolutely against the Windsors' acceptance came as no surprise to the Duchess. 'The reign of George VI,' she said bitterly, 'is a split level matriarchy in pants. Queen Mary runs the King's wife, and the wife runs the King.'[32]

But there were more serious reasons for the royal family's attitude. There was a feeling, at the Palace, that the Duke of Windsor could not be relied upon to behave with the necessary royal circumspection. On several occasions since the Abdication – by a highly publicised visit to Nazi Germany in 1937, by a broadcast appeal for peace in the United States in 1939, by a direct approach to Hitler to prevent war, and by a series of other, minor, indiscretions – he had broken the royal code by which no king, not even an ex-king, should involve himself in controversial political issues. The Duke was considered to be too outspoken, too impulsive, too meddlesome; he could not be trusted to observe the monarchal conventions.

And so, in spite of a torrent of sometimes plaintive, sometimes aggressive letters to the King, the Duke of Windsor was kept at arm's length. Not for many years, and then only up to a point, did the royal family become reconciled to the Duke and Duchess of Windsor.

By the outbreak of war, the Duke and Duchess of Kent had established themselves as the royal family's most decorative couple. With his good looks, impressive bearing and social aplomb, the thirty-six-year-old Duke fulfilled the largely ceremonial demands of his position to perfection; while the thirty-one-year-old Duchess was not only one of the most charming but far and away the best-dressed woman in the family. 'The Duchess has made fashion history,' claimed the *Sunday Express*. 'She has given London the leadership which belonged to Paris . . .'[33]

Yet the Duchess of Kent was not quite what she seemed. Contrary to the general impression, she was a shy, essentially domestic woman, devoted to her two children (Prince Edward, born on 9 October 1935 and Princess Alexandra, born on Christmas Day 1936) and to her many Continental relations. Like the equally *soignée* Queen Alexandra before her, the Duchess of Kent was, at this stage of her life, a loyal, gentle, unpunctual, somewhat indolent person, happiest in the company of those whom she knew well. She tended to leave everything, even the running of their two homes – 3 Belgrave Square and a mansion called Coppins in Buckinghamshire – to her husband.

When the visiting Lady Airlie once complimented her on 'the beautifully arranged rooms and the perfectly chosen meal', the Duchess laughed. 'I am really a very bad hostess,' she admitted. 'My husband chose the dinner and the wine – and the flowers and everything else. He enjoys doing it, and so I always leave the household affairs to him. I let him make all the decisions over furniture and decorations. He has a wonderful sense of colour and design.'[34]

An opportunity for the couple to exercise their talents on a wider stage – by the Duke of Kent's appointment as Governor-General of Australia in 1939 – was prevented by the outbreak of war. Much to the Duke's disappointment, the appointment was postponed. Although he was not expected to be involved in any fighting, it was essential that a Prince of the Blood be seen making some sort of contribution in the coming struggle.

In fact, the Duke of Kent was only too ready to be actively engaged in the war. He found the Admiralty desk job, to which he was posted on rejoining the navy, boring in the extreme; before long, he transferred to the Royal Air Force. He later became Chief Welfare Officer of the RAF with the rank of Air Commodore. But he found his new duties hardly more stimulating than the old. In many ways, they were simply a wartime version of what his brother, as Prince of Wales, used to call 'princing': inspecting factories, touring civil defence installations, looking at bomb sites and visiting RAF bases. 'It's not very exciting to spend one's time looking at ablutions,'[35] he once sighed. He resented the royal restrictions which kept him from being more usefully and interestingly employed.

The Duchess of Kent was suffering from no such frustrations. As Commandant of the Women's Royal Naval Service, the Wrens, she was enjoying great success. Although, like Queen Elizabeth, she disliked wearing uniform, it was for the elegance with which she wore hers as much as for the grace and efficiency with which she carried out her duties that she won such popularity. Her association with the Wrens changed its image overnight. Such was the attraction, both of her personally and of the monarchy generally, that it needed only one broadcast appeal (coupled with press photographs of her in uniform and stylish hat) for volunteers, for the Admiralty to be flooded with applications. Over three thousand came in on the first day. 'Whatever you do,' begged one despairing Admiralty official, 'don't on any account let the Duchess broadcast again.'[36]

The couple's third child, a son, was born on 4 July 1942. He was christened Michael George Charles Franklin: Franklin after one of his godfathers, the President of the United States. In later years, sporting a full beard, Prince Michael of Kent came to look astonishingly like his grandfather, King George V.

In spite of his manifold, if unfulfilling, wartime duties, the Duke of Kent still found time to pursue one of his chief interests: the collecting of paintings, furniture, porcelain and silver. His home, says 'Chips' Channon, was 'full of rich treasures, and gold boxes, étuis and pretty expensive objects always being exchanged and moved about.'[37] Whenever possible, the Duke would visit Queen Mary at Badminton. Together, mother and son would explore the antique shops of Bath. With each passing year, the old Queen found the company of her artistic and animated youngest son more and more congenial. She could talk to him, she admitted to her brother Lord Athlone, 'openly and with ease'. Her two other sons, the King and the Duke of Gloucester, she complained, 'are *boutonnés.*'[38]

'He often used to say I looked nice,' sighed Queen Mary after the Duke of Kent's death. 'Nobody else ever did.'[39]

In the summer of 1942, the Duke of Kent was due to carry out a tour of inspection of RAF bases in Iceland. He set off, from the RAF station at Invergordon in Scotland, in a Sunderland flying boat just after 1 p.m. on Tuesday 25 August. Half an hour later the seaplane crashed into a remote and mist-shrouded mountain side. Help, in this rough, desolate and misty terrain was a long time coming. When it did, it was too late. Of the fifteen men aboard, only one – a gunner in the rear turret – had survived. The aircraft was unrecognisable. The Duke of Kent must have been killed instantly.

The news was telephoned to the King at Balmoral that evening. His first thought, on being called away from the dinner table, was that the call might concern Queen Mary. 'The news came as a great shock to me,' wrote the King in his diary that evening, 'and I had to break it to Elizabeth, and Harry and Alice [the Duke and Duchess of Gloucester] who were staying with us.' After the Duke of Kent's funeral service, in St George's Chapel on 29 August, the King admitted to being more moved than he had been at any previous family funeral. 'Everybody was there,' he confided to a friend, 'but I did not dare look at any of them for fear of breaking down.'[40] Kings do not weep in public.

The Duchess of Kent was desolate. She had been devoted to her debonair husband. 'Her whole life,' said one of her relations afterwards, 'revolved around him and she had no one else.'[41] For days after his death, she refused to leave her room, alternating between bouts of uncontrollable weeping and complete apathy. She seemed to have lost interest in everything, even her children.

It needed Queen Mary – herself heartbroken at the death of this dearly loved son – to reawaken the Duchess's interest in life. Exercising that phenomenal self-control which had seen her through so many crises, Queen Mary suppressed her own grief and drove from Badminton to Coppins to comfort and hearten her daughter-in-law. No one knows exactly what she said to the Duchess but the old Queen later revealed that she had spoken of the indulgence of 'self-pity' and the imperatives of 'duty'.[42] Queen Mary would have made it clear that the Duchess of Kent was more than just a woman who had lost her husband on active service. As the widow of a prince of the reigning House and as the mother of princes, she had special obligations: she had an all-transcending duty to the royal family, and to that most sacrosanct of institutions, the British monarchy.

Within a few weeks the Duchess of Kent was back, in naval uniform, inspecting a Wren training centre in London.

The death of the Duke of Kent had an immediate effect on the life of the Duke of Gloucester. The forty-two-year-old Duke was now the only adult prince left in a position to give full support to the monarch. Already Regent Designate (and so he would remain until Princess Elizabeth turned eighteen on 21 April 1944) the Duke of Gloucester was from now on obliged to devote still more time to royal duties. His soldiering days were effectively over. Writing to the Secretary of State for War, the Duke explained that the King had decided that he could 'no longer have a permanent position at the War Office.'[43]

Not that his military career had been in any way spectacular. His greatest ambition – to command his regiment, the 10th Royal Hussars – had never been realised. On the accession of George VI, and on his own nomination as Regent Designate, the Duke had been obliged to give up his career and to accept a purely ceremonial promotion to Major-General. But the outbreak of war had called for a more active military commitment: it had also raised the perennial problem of what to do with a soldier-prince in wartime. In recent times King George VI had been the only son of a sovereign to take part in battle. Not for another two generations, until Prince Andrew went to fight in the Falklands, was a monarch's son treated like any other soldier.

So, in order to keep him out of harm's way, the Duke of Gloucester was appointed Chief Liaison Officer with the British Field Force in France. By no means, though, did this posting keep him out of harm's way. The Duke's ill-defined duties, coupled with his determination to involve himself more actively in whatever was going on, ensured that he was constantly being caught up in dangerous situations ('I've got royal blood on me,'[44] exclaimed one soldier proudly after dressing the Duke's wounds) and in the end he was ordered home. As he explained to Queen Mary, his presence had been an embarrassment to GHQ, 'because wherever I went, or had been, I was bombed.'[45]

The frustrations of his life in France were as nothing compared with the frustrations of his life back in England. First as Chief Liaison Officer GHQ Home Forces and then as a colonel in the 20th Armoured Brigade ('If I made him a Major General,' the King very sensibly assured the brigadier commanding the 20th Armoured Brigade, 'I can now make him a Colonel.'[46]) the Duke of Gloucester's days seemed to be restricted, almost entirely, to tours of inspection. And when he was not inspecting at home, he was inspecting abroad. He went to Northern Ireland, he went to Gibraltar and, in April 1942, he set off on a four-month-long military and diplomatic tour which took him to the Middle East and India.

The purpose of this mission was twofold: Britain, in the person of the monarch's brother, would be underscoring its friendship with the not always reliable countries of the Near and Middle East; and the troops – both British and Commonwealth – would be reminded that their efforts were not going unappreciated. It was yet another way in which the monarchy, standing high above party or government, could fulfil its functions.

Typically, the Duke of Gloucester did not see the tour in such grandiose terms. 'Anyway,' he wrote to the King as he flew on towards India, 'it might do more good than harm.'[47]

It was while the Duke was away that he became the object of a certain amount of ridicule at home. At a time when a succession of military defeats was making Churchill's position increasingly shaky, a Conservative member of parliament, Sir John Wardlaw-Milne, moved a Vote of Censure. In the course of it he suggested that, in order to separate the military and political spheres, the Duke of Gloucester be made Commander-in-Chief of the British forces. He was implying, naïvely perhaps, that with a member of the royal family as nominal head of the armed forces, there would be less opportunity for Churchill's intervention in military matters. 'The House,' wrote 'Chips' Channon, 'roared with disrespectful laughter, and I at once saw Winston's face light up, as if a lamp had been lit within him and he smiled genially. He knew now that he was saved . . .'[48]

Wardlaw-Milne's suggestion gave the *New Statesman* a splendid opportunity to pass judgement on the Duke of Gloucester. Calling the proposal 'fantastic' and 'preposterous' and claiming that the House of Commons had been dumbfounded, it asked how anyone could seriously imagine that at 'this grave crisis in our history the appointment as Commander-in-Chief of a Royal Duke is a suitable remedy for the disease that affects our society?'[49]

Domestically, the Duke of Gloucester's career was proving less chequered. If he had seemed, at the beginning, to have married for marrying's sake, he had by now developed a close and loving relationship with his wife. His letters to Alice, Duchess of Gloucester were warm and intimate; both in taste and in temperament the couple were very well matched. By now they were established in two homes: York House in St James's Palace, in which so many of King Edward VII's descendants had lived, and Barnwell Manor in Northamptonshire.

Although the Duchess did her full share of wartime duties, much of her time was taken up with the birth of her two children. After a series of miscarriages, the Duchess finally gave birth, by Caesarian section on 18 December 1941, to a son. 'Oh, the joy I felt when I heard you and Alice had got a boy,' wrote Queen Mary from Badminton, 'and that your great wish had been fulfilled after all these years.'[50] The baby was christened by the Archbishop of Canterbury at Windsor and given the name William. The life of Prince William of Gloucester was tragically short.

A second son was born on 26 August 1944. Again Queen Mary was overjoyed. She hoped that they would give the Prince the name of Richard; it sounded so well with Gloucester. The Duke was not so sure. As he could never pronounce his 'Rs', Richard presented difficulties. But in the end the baby was named Richard, and the Duke had to be content with 'William and Wichard'.[51]

What the Duke of Gloucester's biographer calls 'a twilight phase of his life and career'[52] – a phase in which he seemed to be fulfilling no useful function – ended when Princess Elizabeth turned eighteen on 21 April 1944. Although the Princess would not come of age officially until she turned twenty-one, the Regency Act of 1937 had recently been amended so as to allow her to serve as a Counsellor of State if necessary. This ended the Duke of Gloucester's term as Regent Designate. No longer obliged to remain close at hand, and with the tide of war having turned, the Duke could now render the Crown a different sort of service. It was decided that he should take up the post at one time intended for the late Duke of Kent: the Governor-Generalship of Australia.

Daunted, perhaps, by the prospect of this high office – for both the Duke and Duchess were shy, domestic, country-loving people – they nonetheless accepted it without question. For if the couple lacked the strong public images of some other members of the family (Queen Mary was always complaining that their manifold public duties were not nearly well enough publicised) their sense of duty was no less strong. They would be able, thought the Duke, 'to help Bertie'[53] more effectively in Australia than at home. 'I have felt that I have been doing very little,' admitted the Duke to Queen Mary. 'Now I feel I have something definite to do makes all the difference.'[54]

The old Queen was in full agreement. 'I hope they will be a success,' she wrote to Lord Athlone after the Gloucesters and their two little sons had sailed away on 16 December 1944, 'it may give Harry a chance of showing what he is made of.'[55]

'A victory at last,' wrote George VI in his diary on 4 November 1942 on hearing of the 8th Army's defeat of Rommel's forces in North Africa, 'how good it is for the nerves.'[56]

With this gradual turning of the tide of war – the German retreat in North Africa, the Russian advance in Europe, the American victories in the Far East – the King was able to think of associating himself more actively with the armed forces. By his close identification with the sufferings of his subjects at home, he had established himself as a new sort of warrior-king. Now he felt that he should use the great prestige of his office to encourage the fighting men. 'He feels so much at not being more in the firing line,'[57] admitted the Queen to Queen Mary. The less dangerous, more hopeful military situation would allow him, without overstepping the bounds of his constitutional position, to be a warrior-king in the more generally accepted sense.

So the King paid a series of official visits to the various battle fronts. Between June 1943 and October 1944 he visited North Africa, Malta, France, Italy and the Low Countries. Everywhere he went he was enthusiastically welcomed. It did not matter to the thousands upon thousands of troops who cheered him so heartily that King George VI was not a particularly impressive-looking man, that he did not have a striking public presence; he was being cheered for what he represented. The King understood enough about the mystique of monarchy to appreciate the elevating effect of his presence on the troops. It had another, no less valuable effect as well. As a young soldier, writing home to his mother from North Africa, claimed, the sight of the King made him feel that he was 'not quite so far from home'.[58]

These tours of inspection had an equally elevating effect on the King

himself. The warmth of his welcome touched and heartened him considerably. His arrival in the bomb-scarred island of Malta moved him almost to
tears. The cheers, as he stood on the bridge of the cruiser *Aurora* as it entered
the Grand Harbour of Valletta, were overwhelming. When the Lieutenant-
Governor of the island assured the King that he had made the people of Malta
very happy that day, the King replied that, on the contrary, *he* was the
happiest man on Malta.

A source of continuing gratification to the King was the cordiality of his
relationship with Winston Churchill. Not since Queen Victoria's intimate
relationships with Lord Melbourne and Benjamin Disraeli, had monarch and
prime minister enjoyed a closer rapport. King George VI and Winston
Churchill had complete confidence in each other. 'I valued as a signal
honour,' wrote Churchill grandiloquently, 'the gracious intimacy with
which I, as first Minister, was treated,'[59] while the King proudly admitted to
Queen Mary that Churchill told him 'more than most people imagine'[60]
about his future plans and ideas. On one occasion, an exchange of complimentary telegrams between King and Prime Minister moved *The Times* to
pay tribute to the skill and scrupulousness with which the monarch carried
out his constitutional duties.

'Mr Churchill's telegram . . .' read the leading article on 18 May 1943,
'revealing the help that one of the strongest Prime Ministers has received
from his Sovereign, is a powerful reminder that King George VI is doing a
work as indispensible for English governance as any of his predecessors, just
as he has set his peoples from the first day of the war an unfailing public
example of courage, confidence and devoted energy; and it conveys a hint of
how much His Majesty's advisers continue to owe to His Majesty's advice.'[61]

Only once was there a clash of wills between the two men. Both favoured
the idea of playing a part in the D-Day landings, of actually accompanying
the invading troops. It did not take long for the King's private secretary, Sir
Alan Lascelles (he had replaced Sir Alexander Hardinge, who had previously
served George V and Edward VIII) to talk his sovereign out of this hazardous
scheme. Who, asked Lascelles drily, should Princess Elizabeth choose as her
prime minister in the event of both the King and Churchill being killed? But
Churchill was not so easily dissuaded. Only after the King had written him a
couple of forcefully-argued letters and had even tackled him face-to-face on
the subject, did Churchill back down. 'He has decided not to go on the
expedition only because I asked him not to,'[62] noted the relieved King.

So it was only fitting that when peace in Europe was formally announced
on 8 May 1945, Winston Churchill was invited to appear on the balcony of
Buckingham Palace with the King and Queen and their daughters. Although
the celebrations lacked the abandon of those of November 1918 – the news
had been known for several days and the war in the Far East had another three
months to run – the scenes outside the Palace were no less jubilant. Time and

22 Princess Elizabeth's eighteenth birthday, 21 April 1944. Standing, from the left: the Duke and Duchess of Gloucester, Princess Margaret, the Princess Royal, the widowed Duchess of Kent, the Earl of Harewood. Seated: Queen Mary, George VI, Princess Elizabeth, Queen Elizabeth

23 South Africa, February 1947. Princess Margaret, George VI, Queen Elizabeth and the secretly engaged Princess Elizabeth

24 The country-loving Duke and Duche of Gloucester with their sons, Prince William and Prince Richard at Barnv Manor, 1950

25 George VI's last Christmas. Standing from the left: the young Duke of Ken Princess Margaret, Princess Alexandr Kent, the Duchess of Kent, the Duke Gloucester, Princess Elizabeth, the D of Edinburgh, the Duchess of Glouce Seated: Queen Mary, George VI hol Princess Anne, Queen Elizabeth hold Prince Charles. Front row: Prince Richard of Gloucester, Prince Micha Kent, Prince William of Gloucester

again, with and without Churchill, the royal family were called back onto the balcony.

'We have been overwhelmed by the kind things people have said over our part in the War,' wrote the King a few days later. 'We have only tried to do our duty.'[63]

10

A People's King

KING GEORGE VI, at the end of the Second World War, faced a very different world from that faced by his father, King George V, in 1918. Then, the British Empire was still regarded as the greatest power on earth; now it was overshadowed by the two new super-powers, Russia and the United States. And during the years that were left to him, George VI was to see a further diminution of his country's might and status: for the King was to preside over the first moves whereby Great Britain divested itself of its colonial power.

Domestically, too, the political situation was very different. For all the social unrest and democratic fervour that had characterised Europe in 1918, King George V had drawn comfort from the fact that his post-war coalition government was predominantly Conservative. Indeed, for most of his reign, George V had worked with governments that were conservative in tone. But Churchill's wartime coalition government did not long outlast the war in Europe. Peace brought with it a widespread desire for greater social justice, and the general election of 1945 returned a Labour government with a substantial majority. So George VI was to find himself presiding over, not only the beginnings of the dissolution of the old Empire abroad, but the establishment of the welfare state at home.

The King did not face the prospect of social revolution with much equanimity. For all his humanity, fair-mindedness and genuine concern for the underprivileged, the King's views were those of the old ruling classes; like his predecessors – Edward VII, George V and Edward VIII – George VI was essentially conservative in outlook. It would have been astonishing had he not been so. As a constitutional monarch the King might have been above party, but to be above class, when British society was so structured that he formed the very summit of the class system, was not quite so easy. So the King could hardly welcome the coming of a social order which planned to eliminate that very system.

But not for a moment did the King allow his misgivings to affect his dealings with his new Prime Minister, Clement Attlee, or the other Labour ministers. The King had been greatly encouraged by the reminder, from that staunch Imperialist, South Africa's General J.C. Smuts, that the Crown was always a stabilising factor in British politics, and by the assurance, from his cousin Lord Louis Mountbatten, that the King would find his position greatly strengthened, 'since you are now the experienced campaigner on whom a new and partly inexperienced government will lean for advice and guidance.'[1]

'Ministers come and go,' *The Times* reminded its readers, 'but the King remains, always at the centre of public affairs, always participating vigilantly in the work of government from a standpoint detached from any consideration but the welfare of his peoples as a whole. He is the continuous element in the constitution, one of the main safe-guards of its democratic character, and the repository of a knowledge of affairs that before long comes to transcend that of any individual statesman.'[2]

At first it was not easy. 'The people,' complained the King to the Duke of Gloucester of his new ministers, 'are rather difficult to talk to.'[3] Most difficult of all was Attlee. Lacking the courtliness of Churchill, he felt shy and awkward in the presence of the monarch; as shy and awkward as the monarch felt in his. Their meetings were marked by long silences. And although, in time, the King came to understand and appreciate his Labour ministers rather better, he always felt that they were implementing what he regarded as their radical policies too fast. Always a worrier, he now worried more than ever.

'I do wish one could see a glimmer of a bright spot anywhere in world affairs,' he once wrote to Queen Mary. 'Never in the whole history of mankind have things looked gloomier than they do now, and one feels so powerless to do anything to help.'[4]

There were times when, like his grandfather and father before him, George VI despaired of the future of the monarchy. 'Everything is going nowadays,' he once sighed on hearing that a famous ancestral home had gone to the National Trust. 'Before long, I shall also have to go.'[5]

But the King, in his self-deprecating way, was underestimating the firm hold which the institution of monarchy had on the hearts of the British people. He did not appreciate how much his own conduct during the war had enhanced the popularity of the Crown; nor did he appreciate that, far from weakening the position of the monarch, the post-war social revolution was ultimately to strengthen it. The gradual levelling of society helped dissociate the Crown, in the minds of the general public, from the old ruling class. The process begun by George V, of gradually converting the monarchy into a supra-national institution rather than the apex of a pyramidal class system, was accelerated during George VI's reign.

Most of the monarchies of Europe, as the King's future son-in-law, Prince Philip, once explained to an American television audience, 'were really destroyed by their greatest and most ardent supporters. It was the most reactionary people who tried to hold on to something without letting it develop and change.'[6]

And in the 1970s Richard Crossman, the Labour cabinet minister, claimed that 'roughly speaking, it is the professional classes who in this sense are radical and the working-class Socialists who are by and large staunchly monarchist.'[7] Today, the monarchies of Europe (Spain always excepted) tend to be countries with strongly democratic, socialist traditions.

Nor, paradoxically, was the loss of Britain's power and prestige to lead to a corresponding loss of prestige for the Crown. On the contrary, it was to be enhanced. George VI would probably have been astonished at the reverence, loyalty and affection in which, thirty years later, his daughter Queen Elizabeth II was to be held.

'Poor darlings,' wrote King George VI of his two daughters at the end of the war, 'they have never had any fun yet.'[8]

And not only had Princess Elizabeth and Princess Margaret had no fun, they had been obliged to lead an even more secluded life than was customary for royal children. Once adolescent, the sons of King George V had mixed freely with others; just as, in time, Queen Elizabeth II's children mixed even more freely. But five-and-a-half years of war had ensured that the two princesses spent most of the time at Windsor Castle in the company of their governess, Marion Crawford, and of their nursemaid and dresser, Margaret MacDonald. They did not even see much of their parents, for although the King and Queen spent weekends at Windsor, they were usually up in London or away on official duties. Too young to play any part in the war, the princesses had simply continued with their education. Not until the spring of 1945, when Princess Elizabeth was almost nineteen, were her horizons widened when she joined the Auxiliary Territorial Service. She completed her ATS course in vehicle maintenance just before war ended.

Princess Elizabeth emerged from these years of seclusion – the most impressionable years of her life – as a shy, serious, conscientious young woman, somewhat stiff in her manner and conventional in her attitudes. Princess Margaret, already more extrovert, was still young enough, at fourteen, to throw off the effects of this unnaturally restricted period. Although both were small and attractive, with dark brown hair and superb complexions, Princess Margaret had the livelier, more piquant face. Princess Elizabeth often looked grave. In journalistic shorthand, Princess Elizabeth's looks were described as 'Hanoverian', Princess Margaret's as 'Stuart'. The war years had bound both sisters, even more securely, to their parents. The four of them remained a self-contained, utterly devoted little group.

In their determination that their daughters should now enjoy some of that long-denied fun, the King and Queen created as informal an atmosphere as was possible within the confines of a court. The eighty-year-old Lady Airlie, having experienced court life during the reigns of Edward VII and George V, found herself, after some initial reservations, delighted by the friendliness and homeliness surrounding the royal family. They were more like an 'ordinary family';[9] all the old stuffiness was gone. 'You must ask Mummy,'[10] the King would say – as any father would have said – when his daughters came to him with requests. And Princess Margaret would pout – as any other daughter might have pouted – when her mother sent her back to put on a thicker coat.

At Balmoral, while the Queen, in thigh-length waders, went fishing for salmon, the King initiated Princess Elizabeth into the skills and pleasures of deerstalking. The King, like his father, was an excellent shot. The family enjoyed elaborate picnics in an old abandoned schoolhouse, trooping down afterwards to the burn to wash up the cups and plates. At Sandringham, surrounded by batches of Guards officers with whom they kept up a bantering relationship, the two princesses played records, listened to the radio and danced. Even the eighty-year-old Queen Mary, by now re-established at Marlborough House, joined in the dancing; and she would keep dancing until everyone went to bed at one in the morning.

While Lady Airlie pronounced Princess Elizabeth to be 'one of the most unselfish girls I have ever met', Queen Mary described the arch and mischievous Princess Margaret as *espiègle*. 'All the same,' the old Queen said, 'she is so outrageously amusing that one can't help encouraging her.'[11]

Fascinated by his younger daughter, the King tended to spoil her; but it was Princess Elizabeth who was his soul-mate. She was his constant companion in his outdoor pursuits. His affection for his elder daughter was very deep. Those about him realised that he was secretly dreading the day when marriage would take her from him. His fears were not without foundation. For it was during these post-war years that Princess Elizabeth fell in love with her future husband, Prince Philip of Greece. The two of them had met on several occasions in the past, for they were related, but by 1946 it was clear that the shy Princess Elizabeth was set on marrying the handsome Prince Philip. For a variety of reasons, not least because he could not bear the thought of parting from her, the King discouraged any talk of an early engagement. It was not that he was exceptionally possessive; it was simply that, having suffered so bleak a youth himself, the King was anxious to prolong this period of idyllic family happiness. With a wife whom he adored and two daughters to whom he was devoted, King George VI can be forgiven for wanting to keep this unit intact for as long as possible.

An opportunity for doing so came early in 1947. The King had been invited to pay a state visit to South Africa. He was determined that this should be a family venture and that all four of them should travel together. The idea was welcomed by the South African Prime Minister, General Smuts, and, at the end of January 1947, the royal family set sail for their three-month-long journey. It was to be the first time, not only that a reigning sovereign had visited South Africa but that the royal family had toured in full strength.

It was also an example of the way in which royal tours can be used to further political ends. For the South African visit was not merely a much-needed holiday in the sun, nor even a way of thanking South Africa for its contribution towards winning the war. Smuts, with his great faith in the power of the monarchy to influence public opinion, hoped that the tour would counteract the growing threat of Afrikaner republicanism. Surely in the face of this charming family – the unassuming King, the friendly Queen, the unspoilt princesses – some of the opposition to the concept of monarchy would melt. Who could possibly resent such kindly, well-meaning people? What republican could resist the Queen's radiant smile?

So the royal family was launched on a full-scale tour of the country. At times, the pace was little short of gruelling. For day after day, for weeks on end, during the hottest months of the year, the royal family was obliged to fulfil an exhausting round of public engagements. The Queen admitted that the tour was 'very tiring';[12] the King lost over a stone in weight. It was a wonder that they could do it all so gracefully and so uncomplainingly.

Although, as always, the Queen made the greatest impression, it was as a family group that they won so many hearts. Whenever the White Train, in which they travelled, stopped at some remote, sun-baked railway siding, the family would alight and talk to the little knot of people gathered there. 'These informal meetings were the most valuable of the tour,' the Queen said afterwards. 'One felt that one was really getting to meet ordinary people.'[13]

Successful in so many ways, the tour's political success was difficult to estimate. Deeply conscious of Afrikaner Nationalist coolness, even hostility, the royal family did what they could to combat it. Often, by their charm and their simplicity and their frankness, they seemed to melt the antagonism. One old Nationalist, who had fought in the Anglo-Boer War, was so impressed by his talk with the King that he tore off his ornamental leather belt (which the King had admired) and, running alongside the moving White Train, passed it up to one of the equerries shouting, 'Here, give it to him.'[14] To another Boer veteran, who had told her that he could never forgive the British for fighting against the Boers, the Queen deftly admitted that, as a Scot, she understood his attitude perfectly.

Just before leaving South Africa, the King and Queen arranged a private meeting with the Leader of the Opposition, Dr D.F. Malan and his wife. 'As was only right,' Malan said afterwards, 'nothing was discussed that had any political meaning. Our conversation was quite informal and friendly.'[15] After a while, the two princesses were called into the room. They all parted on the most amicable of terms.

'If, and I firmly believe it has,' wrote the King to Smuts on the voyage home, 'our visit has altered the conception of monarchy to some South

Africans and has given them a new viewpoint from our personal contacts with them, then our tour has been well worth while . . .'[16]

It was a vain hope. Just over a year after the royal visit, South Africa went to the polls. Although Smuts's United Party won more votes, Malan's National Party won more seats. From that time on, the National Party became ever more firmly entrenched until, in 1961, in the tenth year of Queen Elizabeth II's reign, South Africa became a republic and ceased to be a member of the Commonwealth.

So it was paradoxical that Princess Elizabeth, on coming of age in Cape Town on 21 April 1947, broadcast from South Africa an appeal to all the nations of the British Commonwealth to witness what she called her 'solemn act of dedication'.

'I should like,' she said in that still-girlish voice, 'to make that dedication now. It is very simple. I declare before you all that my whole life, whether it be long or short, shall be devoted to your service and the service of our great Imperial Commonwealth to which we all belong . . . God help me to make good my vow and God bless all of you who are willing to share in it.'[17]

In a different part of the Commonwealth, as Governor-General of Australia, the Duke of Gloucester had been implementing another of the traditional methods by which the monarchy fulfils its functions and spreads its influence.

A governor-general is the monarch's personal representative, with powers similar, in all essentials, to those of the sovereign. Rendered completely independent of the British government by the resolutions of the Imperial Conference of 1926, a governor-general holds almost exactly the same position in relation to his country's affairs as the sovereign holds in Britain. In Australia, therefore, the Governor-General is the representative of the King, or Queen, of Australia.

Where, until after the Second World War, a governor-general was a member of the royal family, his standing was undoubtedly enhanced. Valid or not, the idea that a royal governor-general was somehow superior to a non-royal or a local one, died very hard. By 1945, the twentieth century had seen four royal governors-general: the Duke of Connaught and the Earl of Athlone in Canada, and Prince Arthur of Connaught and again the Earl of Athlone in South Africa. With the late Duke of Kent's appointment having come to nothing, the Duke of Gloucester was Australia's first royal governor-general. Only as the century progressed, and feelings of national identity increased, did the practice of importing governors-general, whether royal or not, fall away. A plan for Prince Charles to be appointed Governor-General of Australia soon after his marriage in 1981, met with a luke-warm response.

In the 1940s, the majority of Australians were still happy enough to have a member of the royal family as Governor-General. The *Sydney Herald* hailed the prospect as 'a magnificent gesture' and the *Sydney Sun* considered it 'the greatest compliment the Throne can pay to the Australian people.'[18] In her old age, Princess Alice, Duchess of Gloucester, felt certain that they had been appreciated for what they had done in Australia.

In the two years that the Duke and Duchess of Gloucester spent in Australia – from January 1945 until January 1947 – the couple certainly did a great deal. 'No Governor-General in the past has travelled so far, or met so many people in two short years in this vast country,'[19] claimed the wife of one state governor. As the monarch's representative, the Duke was obliged to carry out all the customary duties: opening parliament, holding investitures, receiving foreign dignitaries, talking to ministers, attending banquets and receptions, giving garden parties, inspecting troops, taking the salute and applying himself to hour upon hour of desk work.

Making the Duke's job even more arduous was his shyness, for he had inherited his full share of the family affliction. He was always nervous on formal occasions and never conquered his distaste for public speaking. And, just as George VI's first audiences with Attlee were notable for their awkward silences, so were the Duke of Gloucester's first meetings with his two prime ministers. The King's injunction to his brother that 'your PM has got to tell you everything and get all the information from him'[20] was not so easily carried out when neither the Governor-General nor his prime ministers were especially articulate men.

When the Duke was not doing his job in Canberra, he and the Duchess toured the country. In spite of searing heat, inadequate accommodation, bumpy aeroplane flights, exhausting schedules and frequent ill health, the Gloucesters pushed on uncomplainingly. In fact, in their self-effacing way, the Duke and Duchess of Gloucester were shining examples of that devotion to duty which characterises the House of Windsor. With very little taste, temperament or natural talent for their calling, the couple did their job to the very best of their abilities. It had been the same with King George V; it was the same with King George VI; it became the same with Queen Elizabeth II. All of them would probably have been far happier out of the public eye, living quiet lives in the country with their dogs and their horses, restricting their public appearances to the occasional opening of a fête or the reading of a lesson. None of them really relished their high office. What kept them at their task – and what King Edward VIII so conspicuously lacked – was a dogged, unselfish, unquestioning sense of obligation.

This is what made the occasional criticism so difficult to accept. The Gloucesters had their share of it. The Duke, with his bluff manner and short temper, sometimes made an undiplomatic remark. The Duchess, with her innate modesty, lacked the necessary flair for the showier aspects of her task. All four members of the family, and particularly young Prince William, suffered spells of ill health. And when it became known that the Duke's term was not to be extended beyond two years, there was widespread speculation as to the reason. Was the Duke longing to leave Australia? Had his term been unsuccessful? 'Have the Gloucesters failed?' trumpeted one newspaper head-line.

The simple explanation was that George VI had insisted on his brother's return to Britain. With the King about to set out for his tour of South Africa, it was essential that the Duke of Gloucester, as senior Counsellor of State, be at home in his absence. The deputising for an absent monarch was one of the major duties of a member of the royal family. This meant that the Duke had to return to Britain before the King and his family set sail. As always, the Duke of Gloucester, who very much wanted to remain in Australia, was obliged to put national interests before personal preferences.

When he left on 18 January 1947 (the Duchess and their two sons followed by sea) the Duke left behind him a reputation as a conscientious worker, a sympathetic listener and an unpretentious personality. His honest-to-goodness qualities had made a good impression on the Australians. Wherever he went, the crowds had always proved gratifyingly enthusiastic. 'God bless you,' the Duchess would sometimes hear the people shout as they drove by; 'they seemed very excited and pleased to see us,'[21] she could report.

Perhaps the Duke of Gloucester's achievement was best summed up in the newspaper cartoon showing him setting off on his final flight home. 'There goes a good bloke,'[22] read the caption.

Princess Elizabeth's engagement to Lieutenant Philip Mountbatten, officially announced on 10 July 1947, promised both a dynastic alliance of the traditional kind and a marriage that was very much in tune with the changing image of the British monarchy. For Philip Mountbatten, while being a member of that great clan of Europe's inter-related royals, was a British subject, a serving sailor and a personality of progressive and outspoken views. Through the still somewhat stultified atmosphere of the court, this new addition to the family was to blow like a gust of fresh air.

The couple were doubly, if distantly, related. Born Prince Philip of Greece, the young man's paternal grandfather had been Queen Alexandra's brother: the Danish prince whom the Greeks had accepted as their King in 1863. His maternal grandmother had been one of Queen Victoria's many grand-daughters. This maternal grandmother, Princess Victoria of Hesse, had married Prince Louis of Battenberg who, in spite of a lifetime's distin-guished service with the Royal Navy, had been forced to resign as First Sea Lord at the outbreak of the First World War because of the public clamour against his origins. A subsequent clamour had compelled the Battenbergs to change their name to Mountbatten. But it had been as Princess Alice of

Battenberg that the eldest daughter of this marriage had married Prince Andrew of Greece in 1903.

The marriage of Prince and Princess Andrew of Greece had not been a great success. Temperamentally ill-suited, the couple's chances of establishing a stable relationship had not been helped by the volatile nature of Greek politics. By the time their fifth child and only son, Prince Philip, was born on the island of Corfu on 10 June 1921, the Greek royal family had already experienced a succession of violent deaths, abdications and restorations. The couple drifted apart. The debonair Prince Andrew eventually settled for life in the South of France while the deaf and deeply religious Princess Alice lived an increasingly withdrawn existence.

Living apart from her husband, Princess Alice was obliged to rely on her brothers, George and Dickie – by now Marquess of Milford Haven and Lord Louis Mountbatten – to help her raise young Prince Philip. The boy, who had been to school in Paris, was now sent, first to the preparatory school at Cheam in Surrey and then to Salem, the famous experimental school started by Kurt Hahn in Bavaria. After Hahn's opposition to the Nazi regime had forced him to leave Germany and open a new school at Gordonstoun in Scotland, Prince Philip followed him.

In the spartan, high-minded, mentally and physically competitive atmosphere of Gordonstoun, the young Prince Philip more than proved himself. When one member of the royal family asked Queen Mary whether the fact that Prince Philip had been to 'a crank school with theories of complete social equality where the boys were taught to mix with all and sundry' would prove useful or unwise, the old Queen's answer was unequivocal. 'Useful,' she snapped. 'And it will be . . .' she went on to explain, on repeating the conversation to Lady Airlie. 'The world has changed since you and I were born into it, and it will change still more.'[23]

In this way, by the choice of Cheam and Gordonstoun for Prince Philip, was a pattern laid down for the education of future generations of princes. The days of sheltered royal education conducted by governesses and tutors were now numbered: Queen Elizabeth II's three sons were all, in turn, subjected to the rigours and challenges of Gordonstoun.

From Gordonstoun, Prince Philip entered the Royal Naval College at Dartmouth. So far, the characters of three kings – George V, Edward VIII and George VI – had been partly shaped by Dartmouth; the college played a similar role in the careers of Prince Philip and his two eldest sons, Prince Charles and Prince Andrew. And it was at Dartmouth, just before the outbreak of the Second World War, that the young, strikingly good-looking Prince Philip had his first recorded meeting with Princess Elizabeth. They must have met before, on great family occasions, but this was the first time that their coming together had been noticed and commented on. The Princess and her sister, in the company of their parents, were visiting the Naval

College. Although the meeting seems not to have meant a great deal to the eighteen-year-old Prince, the thirteen-year-old Princess was clearly deeply impressed.

And impressed, whenever the two of them met during the war years, she remained. While Prince Philip was caught up in the dangers and diversions of active service, Princess Elizabeth, in the seclusion of Windsor Castle, kept his memory very much alive. 'This was the man,' wrote George VI's official biographer, 'with whom Princess Elizabeth had been in love from the first meeting.'[24]

Once the war was over and the two met more frequently, the Princess became more than ever determined to marry her handsome Prince. But although the King approved of Prince Philip he had certain reservations. Not only did he not want to lose his adored daughter too soon but there was the vexed question of the Prince's nationality. With Greece in its customary state of turmoil, marriage to a Greek prince – although the Greek Royal House was actually Danish – could bring complications. Yet, for various reasons, the time did not seem opportune for the renouncing of his Greek nationality. Nor was the British public too happy about his Greek origins. An opinion poll proved that forty per cent resented the fact that the Prince was a foreigner.

All these difficulties the Princess swept aside. When, in the autumn of 1946, Prince Philip proposed to her, she accepted.

But with her ingrained sense of royal obligation, Princess Elizabeth acceded to her father's wish that the engagement be kept secret until after the South African tour. It would be better to get that, and her official coming-of-age, over before making the announcement. So the Palace issued a denial of newspaper rumours about the engagement. The Princess's answer to un-inhibited South African questioning about her engagement was a smiling 'Wait and see', and only a handful of people knew about her telephone calls to the Prince whenever the White Train was drawn up for the night. (Her future son and heir, Prince Charles, was less fortunate: tapes of his supposedly secret telephone calls to his future wife, while he was on tour in Australia, were sold by a journalist to a German magazine.)

Not until two months after the family's return from South Africa was the official announcement made. By then Prince Philip had changed his nationality, his name and his title. On becoming a naturalised British subject he had ceased to be a Prince of Greece and Denmark with the resounding name of Schleswig-Holstein-Sonderburg-Glücksburg and had adopted the Anglicised version of his mother's name, Mountbatten. He became, quite simply, Lieutenant Philip Mountbatten. Not until his wedding morning was he created Duke of Edinburgh and not until ten years later, on 22 February 1957, was he accorded the style and title of Prince of the United Kingdom by his wife.

The wedding, on 20 November 1947, was the first great royal occasion to recapture something of the splendour of pre-war years. As always, it provided a glittering focal point for national loyalties; it heightened, as the *Daily Express* leader column said at the time of the Princess's engagement, 'the ordinary man's sense of history. It enables him to project the past into the future.'[25] In grey, war-racked Britain, the wedding seemed like the herald of better times; almost like a reaffirmation of Britain's place in the world.

As the date approached, public interest increased enormously. One observer saw the wedding as 'some sort of symbol of what is, emotionally, the most important part of our way of life – the family',[26] while a great many others regarded it as the symbol of something more significant: their country's enduring importance in a changing world. For as British power waned, so did British pride in the royal family wax. Here was something which no other country, no other monarchy, could match. Britain might no longer be a first-rate power but there was nothing second-rate about its monarchy. 'It was a sentiment,' writes Philip Ziegler, 'that was to grow in stridence over the next twenty-five years.'[27]

The press had at one stage predicted an austerity wedding. But there was no sign of austerity in the day's ceremonial. For the first time in a decade, the Sovereign's escort of the Household Cavalry was in full ceremonial uniform; the European royals, regnant and exiled, who had come pouring into London, were all lavishly dressed; the bride's dress, by Norman Hartnell, was as sumptuous and intricate as any he had ever made. And bringing the glories of the ceremony closer to the general public was the fact that it was filmed.

In his address, the Archbishop of York claimed that 'notwithstanding the splendour and national significance of the service . . . it is the same as it would be for any cottager who might be married this afternoon in some small country church.'[28] And the touching letter which the King wrote to his daughter when it was all over, captures something of the flavour of the simple family occasion.

'I was so proud of you and thrilled at having you so close to me on our long walk in Westminster Abbey, but when I handed your hand to the Archbishop I felt I had lost something very precious . . .

'Our family, us four, the "Royal Family" must remain together with additions of course at suitable moments!! I have watched you grow up all these years with pride under the skilful direction of Mummy, who as you know is the most marvellous person in the World in my eyes, and I can, I know, always count on you, and now Philip, to help us in our work. Your leaving has left a great blank in our lives but do remember that your old home is still yours and do come back to it as much and as often as possible. I can see that you are sublimely happy with Philip which is right but don't forget us . . .'[29]

*

If, in the main, Princess Elizabeth's marriage had been a conventional royal alliance, the same could hardly have been said of the marriage of her cousin George Lascelles, the 7th Earl of Harewood. His was to be the first of the kind of marriage that became increasingly accepted in the years ahead.

This eldest son of King George VI's sister, the Princess Royal, and the 6th Earl of Harewood, had succeeded to the title, and to the ownership of the stately Harewood House, on the death of his father in 1947. Even by this stage, the twenty-four-year-old Lord Harewood was something of the family odd-man-out. His background and education had been traditional enough. His father, in spite of his extensive art collection and his talent for needlework, had lived the usual, countrified life of an aristocratic landowner; his mother, in addition to her occasional royal duties, confined herself to such conventional pursuits as gardening, letter-writing and, above all, race-going – for which she had inherited the family passion.

Another of the Princess Royal's family legacies was her shyness. This, allied to an upbringing at the hands of King George V and Queen Mary which had discouraged, as her son was later to put it, 'direct discussion or any displays of emotion',[30] made communication, except on the most basic level, very difficult. 'We did not talk of love and affection and what we meant to each other,' remembers Lord Harewood, 'but rather – and even about that not easily – of duty and behaviour and what we ought to do . . .'[31] It was often rumoured that the Princess Royal's marriage had not been a success; that her husband was a cold and cruel man. This, her son has denied. His parents, in their undemonstrative way, were fond of each other, with many friends and interests in common.

Educated at Eton, the young Viscount Lascelles, as he then was, went on to serve as a captain in the Grenadier Guards during the Second World War. He was captured and imprisoned at Colditz where, as the nephew of King George VI, he was regarded as a *Prominente*, one of a group of well-born prisoners, highly valued for their possible future use as hostages. It never came to that and, on his release in 1945, George Lascelles went to Canada as an ADC to the Governor-General, his great-uncle, Queen Mary's brother, Lord Athlone. There then followed eighteen months at King's College, Cambridge.

All this, with the exception of his time as a prisoner of war, was familiar enough territory for a minor member of the royal family. But it was the young man's burgeoning interest in opera that set him apart from the rest of them. Not even his father's death in 1947 and his assumption of the responsibilities of Harewood House, could dampen his musical enthusiasms. He was to devote his life to them. An efficient, talented and knowledgeable musical director, Lord Harewood became, in time, the managing director of the English National Opera.

'It's very odd about George and music,' a perplexed Duke of Windsor once said. 'You know, his parents were quite normal – liked horses and dogs and the country.'[32]

His musical career was his first break with royal tradition; the second was his turbulent marital career. It began in 1949 when the twenty-six-year-old Lord Harewood announced his intention of marrying, not some aristocratic girl from the shires but a beautiful, dark-eyed, Viennese-born Jewess by the name of Marion Stein. The daughter of cultured Austrian refugees, Marion Stein shared Lord Harewood's musical interests. Although apparently admirably suited, the couple could not be married without the formal permission of the Sovereign. Not for the last time in his life had Lord Harewood come up against the stipulations of the Royal Marriages Act of 1772.

This Act, designed by King George III to prevent members of the family in line of succession from contracting unsuitable alliances, was still very much in force, although there had been no cause to invoke it for several generations. (As a reigning monarch, Edward VIII had not been subject to the Act.) Nor was there any cause to do so now. If Marion Stein was a somewhat exotic choice, she was by no means an unacceptable one. The King had no objections to the match. Such objections as there were – and they were said to be vehement – came from Queen Mary. She would not hear of the marriage. And until such time as she would, the King refused to give his permission. He advised his nephew to wait.

When Lord Harewood could wait no longer, he tackled Queen Mary himself. 'Barriers within the family were neither stiff nor high . . .'[33] he once explained; and his grandmother proved to be as sympathetic on this occasion as she had been on others. In any case, her initial opposition had by now abated somewhat and she allowed herself to be talked round. This left the King free to give his permission. The engagement was announced on 19 July 1949.

The marriage was solemnised in St Mark's Church, North Audley Street on 29 September that year. One untoward incident only marked the otherwise impeccably organised reception, attended by the entire royal family, in St James's Palace. The ageing and short-sighted novelist, E.M. Forster, was discovered bowing to the wedding cake in the understandable misapprehension that it was Queen Mary.

Few things illustrated better the British genius for compromise or the monarchy's capacity for adjusting to changing circumstances than the postwar formula worked out for a new relationship between Crown and Commonwealth.

King George VI was fond of saying that an outsider, faced with the anomalies of the British Commonwealth, would feel exactly like the man who, on first seeing a giraffe, exclaimed, 'There ain't no such animal.'[34] If this had been apposite in the years before the Second World War, it was to become doubly so in the years after. Since the Imperial Conference of 1926, the Commonwealth (apart from the various colonies and dependencies) had been made up of a group of independent white, or white-ruled, nations, united by a common allegiance to the Crown. Each nation had recognised George VI as King. But by 1949 it was realised that a new Commonwealth arrangement, embracing all Britain's one-time colonial possessions, would have to be worked out.

By the end of the war the whole concept of colonial rule – of one country having the say over the destinies of another – had become distasteful to Western democracies, and so the British government set about granting independence to its remaining colonial possessions. The most important of these was India. Attlee's choice of Lord Mountbatten for the difficult task of bringing down the curtain on the Raj was masterly: not only did Mountbatten have the necessary dash, drive and ruthlessness for the mission but he was a member of the royal family. The last Viceroy of India would be, not only the monarch's personal representative, but his cousin.

Mountbatten's negotiations concluded, power was transferred to the newly created dominions of India and Pakistan on 15 August 1947. From that time on King George VI ceased to sign himself George RI. Queen Mary, who over thirty-five years before had stood beside King George V beneath that golden-domed pavilion at Delhi to receive the homage of their Indian subjects, could not help being upset by the change. On the back of an envelope of a letter from her son, received on 18 August 1947, she wrote: 'The first time Bertie wrote me a letter with the I for Emperor of India left out, very sad.'[35]

There was sadder to come. India, not content with independence from Britain, no longer wished to owe allegiance to the Crown. She intended to declare herself a republic. On the other hand, she did not want to leave the Commonwealth, a Commonwealth whose essential unifying factor *was* a common allegiance to the Crown. How could this circle possibly be squared? For squared it would have to be, if all former British possessions, on gaining independence and becoming republics, were to stay in the Commonwealth.

A solution was worked out. A conference of Commonwealth prime ministers, held in London in 1949, devised a formula whereby the British monarch would become 'the symbol of the free association of the independent member nations of the Commonwealth, and as such head of the Commonwealth.'[36] In future, any country with some British association in its past, whether presided over by its own monarch, governor-general or president, would acknowledge the British sovereign, not necessarily as sovereign, but as 'Head of the Commonwealth'.

Queen Elizabeth II, at her Coronation, was proclaimed, in the new style, as: 'Queen Elizabeth the Second, by the Grace of God, Queen of this Realm and of all her other Realms and Territories, Head of the Commonwealth . . .'[37]

And just as the Statute of Westminster had, at one and the same time, relieved George V of some of his powers while enhancing his prestige, so was the status of future British sovereigns elevated by this new, ingenious formula. It was a milestone, not only in the evolution of the Commonwealth but of the monarchy. While the rest of the monarch's diplomatic influence has gradually waned and Queen Elizabeth II cannot hope to play the sort of role played by her great-grandfather, King Edward VII, her international prestige, as head of a vast, multi-racial community of peoples, has increased enormously. In 1877, a gratified Queen Victoria had been created Queen-Empress; a century later, her great-great-granddaughter, celebrating the Silver Jubilee of her reign, occupied, as Head of the Commonwealth, a hardly less glorious position.

In less dramatic ways, also, the monarchy continued its process of adjustment to changing times. Not only had George VI introduced a more relaxed atmosphere into the daily life of the family but the court had become less formal. In fact, the King did not even like the use of the word 'court'; it smacked too much, he protested, of 'courtiers lounging about'[38] whereas, in reality, it was a hard-working, business-like institution. The levees – those all-male assemblies dating back to the days when various favoured gentlemen had gathered to greet their sovereigns on getting out of bed in the morning – were discontinued. The rules regarding court dress – the tunics, knee-breeches and stockings which had been compulsory for any man dining with the King – were relaxed. Guests found the King and Queen friendly and approachable. Whereas Queen Mary would sit uncompromisingly erect, bestowing no more than a minute's stilted conversation on the nervous ladies who were led up to speak to her, Queen Elizabeth would greet them like friends, giving them the full benefit of her clear blue eyes, her tilted head, her beautifully modulated voice.

When the American Ambassador, Joseph Kennedy, with cheerful disregard for the custom whereby the royal family always opened court balls, simply dashed across the room to ask the Queen to dance the minute the band struck up, she unhesitatingly accepted his invitation. At private dances, the King was quite likely to be found leading conga lines along the corridors of Buckingham Palace or Windsor Castle. The members of the household, although occasionally subjected to the King's violent temper, found him acutely sensitive to their welfare and sympathetic to their problems.

In common with his grandfather, Edward VII, and unlike his father, George V, the King welcomed new inventions. He took the keenest interest in the use of the relatively new medium, television, for the recording of royal occasions. He would even give instructions as to where the cameras should be placed for the most effective results.

More than any previous twentieth-century sovereign had George VI struck exactly the right balance between the mystique and majesty of his position and the identification with his subjects. Both Edward VII and George V had been popular kings but somewhat remote personalities, far removed from the everyday life of their subjects. Edward VIII, on the other hand, had yielded some of the dignity of his position. King George VI understood all this and, for his time, drew the line with great expertise. In the early days of his reign, his awareness of his own limitations had encouraged him in the conviction that 'a crowned and anointed King must not be too ready to step down from his pedestal'[39] and that any unbending should be left to the Queen, but by now he had become what he had resolved to become after his Canadian tour of 1939: a people's King, a man with a common touch.

In many ways, and in spite of his fretful, sensitive nature, King George VI was not unlike the vast majority of his subjects. Neither an intellectual nor an aesthete, he shared a great many of their philistine tastes. His humour was salty, he loved re-telling old jokes, he roared at the Crazy Gang, he never missed an ITMA programme on the radio. On seeing John Piper's newly painted studies of Windsor Castle, with their typically lowering, atmospheric skies, the King is said to have commiserated with the artist for not having had better weather during his stay. He was, in short, an ordinary person in an extraordinary position – as his father had been, and as his daughter became.

The King's greatest pleasures, again like those of his subjects, came from his home life: from the love and support of his family, his garden at Royal Lodge, his shooting at Balmoral, his concern for the Sandringham estate. Like his father, and grandfather, he loved Sandringham best of all his homes. And he liked to think of this love being passed on to future generations. 'I want Lilibet and Philip to get to know it too,' he once wrote to Queen Mary, 'as I have always been so happy here . . .'[40]

Four generations of monarchs and their heirs had spent their Christmases at Sandringham and by the end of 1948 there were the beginnings of a fifth generation. On 14 November 1948 Princess Elizabeth gave birth to a son. His birth was marked by the scrapping of yet another ancient royal tradition: the King had abolished the custom whereby the Home Secretary was obliged to attend and verify each royal birth. The baby was given the names Charles Philip Arthur George. The choice of the name Charles was widely regarded as a deliberate attempt to emphasise the family's Stuart, and therefore British, as opposed to its Hanoverian, or German, connections.

Just under two years after the birth of Prince Charles, Princess Elizabeth gave birth to a second child, a daughter who was christened with the equally Stuart-sounding name of Anne.

It was as the centre of this happy and exemplary family circle that George VI had come to be so highly regarded. There was no doubt that, in the public mind, the royal family epitomised all that was admirable in national life. As much as ever, the King was expected to be the symbol of domestic virtue. He was known to be a man of simple religious faith and a devoted husband and father. 'I make no secret of the fact,' he once admitted in a broadcast to his subjects, 'that there have been times when [the burdens of kingship] would have been almost too heavy but for the strength and comfort which I have always found in my home.'[41]

His chief source of strength and comfort remained, of course, the Queen. Theirs was an ideal, perfectly balanced partnership. To imagine that she, because of her more assured public image, dominated him, was to misunderstand their relationship. Just as Queen Mary had adapted her personality to serve King George V, so did Queen Elizabeth adapt hers to lighten her husband's load. Although her interests were wider and deeper than his – she had a taste for music, painting, ballet and a greater knowledge of the turf – she never allowed them to intrude on her married life. If anything, the King had the stronger personality. 'The King was a rock to her . . .' claimed one of the Queen's sisters. 'In fundamental things she leant on him: I have always felt how much the Queen was sustained by the King.'[42]

Yet there was no denying that, in public, it was she who appeared to be sustaining him. Where the King invariably looked tense and preoccupied, the Queen was never anything less than graceful, interested and vivacious. Her famous smile never faded; her famous wave never faltered. By now, the art of being a queen was as natural to her as breathing. She had come, well and truly, into her own. It was in these post-war years that Queen Elizabeth perfected – as Queen Mary had perfected – the distinctive appearance that has remained hers for the rest of her life. She had become – with her elaborate hats, her floating draperies and her high heels – an instantly recognisable figure. She could surely never have been mistaken for anything other than a queen.

And to her individual appearance, social talents and professional manner, Queen Elizabeth brought something more: a strong personal magnetism. It seemed to have an almost physical quality. The crowds could sense it at once; they responded to her immediately. A Commonwealth cabinet minister once spoke to her about this phenomenon. 'Your Majesty,' he said, 'may I say something, I am not trying to flatter, but we all feel a warmth radiating from you. I can't describe it, something intangible. Do you feel that you are giving something out?'

Her answer was charmingly frank. 'I must admit that at times I feel something flow out of me. It is difficult to describe what I mean. It makes me feel very tired for a moment. Then I seem to get something back from the people – sympathy, goodwill, I don't know exactly – and I feel strengthened again, in fact, recharged. It's an exchange, I expect; I don't know . . .'[43]

Yet no less than the King was the Queen surprised by the outpouring of public affection on the occasion of their Silver Wedding on 26 April 1948. 'We were both dumbfounded over our reception,'[44] admitted the King to Queen Mary. The same had been true of King George V on the occasion of his Silver Jubilee in 1935; the same was true of Queen Elizabeth II on hers in 1977. The procession to and from St Paul's, the twenty-mile-long drive through the streets of the capital, the appearances on the Palace balcony, all in bright spring sunshine, gave the public an opportunity to demonstrate their love and loyalty towards the royal couple.

Inevitably, there was some criticism. 'He had no wit, no learning, no humour, except of a rather schoolboy brand,'[45] complained 'Chips' Channon. The servants dreaded the King's sudden bursts of anger; guests were sometimes discomforted by the caustic comments by which he masked his persistent feelings of inadequacy. But when set against the general air of approval, such carpings were negligible.

The British dearly love long-established institutions and long-lived public figures. Had he lived another twenty or so years, King George VI, with his inimitable Queen beside him, would have ended up as a greatly revered and admired monarch. Year by year, he was growing in stature. As it is, Queen Elizabeth the Queen Mother has established herself as one of the most remarkable members of the royal family. Together, given a thirty-five-year-long instead of a fifteen-year-long reign, King George VI and Queen Elizabeth could have developed into the most popular King and Queen Consort of the twentieth century.

But it was not to be. Even before the birth of his first grandson in 1948, the King began to show signs of the illness that was to kill him. Cramp and pain in his left leg was diagnosed as arteriosclerosis and he was forced to cancel a proposed tour of Australia and New Zealand. The amputation of his left leg was narrowly avoided but a few months later he underwent an operation. He seemed to be making a good recovery and the tour was rescheduled for 1952. In the spring of 1951 – the Festival of Britain year in which he bravely played his part – the King again showed signs of failing health and in September he underwent another operation. This time his entire left lung was removed. Although the King did not know it, the operation had been for cancer. Once again, he seemed to be making a satisfactory recovery but the threat of another thrombosis always hung over him. There was no possibility now of a tour of Australia and New Zealand.

For a man who had suffered so many strains, frustrations and misfortunes, and who had always shown such courage, these years of illness were yet another cross to be borne stoically.

*

One thought which must have brought the ailing King consolation during these last years was that the future of the dynasty was in good hands. Not only was another generation growing up in the royal nursery but Princess Elizabeth and her husband were proving to be dedicated members of what the King always referred to as 'the firm'.

For the Duke of Edinburgh, it was not always easy. The couple had spent some of their early married life in Buckingham Palace. In spite of George VI's more relaxed regime, the Palace remained a formal, impersonal and tradition-bound institution; it was certainly no place for the bluff and independent-minded husband to establish himself as master of his own home. His opportunity to do so did not come until 4 July 1949 when the couple and their baby moved into nearby Clarence House. Aptly and understandably, the Duke dubbed it 'Independence Day'.

But by now the young husband was experiencing another of those classic royal dilemmas: the tug-of-war between his royal obligations and his wish to pursue his own career. It had been the same for someone like the Duke of Gloucester; later, it was the same for someone like Princess Margaret's husband, the Earl of Snowdon. By day the Duke of Edinburgh did a boring desk job at the Admiralty; by night he carried out a variety of public duties, either alone or a pace or two behind his wife. His overriding ambition was to command his own ship and, in the autumn of 1949, he moved a step nearer towards fulfilling it: the Duke was posted to Malta as first lieutenant and second-in-command of HMS *Chequers*. On Malta he was joined, for two longish periods, by Princess Elizabeth (the infant Prince Charles and, in time, Princess Anne, were cared for by the King and Queen) and in August 1950 the Duke achieved his ambition by being gazetted lieutenant-commander and given the command of the frigate HMS *Magpie*.

His gratification was short-lived. With the King so ill, it was imperative that the couple return home to shoulder some of their responsibilities. The Duke of Edinburgh was obliged to leave the navy on indefinite leave. He is on it still.

The couple's first major engagement was a tour of Canada, with a visit to the United States, in the autumn of 1951. It started with the breaking of yet another royal taboo. With the King's connivance, the Duke of Edinburgh overcame the opposition to the heir to the throne flying the Atlantic, and they set off by air rather than by sea. It was the first of the numberless flights that the couple were to make to Commonwealth countries in the years ahead.

As on all royal tours, the couple were subjected to a more rigorous programme and to more intensive scrutiny than was usual at home. In this heightened, more demanding atmosphere, they acquitted themselves well. The Princess, with her glowing complexion and vividly-coloured clothes, looked radiant; the Duke won praise for his good looks and relaxed manner. The couple were also exposed to greater informality and considerably less reverence than was customary in Britain. In few places was this more noticeable than in the home of President Truman. One of the royal visit's more memorable moments came with the meeting between Princess Elizabeth and the President's deaf and aged mother-in-law.

'I'm so glad,' chirped the old lady, who had just heard that Winston Churchill had once again become Prime Minister, 'that your father's been re-elected.'[46]

With no chance now of King George VI being able to face the rigours of the Australian tour, it was decided that his daughter and son-in-law should represent him. So, leaving Prince Charles and Princess Anne once more in the care of their grandparents, the couple set off, again by air, on 31 January 1952, bound first for East Africa. They were seen off at London airport by the King, the Queen and the twenty-one-year-old Princess Margaret. This was the last public glimpse of the King, standing frail and hatless in the bitter winter wind, as he waved goodbye to the daughter he loved so dearly.

He returned almost immediately to Sandringham and to his hare shooting. And it was here, in the early hours of 6 February 1952 after a particularly satisfying day's shooting, that the fifty-six-year-old King died, peacefully in his sleep.

Perhaps the general feeling on George VI's death was best summed up in the words of one young artisan. 'I think we all liked the King a great deal. Never wanted to be King. Sacrificed practically everything for his country. I think if anybody died for his country it was the King.'[47]

It was not until 2.45 p.m. (East African time; the time in London was 11.45 a.m.) that Princess Elizabeth was told, by her husband, that her father had died and that she was now Queen. She was then at the Sangana Hunting Lodge in Kenya where the royal party was having a short rest from the round of official engagements. Her calm, in the face of this tragic and momentous news, was little short of phenomenal. With a composure that would have done credit to her grandmother, Queen Mary, and which was very much part of the royal stock-in-trade, the new Queen prepared for the 4000-mile flight that would take her back to her kingdom.

And Queen Elizabeth II was no less composed as, on the afternoon of Thursday 7 February, she came slowly down the steps of her aircraft to receive the homage of a past, a present and a future prime minister: Clement Attlee, Winston Churchill and Anthony Eden. Dressed all in black, she formed the central figure of a set-piece which was in every way as memorable as that of the young Queen Victoria being greeted by the Archbishop of Canterbury and the Lord Chamberlain on the morning of her accession.

Was this the dawn, people wondered, of an equally glorious reign?

Part Five

QUEEN ELIZABETH II
1952 –

New Beginnings

EACH twentieth-century monarch, on ascending the throne, has been faced by different public expectations. Edward VII was confronted by the impossible-seeming task of filling the vacuum left by the awe-inspiring Queen Victoria. George V was obliged to follow a reign of exceptional social and diplomatic brilliance. Edward VIII was looked upon as a progressive, modernising monarch. When his bubble burst, it fell to George VI to restore the stability, and respectability, of the monarchy. Queen Elizabeth II came to the throne amid the highest hopes of all.

Here, surely, was an opportunity for new beginnings. At twenty-five, Queen Elizabeth II was the youngest monarch to ascend the British throne since Queen Victoria, well over a century before. Her three predecessors had all been over forty; King Edward VII had been almost sixty. With her accession coinciding with the end of the country's post-war period of austerity, the new Queen seemed to represent the spirit of youth, the hopes for the future. Britain had enjoyed its periods of greatest national achievement during the reigns of previous queens; would the new Queen turn out to be another Elizabeth I, another Victoria? The air was full of heady talk about national regeneration, about political and economic revival, about 'New Elizabethans'. The press sounded fanfares for the dawn of a new golden age, presided over by a new Gloriana. Churchill, in his orotund fashion, hailed the Queen as 'a young, gleaming champion'.[1]

That this mood of national euphoria very soon evaporated was no fault of the new Queen. There was nothing that she could do – other than fulfil her functions as gracefully and efficiently as possible – to reverse the trend of history. Yet, interestingly enough, while Britain continued its decline as a great power, the Queen herself went a long way towards fulfilling these extravagant expectations. Her realm might not be about to recapture its former glory, but the monarchy was set, not only on retaining its glory, but on enhancing it.

What was she like, this young woman on whom so many unrealistic hopes were centred? At this early stage, her subjects did not know a great deal about her. She was still too young to have established a definite public image. Although no great beauty, she was certainly very attractive, with a lustre that was not entirely due to her status. When she smiled, she looked radiant. But people complained that she did not smile enough. When asked about this, she said that she had not realised that as a working monarch she was meant to smile. In the same way had her grandfather, George V, on being tackled about his solemn public manner, replied that sailors did not smile when on duty. Nor did the new Queen have anything like her mother's social aplomb. In public she could look stiff, aloof, uninterested. Her speeches were stilted, her voice immature. The truth was that, like so many members of her family, Queen Elizabeth II was painfully shy; and again, as with so many of them, a considerable effort of will was needed to master this shyness.

In private, it was another matter. Then the Queen was relaxed, amusing, quick-witted. She had strong opinions; she knew her own mind. Those who worked with her found themselves impressed by her conscientiousness and her common sense. Her thoughts were highly organised. She worked on her 'boxes' with a diligence worthy of her father or her grandfather. Her first Prime Minister, the ageing Winston Churchill, frequently found that she was better informed on certain subjects than he was. A later Prime Minister, Harold Macmillan, pronounced her to be quick, well-informed and in possession of an exceptionally retentive memory. R.A. ('Rab') Butler described her as clever.

Contrary to public expectations, Queen Elizabeth II did not profess to be a reforming monarch in the mould of her uncle, Edward VIII. 'Let us hope that there will now be a clean-out, a clean sweep,'[2] wrote 'Chips' Channon on the Queen's accession. He should have known better. All King Edward VIII's talk of modernising the monarchy had come to nothing; Queen Elizabeth II was more intent on retaining, in broad outline, the monarchy as established by her grandfather, King George V. What she was determined to uphold – by instinct rather than design – was the dignity, dependability and respectability of the Crown.

It was true that with the Duke of Edinburgh's active encouragement, the Queen made certain changes: for one thing, Buckingham Palace was modernised and made more efficient. But she made a point of retaining, intact, the household personnel inherited from her father. Sir Alan Lascelles, who had been George VI's private secretary, became her private secretary; Sir Michael Adeane, who had been the King's assistant private secretary, became hers until, in turn, he succeeded Lascelles. It was not so much that the Queen felt too young and inexperienced to choose new personnel; it was mainly because these men fitted admirably into the sort of monarchy which she planned to maintain. What she was after was continuity.

By few things, of course, is the continuity of the monarchy better emphasised than by a Coronation. The crowning of Queen Elizabeth II, in Westminster Abbey on 2 June 1953, aroused even more public interest and enthusiasm than usual. Not only was this Coronation the first to be televised, it was the first great public occasion at which the television audience out-numbered the radio audience. Few could resist the allure of a young woman playing the central role in so solemn, sumptuous and anachronistic a ceremony.

For it seemed scarcely believable that in the middle of the egalitarian twentieth century there should be enacted this glittering pageant: that the Queen, in her intricately embroidered white satin dress and ermine-lined velvet robes, with the St Edward's Crown upon her head and the orb and sceptre in her hands, should be able to look forward to a long and glorious reign. Or that her four-year-old son, in his white satin suit and brilliantined hair, fidgeting between the shimmeringly-dressed figures of his grand-mother, now Queen Elizabeth the Queen Mother, and his aunt, Princess Margaret, would one day inherit that crown.

Notably absent from Queen Elizabeth II's Coronation was her grandmother, Queen Mary. The eighty-five-year-old Queen had died, less than three months before, on 24 March 1953.

During the last years of her life, Queen Mary had established herself as an apparently indestructible part of the national scene: she had become, as one observer put it, 'like St Paul's Cathedral'.[3] Indeed, there was about Queen Mary's lifestyle something of the grandeur, precision and wealth of detail of a Baroque cathedral.

By now Marlborough House had been fully restored to its pre-war glory: it was crammed with the treasures that she had spent a lifetime collecting. Seated in their midst, the old Queen herself looked not unlike some pains-takingly executed work of art. For there was an almost unreal perfection about Queen Mary's appearance: it was stylised to a degree. Everything – that elaborately coiffured head, those ropes of pearls, those lavish dresses – gave her, claims Osbert Sitwell, 'a particular sort of film-star glamour'.[4] Queen Mary looked flawless, impeccable, other-worldly.

But there was nothing ossified about her day-to-day life. Even in her eighties, her interest in the world about her was unimpaired. She still carried out her public engagements, she still visited exhibitions, she still scoured antique shops, she still attended courts for juvenile delinquents. The theatre remained one of her great loves. No musical was too rowdy; no play too shocking. The news that Queen Mary was in the box always heightened the atmosphere backstage. Invariably she came round to meet the actors.

On one occasion she visited the Aldwych Theatre to see Gertrude Lawrence in Daphne du Maurier's *September Tide*. Afterwards she passed slowly down the line of actors, until she reached Gertrude Lawrence. She had enjoyed the evening immensely, the Queen assured Miss Lawrence, but she had found it difficult to hear the ends of the sentences.

'Do you hear,' said Gertrude Lawrence brightly, turning to the rest of the cast, 'now you've all got to speak up.'

'Not all of them,' said Queen Mary firmly, 'just you.'[5]

Less frequently, the Queen would dine out. With her would come a uniformed footman, carrying two half-bottles of hock. One of these he would open and, throughout the meal, would keep his mistress's glass – but hers alone – replenished. If she asked for the second bottle to be opened, her hosts would know that their dinner party had been a success.

Of great interest to Queen Mary were the visits of her great-grandson, Prince Charles. Whereas Princess Elizabeth and Princess Margaret, on similar visits, had never been allowed to touch any item in her collection, Prince Charles could play with certain selected objects. He retains a vivid picture of the dignified old lady sitting, 'always bolt upright',[6] either in her drawing-room at Marlborough House or in the back of the Daimler when she took him for drives in Richmond Park. It must have been a source of great pleasure and comfort for this royal matriarch to know that there was now an heir in the fourth generation.

The death of her son, George VI, marked the beginning of the end for Queen Mary. She had already outlived two of her sons – Prince John and the Duke of Kent – and now there was a third, King George VI. She had mourned the passing of four British sovereigns, and her granddaughter, Queen Elizabeth II, was to be the sixth sovereign to reign in her lifetime. As in Queen Mary's youth, Britain was once more ruled by a queen. Ever conscious of her dynastic obligations, the old Queen lost no time in paying homage to her new sovereign. On the afternoon of the Queen's sudden return from East Africa, Queen Mary drove over to Clarence House. 'Her old Grannie and subject,' she said, 'must be the first to kiss Her hand.'[7]

So often, in the history of the House of Windsor, it is the women who are left behind, and few sights were more poignant than that of the three black-clad, heavily veiled queens – Queen Elizabeth II, the Queen Mother and Queen Mary – at the lying in state of King George VI's coffin in Westminster Hall.

Always methodical, Queen Mary set about making a new will and cataloguing the possessions which would now have to go to the new sovereign. And she let it be known that, in the event of her own death before the Coronation, no court mourning should be allowed to dim the splendour of the occasion. It was to be Queen Mary's last act of self-sacrifice for the monarchy to which she had devoted her life.

'There has not been a word of criticism of the grand old lady . . .' wrote 'Chips' Channon on Queen Mary's death. 'The world will be the poorer.'[8]

And so would the monarchy. Queen Mary, by her dignity, her high standards and her unwavering sense of duty, had imbued the throne with an awesome, almost irreproachable venerability.

'I wonder if you realise it,' a fellow guest had once remarked to Osbert Sitwell as the Queen, blazing with jewels, had led the way out of the dining-room, 'but after that old lady has gone, you'll never see anything like this, or like her again.'[9]

He might well have been right but one wonders if Queen Elizabeth II – whose character owes so much to Queen Mary, whose reserved public manner can be so like Queen Mary's and whose features, as she ages, are beginning to resemble Queen Mary's – will not, in her old age, give off something of the aura of this indomitable old Queen.

If Queen Elizabeth II's grandmother, Queen Mary, had been symbolic of the sort of monarchy which was passing into history, the Queen's sister, Princess Margaret, represented the royal family's more informal, more adventurous, more emancipated attitudes. Twenty-two at the time of the Queen's Coronation, Princess Margaret was very much a young woman of her time. There was nothing stuffy about her. Small, attractive, always fashionably dressed, she was something of a trend-setter. Her tastes – for popular music, for night clubs, for the theatre, for current catch phrases, for *outré* company, even for smoking in public through a long cigarette-holder – made her far more newsworthy than her more conventional elder sister. At times it was easy to forget that this *soignée*, effervescent and articulate young woman was a princess.

But she was. And it was said that one forgot it at one's cost. For Princess Margaret, in spite of her somewhat unconventional attitudes, was very conscious of being a king's daughter. Yet since the death of her father, her royal role had not been very clearly defined. Whereas some sort of shape can be given to the lives of even the most amorphous of princes by putting them into one of the armed services, a princess – particularly an unmarried princess – needs to have an especially strong sense of royal direction if she is not to lose her way. As the younger sister, free of the disciplines and responsibilities of future sovereignty, Princess Margaret had always been indulged; this indulgence had left her without any clear sense of identity. How best could this modern, independent-minded young woman fit into the ancient, tradition-bound institution of monarchy? Would it be possible for her to have her cake and eat it?

None of this is to say that Princess Margaret did not – and has not since – carried out her full share of public engagements. The aura of glamour in which she moved always tended to obscure her more mundane, less newsworthy activities: her association with nursing, with girl guides, with various regiments; her visits to schools, her lunches with mayors, her tours of factories. The public preferred to see her as the press pictured her: as a royal maverick. 'I wonder what will happen to her?' mused the ubiquitous 'Chips' Channon on one occasion. 'There is already a Marie Antoinette aroma about her.'[10] It was not so much a frivolous, ill-fated, Marie Antoinette aroma as an unresolved, Edward VIII aroma. For Princess Margaret was then on the threshold of a career that has been plagued by that recurring royal dilemma: personal happiness versus public responsibility.

The first test came at the beginning of Queen Elizabeth II's reign. Princess Margaret let it be known that she wanted to marry Group Captain Peter Townsend, the Comptroller of her mother's household.

In many ways, it would have been a suitable, if somewhat unconventional, match. Peter Townsend was very much part of the royal establishment. During the course of the last decade, first as equerry to the late King George VI and then as Comptroller to the Queen Mother, Peter Townsend had endeared himself to the entire royal family by his good looks, his efficiency and his charm. That Princess Margaret should have fallen in love with this discreet and dependable royal servant is not surprising. Particularly after the death of her father, Townsend had provided the high-spirited Princess with a strong and steadying arm. It was true that he was almost sixteen years her senior and that his background was neither royal nor aristocratic but these were relatively minor considerations. Had not George V's daughter, Princess Mary, married a man fifteen years older? Indeed, it is an indication of the rapidity with which royal attitudes were changing that there were few objections (and these from the older generation at the Palace) to Peter Townsend on the grounds of birth or position. George VI would have baulked at the idea of his daughter marrying his equerry; George V would have forbidden it.

No, the chief objection to Group Captain Peter Townsend was the apparently insurmountable one: he had been party, albeit the innocent party, to a divorce. The rock on which Edward VIII's career had foundered in the 1930s looked no less immovable in the 1950s. The stage seemed set for one of history's repeat performances.

Both personally, and in her capacity as an anointed monarch and supreme governor of the Church of England, Queen Elizabeth II could not possibly countenance divorce. It was up to the monarchy, she reckoned, to set an example in the upholding of the sanctity of marriage. Yet she was devoted to her sister, fond of Townsend and anxious to see them happy. What was she to do?

What the Queen was obliged to do – for by the stipulations of the Royal Marriages Act no member of the family in line of succession to the throne under the age of twenty-five could marry without the sovereign's permission – was to consult her Prime Minister, Winston Churchill. He advised against the marriage. Parliament would never sanction it, he said. The attitude of the general public towards divorce might have been far more tolerant these days than it had been in Edward VIII's time but there was still a powerful section of the cabinet strongly opposed to it.

As the Queen was constitutionally bound to accept the advice of the Prime Minister, she had no choice but to refuse to give her consent. Her sister would have to wait until she turned twenty-five, at which time, if the Queen still disapproved, permission could be sought from parliament. To this Princess Margaret agreed. The royal family no doubt hoped, as they had hoped at the time of Edward VIII's obsession with Mrs Simpson, that the affair would simply run its course.

But the two-year wait resolved nothing. Princess Margaret was as determined as ever to marry Peter Townsend. And from out of the hurricane of rumour, speculation and gossip that followed the breaking of the news of the Princess's romance, one stark fact emerged: parliament would not sanction the marriage. If the Princess persisted in her plans, she would almost certainly lose her rank, her status and her income. All the luxuries, pleasures and privileges of a royal princess would have to be exchanged for the uncertainties and impecuniosity of life as Mrs Peter Townsend.

Still more serious was the moral issue. Princess Margaret was, and is, in spite of general opinion, a woman of strong religious convictions, great family loyalty and unquestioned royal dedication. She was as much concerned with the ethics as with the practicalities of the choice which now faced her. The attitude of the press and the public ranged from those who saw the affair as nothing more than the perfectly natural wish of a young girl to marry the man of her choice to those who saw it as a dereliction of duty, a flouting of the Church's teachings and a deplorable example to others.

In an influential leader *The Times* of 24 October 1955 threw its considerable weight behind those who opposed the match. Princess Margaret, it pointed out, was not just another young woman but the sister of the Queen 'in whom the people see their better selves reflected, and since part of their ideal is of family life, the Queen's family has its own part in the reflection. If the marriage which is now being discussed comes to pass, it is inevitable that this reflection becomes distorted.' *The Times* felt sure that people wished the Princess every possible happiness: 'not forgetting that happiness in the full sense is a spiritual state and that its most precious element may be the sense of duty done.'[11]

In the end, there was really no choice. If Princess Margaret did not want to become another Duke of Windsor, trailing a shameful aura of duty shirked and self indulged, she would have to renounce Peter Townsend. And so, on 31 October 1955, she issued a moving statement to that effect.

If, in some ways, the Townsend affair was an echo of the Abdication crisis, it also represented a last-ditch stand for the attitudes which made any possibility of divorce within the royal family unthinkable. Although it is highly unlikely that Prince Charles, as heir to the throne and future supreme governor of the Church, would have considered marrying a divorcee, divorce within the royal family itself has been accepted to an extent that would have appalled King George V and Queen Mary. Three of their grandchildren – the Earl of Harewood, Prince Michael of Kent and Princess Margaret herself – have either been divorced or married divorced people, or both; and if Prince Charles did not marry a divorcee, his wife – Britain's future Queen – is the daughter of divorced and remarried parents.

But at the time, and in the short term, Princess Margaret's sacrifice reflected great credit on herself and on the monarchy. The press was almost unanimous in its approval. *The Times* announced that 'all the peoples of the Commonwealth will feel gratitude to her for taking the selfless, royal way which, in their hearts, they expected of her.'[12]

As the years went by and this controversial princess – torn between her not unreasonable determination to lead her own life and her no less determined sense of royal duty – was forced to move through a cloud of press-inspired scandal worthy of Edward VII or Edward VIII, people blamed it all on her frustrated first romance. To any report of Princess Margaret's latest escapade there was always the stock answer: 'They should have let her marry Townsend.'

More than ever, as Queen Elizabeth II's reign unfolded, and the royal family expanded, did the monarchy come to resemble what George VI used to call a family firm. There was always some member on hand to carry out one or other public engagement; to become patron of this charity or colonel-in-chief of that regiment. In the early years, one of the most valuable of these members was the widowed Duchess of Kent.

In some ways, the tragic death of the mercurial Duke of Kent had been the making of his wife. Forced to carry on alone, the Duchess had realised her full potential. From being a home-loving, unpunctual, somewhat dependent personality, she developed into a conscientious, hard-working and self-assured member of the family. She began by taking over a great many of her late husband's responsibilities; from this she graduated into a fully involved member of the royal team, very much of a personality in her own right. Eventually, the Duchess of Kent was actively connected with well over a hundred different organisations.

One of her husband's positions which she took over with considerable relish and with which she was always closely associated, was the Presidency of the All England Lawn Tennis and Croquet Club. The Duchess had always been interested in tennis and for year after year she was a regular spectator

27 The adored Queen Mother with her grandchildren, Prince Charles and Princess Anne

26 The photograph chosen by Queen Elizabeth II as her private Christmas card in 1952 showing the Queen, the Duke of Edinburgh, Prince Charles and Princess Anne

28 The Queen with one of her corgis, Sugar

during Wimbledon fortnight. The sight of the beautiful, always fashionably dressed Duchess of Kent, presenting the prizes for the singles finals on the centre court, became a familiar part of the annual royal pattern. Her role has since been taken over by her daughter-in-law, the present Duchess of Kent.

Making the Duchess of Kent's contribution to the monarchy all the more admirable was the fact that for eleven years – from the death of the Duke in 1942 until the passing of the new Queen's Civil List in 1953 – she received no income whatsoever from the state.

On the death of the Duke of Kent, his annual income of £25,000 from the Civil List ceased. By an unfortunate oversight, no provision had been made, on the Civil List drawn up at the start of George VI's reign, for the widows of younger sons. No doubt parliament would have granted the widowed Duchess an allowance but it was considered inadvisable to apply for one in wartime. Nor, when the war ended and the country was plunged into its period of post-war austerity, was anything done about it. The time never seemed quite right. The result was that one of the most popular and publicly active members of the royal family was obliged to carry out her duties without any official income.

Nor did the Duchess of Kent (unlike the Duchess of Gloucester) have any personal fortune. She had inherited very little from her father, Prince Nicholas of Greece, and the late Duke of Kent had spent a great deal of the money bequeathed him by George V on his collection of antiques and paintings. He had left his home, Coppins, to his elder son and the rest of his inherited money was bound up in trust for his three children, Prince Edward, Princess Alexandra and Prince Michael. Both King George VI and Queen Mary (her annual income was £70,000) behaved very generously towards the widowed Duchess but charity can never take the place of an independent income.

There was only one thing that the Duchess of Kent could do: she had to sell her husband's collection of art treasures. The three-day auction at Christie's, in March 1947, realised over £92,000. The sum, the Duchess is afterwards reported to have said, hardly compensated for her humiliation. Nor, with three children to raise and educate, a large country home to run and a royal standard to be maintained (which included dressing with an elegance expected of her) could the Duchess's financial troubles be said to be over. In 1960 she was obliged to have another sale. Her celebrated Fabergé collection went under the hammer at Sotheby's.

So, for many years, the Duchess of Kent was obliged to practise the most rigid economy. Those girlhood days of impoverished exile in Paris now stood her in good stead. At the risk of appearing mean, she cut down on servants, entertaining, even everyday comforts. She is once reported to have removed the card from a bouquet of roses sent to her by Sir Malcolm Sargent, replaced it with one of her own, and then sent the roses round to old Princess

Marie Louise, who was ill. Very few realised that some of the clothes which the Duchess wore with such style and assurance were bought off-the-peg in department stores. She was the first woman in the family not to rely exclusively on couturier-designed clothes. That she remained the best-dressed among them says a great deal for her innate good taste.

Not until the Civil List was revised on the accession of Queen Elizabeth II was the Duchess granted an official allowance. A fund of £25,000 was put at the disposal of the Sovereign for the benefit of those members of the family who received no direct parliamentary grant. From this, the Duchess of Kent was given an annual allowance of £5,000. It was not much but it helped cover, as it was designed to do, the expenses incurred in the carrying out of her public engagements.

With the new reign, these engagements steadily increased. The royal family appreciated that in the Duchess of Kent they had a representative who was not only dignified and diligent but whose aura of glamour presented to the world yet another facet of a many-faceted monarchy. Not only at home but abroad, the Duchess's particular qualities were put to good use. Sometimes alone, sometimes accompanied by her elder son, the young Duke of Kent, or her daughter Princess Alexandra, she undertook official tours throughout the world.

Yet out of the public eye, the Duchess of Kent led a relatively simple life. Part of this was due, of course, to financial reasons; part to personal preference. For the Duchess was a complex, somewhat deceptive character. In spite of her glossy appearance and cosmopolitan air, she remained, at heart, a warm, kindly, almost unsophisticated woman. She liked to think of herself as 'cosy'.[13] She might have been very conscious of her royal lineage and had the usual royal knack of remaining always one stage removed but she was surprisingly modest and self-deprecating. More cultured, less of an outdoor type than the rest of the royal family, she nonetheless shared their knock-about brand of humour and avoidance of abstract or philosophic discussion. Her greatest pleasures still stemmed from family life: from her own children and from her many Continental relations.

The Duchess was an excellent mother. Her three children were raised simply, informally and with great affection. Princess Alexandra was the first British princess to enjoy an ordinary schooling: she attended a boarding school at Heathfield, near Ascot. In time, the Princess developed into a good-looking, engaging and accomplished member of the dynasty; very much her mother's daughter, even to the whimsical smile.

The young Duke of Kent went to Eton, to Le Rosay in Switzerland and on to Sandhurst. He was commissioned into the Royal Scots Greys. Prince Michael followed his brother to Eton and subsequently joined the 11th Hussars. As young men, their image was that of the conventional royal duke – fast cars, winter sports, girl friends – but both were dedicated professional soldiers and no less dedicated members of the royal team, always on hand for minor engagements.

All in all, the Kents were proving as valuable to the new Queen as any other members of the family. Each, in his or her own way, was fulfilling a different role in the new style of monarchy which had been evolving over the last half-century, and which was being perfected by Queen Elizabeth II.

But the going was not always smooth. The opening years of the new reign brought their share of troubles for the royal family. Once the assumption that the accession of a new queen would mean the dawn of a new age proved unfounded, a sense of disillusionment set in. It was deepened by the continuing loss of national prestige, and particularly by the Suez crisis of late 1956, in which the Queen became directly involved. She was criticised for remaining at the Goodwood races instead of returning to London to sign the proclamation calling out the army reserves. There was still more criticism of the manner in which she selected a new Conservative prime minister to replace Sir Anthony Eden, whose health had been broken by the strain of Suez. Faced with a choice between Harold Macmillan and 'Rab' Butler, the Queen took the advice of two elder statesmen, Lord Salisbury and Sir Winston Churchill, and chose Macmillan. This immediately laid her open to the accusation that she had allowed herself to be influenced by the old aristocratic order, that she was still very much part of what was coming to be called 'The Establishment'.

Indeed, with Britain on the threshold of the 'Swinging Sixties', Queen Elizabeth seemed to belong, in the eyes of her detractors, to an age that was passing. Her unadventurous clothes, her staid manner, her country interests, her colourless speeches, her schoolgirlish voice – all these came in for censure. Furthermore, she was accused of having no intellectual or cultural tastes. She was surrounded, it was claimed, by a tweedy, conventional, hopelessly old-fashioned entourage. The court, as Lord Altrincham put it in his celebrated tirade against the monarchy in the *National and English Review* of August 1957, 'has remained a tight little enclave of English ladies and gentlemen.'[14] Writing more, he implied, in sorrow than in anger, Lord Altrincham regretted that the Queen was not taking advantage of her unique position to establish herself as a more assertive, articulate and enlightened personality.

His views were publicly echoed by several others, including Malcolm Muggeridge. Letters to the *Daily Mirror* showed that four to one of the correspondents agreed with Lord Altrincham; a *Daily Mail* poll revealed a majority in favour of a less exclusive, less traditionally based royal household.

'She's a bit set in her ways,' summed up one observer. 'Maybe it's because of the position she's in. But I think she ought to mix more with people not in her own set.'[15]

It was even suggested that the Queen might be too sedate for her more dashing husband. There were rumours of a rift between the couple. It seemed confirmed when the Duke of Edinburgh set off on a four-month-long voyage on the royal yacht *Britannia* in the autumn of 1956. The Duke's answer to journalistic speculation about his married life was characteristic. 'Those bloody lies that you people print to make money,' he stormed. 'Those lies about how I'm never with my wife.'[16]

If the Duke's reaction to press intrusion was to rail against it, the Queen's was to protect herself from it. The relationship between the royal family and the press became increasingly uneasy during the 1950s. As social reporting, and long-lens photography, intruded ever more remorselessly into private lives, the Palace showed understandable signs of resentment. Still unsure of herself, still appalled by the frenzied media coverage of the Townsend affair, desperately anxious to preserve her own and her family's privacy, the Queen and her advisers tended to treat the press with great wariness. Their suspicions were justified. When, in a laudable effort to break new ground, the Queen sent Prince Charles first to a London day-school, Hill House, and then to his father's old school Cheam, in Berkshire, the press followed in full cry. So dense was the pack of newshounds during the Prince's first days at Hill House that the Queen was obliged to keep him home while her press secretary telephoned various editors, begging them to recall their representatives. And during the eighty-eight days of the Prince's first term at Cheam, newspapers carried no less than sixty-seven stories about him.

Small wonder that the Queen became increasingly protective, increasingly determined to keep her private life private. This, in turn, encouraged the public view of her as a remote, somewhat impregnable figure.

It was a pity that her subjects could not get some different views of their monarch: romping with her children, bantering with her husband, rocking on her heels at some joke, dishing out food for her frenetic corgis, chatting animatedly to stable boys, talking easily to prime ministers, bestowing honours with a smiling informality which would have astonished George V or even George VI. She could always, said those who knew her well, see the funny side of things.

And gradually, as her confidence grew, the Queen began to make changes. Her voice improved. 'She came across quite clear and with a vigour unknown in pre-Altrincham days,'[17] judged Harold Nicolson after listening to her Christmas broadcast of 1957. Another change that year was the televising of the Christmas message. No more than King George VI had the Queen enjoyed these annual radio broadcasts, but to appear on television was infinitely more nerve-racking. Yet she did it. And with each year her performance became more polished and more self-assured; her message delivered more convincingly.

In fact, television was developing into a two-way advantage for the Queen and her family. Not only at Christmas but on almost every occasion that a member of the royal family carried out some important public duty, the event was televised and brought into homes throughout the land. Every other day, housewives could see the Queen, the Duke of Edinburgh, the Queen Mother, Princess Margaret or other members busily fulfilling engagements that ranged from triumphant state occasions to modest ribbon-cutting. In turn, the family was able to watch, in conditions of complete privacy and relaxation, the sort of programme that everyone else in the land was watching. It exposed many of them, for the first time in their lives, to the honestly-expressed views, and to an approximation of the daily life, of ordinary people. A cabinet minister was once intrigued by the Queen's animated description of an all-in wrestling match she had seen on television. 'It was interesting to hear what a vivid description she gave of the whole scene, writhing herself, twisting and turning, completely relaxed.'[18]

By this time the Queen had already initiated a new way of meeting, if not exactly ordinary people, people to whom she would not normally have had a chance of speaking. She began to give small, informal luncheon parties to which she invited an assortment of guests: newspaper editors, actors, clergymen, broadcasters, headmasters, businessmen, writers, industrialists. While their conversation would take her into a different, much wider world, they would find themselves impressed by her ease and friendliness. Often other members of the family – Princess Margaret or later Princess Anne – would be at the table.

The innovation might have been far from daring but by no stretch of the imagination could one visualise King George V in happy lunchtime conversation with some male ballet dancer or Queen Mary swopping anecdotes with the president of a trades union.

At about the same time the Queen put an end to the long-established, highly formalised and infinitely more tedious way of meeting people: the presentation parties at which hundreds of well-born or well-heeled debutantes would file past her in order to 'come out' – to be officially launched on their London 'season'. By the late 1950s these socially divisive presentation parties struck an extremely false note in Britain's increasingly egalitarian society. By abolishing them, the monarchy continued its policy of distancing itself from the old ruling classes.

With the abandonment of the presentation parties, the number of garden parties was increased. At these less formal occasions, the Queen was able to meet a much wider cross-section of people. With some eight thousand guests being invited to each of these three parties in the grounds of Buckingham Palace (and one at Holyroodhouse in Edinburgh) the Queen, trailing a selection of her relations – the men in morning dress, the women in flowered hats and chiffons – could exchange a few words with members of the public who had been invited because of their contribution to national life rather than for their social status. In earlier days, when royal garden parties had been strictly 'society' occasions, George V would have known almost all the guests; nowadays, almost every face is new to the Queen.

If none of these changes could be called revolutionary, they were indicative of the pace at which the Queen was prepared to modernise the monarchy. No less than her father, King George VI, was Queen Elizabeth II conscious of the delicacy of the balance that had to be struck between the mysticism of the monarchy and the public accessibility of the monarch. It would be wiser, at this early stage, to hold a traditional position: to remain somewhat aloof, to adhere to the established values, to screen at least some of Bagehot's forbidden daylight. All going well, the Queen could expect a long reign; it would be better to let things evolve gradually. In any case, hers was not a nature to court popularity or to follow current trends. If people were looking for something more dynamic, something more innovative from the monarchy, there were other members of her family on hand to supply them; not least of all her consort, the Duke of Edinburgh, whom she had created Prince of the United Kingdom and Northern Ireland in 1957.

The role of a queen's consort is a loosely-defined one. Whereas the wife of a king automatically becomes queen and is crowned and anointed beside him, the husband of a queen regnant has no constitutional powers, no official position, no clearly prescribed job. His role is very much what he makes of it. The husbands of reigning queens have ranged from those who rule as joint sovereigns to those who make no national contribution whatsoever.

The consort with whom Prince Philip is most frequently compared is, of course, Queen Victoria's husband, Prince Albert. Hard-working, well-intentioned, and capable, Prince Albert certainly made the most of his position. By the time of his premature death, he was king in all but name. Politically, Prince Albert wielded far more power and influence than does Prince Philip, for not only did he have access to the 'boxes' (which Prince Philip does not) but it was he who defined the ideal of constitutional monarchy – of lifting the Crown above politics. The monarchy which Queen Elizabeth II inherited – a monarchy shorn of political power but dedicated to the service of all the people – was very much Prince Albert's creation.

At the very start of her reign the Queen regulated her husband's position by issuing a statement to the effect that he would henceforth 'hold and enjoy Place, Pre-eminence and Precedence next to her Majesty.' This ensured that her consort would never be subjected to the sort of crude elbowing out of the way to which the young Prince Albert had been subjected by Queen

Victoria's envious male relations. Five years later, on the 100th anniversary of the creation of Prince Albert as Prince Consort, Queen Elizabeth II gave her husband the title of Prince to replace the title of Prince of Greece and Denmark relinquished when he became a British subject ten years before.

But with the job itself, as Michael Parker, Prince Philip's private secretary once put it, 'starting from the very beginning, when there was nothing at all, he had to build it up brick by brick . . . He had to think it out alone.'[19]

Prince Philip's main task was, and is, the task of any royal consort, male or female: to accompany, encourage and support the sovereign, both in public and in private. This he does admirably. The Queen could not have hoped for a more impressive-looking husband. With his tall, upright figure, his handsome, clear-cut features and his blue-eyed, penetrating glance (rendered penetrating, it must be admitted, by contact lenses) Prince Philip has a natural air of command. More assured, more articulate, more gregarious than the Queen, he is of inestimable help to her on public occasions. He can always be relied upon to crack jokes, to ask intelligent questions, to prevent things getting bogged down. He has a spontaneity and lightness of touch notably lacking in his more reserved wife. The Prince can get away with the sort of off-the-cuff remark that would be, not only unseemly, but positively insulting from a reigning sovereign.

There are times, though, when he does *not* get away with them; when his efforts to prick pomposity are too crude by half. 'Where did you get those?' he once asked a dazzlingly bemedalled Brazilian general. 'In the war? I didn't know Brazil was in the war that long.'

'At least, Sir,' came the dry reply, 'I didn't get them from marrying my wife.'[20]

In private, Prince Philip remains master of the house, playing the accepted husbandly role. It is he who makes the decisions on things like running the estates or buying the cars. As the Queen dislikes formal evening engagements, Prince Philip sallies quite happily forth to attend regimental dinners or gatherings of scientists while she stays at home. Unlike the Queen, he is only too ready to stand up in the drifting cigar smoke to deliver one of his hectoring after-dinner speeches.

But for a man of Prince Philip's abounding energies, acute mind and strong opinions, a merely supportive role would never have been enough. He needed to make his own mark. This he has done in no uncertain fashion. The public image of Prince Philip – as a hearty, forceful, outspoken, arrogant and highly intelligent man, intolerant of red tape and outmoded traditions – is very largely an accurate one. No member of the royal family during the twentieth century has done more to give the monarchy a progressive air; none of them have seemed more in touch with ordinary people. 'I haven't come here to see your bloody mayors. I came to meet the dockers,'[21] is the sort of remark that tends to win him public approval. That one of the mayors happened to be a docker and the other a railway worker was neither here nor there.

No one could deny that Prince Philip – piloting his own helicopter, driving himself in fast cars, jetting to conferences half-way across the world, excelling in sports like squash, skin-diving and sailing – is representative of the age in which he lives. Like Edward VIII in his days as Prince of Wales, Prince Philip is the monarchy's answer to the modern world.

The list of his independent activities is formidable. As well as making overseas tours as the Queen's representative (he has seen countless flags of independence run up and countless heads of state buried) Prince Philip has toured on behalf of his own innumerable projects. There are few countries in the world that he has not visited. Each year he travels about 75,000 miles; each year he delivers about eighty major speeches, written, jokes and all, by himself. His public interests are wide-ranging, but it is in the fields of conservation, wild life, youth, science, industry and technology that he is most deeply involved. With the passing years he has developed into a self-appointed, one-man prodder of the national will. In speech after speech he exhorts his fellow countrymen, particularly industrialists and businessmen, to work harder, to plan more efficiently and, in the phrase that has come to typify his straight-talking style, to 'pull their fingers out'.

His tactlessness, his tendency to put his foot in it, his running battle with the press – all these are now part of the Prince Philip legend. There are numerous examples of his crass remarks and explosive reactions. 'As so often happens,' he once said with cheerful frankness, 'I discovered that it would have been better to keep my trap shut.'[22] This honesty, this self-awareness, this readiness to admit his mistakes is one of his saving graces. And there are many more. His bark is much worse than his bite. He is not just, as he suspects many people think him to be, 'an uncultured polo-playing clot'.[23] The hearty façade screens an incisive mind, an interest in the arts (he is an enthusiastic painter) a concern for spiritual and religious matters and a great kindness.

His dedication to his job – the serving of the monarchy – is absolute. 'You might ask whether all this rushing about is to any purpose,' he once wrote to his biographer, Basil Boothroyd. 'Am I just doing it to make it look as if I'm earning my keep, or has it any national value?'[24] He clearly thinks that it has. And he is right. Obsessed by making what he calls a 'sensible contribution', Prince Philip has made a far greater contribution to the monarchy, the country and the Commonwealth than was ever expected of him. The zeal and energy with which he throws himself into his task are apparently inexhaustible. 'I gave up trying to stop him years ago,'[25] says the Queen smilingly. Besides, asks the Prince in that self-depreciating manner, what else would he do? 'Sit around and knit?'[26]

The remark comes as a reminder that all his efforts are, in a sense, voluntary: that there is really no need for him to make so immense a contribution.

In the final analysis, members of the royal family can do as much, or as little, as they choose. They can turn down proposed engagements; they can keep their commitments to a minimum; they need initiate nothing. 'There's no reason,' once said a member of Prince Philip's staff, gazing out across some sunlit beach, 'why he shouldn't spend most of his time lying around in places like this.'[27]

In the early years of the Queen's reign, until he had fully adjusted himself to his role, the frustration of having no real job sometimes showed. It was, perhaps, in order to get out of the Queen's shadow that Prince Philip went off on those long journeys alone; this, in turn, gave rise to the rumours of a rift between them. But there was no real evidence of a rift, neither then nor since. On the contrary, the relationship between husband and wife is close and affectionate. Their differences, in style and temperament, are complementary. Where he is reckless, she is circumspect; where he is abrasive, she is compassionate; where he is trenchant, she is diplomatic. If he has the more philosophic turn of mind, she has the more sensitive. Both are sensible, well-informed, honest-to-goodness people. That they have been referred to, satirically, as 'Keith and Brenda' – the archetypal, middle-class, middle-brow couple – would not bother either of them unduly: royals have had to put up with worse names than this.

Although the couple sleep in separate bedrooms, they see a great deal of each other during the course of an ordinary working day. At weekends, or on holiday at Sandringham or Balmoral, they share many interests and activities. Both are outdoor people; both love country pursuits. To see the Queen's normally grave face break into a dazzling smile as her husband makes some quip, is to appreciate the warmth of feeling and depth of understanding between them.

On 19 February 1960, ten years after the birth of Princess Anne, the couple had another child, a son who was given the name of Prince Philip's father, Andrew. And on 10 March 1964 came a third son, whom they called Edward. Before then, however, the Queen had given public proof of her appreciation and love for her husband. She declared that, in future, while the name of her House and Family would remain 'Windsor', the surname of her children and their descendants would be 'Mountbatten-Windsor'.

'The Queen has always wanted,' she explained, 'without changing the name of the Royal House established by her grandfather, to associate the name of her husband with her own and his descendants.' The idea, she added touchingly, had been in her mind for a long time; it lay 'close to her heart'.[28]

In few ways did Princess Margaret illustrate more vividly the monarchy's continuously changing image than in her choice of a husband. For in spite of her reputation as a colourful, unorthodox and emancipated princess, the announcement of her engagement, on 26 February 1960, took the public by surprise.

For one thing, she had kept the affair secret; for another, the young man's background and lifestyle were, to say the least, unusual in a royal suitor. Born on 7 March 1930, Antony Armstrong-Jones was the son of a three-times married Welsh barrister; his mother, sister of the designer Oliver Messel, had remarried an Irish peer, the Earl of Rosse. After a conventional education – Eton and Cambridge – Antony Armstrong-Jones had set himself up in an unconventional career: as a photographer in Pimlico. Talented, hard-working and successful, moving in a world of advertising, fashion photography, theatrical designing, pop music, informal parties, casual love affairs, Armstrong-Jones was a far cry from the sort of landed aristocrat whom Princess Margaret would ordinarily have been expected to marry. He was certainly not another Viscount Lascelles, husband of King George V's daughter, Princess Mary; nor did he have anything in common with Princess Margaret's previous escorts.

'There is,' as *The Times* put it, 'no recent precedent for the marriage of one so near to the Throne outside the ranks of international royalty and the British peerage.'[29] And even the *New Statesman* decided that the young man's qualifications for becoming a member of the royal family had to be judged 'with a leniency which only a few years before would have been unthinkable.'[30]

But there it was. The couple were patently fond of each other, they shared many tastes and interests, they were both lively, talented, sophisticated. And if Armstrong-Jones was drawn as much by the Princess's dazzling position as by her many attractions, who can blame him? And who can blame her, at the vulnerable age of twenty-nine (and having just heard that Peter Townsend, whom she had been seeing intermittently, was to marry a Belgian heiress) for wanting to cock a snook at convention by marrying this handsome, intelligent and engaging young man?

The royal family, swallowing hard, accepted Princess Margaret's choice. There was not much else that they could do. In any case, both the Queen and the Queen Mother were fond of Armstrong-Jones and they were only too pleased that the ghost of the Townsend affair was being laid to rest. And if the young man did not quite match up to the sporting, soldierly image of the rest of the royal menfolk, he seemed ready enough, in these early days, to adapt to their way of life.

The family either did not think, or did not want to think, of the possible pitfalls that lay ahead for the couple. Princess Margaret, for all her free-and-easy attitudes, was still very much a princess: indulged, imperious, used to getting her own way. Antony Armstrong-Jones was an equally independent personality: an energetic, ambitious and successful career-man, no less accustomed to leading his own life. The truth was that Princess Margaret would have been far better off with someone like Prince Philip, a man totally dedicated to helping her in her royal calling, or with someone like Princess Alexandra of Kent's future husband, Angus Ogilvy, who was content to leave his wife to get on with her public engagements while he concentrated on his own career.

There is, as Princess Margaret's niece, Princess Anne, was later to say, 'a special difficulty' about the status of a princess's husband. 'After all, we normally still think of the husband as number one and the wife as number two, whereas in the case of a royal female who has public duties to perform, it's rather the other way round.'[31]

About these future marital hazards the general public were blissfully unaware. They were only too delighted that the bewitching Princess Margaret, cheated of happiness with Peter Townsend, had found it at last with this man of the people. For, in its customarily perverse way, the public both admired the bride for being royal and the bridegroom for being a commoner. The wedding, in Westminster Abbey on 6 May 1960, was, in spite of some cold-shouldering on the part of various less enlightened Continental royals, an occasion for great public enthusiasm. The date happened to be the fiftieth anniversary of the death of Edward VII and the twenty-fifth anniversary of George V's Silver Jubilee. The always fashion-conscious bride wore a dramatically simple, full-skirted dress of white silk organza; the bridegroom, as though to underline his non-royal, non-Establishment status, wore morning dress instead of the more customary uniform. Both looked small, *soignés*, strikingly attractive.

Few could doubt, as the couple sailed away on the royal yacht *Britannia* for a honeymoon in the fashionable Caribbean, that the marriage marked yet another milestone in the evolution of the monarchy. Together this quasi-bohemian, quasi-intellectual couple bridged the gap between the monarchy and the nation's cultural life, bringing it closer to the professional contemporary world. They were the monarchy's contribution to the 'Swinging Sixties'.

The Royal Firm

IF QUEEN ELIZABETH II had any doubts about the way in which her heir should be raised, she could have had none whatsoever about the way in which he should not be raised. Edward VII and Edward VIII had provided two regrettable examples of what could go wrong with the upbringing of eldest sons. The force-feeding methods applied to Queen Victoria's heir and the combination of unimaginative schooling and naval discipline applied to George V's heir had produced unhappily similar results: both princes had emerged as ill-educated, immature, unresolved young men, obsessed with fashion and hungry for pleasure. Different in some ways, these two Princes of Wales had led similarly frustrated and unfulfilled lives.

In the main, two things ensured that Prince Charles – created Prince of Wales at the age of nine in 1958 – would not follow this same road. He was raised in a warm and loving atmosphere, and he was given as normal an education as possible. Except for the presence of his undeniably masculine father, Prince Charles spent his early years very largely in the company of devoted women: the Queen, the Queen Mother, Princess Margaret, his nurses and his governess. His closest companion was his sister Princess Anne. Of the two royal children, it was Princess Anne who was the more forceful, extrovert personality. Prince Charles was more like his mother, and like his grandfather, King George VI – shy, retiring, self-effacing.

In an effort, not only to counteract this feminine atmosphere but to raise the Prince in a relatively natural fashion, the Queen and Prince Philip decided that the traditional pattern of royal upbringing must be changed: not for Prince Charles (nor for his sister and later his two brothers) that circumscribed, somewhat cosseted education at the hands of carefully selected tutors. They must grow up, as much as possible, like other children.

It was a bold decision. That it had been made, very largely, by Prince Philip was not surprising. Yet he was fully alive to the difficulties. In an eminently sensible way, the Prince once outlined his views on the education of his children. 'People talk about a normal upbringing,' he said to Basil

Boothroyd. 'What is a normal upbringing? What you really mean is: was I insisting that they should go through all the disadvantages of being brought up in the way other people are brought up? Precisely that – disadvantages. There's always this idea about treating them exactly like other children. In fact it means they're treated much worse, because they're known by name and association . . . It's all very well to say they're treated the same as everybody else, but it's impossible.'[1]

Yet Prince Philip felt that the risk was worth taking; but only with the co-operation of his children. For all his strong-mindedness, Prince Philip was not a strict disciplinarian in the mould of George V. On the contrary, he was tolerant and understanding. The royal children always felt that they could go to both their parents for advice and sympathy. Prince Charles's system of education was not imposed upon him: he was consulted about it at every step. That this sensitive boy of above average intelligence never resented being subjected to the rigours and challenges of open competition at a place like Gordonstoun says a great deal for the relationship between parents and son. 'My parents were marvellous in this way,' claimed Prince Charles. 'They'd outline all the possibilities, and in the end it was up to you.'[2]

One could hardly imagine such sentiments coming from the lips of either of the two previous Princes of Wales.

So Prince Charles set a precedent by being the first heir-apparent ever to go away to school. In the decade between 1957 and 1967 he progressed from being a day-boy at Hill House school, to being a boarder at Cheam preparatory school, to joining his father's old school, Gordonstoun, broken by a couple of terms at Timbertop in Australia. Granted that they were all schools for privileged children and not the state schools urged by some Socialist politicians, the Prince's education did allow him to compete on equal terms and to develop some normal relationships with other boys. The result was that he emerged far better educated and far better adjusted than any recent heir to the throne.

'I suppose I could have gone to a local comprehensive or the local grammar but I am not sure it would have done me much good,' the Prince said afterwards. 'I think a public school gives you a good deal of self-discipline and experience and responsibility; and it is this responsibility which is worthwhile. In these times, the organisation I work for is called into question; it is not taken for granted as it used to be. One has to be far more professional at it than one ever used to be. And I hope that my education and upbringing and all these various schools and establishments will in some way equip me for this role.'[3]

Not until he went up to Cambridge, at which – unlike any other heir to the throne – he won a place by his own right, did the Prince of Wales begin to show signs of the alert and agreeable personality he has become. Until then he had been a shy, staid, serious-minded youngster, with none of the flair of his two predecessors. Walter Bagehot's dark warnings against the temptations which lay in wait for Princes of Wales ('All the world and the glory of it, whatever is most seductive, has always been offered to the Prince of Wales of his day . . .'[4]) were unnecessary in the case of this latest Prince of Wales. Far from being the usual pleasure-seeking royal rebel, Prince Charles was a conscientious prince and a dutiful son: 'happier,' as he once touchingly put it, 'at home than anywhere else.'[5]

By opting for Cambridge, the Prince was following a family tradition. In the course of the previous century or so, King Edward VII, his ill-fated son Prince Eddy, King George VI and his brother Prince Henry, Duke of Gloucester had all been to Trinity College, Cambridge. Unlike them, however, Prince Charles insisted on living in college and on taking a degree. And, again unlike them, he applied himself to his three-year-long course of study with a dedication and a success that had been notably lacking in his predecessors. Having read archaeology, anthropology and later history, Prince Charles was the first Prince of Wales to win a University degree.

To the extra-curricular activities of University life, Prince Charles applied himself with equal dedication. He joined the Madrigal Society, playing his cello in public; he contributed to an undergraduate magazine; he took part in amateur dramatics, notably the Trinity revues, diverting the world with a picture of himself sitting in a dustbin; he became noted for his imitations of those manic-voiced radio comedians, the Goons; he even attended, incognito, a student demonstration. 'I do try to understand what they're getting at,' was his characteristic comment on the demonstrating students, 'but I can't help feeling that a lot of it is purely for the sake of change, and for the sake of doing something to change things – which, from my point of view, is pointless.'[6]

And if these extra-mural activities seemed a trifle effete, the Prince could always point to his sporting achievements. Fishing, shooting and polo were his passions; in 1968 he won a half-blue for representing Cambridge at polo.

Hand in hand with this broadening of the Prince's horizons went an increasing awareness of his royal position and obligations. Prince Charles had not been forced too early to play his royal role; only gradually was he drawn into the performance of what the Master of Trinity, Lord Butler, testily referred to as 'balcony jobs'.[7] He had driven in various carriage processions, appeared on the Palace balcony and rewarded waiting crowds with a few words, but not until he turned eighteen, on 14 November 1966, when he became eligible to succeed to the throne in his own right and was made Counsellor of State, did Prince Charles begin to make formal public appearances. He attended his first Opening of Parliament in 1967, taking the heir's traditional place on the sovereign's right. In the following year he was formally invested as a Knight of the Garter. He attended his first Buckingham Palace garden party, he gave his first radio interview, he made his first television appearance. But his most important public function came in the summer of 1969 when, at the age of twenty, he was invested as Prince of Wales at Caernarvon Castle.

Whereas, fifty-eight years before, the seventeen-year-old Prince Edward had simply been taken to Caernarvon to be presented, in his 'preposterous rig', to the Welsh people, Prince Charles underwent a far more thorough course of preparation. But the underlying motive was equally political. Anglo-Welsh unity was no more assured in 1969 than it had been in 1911. In fact, the fires of Welsh nationalism were raging far more fiercely then than before. To help, not only to contain them but to prepare the Prince for his Investiture, he was sent for one term to study Welsh at the University College of Wales, Aberystwyth.

This bold experiment made precious little difference to Welsh nationalist feeling. Plans for the Investiture had to go forward in the face of protests in parliament, a rash of anti-English slogans and defacements and, finally, the horror of exploding bombs. Through it all, the Prince remained astonishingly calm. By his unaffected manner, his patently honest intentions and the diligence with which he applied himself to learning the Welsh language, Prince Charles overcame a great deal of resentment. In the end – for Welsh nationalism was a minority sentiment and few can resist the glamour of a royal occasion – the Investiture was a resounding success. 'It was a far greater triumph than we had a right to expect,' claimed George Thomas, Secretary of State for Wales, to the Queen. 'He really was the Prince Charming.'[8]

If, in his military uniform, ermine-trimmed surcoat and golden coronet, Prince Charles did not quite match the good looks and romantic air of the previous Prince of Wales, he struck observers as being an eminently more mature, intelligent and good-natured young man. He was also more happily attuned to his place in the world. Not plagued by insecurities, not embarrassed by homage, not ashamed of his status, as the future King Edward VIII had been, Prince Charles responded to the ceremony with due solemnity.

But he was not prepared to take himself too seriously. As he knelt before the Queen to intone his oath of fealty – 'I Charles, Prince of Wales, do become your liege man in life and limb and of earthly worship, and faith and truth I will bear unto you to live and die against all manner of folks' – mother and son were seen to exchange relieved, amused, affectionate smiles.

Throughout these years, the family of Princess Marina, Duchess of Kent, was multiplying. In the summer of 1961 her eldest son, the tall, twenty-five-year-old Prince Edward, Duke of Kent, married Katharine Worsley, only daughter of Sir William Worsley, wealthy Yorkshire landowner and Lord Lieutenant of North Riding. Earlier reservations about the match – the Duke

29 The royal family at the funeral of Princess Marina in 1968. In the foreground, from the left: the Duchess of Kent, the Duke of Kent, Princess Alexandra, Angus Ogilvy, Prince Michael of Kent

30 The Queen at her most relaxed, with her horses

31 The Prince of Wales, flanked by the Queen and Prince Philip, at his Investiture at Caernarvon Castle in 1969

was some three years younger than his bride and she, like the young Lady Elizabeth Bowes-Lyon, baulked at the idea of a life of royal obligations – proved groundless. The blonde, beautiful, serenely mannered young Duchess of Kent quickly established herself as one of the most accomplished members of the family. 'It can't be easy, marrying into *this* family,'[9] once remarked one of its number; for the young Duchess of Kent, it seems to have proved all too easy.

The couple, whose homes are York House, St James's Palace (once the home of the Duke's father and grandfather) and Anmer Hall, near Sandringham, have three children: George, Earl of St Andrews, born in the year after their marriage; Lady Helen Windsor, born in 1964; and Lord Nicholas Windsor, born in 1970, the first royal baby to be born in hospital.

As a serving soldier in the Royal Scots Dragoon Guards, the young Duke of Kent eventually came up against one of those perennial royal problems: whether a Prince of the Blood should be involved in serious fighting. Early in 1971, soon after his regiment had been posted to Northern Ireland, the Duke was hastily withdrawn. It was not so much that the authorities feared the risking of his life; what bothered them was the inadvisability of a member of the royal family becoming involved in what was tantamount to a civil war, aggravated by the possibility of the Duke being kidnapped by the IRA.

'The fact that I am a member of the royal family makes no difference whatsoever,' the Duke is reported to have argued. 'I have a job to do, like anyone else in the Army.'[10] But he was overruled.

Due, in part, to such frustrations, the Duke of Kent left the army. In 1975 he embarked on another career, so becoming one of that new generation of princes prepared to go out and earn their own livings. It was a significant step forward. Not until after the Second World War did working for one's living come to be regarded as one of the essentials of a truly fulfilled and dignified life. As late as the 1930s few well-born young men would have felt it necessary to justify their existence by doing a day's work. Certainly, no prince would have felt it. But by the 1970s, the idea of a prince leading the sort of self-indulgent life that Edward VII had led, or even the countrified sort of life led by George V, before they became kings, was out of the question.

Appreciating this, the Duke of Kent joined the British Overseas Trade Board where he soon established a reputation as a shrewd, knowledgeable and hardworking promoter of British technical skills abroad. And although the Duke's busy career is a far cry from the sort of protected, well-ordered, uncompetitive life led by the princes of a previous generation, he is still expected to fulfil various royal commitments. Both the Duke and Duchess of Kent play their part on state occasions, represent the Queen abroad, and carry out numerous public engagements.

The Duke of Kent's sister, Princess Alexandra, also married a commoner. In 1963, at the age of twenty-six, the graceful, good-looking, lop-sidedly smiling Princess married Angus Ogilvy, second son of the twelfth Earl of Airlie. The match again illustrated the closeness of the bonds between the royal family and those who serve them; for Angus Ogilvy's grandmother had been Queen Mary's close friend and lady-in-waiting, Mabell, Countess of Airlie, while his father was for many years Lord Chamberlain to Queen Elizabeth the Queen Mother.

At the time of the marriage, Angus Ogilvy was well established in the City, a company director holding something like fifty directorships. A mature, independent, well-adjusted man, Ogilvy expected neither wealth nor title nor quasi-royal status from the marriage. Although he sometimes accompanies his wife on tours abroad or official engagements at home, he is quite content to let her get on with her royal obligations while he gets on with his business career. At present he is chiefly concerned with his work as adviser-director at Sotheby's, the celebrated auctioneers.

'I don't bore her with my daily routine and she doesn't bore me with hers,'[11] is his frank summing-up of their marital arrangement.

By all accounts, their private life is equally successful. Princess Alexandra is as engaging and spontaneous a personality at home as she is in public. They live in Thatched House Lodge in Richmond Park and have two children, a son born in 1964 and a daughter born in 1966. These great-grandchildren of King George V are known simply as Mr James Ogilvy and Miss Marina Ogilvy.

This new generation was a source of great joy to their grandmother who, on the marriage of her eldest son, had reverted to her girlhood title of Princess Marina. The title of Dowager Duchess of Kent would have sat very oddly on the still youthful-looking Princess Marina. Her son's marriage brought another change as well. Princess Marina handed over her old home Coppins to the newly-married pair (who subsequently sold it) and moved into an apartment in Kensington Palace. This she shared with her youngest, as yet unmarried son, Prince Michael.

In no sense, though, did this move mark a retirement from public life. From Kensington Palace Princess Marina set out on overseas tours, public engagements and private appointments. Often she was to be seen, quite alone, walking her dog in Kensington Gardens. She used to enjoy telling the story of the American tourist who, armed with a camera, once approached her in the gardens; assuming that he was about to ask her to pose for a picture, she was highly amused when he asked her if she would be good enough to take a photograph of him, with his wife and sister. For, no more than her elegance or her sweetness of nature, did Princess Marina's sense of fun ever desert her.

She died, of a brain tumour, at the age of sixty-one on 27 August 1968. On the night before she was buried, her husband's body was taken from the crypt of St George's Chapel to be buried, as she had always wished it to be, in the royal family's private burial ground at Frogmore. This 'dazzling pair', as 'Chips' Channon once called them, now lie side by side under the green lawns and spreading trees below Windsor Castle.

'I want to show,' said Queen Elizabeth II from New Zealand in 1953, in the course of the first Christmas broadcast ever made outside Britain, 'that the Crown is not merely an abstract symbol of our unity but a personal and living bond between you and me.'[12]

In the decades that have passed since that triumphant Coronation tour (it was the first time that a British sovereign had travelled round the world) the Queen has proved as good as her word. More than any previous British monarch has she established herself as 'a personal and living bond' between Crown and people. She takes her role as Head of the Commonwealth very seriously indeed. Those who have worked with her, or who know her well, claim that Queen Elizabeth II regards the upholding of the ideals of the Commonwealth as one of her most important trusts. 'She has great faith in the work she can do for the Commonwealth,'[13] noted one of her prime ministers. Indeed, the Commonwealth is the one sphere in which the Queen has actually managed to extend the monarchy's influence. Just as her great-grandfather, King Edward VII, won his somewhat inflated reputation as the supreme royal diplomat, so has Queen Elizabeth II won a far more richly deserved reputation as a dedicated and influential Head of the Commonwealth.

Yet the Commonwealth remains a bewilderingly amorphous institution. Its forty or so members range from tiny islands to vast sub-continents; its people from the most primitive to the most highly civilised individuals; its forms of government from the most simple to the most sophisticated; it embraces almost every race, religion and culture on earth. Some of these countries are republics with presidents as heads of state. Some are monarchies with kings of their own. Some countries, such as New Zealand, recognise the Queen as head of state as well as head of the Commonwealth: so that she is Queen of New Zealand at the same time as being Queen of Great Britain.

All in all, the Commonwealth is a very different institution from the Empire once presided over by King Edward VII. Two things only now link this assortment of territories. One is an association, at some time or other in the past, with Britain; the other is the recognition of the Queen as their Head. The Crown, as the Queen herself once put it, 'is a human link between all peoples who owe allegiance to me – an allegiance of mutual love and respect and never of compulsion.'[14]

It is then, as this 'human link' that the Queen so tirelessly fulfils her Commonwealth role. Her private secretary, on once being asked in what respect the public life of the Queen differed from the lives of her predecessors, had a concise answer. 'First,' he said, 'the Queen has come to stand much nearer to her people in all her realms . . . Secondly, and this follows to some extent from the first answer, the mobility of the monarch has enormously increased since 1952.'[15]

How much more, then, has it increased since the beginning of the century. When King George V and Queen Mary – at that stage still Duke and Duchess of York – embarked on the first great Empire tour in 1901, they were to be away from home for eight months. Today, Queen Elizabeth II can fly to New York in less time than it took her grandparents to travel from Marlborough House to Portsmouth to board their ship.

It is this mobility that has made possible the Queen's close and successful association with the Commonwealth. She has become the most travelled monarch in British history. She makes at least two major foreign tours each year; and of the more than one hundred countries she has visited the states of the Commonwealth make up the majority. By plane, by ship, by train, by car, she has travelled thousands upon thousands of miles. She has ridden on elephants, been rowed in canoes, been whisked' aloft in cable cars, 'gone walkabout' in remote towns and cities. In evening dress and jewels she has watched warriors cavorting in the African sun; in fur coat and snow boots she has chatted to Red Indians; in straw hat and floral dress she has attended tropical garden parties; in white brocade and flashing tiara she has opened parliaments.

But these tours are not all bouquets and applauding crowds. There is always an element of risk, even danger. Besides the ever-present threat of an attack by some unbalanced fanatic, there is the chance of a politically motivated assassination attempt. On occasions, a political crisis can place the Queen in an embarrassing, even hazardous position. In 1961 there was considerable pressure for her to cancel a visit to the Republic of Ghana. Ruled by the dictatorial President Kwame Nkrumah, Ghana was in a particularly unstable state – just ripe, it was said, for the picking by Russia. This made the Queen all the more determined to go on with the visit. Not even a bomb which rocked the Ghanaian capital five days before the visit could change her mind.

'How silly I should look if I was scared to visit Ghana,' she announced serenely, 'and then Kruschev went a few weeks later and had a good reception.'[16]

So she went, and the visit was a great success.

'The Queen has been absolutely determined all through,' wrote Prime Minister Harold Macmillan admiringly in his diary. 'She is grateful for MPs' and Press concern about her safety, but she is impatient of the attitude towards her to treat her as a *woman* and a film star or mascot. She has indeed "the heart and stomach of a man".'[17]

Three years later, a state visit to Canada had to be undertaken in the teeth of French separatist opposition. But as imperturbably as ever, the Queen went through it all: facing death threats, newspaper antagonism, insulting placards, noisy demonstrations, and disapproving crowds. It was left to Prince Philip, on a later tour, to give the rebellious Canadians a blunt answer to what he called 'this question of monarchy'. If the people did not want it, they could change it. 'The monarchy exists not for its own benefit, but for that of the country. We don't come here for our health. We can think of better ways of enjoying ourselves.'[18]

In 1979, on a tour of several central African countries, fighting broke out on the Zambian border between Rhodesian forces and guerrillas. With the Queen due to arrive in Zambia from Tanzania the following day, it was wondered whether the visit should be cancelled. The Queen was consulted. Her answer left no room for doubt. There was no reason, announced her press secretary blandly, 'to suggest the Queen's plans should be altered.'[19]

And when the Queen herself is not on tour, she is represented by other members of her family. There is hardly a week in which one or other of her relations is not standing to rigid attention, in the blazing sunshine or the pouring rain, as a local military band thumps out a not always happy rendering of 'God Save the Queen'.

These tours, undertaken so conscientiously by the Queen and her family, are one side of the Commonwealth coin; the other is the less public side – the work which the Queen does behind the scenes. Sometimes abroad, more often at home, the Queen hosts the Commonwealth Conference. Year after year she is photographed – a small, slim figure in long dress and glittering jewels – seated in the middle of a group of black, brown, yellow and white politicians. Although she plays no part in their deliberations, her influence is considerable, and is becoming more considerable with each year that passes. At the Commonwealth Conference held in Lusaka, for instance, it is claimed that her private talks with various heads of government did a great deal towards smoothing the always turbulent waters of African politics.

For gradually, in the thirty or more years that have passed since her accession, Queen Elizabeth II has emerged as the one constant factor in the ever-shifting kaleidoscope of Commonwealth affairs. She has lived through so much. She has seen colonies change into self-governing states, protectorates change into monarchies, dominions change into republics, parliamentary democracies change into police states and back again. She has seen constitutions altered, *coups* crushed, politicians come and go, tyrants rise and fall, heads of state superceded, deposed or assassinated. She can remember most things happening before. It is no wonder that, over the years, the Queen has developed into a person of considerable expertise, experience and aplomb.

To an outsider, the Commonwealth is a highly irrational organisation, its only common denominator being the Queen. She remains the one unifying symbol. Whatever the monarchy may have lost in the way of political power and influence in Great Britain, the Queen has more than made up for as Head of the Commonwealth. No other figure in public life, no other head of an international organisation, not even the President of the United States, is as well known as she. Queen Elizabeth II has become as familiar a figure in today's world as Queen Victoria was in hers.

Representing Queen Elizabeth II abroad as dutifully as he had represented his father George V and his brother George VI, was the Queen's uncle, the Duke of Gloucester. Better than any other surviving, fully involved member of the royal family had the Duke of Gloucester known the British Empire in its heyday. Now, more often than not, he found himself presiding over the transition to independence of this or that Commonwealth country. Looking, in his bemedalled Field-Marshal's uniform 'like an anxious porker which had escaped from the Cavalry Club'[20] and with his sweetly smiling Duchess by his side, the Duke of Gloucester would uncomplainingly endure the elaborate ritual that always marked these occasions.

What he thought of this dismantling of the Empire one does not know. The Duke of Gloucester was a man of few words and of even fewer analytical or ideological thoughts. His was not, he would probably have said, to reason why. The Duke carried out his duties brusquely but with a thoroughness and a tact that was seldom appreciated at home. As his assistant private secretary once reported from Malaysia, not everyone in Britain realised 'how well the Duke can put himself over if he is so willed and encouraged or indeed how well he can carry off important occasions.'[21] Even if he were feeling ill, the Duke would carry on: 'it would never have occurred to him not to,'[22] says one of his equerries.

If the Duke of Gloucester did have any strong feeling about the Commonwealth, it was his affection for Australia. His youthful tour and his term as Governor-General had left him with an abiding interest in this vast and fascinating country. He always enjoyed presiding over the annual Australia Club dinner and in 1965 he and the Duchess paid the country another visit. He hoped, the Duke once told an Australian audience, that his eldest son, Prince William, would one day become their Governor-General.

In his undemonstrative way, the Duke was devoted to his two sons, Prince William and Prince Richard. 'He was determined,' remembers one of his equerries, 'that his children should not be as afraid of him as he had been of his father. He wanted them to feel that they could always talk to him about their problems.'[23] It was in the country, at Barnwell Manor, his efficiently run farm in Northamptonshire ('My father was a gentleman farmer at heart,'[24] claimed Prince William) and at the House of Farr in Scotland, where he went for the shooting, that the Duke was able to get to know them better.

Although both princes had inherited their mother's distinctive, high-cheekboned looks and both had been educated at Eton and Magdalen College, Cambridge (where, like Prince Charles, they lived in) they were somewhat different types. Prince William had more *élan*; Prince Richard was more academically-minded. But the frustrations that had characterised the Duke of Gloucester's life characterised theirs as well: father and sons were all obliged to sacrifice their preferred way of life on the altar of duty.

Prince William has been called 'the Pioneer Prince'. Good-looking, gregarious, extrovert, he set many precedents. He was the first member of the royal family to attend an American university, Stanford in California, where he studied economics, business and political science. He was the first to earn his living by joining the Foreign Office as a professional diplomat, serving in such far-flung posts as Nigeria and Japan. He was the first to undertake a series of adventurous journeys, travelling in conditions of discomfort and freedom hitherto undreamed of. He was a skilled and enthusiastic pilot. 'I need the freedom of flying,' he once explained. 'If you are royal, everybody gets scared of you taking risks.'[25]

There was the rub. More perhaps than most did this restless, unconventional Prince feel the restrictions of his position. 'Throughout his life,' wrote one friend, 'he was torn between the yoke of his birth and his longing for freedom.'[26] 'I think freedom is what I miss most of all,'[27] the Prince once sighed. It was almost inevitable then, that this tug-of-war should affect the Prince's love life. Like the Duke of Windsor, when Prince of Wales, Prince William was drawn to older, sometimes divorced or married women. One of them, a sophisticated and attractive divorcee by the name of Zsuzui Starkloff, with whom the Prince had fallen in love in Japan, was brought to England to meet the Duke and Duchess of Gloucester. It did not take her long to realise that any idea of marriage was out of the question. 'William's devotion to his parents, and his sense of responsibility towards what he is' was, she admitted, too strong.

'He's too much of a man to be happy in the Prince's role and he's too much of a Prince to be happy in an ordinary man's role,'[28] was her summing-up of Prince William's dilemma.

But even the small measure of freedom enjoyed by Prince William was severely threatened when, in 1968, his father suffered the first of a series of strokes. For the last six years of his life the Duke of Gloucester was confined to a wheelchair, unable to speak or to respond to conversation. His long illness saw his Duchess at her most admirable. On the one hand she shouldered a great many of his burdens; on the other she insisted that he be treated as though he were still a fully involved member of the family.

The Duke's illness helped make up Prince William's mind. 'I suppose,' he declared, 'I've spent my time running away from what I knew was the inevitable: a full time job as a Royal Prince. Now the time has come when I know I can't run away any longer. One of the things that no one ever understands is that it's not easy being Royal . . .'[29]

Yet at the time, it looked as though the younger son, Prince Richard, might be able to escape the royal treadmill. Slight and bespectacled, Prince Richard was more studious, more artistic, more politically aware than Prince William. But, like his brother, he belonged to the generation of princes who are not only prepared but anxious to make their own mark. He trained and practised as an architect and wrote on London architecture and statuary. In July 1972, at the age of twenty-seven, Prince Richard took another unconventional step by marrying, not into the British aristocracy, but a secretary at the Danish Embassy in London, Birgitte van Deurs, the daughter of a Danish lawyer. To further emphasise their bid for independence, the couple planned to set up home in a converted warehouse in London's dockland.

Within weeks of the wedding, the course of their lives was altered dramatically. On 28 August 1972, the thirty-year-old Prince William was killed in a flying accident, while taking part in the Goodyear Air Race near Wolverhampton. This meant that Prince Richard was now heir to the dukedom. Resigning themselves to the inevitable, the newly-married couple gave up their dream of a dockland home and moved into Kensington Palace. On the death of his father, on 10 June 1974, Prince Richard became Duke of Gloucester.

Just as uncomplainingly as his father and brother had given up their careers for more onerous 'princing', did the new Duke of Gloucester forsake his full-time architectural practice to devote himself to the family 'firm'.

Among his many commitments, however, are some which reflect his relatively unorthodox, humanitarian and artistic tastes: Action on Smoking and Health, the Cancer Research Fund, St John Ambulance Brigade, Architect-Artists, the Victorian Society.

His Danish-born Duchess (the Dowager Duchess, like Princess Marina before her, took her own name and is now known as Princess Alice, Duchess of Gloucester) whom some had been inclined to dismiss as unremarkable, revealed herself to be a young woman of resilience and determination. Very soon adapting herself to her new role, she proved that she could fulfil her many engagements with efficiency and aplomb. The couple have one son, Alexander, Earl of Ulster, born in 1974, and two daughters, Lady Davina Windsor, born in 1977, and Lady Rose Windsor, born in 1980.

There can be little doubt that this earnest, unassuming, domesticated couple (the Duke is often to be seen around London on his motor-cycle) would have been far happier living their own life in dockland. But it was not to be. 'There's no escaping it, you know,'[30] the aged Princess Alice, Countess of Athlone, their Kensington Palace neighbour, used to say when discussing royal responsibilities. Nor is there; not, at any rate, without considerable family upheaval. In the end, almost everything must be sacrificed to the demands of the dynasty. And two generations of Gloucesters have sacrificed as much as anyone.

There was one important aspect by which the image of a dedicated and united family on the throne was rendered less than perfect: the Duke and Duchess of Windsor remained very much beyond the family fold. And not only beyond it, but living the sort of smart, showy, self-indulgent life that was the very antithesis of everything that the British monarchy had come to represent. Free of the matrix of royal obligation that has kept, and keeps, several members of the royal family in check, the Windsors lived out their days in self-centred ease.

The couple had two homes, both in France. One was an impressive mansion in the Bois de Boulogne; the other was an old mill, not far from Paris, which they had bought and renovated. In this way their opposing tastes – hers for the city and his for the country – could be accommodated. These two permanent homes secured, the Duchess was able to exercise her talents for decorating and entertaining to the full. With money being no object (the Duke had secured a generous financial settlement before his abdication and he was knowledgeable about investments) her homes became rightly celebrated for the elegance of the decor and the magnificence of the food.

The couple lived on a royal scale. It was a world of liveried servants, aides, secretaries, chauffeurs, detectives, maids and personal hairdressers. They travelled ceaselessly: New York, Palm Beach, Biarritz, the Riviera. Epitomising everyone's idea of high life, they moved in an aura of luxury and excitement. Everything they did made news. Each journey, each party, each interview meant another series of photographs: they would be pictured boarding ocean liners, dancing at charity balls, eating in restaurants, strolling in their gardens, feeding their pugs. Every indiscretion was magnified; every scrap of gossip was repeated. It was as if they lived in a permanent spotlight.

Seen from a distance, the famous couple seemed ageless, like flies trapped in amber. While other men grew bald and jowly and paunchy, the Duke of Windsor kept his hair, his boyish features and his slight figure. Only on coming closer could one see that cross-hatching of fine lines and that expression of deep melancholy. No less than his wife was the Duke obsessed with clothes. The jackets of his suits he had made in London and, because he preferred the cut of American trousers, these he had made in the States; 'pants across the sea'[31] was the Duchess's little joke about her husband's idiosyncrasy. This sartorial concern helped to enhance his youthful image.

The Duchess's apparent youthfulness was even more remarkable. She lost neither her bandbox elegance nor her supple figure. For year after year, for decade after decade, the Duchess of Windsor stepped forth – slender, svelte, with never a hair out of place nor an accessory wrongly chosen. Those hours

spent with the beautician and the hairdresser and the dressmaker were indeed
well spent. One had to come up very close indeed to appreciate that she was
any older than she had been at the time of her marriage. Seldom has art, and
science, triumphed so successfully over nature.

Although, not unnaturally, the Duke and Duchess had their shortcomings,
they were an engaging couple to meet – interesting, articulate and amusing.
They were neither of them intellectuals but, in their different ways, they were
both very capable people. The pity of it all was that none of this ability was
put to any worthwhile use. The Duke had status, a good financial brain, a flair
for organisation and a talent for inspiring loyalty. He could have been the
patron of any number of international societies; they could both have done so
much to encourage the arts or alleviate suffering or foster international
goodwill. But they preferred, it seems, to dedicate themselves to the pursuit
of their own pleasure. Of the royal family's sense of public service, the couple
had nothing.

How much truth was there in the legend, so dear to the hearts of the
popular press, that this was 'the greatest love story of the century'? That the
Duke of Windsor was deeply in love with his wife there can be no doubt.
Never, apparently, did he feel that in giving up his throne for love he had
made the wrong choice. Anyone who had anything to do with the couple
testified that she was the centre of his world. She was constantly in his
thoughts; if she were in the room he had eyes for no-one else; if she were out,
he fretted until she came home. His will was entirely subjected to hers; to the
end of his life she dominated him. None of this is to say that she was a virago.
It was simply that, in the partnership, she was the stronger personality.

And the Duchess? Did she love him? Only she, of course, can answer this.
'Any woman who has been loved as I have been loved, and who, too, has
loved,' she once wrote, 'has experienced life in its fulness.'[32] Naturally
disciplined, increasingly dignified, always conscious of the fact that she was
under critical scrutiny, the Duchess of Windsor made very little display of her
innermost feelings. But one can safely assume that her love was not as
obsessive as his. Perhaps to have been the object of that all-consuming
passion was enough. 'He had everything,' she kept repeating to a guest one
evening, 'and he gave it all up for me.'[33]

Although the Duke of Windsor had played his part in two royal ceremonies
– the funerals of his brother King George VI and of his mother Queen Mary –
the family frigidity persisted. Only in the mid-1960s, thirty years after the
Abdication, were there signs of a gradual thaw. Early in 1965 the Duke,
accompanied by the Duchess, came to London for an eye operation. He was
visited in hospital by the Queen and, for the first time as an adult, the Queen
spoke to the Duchess of Windsor. Another of the Duke's visitors was his
sister, the sixty-eight-year-old Princess Royal. Within a few weeks she had
died, and the Duke and Duchess attended her memorial service.

The first public show of reconciliation came some two years later when the Queen invited the Duke, and the Duchess, to attend the unveiling of a memorial tablet to Queen Mary at Marlborough House. It was ironic that it should have been at a ceremony to pay homage to the Duchess's most implacable opponent that this scene of family hatchet-burying should have taken place. Not that the Duchess of Windsor would ever have been taken for a member of the family. Surrounded by the royal women in their flowery hats and pastel colours, the strikingly-dressed Duchess could hardly have looked more alien. After the ceremony, both the Queen and the Duchess's other implacable opponent, the Queen Mother, stopped to speak to her. It was noticed that the Duchess curtsied to neither.

A few years later, the twenty-one-year-old Prince Charles, on a private visit to Paris, suddenly decided that he would like to see his celebrated great-uncle. A meeting was arranged and in what has been called 'a moment of history',[34] the fallen and the future monarch chatted happily together and parted emotionally.

During Queen Elizabeth II's state visit to Paris in May 1972 to mark Britain's entry into the Common Market, the Queen herself paid a call on her uncle. By now the seventy-seven-year-old Duke of Windsor was dying of cancer of the throat. While Prince Philip and Prince Charles had tea with the Duchess, the Queen went up to see the Duke. She remained with him for half an hour.

In less than a fortnight, on 28 May 1972, the Duke of Windsor was dead. Only now, in death, was he accorded a ceremonial home coming. He had asked to be buried, not beside Edward VII, George V and George VI in the crypt of St George's Chapel but at nearby Frogmore. This would mean that his adored wife could one day be buried beside him. The Duke's body was flown to England and, two days later, the Duchess arrived in an aeroplane of the Queen's Flight. She was accommodated, at last, in Buckingham Palace as the guest of the Queen. Throughout her stay, the Duchess was treated with every kindness and consideration. Heavily sedated and deeply distraught, the Duchess remained veiled during all her public appearances, including the funeral service in St George's Chapel on 5 June. As soon as the Duke had been buried, she flew back to France.

In its obituary columns, the press concentrated, for the most part, on the first half of the Duke of Windsor's life: on his golden years as Prince of Wales and on the details of the Abdication. He was praised for the dignified way in which he had renounced the throne.

The general public was ready to grant him more than this. By the way in which the crowds flocked to the funeral and by the tone of public comments and letters to the press, it was apparent that there was a feeling that the Duke had been shabbily treated. The quarrel, it was said, should have been patched up years ago. The royal family should have been more understanding, more sympathetic, more forgiving. They could have shown a little more warmth.

These were obviously the Duchess of Windsor's views as well. 'They were polite to me,' she afterwards said, 'polite and kind, especially the Queen. Royalty is always polite and kind. But they were cold. David always said they were cold.'[35]

No one could accuse the Queen's daughter, Princess Anne, of not pulling her royal weight. Robustly and directly, this controversial Princess has contended with at least three of the problems which beset members of the royal family. By her equestrian achievements, she has proved her individual worth. She has successfully reconciled her public duties with those of a wife and mother. And she has fought a running battle with the press. At the same time, Princess Anne has helped move – or 'shove' as she might put it – the monarchy forward along its evolutionary course. Faced by her no-nonsense attitudes, precedents have gone down like nine-pins.

Princess Anne is very much her father's daughter: restless, quick-tempered, competitive, imperious. Her strength of personality and stubborn individualism have been apparent throughout her life. It was always she who initiated any childhood pranks while her tamer, more conventional brother, Prince Charles, followed. They used to fight, she admits cheerfully, 'like cat and dog'.[36] She was the first daughter of a reigning sovereign to attend boarding school, Benenden. From the start of her public life she cultivated a highly distinctive appearance: not for her the obligatory, pretty-as-a-picture look of her royal relations; her clothes were always bold and dashing. Among the generally discreet, ultra-feminine women of the British royal family, Princess Anne remains very much the odd-one-out. Her air is less decorous, more natural; she has an almost hoydenish quality. Anything mechanical fascinates her: she has an abiding interest in anything that goes, as she puts it, 'chug'. Shrewd and intelligent she might be, but she is no intellectual.

Riding remains Princess Anne's obsession. In her the royal family's interest in horses, be it riding, racing, 'eventing', or four-in-hand driving, has found the fullest expression. Riding, particularly in horse trials, represents the one field in which she can make her mark quite irrespective of her royal status. On the back of a horse she is simply another individual. Here, everything depends on her own abilities. Throughout her remarkable equestrian career, the Princess has shown courage, toughness and determination. No number of accidents – jolts, tumbles, crashes or even cracked bones – can dampen her enthusiasm or lessen her will to excel.

For excel she certainly has. Among the Princess's many achievements, she can claim to be the first member of the immediate royal family to win a place in the British team at the Olympic Games. With her, horse riding is more than a sport: it is a challenge to prove herself as a person.

Her choice of husband emphasised her strongly independent streak. When she married, on 14 November 1973 at the age of twenty-three, the Princess chose, not a princeling or an aristocrat, but the relatively obscure and humbly-born army officer, Mark Phillips, because he shared her interest in equestrian sports. The wedding ceremony, for all its splendour, was a family as opposed to a state occasion; the bridegroom was not given a title. On leaving the army some years later, Captain Mark Phillips devoted himself to the running of their farm, Gatcombe Park in Gloucester. They have two children, Peter Phillips, born in 1977, and the more exotically named Zara Phillips, born in 1981.

In the main, Mark Phillips, like Angus Ogilvy, leaves his wife to get on with her many royal engagements while he runs the farm. With this arrangement the Princess has to be content. 'Sometimes I feel I would like to lead a different life from the life I'm living now, which is in great part a very public life . . .' she once admitted. 'But I don't feel I've got any choice. I was born into a kind of life with duties and obligations and opting out isn't on.'[37]

Her range of public duties is more extensive than is generally realised: she carries out something like 150 engagements a year, some of which include tours abroad. Not only to her work for the Save the Children Fund, which she has made particularly her own, but to all her official commitments, she brings a vigour and a professionalism. More patiently than most – for she is less patient than most – she puts up with the small talk, the tedium, the repetition, the necessity to look alert and interested. On state occasions she is equally impressive. At ceremonies such as the Opening of Parliament she looks, in her flashing tiara and glittering dress, unmistakably regal.

Yet such is the way of the world that Princess Anne is better known for her stormy relations with the press than for her devotion to duty. More and more, as the twentieth century progresses, has the royal family been obliged to live a great deal of its life in public. There is now hardly an aspect of their lives which is not subject to press scrutiny or press comment. Every holiday is ruined by clamouring photographers; every minor indiscretion is blown up into a major scandal. 'Today,' as *The Spectator* wryly puts it, 'the public's "right to know" is circumscribed only by the capacity of security men to stop photographers climbing into bedrooms.'[38] Overworked royal press secretaries are either begging newsmen to leave the family in peace or denying the more outrageous stories about them.

All this harassment on the part of the *paparazzi* – the impertinent questions, the frantic mobbing, the shouted demands, the relentlessly probing cameras – try Princess Anne's notoriously short temper. Invariably she shouts back. Indeed, she is often goaded in the hope that she will shout back. One sharp word to a reporter is infinitely more newsworthy than a hundred conscientiously fulfilled engagements.

If the Princess's outbursts are understandable, they are regrettable. She could take a lesson from the Queen Mother or Princess Alexandra. By co-operating with the press, by never being anything less than smiling, good-humoured and gracious, they have drawn their teeth. Princess Anne's method – to give as good as she gets – is not nearly as effective.

But there is no denying that Princess Anne has established herself as a personality to be reckoned with; one whose very outspokenness helps concentrate public attention on the monarchy. 'It is, I think, fair to say,' she once remarked smilingly, 'that I probably attract slightly more attention than the average.'[39] She might not be the most popular member of the royal family but it is her particular combination of qualities – a dynamic individualism allied to a royal conscientiousness – that will help carry the British monarchy into the twenty-first century.

Seldom is the royal family subjected to more ill-informed criticism than in a discussion of its finances. The misconception – that the Civil List is the monarch's personal salary rather than the means by which the running expenses of the monarchy are met – dies very hard indeed. During the 1970s this question of the family's finances became the subject of a particularly heated public debate.

Gone were the days when a Civil List could be fixed at the start of a reign in the certainty that its provisions would be adequate at the end of it. By the year 1970, with inflation rampant, the monarchy was, as Prince Philip bluntly put it, 'in the red'. The annual £475,000 established by the Civil List Act of 1952 was proving hopelessly inadequate; the deficit for the year 1970 alone was £270,000. The same was true of the provisions made for the other leading members of the family.

To meet the Queen's request for an increase in the Civil List, the Prime Minister, Harold Wilson, set up a Select Committee to examine the subject. Its investigations brought the whole complicated and controversial question of the royal family's financial affairs into the open.

The question had two main components: the Queen's private wealth (which was not under investigation) and the expenses incurred in the carrying out of her functions.

Queen Elizabeth II is, by any standards, very rich. Her fortune, which is not subject to tax or death duties, is probably worth several million pounds. Even so, she is not as rich as many people imagine. 'Her Majesty has been much concerned,' protested the Lord Chamberlain to the Select Committee, 'by the astronomical figures which have been bandied about in some quarters suggesting that the value of these funds may now run into fifty to a hundred million pounds or more. She feels that these ideas can only arise from confusion about the status of the royal collections, which are in no respect at her private disposal. She wishes me to assure the Committee that these suggestions are wildly exaggerated.'[40]

The Lord Chamberlain went on to remind them that such things as the royal palaces (with the exception of Sandringham and Balmoral, which are the Queen's personal property), the crown jewels, the collections of pictures, furniture, china and silver, and King George V's famous stamp collection, belonged to the monarchy and not to any individual monarch. But the fact that it was not the Queen's private fortune that was being investigated did not prevent a great many people, headed by that arch-castigator of the monarchy, the Labour member of parliament, Willie Hamilton, from attacking the monarch's store of inherited, shrewdly invested and enviably untaxed wealth.

Not that the Queen's critics did not find plenty to attack in the matter of her public funds. The half-million pound Civil List, they could rightly claim, represented only one portion of the monies granted to the Crown. When one added in the cost of things like the royal yacht, the Queen's Flight, the royal trains, the upkeep of the various palaces – all met by other departments of state – the total cost of the monarchy was closer to £3.5 million a year.

Further bedevilling the issue was the fact that public funds went towards the maintenance of the Queen's private homes of Sandringham and Balmoral. Did the fact that she used them in the course of her duties – receiving ministers, working on her 'boxes', entertaining state visitors – justify this spending of public money on private property? On the other hand, had the Queen not, on occasion, used her private funds to augment the Civil List?

But as it was only the Civil List – and not the contributions of the other departments of state – that was being considered, and as it was clearly inadequate to cope with inflation, the Committee decided to more than double it, to £980,000 a year.

Nor was the Queen the only member of the family to find her allowance inadequate to meet her official expenses. During the last few years she had been obliged to subsidise her relations from her private funds. The Committee therefore decided that the provision made for the other members of the family should also be increased. An additional £89,000 was to be divided annually between the Queen Mother, the Duke of Edinburgh, Princess Anne, Princess Margaret and the Duke of Gloucester, with provision being made for future payments to younger sons and widows.

The Prince of Wales, already in receipt of the handsome, and untaxed, revenues of the Duchy of Cornwall, was not included. Like the previous Prince of Wales (King Edward VIII), Prince Charles paid half of the income of the Duchy of Cornwall to the government; this left him with a healthy enough sum to make his inclusion on the Civil List unnecessary.

Although the Committee made it quite clear that these revised payments were to meet the increased running costs of the monarchy – chiefly the salaries of a staff which was continuously being pruned – the press, and therefore the general public, found it much easier to think of them in terms of a pay increase for the Queen, almost as though she were being given extra pocket money to spend on herself.

Within five years this seemingly generous increase had, in turn, been swallowed up by inflation. By 1975 the Civil List needed another £775,000 to make ends meet; and this in spite of additional economies and staff cuts. A further request led to a further furore. Once again the indefatigable Willie Hamilton was on his feet to denounce what was generally, and inaccurately, being referred to as the Queen's 'pay rise', and once again the question was hotly debated, in parliament and out. But the increase was granted. This time, though, the machinery for granting such increases was altered: instead of a new bill to sanction each increase, the matter of the royal finances would in future be subject to the same procedure as any other government expenditure.

What so many critics failed to appreciate was how little the monarchy – with all its incalculable benefits for the country – cost in relation to other national expenditure. As Philip Howard, in his book *The British Monarchy in the Twentieth Century* has pointed out, the Civil List for 1975 equalled half the state subsidy for the Royal Opera, Covent Garden, that year. A farthing a month from every member of the British population would make up an amount equal to the annual Civil List.

On the other hand, it is not unlikely that the Queen's private fortune is larger than that of any of her subjects. This has not always been the case. Her great-grandfather, King Edward VII, was merely one rich man – and by no means the richest – among many; Queen Alexandra could express the wistful hope that the new decorations at Windsor would equal the splendour of the Rothschild houses. But the redistribution of wealth after the Second World War finally put an end to this privileged society, leaving only the sovereign's untaxed fortune intact. In the same way that the monarch is above politics and above class, so is she – less acceptably in the eyes of some – above taxation.

None of this is to say that the Queen, or any member of her family, lives in a lavish style; nor that the majority of her subjects would wish to see her stripped of her fortune. It is simply that now, more than ever, is the monarchy expected to justify its existence, to be seen to be earning, not only its keep, but its right to hang on to its wealth. An indolent, scandalous or recklessly extravagant monarch would very soon force the whole question of the royal fortune into open debate. For if the Queen is now more popular than ever, she is also, as one of the wealthiest people in the country, more vulnerable than ever.

32 A family group taken to mark the Queen's Silver Wedding in 1972. Standing, from the left: the Earl of Snowdon, the Duke of Kent, Prince Michael of Kent, Prince Philip, the Earl of St Andrews, the Prince of Wales, Prince Andrew, Angus Ogilvy, and James Ogilvy. Seated: Princess Margaret, the Duchess of Kent holding Lord Nicholas Windsor, the Queen Mother, the Queen, Princess Anne, Marina Ogilvy, Princess Alexandra. Seated on the floor: Lady Sarah Armstrong-Jones, Viscount Linley, Prince Edward, Lady Helen Windsor

33 A relaxed royal family: the Queen with Princess Anne, and Prince Philip with
Prince Edward: in the foreground are Prince Charles and Prince Andrew

'The Daylight and the Magic'

THE CONCEPT of a family on the throne could hardly be better exemplified than in the person of the Queen Mother. Born during the reign of Queen Victoria, she has lived through five subsequent reigns. The daughter-in-law of George V, sister-in-law of Edward VIII, consort of George VI, mother of Queen Elizabeth II, grandmother of the future King Charles III, she has provided a strong and scintillating thread of continuity for something like sixty years. To the public, this matriarch of the royal family is affectionately known as the Queen Mum: the revered mother-figure, not only of her family, but of the entire nation.

The Queen Mother (known to her family and their households as Queen Elizabeth; her daughter is referred to as 'the Queen') prefers to see herself, not so much as a personality in her own right, but as a supporter of the monarch of the day. 'Whatever we do,' Princess Alice, Countess of Athlone used to say, 'we do for the King or Queen, as the case may be';[1] and this is very much the Queen Mother's tenet. Be that as it may, there can be no doubt whatsoever that the Queen Mother *is* very much of a personality in her own right. It is not simply for her longevity nor her experience nor her familiarity that she is so valuable and popular a member of the royal family; it is for her exceptional personal qualities.

A fear (strengthened by her acquisition of a remote castle in Scotland) that the Queen Mother would retire from public life after the death of her husband, was soon dispelled. 'My only wish now,' she announced in a message to the nation, 'is that I may be allowed to continue the work that we sought to do together.'[2] 'I always think,' she explained recently when discussing one of her tours, 'that it's better to keep *on* and *not* have a rest.'[3] And on another occasion, revealing that streak of steely common sense which is as much part of her nature as her sympathy and charm, she told her daughters that their work was 'the rent you pay for life'.[4]

She has certainly never been in arrears. By the ease, grace, apparent enjoyment and undoubted professionalism with which she carries out her many public duties, be they overseas tours or garden inspections, the Queen Mother has brought an unparalleled lustre to the monarchy. Her style is quite different from those of her predecessors: the distrait charm of Queen Alexandra and the unbending majesty of Queen Mary. Harold Nicolson, watching her at the opening of some new buildings at Morley College in 1958, professed himself amazed at her polished performance. 'She was in her best mood and spirits,' he reported to his wife. 'She has that astonishing gift of being sincerely interested in dull people and dull occasions . . . [She] seemed really interested and spoke to almost all of them, putting them instantly at their ease . . . You know how much I like people who are good at their jobs, and she is superb at *her* job. Somehow she creates such an impression (indeed a radiance) of goodwill and good behaviour that no ill feelings could live or breed in such an atmosphere.'[5]

'Wherever you go in the world,' the Queen Mother once remarked, 'there's always a wonderful Scotswoman doing a wonderful job of work.'[6] She could hardly have better summed up her own contribution to national life.

Out of the public eye, the Queen Mother is no less remarkable. She has managed to combine the royal family's traditional outdoor enthusiasms with less customary cultural interests. She is as happy in raincoat, stout shoes and pull-on felt hat as she is in her more usual floating chiffons and trembling ospreys. She shares the dynasty's obsession, initiated by Edward VII, with the Sport of Kings – or, by now, Queens – and from her famous racing stable she derives as much pleasure as from anything else in life. In thirty years she has had more than three hundred winners. Salmon fishing remains one of her passions. Another is for her gardens, whether at Clarence House in London, Royal Lodge at Windsor, Birkhall near Balmoral or the Castle of Mey on the Pentland Firth. No weather is too bad for her to take her collection of scampering corgis out for a walk; or even, to the anguish of her staff, to suggest a picnic. 'Ah!' she will exclaim, standing four-square in a gale force wind, 'this will blow the germs away.'[7]

On the other hand, the Queen Mother is a dedicated patron of the arts, thoroughly at home in the world of music and ballet and painting. Her understanding of pictures and *objets d'art* is more profound than Queen Mary's; she collects the sort of contemporary paintings that would have astonished her predecessor. Her frequent private visits to France are given over, almost entirely, to avid sightseeing: châteaux, churches, gardens. To a dynasty that has often been accused of philistinism, the Queen Mother has brought an informed appreciation of the arts and an unerring taste.

She has also brought a warmth unknown since the days of Queen Alexandra. To her family, no less than to the nation, she is a big-hearted, understanding, eminently sensible mother-figure. Her standards might be rigid but she is never intolerant. The Queen Mother has had her share of personal problems but her daughters, sons-in-law and grandchildren have always found her boundlessly sympathetic. Every day she speaks to the Queen on the telephone ('Your Majesty? Her Majesty, Your Majesty'[8] purrs the Palace switchboard operator as he puts through the daily call) and her relationship with Princess Margaret, for all the vagaries of her younger daughter's life, remains close. 'Isn't she *marvellous*?'[9] Princess Margaret will exclaim; while Princess Anne once admitted feeling depressed at the thought that she would never be able to match her grandmother's remarkable qualities.

Between the Queen Mother and her eldest grandson, the Prince of Wales, the bond has always been very strong. 'He's a darling,'[10] she will say. She is said to see in him some of the characteristics of her late husband. Others see in the Prince some of *her* characteristics. 'He really feels things *here*,' said one long-standing friend of both grandmother and grandson, 'exactly like Queen Elizabeth.'[11] Throughout his life, the Queen Mother has taken a deep interest in Prince Charles's welfare; she is said to have helped choose his future wife.

Her devotion to him is matched by his to her. 'I can only admit from the very start that I am hopelessly biased and completely partisan . . .' he wrote in the Foreword to Godfrey Talbot's biography of the Queen Mother. 'Ever since I can remember my grandmother has been the most wonderful example of fun, laughter, warmth, infinite security . . . For me she has been one of those extraordinarily rare people whose touch can turn everything to gold . . .'[12]

It was during the late 1960s that the royal family's cast-iron attitude towards divorce began to melt. It changed more radically in ten years than it had done in the previous sixty.

Edward VII, while more than ready to sleep with a married woman, resolutely refused to receive a divorced one. George V likewise denied invitations to any technically 'guilty' party in a divorce; his decision to admit 'innocent' parties to the royal enclosure at Ascot was regarded as daringly enlightened. So deep was the wound inflicted by Edward VIII's renunciation of the throne in order to marry a divorcee that the royal family's feelings towards divorce hardened; although neither King George VI nor Queen Elizabeth could be considered narrow-minded people, their high regard for the sanctity of marriage, allied to their experience of the harm wrought by divorce, ensured that the idea of divorce within the family was regarded, for both personal and public reasons, as unthinkable. In 1949 the future Queen Elizabeth II could claim that it caused 'some of the darkest evils in our society today',[13] and as late as 1956 the possibility of Princess Margaret marrying an 'innocent' divorced man could not be countenanced.

Yet so completely had the nation's moral climate changed by the late 1960s that an unyielding attitude to divorce on the part of the Queen would have counted against, rather than for, her.

The first royal divorce concerned the Queen's cousin, Lord Harewood, son of the Princess Royal. During the course of the Queen's reign, Lord Harewood had made a considerable success of his career in the world of music. He had edited the magazine *Opera*, served on the staff of the Royal Opera House, Covent Garden, and was Artistic Director of the Edinburgh Festival and of the Leeds Festival.

His marriage, to Marion Stein, by whom he had had three sons, had proved less successful. Some ten years after the marriage he had fallen in love with an Australian-born divorcee, Patricia Tuckwell. In 1964, while Lord Harewood was still married to his first wife, Patricia Tuckwell bore him another son. Only after this did his wife agree to a divorce. To Lord Harewood's mother, the widowed Princess Royal, the situation must have been extremely painful. Yet, as a true daughter of King George V and Queen Mary, the Princess Royal never raised the subject. Only once, says Lord Harewood, did mother and son discuss it: she listened to what he had to say in complete silence, making no comment except to ask, when he mentioned divorce, 'What will people say?'[14]

She was never to know, for on 28 March 1965, at the age of seventy-seven, the Princess Royal died, very suddenly and quite literally in her son's arms while the two of them were sitting beside the lake at Harewood. 'I suppose she would have wanted that, as, although she liked her due, she also disliked fuss and bother – of any kind,'[15] wrote her sorrowing son. The Princess Royal was buried at Harewood.

Not until January 1967, by which time Lord Harewood was living openly with Patricia Tuckwell and their three-year-old son in a house in St John's Wood, was he sued for adultery by his wife. The granting of a divorce, some six months later, left him free to marry again.

But it was not going to be as easy as all that. By the conditions of the Royal Marriages Act, the Queen's consent would be needed for his re-marriage. This the Queen would have been willing to grant had it not looked as though she, as Supreme Governor of the Church, were condoning divorce. What was she to do? The way out of the impasse was provided by the Prime Minister, Harold Wilson. He put the matter to the cabinet; they advised the Queen to grant permission; and she, as a constitutional monarch, was obliged to take their advice. The divorced Lord Harewood married the divorced Patricia Tuckwell and a royal precedent was duly set.

The Queen's permission, though, had not meant the Queen's approval. For many years after his divorce, Lord Harewood was cold-shouldered by the rest of the royal family.

The next one to take advantage of the possibility of royal divorce was Princess Margaret. By the early 1970s her marriage, too, was in ruins. From the very start, her marriage to Antony Armstrong-Jones (created Earl of Snowdon just before the birth of their first child, David, Viscount Linley, on

3 November 1961) had run into trouble.

There were many reasons for this. The main one, though, was that constantly recurring one: the difficulty of pursuing a full-time professional career while being married to a member of the royal family. Angus Ogilvy and Mark Phillips solved it by distancing themselves from their wives' official lives; Lord Snowdon made the mistake of starting married life as a sort of poor man's Prince Philip. But he had neither the talent nor the temperament for this particular role. When, in his resolve to be more suitably and gainfully employed by resuming his photographic career, Lord Snowdon began to move out of Princess Margaret's shadow, the troubles began.

In any case, the couple were not really compatible. They were too alike. Both were unconventional, mercurial, independent. Princess Margaret's not unnatural insistence on being treated as a princess conflicted with her husband's equally understandable determination to be treated as an artist. From this mutual incompatibility there developed a mutual antagonism. Each began to move in different circles; each found other close companions. Lord Snowdon's name was linked with that of Lady Jacqueline Rufus Isaacs, daughter of the Marquess of Reading; Princess Margaret's with that of a somewhat foot-loose young man, seventeen years her junior, named Roddy Llewellyn.

What little hope there might have been of a reconciliation, or even of keeping up some sort of public front, was ruined by the press. The couple were mercilessly hounded by the *paparazzi*. Once their marital difficulties had become so remorselessly aired, it became almost impossible for them to remain together. In March 1976 they separated. In 1978 they were divorced. The experience has left the Princess with a deeply felt antipathy towards the press.

Lord Snowdon, remarried, now leads an admirably fulfilled and useful life. Princess Margaret remains a controversial figure. Yet she is probably the most interesting member of the royal family – warm, spontaneous, talented, intellectually curious and culturally aware. Busier, more dedicated, more conscientious than she is ever given credit for (her *raison d'être*, she unhesitatingly maintains, is 'to back up the Queen'[16]) Princess Margaret brings a piquancy to a family that has sometimes been accused of stodginess. Colourful characters can serve the cause of monarchy no less effectively than dignified ones.

In spite of the divorce, there has been no family coolness towards Princess Margaret. The Princess, with her two children (Lady Sarah Armstrong-Jones was born on 1 May 1964) both of whom were educated at Bedales, the progressive, co-educational school in Hampshire, remains very much part of the core of the royal family. She is present at all private and public family occasions. 'The high standing and efficient work of the monarchy,' lectured *The Times*, 'does not require that every member of the extended royal family

234   *Queen Elizabeth II*

should be a paragon of virtue or a model of decorum, and that all who fail that test should be withdrawn out of range of royal duties and rewards.'[17] The paper had changed its tune since the days of the Townsend affair.

In the year of Princess Margaret's divorce, the monarchy was faced with yet another complicated matrimonial situation. The dashing, thirty-five-year-old Prince Michael of Kent, a major in the Royal Hussars, announced his intention of marrying the beautiful, thirty-three-year-old, Austrian-born Baroness Marie-Christine von Reibnitz, at that stage working as an interior designer in London. There were two obstacles to the marriage. The Baroness was a Roman Catholic and she was a divorcee.

Her first marriage, to a British merchant banker, having ended in divorce, had subsequently been annulled by the Vatican. This left her free to marry whoever she chose, provided he were not a member of the British royal family. For by the Act of Settlement of 1701, no member in the line of succession could marry a Roman Catholic; nor, by the Royal Marriages Act of 1772, could any royal marriage take place without the sovereign's consent.

The first hurdle was overcome by Prince Michael (only sixteenth in line of succession) giving up his rights to the throne. The second was overcome by the Queen granting her permission.

The Vatican proved less accommodating. With the Church of England opposing the marriage of divorced people in church, the couple had assumed that the Church of Rome would have no objections to a church wedding. After all, the Baroness's first marriage had been annulled by the Vatican. But the Pope refused to grant the necessary dispensation for a mixed marriage to be solemnised in church. The reason for his refusal was the fact that Prince Michael had signed a declaration to the effect that any future children would be raised as Anglicans; in this way, his eldest son would replace him in the line of succession. This the Pope could not countenance. The disappointed couple, who had hoped to be married in Vienna's Schottenkirche, had to content themselves with a civil ceremony in the Town Hall.

Although the Queen kept discreetly silent on the subject, Prince Charles gave his views a public airing by denouncing the 'needless distress' caused by doctrinal argument among Christians. His statement led to yet further doctrinal argument, among both clergymen and members of the public.

In Princess Michael of Kent the royal family has gained another of those non-royal women who take to their royal duties with consummate ease. An exceptionally handsome couple – he bearded in the manner of his grandfather George V, and she fair and stylishly dressed – they are very much working members of the royal team. Their homes are an apartment in Kensington Palace and a country house in that most royal of counties, Gloucestershire. They have two children, Lord Frederick Windsor, born in 1979, and Lady Gabriella Windsor, born in 1980.

Fifty years ago marriage between a British prince and a Roman Catholic divorcee would have meant ostracism, exile and a life of frustrated idleness on the Riviera. Today the couple are fully accepted and fully involved representatives of the sovereign.

Perhaps the ageing Duchess of Windsor may be allowed a wry smile.

In spite of the changes that have taken place in the monarchy during the twentieth century, there are still many aspects of Queen Elizabeth II's life that would be familiar to her predecessors. Her daily routine is very much the same. Most mornings are given over to discussing the mail with her private secretaries and to working on the 'boxes'. She is kept informed of cabinet decisions and of the daily business of parliament; she reads telegrams and despatches; she signs state papers. Her powers, as a constitutional monarch, remain essentially what they were during the reign of her great-grandfather, King Edward VII. She has the right to be informed and consulted and to give advice on national issues. As much as any of the monarchs who immediately preceded her, the Queen remains an essential part of the machinery of government.

Once a week she sees her prime minister. Her first four prime ministers – Winston Churchill, Anthony Eden, Harold Macmillan, Sir Alec Douglas-Home – were Conservatives, all men from a social circle in which she felt at home. But with the Labour victory in 1964 came Harold Wilson, and the Queen was obliged to work, not only with someone from a different background, but with one whose party contained elements that were less than enthusiastic about the monarchy. The same had been true of Edward VII and the Liberals in 1905; of George V and the Labour governments of the 1920s; of George VI and Attlee's post-war government. No less than her predecessors did the Queen accept the change with admirable imperturbability; no less than them did she remain properly impartial. Her attitude towards her subsequent prime ministers, whether Labour or Conservative – Edward Heath, James Callaghan and Margaret Thatcher – has been equally neutral.

The Queen feels more relaxed with some prime ministers than with others. Her relationship with the two Labour prime ministers, Wilson and Callaghan, is said to have been especially good. Callaghan's audiences, at which there was often a great deal of laughter, would sometimes take the form of a stroll round the palace gardens. 'Funny really,' remarked one observer of the Queen's equally warm relationship with Harold Wilson, 'the Royals will often get on famously with a bit of a rum cove. Attraction of opposites, I suppose.'[18] With Margaret Thatcher, things are said to be less relaxed.

Now and then, the Queen has been involved – as the sovereigns before her were involved – in the exercising of her royal prerogative to choose a prime minister: this has invariably been accomplished with tact and discretion.

Without exception, her prime ministers have paid tribute to her industry and her acumen. 'The Queen, after twenty-five years of her reign, knows almost every Head of State and Leader of Government in foreign countries . . .' wrote Lord Home. 'Her experience is readily put at the disposal of the Prime Minister and is invaluable to him . . .'[19]

And James Callaghan claimed that 'Her strength is that she shares the commonsense view of things that distinguishes the British citizen, and she has a true understanding of the significance of her role in the daily lives of the people . . . she has grown immensely in confidence and understanding.'[20]

A great deal of her time, and that of her family, is still spent carrying out the traditional royal tasks: touring factories, visiting hospitals, opening exhibitions, planting trees and laying foundation stones. 'Civic life,' says one member of the family with a rueful smile, 'doesn't change. The mayors and town clerks are *exactly* the same.'[21] Then there are those long-established, elaborately-staged, impeccably organised ceremonial occasions – the investitures, the Opening of Parliament, the Trooping the Colour, the weddings, the funerals, the balls, the banquets – at all of which the Queen's father, grandfather and great-grandfather would feel eminently at home.

In addition to her regular Commonwealth tours, the Queen has undertaken the customary state visits to foreign countries. In turn, she has entertained foreign heads of state with a magnificence and a panache worthy of Edward VII. In spite of the fact that she, like George V and George VI, is a shy, self-effacing person, Queen Elizabeth II has forced herself to play her public role to the full: to talk to strangers, to make speeches, to drive in processions, to deck herself out in glittering regalia, to be always the centre of attention. The widowed Queen Victoria, in her distaste for public life, simply shut herself away from it; Queen Elizabeth II, with hardly more taste for public performance, would never even consider such dereliction of duty.

Much of the Queen's private life, too, would come as no surprise to her immediate ancestors. There is still that annual migration between Sandringham, Buckingham Palace, Windsor, Holyroodhouse and Balmoral. There are still members of the family living in St James's Palace, Clarence House, Kensington Palace, Abergeldie and Birkhall. The three great officers of the royal household are still the Lord Chamberlain, the Lord Steward and the Master of the Horse. The chief working departments remain those of Private Secretary, Comptroller of the Lord Chamberlain's Office, Master of the Household, Keeper of the Privy Purse and Crown Equerry. Among the secretaries, equerries and ladies-in-waiting, the same names continue to crop up. Although the household is now much smaller and everything is more efficiently and economically run, the atmosphere remains luxurious and well-ordered. King Edward VII, coming back, might complain about the smaller staff, the less than fourteen courses served at dinner or the threadbare state of some of the carpets, but life in his great-granddaughter's palaces would present no real hardship, or indeed many surprises, for him.

Equally familiar would be the royal family's amusements and recreations: those mammoth gatherings at Christmas (at Windsor instead of Sandringham these days), the unsophisticated parlour games, the knock-about brand of humour. Hardly more books are read now than were read during the four previous reigns; the choice of music remains cheerfully middle-brow. And, of course, there are all those outdoor activities – walking, riding, shooting, stalking and fishing. The more urban tastes of personalities such as King Edward VII, Queen Mary and Princess Margaret were, and are, the exception; as a rule the British royal family is happiest in the countryside.

Queen Elizabeth II's passion for and knowledge of horses is probably her best-known characteristic. Not since the days of Edward VII has a sovereign been so closely involved with horse racing. With her horses, the Queen can be utterly natural, utterly herself. Dogs too, keep their special place in the affections of the family. Very rarely have the members of the royal clan been photographed out of doors without a pack of dogs at their heels. 'I am Caesar, the King's Dog' were the words inscribed on the collar of Edward VII's adored white terrier; 'Susan, the faithful companion of the Queen' reads the inscription on the gravestone at Sandringham of one of Queen Elizabeth II's many corgis.

But many things have changed. The private life of the family is far more informal. Queen Mary refused to use the telephone; her grandchildren seldom write letters to each other. Royal children go to boarding schools, earn their own livings, use public transport, fly economy class; behave, in short, very like many other members of the public. This relaxation of the old standards has been welcomed, not only by the younger generation, but by those who have experienced life at court through six reigns. 'It's *much* better now,' claimed the nonagenarian Princess Alice, Countess of Athlone, 'not so stiff, much more *natural*.'[22] When necessary, Princess Alice would make her own bed.

And at the same time as the royal family are experiencing life as ordinary members of the public, the public is getting a greater insight into the life of the royal family. This was a conscious decision on the part of the Queen's advisers. By the late 1960s it was realised that, in an age of high-powered publicity and mass communication, it would be positively harmful for the monarchy to keep its back so resolutely turned on modern methods of public relations. 'Don't forget,' said Princess Alexandra on one occasion, 'that nowadays we have to compete with Elizabeth Taylor and the Beatles.'[23] The royal image, in other words, would have to be projected as professionally as any other to avoid its becoming a dispensable anachronism.

Gradually the Queen's tweedier, media-resenting courtiers like her press secretary, Commander Sir Richard Colville, were replaced by men with experience in journalism, marketing and public relations. Her present private secretary, Sir Philip Moore, once worked for the Labour cabinet minister,

Denis Healey; her press secretary, Michael Shea, writes thrillers. Junior members of the family are now far more accessible to the public than before: they give radio, television and newspaper interviews, they make public statements on controversial issues, they co-operate with writers, they make off-the-cuff remarks to strangers, they move far more freely among the crowds, they write books, forewords to books and book reviews. The Queen's speech, at a luncheon at Guildhall to celebrate her Silver Wedding in 1972, was remarkable for a dry, self-depreciating wit that would have been unthinkable in a sovereign's speech even a decade before. It perfectly demonstrated the new, more relaxed relationship between monarch and people.

The *Royal Family* film, in the course of which the general public was given a frank glimpse of palace life behind the scenes, served as another milestone in this process of popularisation. The Queen is said to have sensed a change in the public attitude towards her in the months after its screening. On great ceremonial occasions, too, the television cameras now go into the Palace. The public is able, for instance, to see from the inside, the family going out onto, and coming back from, the central balcony. 'Come on Margaret!' ordered the Queen Mother briskly as, on the occasion of her eightieth birthday celebrations, she stepped out onto the balcony for yet another appearance before the clamouring crowds below.

But hand in hand with this increased public accessibility has gone an increased exposure to public comment and satire. Although Queen Victoria, and still more Edward VII when Prince of Wales, were sometimes subjected to journalistic criticism, not since the early nineteenth century has the royal family been as vigorously satirised as it is now. Continental journalists have always shown a remarkable inventiveness and a less than reverent approach in their articles on the British royal family but since the early 1960s the British media has proved equally merciless. The Queen Mother alone escapes the satirical attentions of press, radio and television. On balance, this is a healthy trend; it is probably of more benefit to the royal family than the sugary, stultifying, sycophantic attitudes of earlier days. It implies that the monarchy is a far from negative or negligible institution; that it is worth criticising and caricaturing.

Yet, in the final analysis, it is not for qualities of ordinariness or for a closer identification with the people that the monarchy is so revered and the Queen so popular. Mystery and magic remain very necessary ingredients. Not too much daylight should be allowed in. Opinion polls prove that the public still prefers to see the monarch as a being apart, as someone not quite real, as an embodiment of all the old-fashioned virtues of dependability, dignity, devotion to duty, marital fidelity, warm-hearted motherhood, private and public morality. In an age of permissiveness and the cult of youth, the Queen has come to represent life's more virtuous and enduring qualities.

With its taste for long-established traditions and personalities, the British public had come to realise, by the second half of the 1970s, that the Queen had been part of the national scene for a surprisingly long time. In fact, a great proportion of the population had grown up, married and had children without knowing any other sovereign. It had become increasingly difficult to remember a time when this small, slight, perfectly groomed figure had not been Head of State. And the fact that her face and figure had changed so little with the passing years seemed to enhance this feeling of continuity. In a fast-changing world, the Queen remained a familiar, constant, stable factor.

This was why, on the occasion of her Silver Jubilee in 1977, Queen Elizabeth II was so rapturously acclaimed. And although it is unlikely that the Queen was quite as astonished by the warmth of public reaction as King George V had been on the occasion of his Silver Jubilee, there can be no doubt that she was highly gratified at the fervent demonstration of national loyalty. As she drove through the streets in her golden Coronation coach on that 7 June 1977, and as she chatted to the crowds outside St Paul's Cathedral, the Queen was clearly touched and delighted by the enthusiasm of the people.

'We have come here because we love you,' said one young office girl.

'I can feel it,' replied the Queen with equal sincerity, 'and it means so much to me.'[24]

No less valuable to the monarchy than the sense of continuity engendered by Queen Elizabeth II are the exceptional qualities of her heir, the Prince of Wales. Prince Philip once said something to the effect that it was a miracle that Prince Charles had turned out so well; it was only to be hoped that, for the sake of the Crown, this miracle would be put to the best use.

As the 1970s drew to a close and the Prince of Wales neared his thirtieth birthday, so did his somewhat equivocal position become more apparent. For the role of a Prince of Wales remained as undefined, and as unsatisfactory, as it had ever been. With the Queen still in her fifties and in the best of health, it seemed likely that Prince Charles, like Edward VII, might well turn sixty before ascending the throne. Would the greater part of his life be spent – as his great-great-grandfather's life had been spent – in a state of vocational frustration and social excess? Or would the fact that he was still unmarried lead him down the ever more slippery path trodden by Edward VIII? Like the previous Prince of Wales, Prince Charles was an object of almost hysterical adulation wherever he went. Might he simply degenerate into an eternally performing, eternally touring, eternally waiting Prince of Wales?

That he did not was due to several factors. His loving family background, his enlightened education, his innate sense of responsibility, his unrebellious nature, have all ensured that Prince Charles is a far more resolved personality than his predecessors. During the six years which he spent in the services after completing his university education, he was allowed to lead a far more adventurous life than any previous heir to the throne. He was the first Prince of Wales to captain his own ship, to fly helicopters and supersonic jets, to make a parachute jump, to train as a frogman and a commando. He faced dangers and ran risks hitherto undreamed of for a future king. What with all that, and with his enthusiasm for polo, riding, shooting, fishing, scuba-diving, windsurfing and skiing, Prince Charles became known as a 'Royal Action Man'.

That was one side of the coin. There is another, far more interesting side. For Prince Charles is not just another swashbuckling, sports-mad princeling. With the derring-do inherited from his father are combined the less aggress-ive, more subtle characteristics of his mother and of his grandfather, George VI. In fact, Prince Charles feels a strong affinity with the grandfather whom he only just remembers; he regrets that he was never able to benefit from the guidance of this earnest and courageous monarch. In conversation, Prince Charles reveals himself to be every bit as modest, considerate and con-scientious as his grandfather.

But there is a great deal more to the Prince of Wales than this. His intelligence is well above average; his interests are wide-ranging. He reads history; he is passionate about music; he is an enthusiastic amateur painter. Acutely aware of the demands and anomalies of his position, he can discuss it with a fluency and an incisiveness that is little short of remarkable. Even allowing for the sycophancy which is likely to colour the judgement of those who come into contact with members of the royal family, Prince Charles is an impressive man to meet.

He also works harder than is generally realised. His public engagements, listed as just over two hundred a year, represent only a proportion of his many official activities: the desk work, the meetings, the audiences, the sittings for portraits. Besides the usual royal functions, including represent-ing the Queen abroad and acting as Counsellor of State at home, the Prince pursues his own particular interests. He speaks out on economic and indus-trial problems; he acts as unofficial salesman for British industry. Like the Queen, he is very aware of the importance and potential of the Common-wealth; he feels that it could become a far more effective world body than the United Nations. He concerns himself with the running of the Duchy of Cornwall, with the problems of the disabled, with the thorny issue of race relations, with the plight of the young and unemployed. Indeed, the Prince has a strongly developed social conscience; one which manifests itself in far more practical ways than the previous Prince of Wales's vaguely expressed sympathies for the underprivileged. He has initiated various schemes and projects; he administers various trusts and charities.

Prince Charles is – and this is of increasing importance to the monarchy – a skilled television performer and an accomplished public speaker. He is equally conscious of the continuing importance of the press. In the face of occasional press harassment, he remains good-natured. He appreciates that there is more than a grain of truth in the newsmen's taunts of 'You need us.' 'If the photographers weren't interested,' he admits, 'that would be the time to start worrying.'[25] In fact, the Prince believes that the monarchy should be more, rather than less, co-operative with the press. 'You scratch my back and I'll scratch yours',[26] is his realistic summing-up of what he feels should be the basis of a more trusting palace-press agreement. By being given more back-ground briefing, by being taken more into palace confidence, the press might regain what the Prince feels is a loss of balance, an inability to differentiate between what is *in* and what is *of* public interest.

To avoid what she called 'the Edward VII situation',[27] the Queen very early on began involving her son in affairs of state. He was given access to some Cabinet papers and Foreign Office telegrams, he was free to discuss political matters with prime ministers, he even sat in on an occasional Cabinet meet-ing. Although all this is better than nothing, the Prince remains very con-scious of the limitations of his position, of the fact that there is really no way in which he can ever become fully involved in the machinery of government. Nothing that he might say could ever alter the course of events. A future Prince of Wales, he muses, should somehow become more closely concerned, and at an earlier age, with the monarch's day-to-day work. 'I hope that somebody reminds me about this in about twenty years' time,'[28] he adds with a characteristically wry smile.

Having resigned himself to the inherent awkwardness of the constitutional status of a Prince of Wales, Prince Charles feels that he must justify himself in other ways. In spite of his manifold public activities and altruistic schemes, he remains alive to the vulnerability of his position. He takes nothing for granted. He is uneasy about his inherited wealth, his unearned privileges, his unreal existence, his personal fallibility. He knows that his job is only what he makes of it; that he must work that much harder to prove that it is relevant in these last decades of the twentieth century. Left to himself, he would just as happily go back to Cambridge to study constitutional history; not for a moment, though, would his ingrained sense of duty permit him to do any such thing.

Hand-in-hand with the Prince of Wales's awareness of the need to adapt to a constantly changing world goes a highly romantic sense of kingship. It is perhaps not too much to claim that his ideal – within the framework of a constitutional monarchy – is of a concerned, involved, almost mediaeval king. There is a great deal to be said, he argues, for the system of hereditary monarchy. A presidency – so temporary, so encompassed by officialdom, so shackled by political considerations – can offer none of the variety, indi-vidualism, eccentricity even, of an hereditary sovereign. Each reign takes on the colour of the monarch in a way that no presidential term could ever do. This is why Prince Charles feels that the ritual and the bravura remain essential aspects of monarchy: they are simply part of the whole. He would change very little. His apparently conflicting views – that the monarchy must be relevant to contemporary life and that the pageantry should be retained – are not really incompatible. After all, the Queen has been very successful in modernising and humanising the monarchy while retaining the ceremonial trappings which enhance the sovereign's position. And Edward VII who, by his approachability, did so much towards abolishing the remote image of royalty, remained a supreme royal showman. There can be little doubt that Prince Charles, as the most intelligent and well-adjusted twentieth-century heir to the throne, will know how to maintain the balance.

The Prince of Wales's home life, throughout his bachelor years, was serene. Unlike Edward VIII as Prince of Wales, Prince Charles had no desire to break free of Buckingham Palace. He was quite content to remain, in his own suite of rooms, under his parents' roof. All in all, the relationship between Queen Elizabeth II and her three sons could hardly have been more different from that between King George V and his sons. If there were squabbles, they tended to be among the brothers rather than between parents and children.

As Prince Charles neared thirty, so did Prince Andrew, twelve years his junior, begin to steal some of the limelight. This could lead to occasional friction. Better looking, more extrovert, more dashing than Prince Charles, Prince Andrew threatened to replace him as the leading royal male idol. Following the pattern set by his brother, father, grandfather and great-grandfather, Prince Andrew joined the Royal Naval College at Dartmouth as a midshipman. In time, his active involvement in the Falklands War earned him the somewhat exaggerated title of 'Warrior Prince' while his no less active love life earned him some less complimentary names. A future, more legitimate title will probably be that of Duke of York. It is now highly improbable, though, that like the two previous Dukes of York, Prince Andrew will suddenly be called upon to replace his elder brother in the line of succession.

It may be just as well. Exactly as, a generation ago, the household expressed relief at the fact that it was the elder sister, Princess Elizabeth, who was Heir Apparent, so is there relief at a kindly Fate which has made the more responsible brother the future king.

The third son, Prince Edward, is very different from Prince Andrew. Sixteen years younger than Prince Charles and processed through the same educational mill as his brothers, Prince Edward is known to be gentler, more artistic and more contemplative than Prince Charles or Prince Andrew. His academic record is better. Taller than Prince Andrew, and as good-looking – in a different way – Prince Edward may well become the first member of a sovereign's immediate family to follow a full-time profession.

In public, as well as in private, all three brothers are relaxed, assertive and articulate to a degree that would have been unimaginable in the sons of

George V. Even in his heyday as Prince of Wales, Edward VIII was never as assured as any of this new generation of princes.

During the years that she lived at home, Princess Anne, too, could hardly have differed more fundamentally from that earlier only sister among brothers – Princess Mary, afterwards Princess Royal. She had always shown more independence. 'When I was a child and up to my teens, I don't think I went along with the family bit,' she says bluntly, 'not until later than everyone else. I know its value now, but I don't think I did up to my middle teens.' In fact, only since her marriage has Princess Anne developed a warmer relationship with her brothers and come to a fuller appreciation of the benefits of her early home life. 'The greatest advantage of my entire life is the family I grew up in. I'm eternally thankful for being able to grow up in the sort of atmosphere that was given to me – and to have it continue now that I am grown up . . .'[29]

If, in spite of all the advantages of an active public life and a happy home background, the Prince of Wales still seemed to suffer from some vague air of unfulfilment, there was one obvious solution: he must marry and settle down. Only then would the ghost of his predecessor be well and truly laid.

In a misguided moment, Prince Charles had once told an interviewer that he thought thirty to be about the right age for him to marry. In November 1978 his thirtieth birthday came and went, and although the Prince's name had been linked with those of several young women – royal and non-royal, suitable and unsuitable – he was still no nearer getting married. Princess Alice, Countess of Athlone, had once bemoaned the fact, in a letter to Queen Mary, that by remaining a bachelor so long, the future King Edward VIII had 'missed his best chances'.[30] The parents of the future King Charles III were beginning to feel the same way.

'You'd better get on with it Charles,' teased Prince Philip, 'or there won't be anyone left.'[31]

With Queen Elizabeth II's three sons grown up, the widows of three of King George V's sons lived on. All three widows had been alive in the first year of Edward VII's reign; all three saw the birth of the Prince who will one day become the seventh sovereign to reign since the death of Queen Victoria.

The most notable of these widows is, of course, the Queen Mother. Her eightieth birthday, in the summer of 1980, was marked by nationwide celebrations. The culmination of these festivities was a procession through the streets of London to a Thanksgiving Service in St Paul's Cathedral. For this triumphant occasion, the Queen ceded first place to her mother; so it was in the last carriage, surrounded by the brilliantly uniformed Sovereign's Escort of the Household Cavalry and with her favourite grandson, the Prince of Wales, sitting beside her, that the Queen Mother drove through the acclaiming streets.

'Royalty,' said the Archbishop of Canterbury in his address, 'puts a human face on the operations of government and provides images with which the people of a nation can identify and which they can love . . . It is very difficult to fall in love with committees or policies but the Queen Mother has shown a human face which has called out the loyalty and the sense of belonging without which a nation loses its heart and disintegrates.'[32]

It was merely one tribute among many. And out of the avalanche of articles, editorials, films and loyal addresses ('Very nice, but they all sound like *obituaries*'[33] was the Queen Mother's characteristically wry comment) was one from an unexpected quarter. For the occasion, that anti-monarchist Labour MP, Willie Hamilton, buried the hatchet. 'Unlike some of her brood,' he conceded, 'she never seems to put a foot wrong. Never a word out of place. With a melting smile turned on at the touch of some invisible switch . . . may God understand and forgive me if I have been ensnared and corrupted, if only briefly, by this superb royal trouper.'[34]

Just over a year later another eightieth birthday was celebrated with much less fanfare: that of Princess Alice, Duchess of Gloucester. For decade after decade, this redoubtable member of the family had been dedicating herself to the business of the monarchy. During her husband's long illness and since his death in 1974, Princess Alice had worked tirelessly at those ceremonial and representative functions in the army and air force which had once been the Duke's main concern. Few members of the royal family have given themselves so unstintingly, and few have received so little public recognition.

Much of this is due to Princess Alice's retiring nature. 'She was painfully shy,' wrote a member of King George VI's household, 'so that conversation with her was sometimes halting and unrewarding, for you felt that she had so much more to say, but could not bring herself to say it.'[35] Almost thirty years later, this shyness remained one of Princess Alice's most apparent characteristics. Less apparent, but no less real, was her exceptional strength of character. 'When you meet my mother you will probably find her very quiet,' her eldest son once said, 'but my goodness she's an incredible person.'[36] And so she is.

The third of these survivors is the most controversial: the Duchess of Windsor. She is also the saddest. For years she has been very ill, confined to one room in her silent, shuttered and closely guarded Paris home, once the scene of all those lavish and elegant parties. That acute mind has gone; that supple body has disintegrated; that taut face has sagged. Her large household staff has been diminished; all her affairs are in the hands of her shrewd lawyer, Maître Suzanne Blum.

The Duchess is said to be very rich, worth several million pounds. What will happen to this fortune, which includes the Duchess's magnificent

34 'Not just an uncultured, polo-playing clot': Prince Philip at his easel

35 Prince Charles, a modern communicator, faces the microphones

36 The Prince of Wales, accompanied by the Queen Mother, Princess Margaret and his future wife, Lady Diana Spencer, leaves St Margaret's Church, Westminster

collection of jewellery? 'The money,' as Lord Mountbatten once pointed out after a visit to the widowed Duchess, 'was *his*, not hers!'[37] Will it revert to the royal family? Lady Monckton, a friend from the abdication days, once tackled the Duchess on the subject of her jewellery. 'Princess Alexandra and the Duchess of Kent are loyal, hardworking girls, both of them, and they haven't many jewels,' she pleaded. 'Unless you've made plans, you might remember them.'[38] The Duchess did not commit herself. But on another occasion, and to another friend, she exclaimed, 'Everything is going to Prince Charles – everything.'[39] However, there are times, in her increasingly rare lucid moments, that the Duchess has claimed that she will leave it all to France, the only country that has been good to her.

There is one legacy, though, that the Duchess of Windsor will definitely be bequeathing to the British royal family: her body. For the Queen has agreed that the Duchess will one day be laid to rest beside her husband, King Edward VIII, at Frogmore. And with her body, warns the Duchess, will come her ghost. Do not be surprised, she tells us, if on certain nights at nearby Fort Belvedere – the setting of what she has called those 'enchanted days' before the Abdication – her ghost is seen wandering among the black and shifting shadows of the cedar walk.

If, in some ways, the choice of a bride for a future king had become easier, in others it had become infinitely more difficult. At the start of Edward VII's reign it would have been unthinkable for an heir apparent to marry anyone other than a princess; by 1980 the Prince of Wales could have married, had he so wished, the most humbly born girl in the world, provided she were neither Roman Catholic nor divorced. But this widening of choice, together with changing public attitudes, has raised an entirely new set of qualifications. Eighty years ago the much narrower field would have ensured that the bride-to-be met most of the necessary requirements. But with no suitable princess on hand, the Prince was obliged to find the sort of girl who was becoming increasingly rare in contemporary society.

Things such as youth, beauty, vitality and grace presented no problem; it was the other qualifications that were becoming so difficult to fulfil. Any future queen would have to come from a stable, respectable background; she would have to know how to cope with press publicity; she would have to be prepared to put up with the restrictions, tedium and artificiality of royal life; and she would have to be a decorous girl without, as it was so euphemistically put, a past: in other words, she had to be a virgin.

That the thirty-two-year-old Prince of Wales managed to find someone tailor-made for the part (only her family background, for all its illustriousness, lacked the necessary stability) was little short of miraculous. The nineteen-year-old Lady Diana Spencer, besides being beautiful, was engaging, discreet, unspoilt, ready to shoulder her royal responsibilities and, as her ineffable step-grandmother, the romantic novelist Barbara Cartland, put it, 'purity itself'.[40] In short, she was an old-fashioned girl for a somewhat old-fashioned young man.

For those who looked for parallels, Lady Diana's family background was not unlike that of an earlier future queen, Lady Elizabeth Bowes-Lyon. Both were daughters of long-established aristocratic houses with royal associations in their past. Lady Diana's father was the eighth Earl Spencer, whose family could claim direct, if illegitimate, descent from the Stuart Kings of England. The link with the Queen Mother was further strengthened by the fact that Earl Spencer had once been an equerry to King George VI (and later Queen Elizabeth II) and that Lady Diana's maternal grandmother, Lady Fermoy, was a lifelong friend and lady-in-waiting to the Queen Mother. Other members of Lady Diana's widespread family had also served the Queen Mother in various capacities. It is not altogether surprising then, that Lady Diana Spencer should have been looked upon as the Queen Mother's choice of bride for her grandson. True or not, there can be little doubt that the Queen Mother would have approved of this fresh, unworldly and warm-hearted girl.

Another point in Lady Diana's favour was her Englishness. That process of Anglicanisation, initiated by Edward VII, was to be given one of its most significant boosts by this alliance with a well-rooted, undeniably English family.

A point against her was one which no longer mattered quite so much. When Lady Diana was eight, her parents were divorced. Her father subsequently married a divorcee, Raine, Countess of Dartmouth, the colourful daughter of that even more colourful mother, Barbara Cartland. Lady Diana's mother had also remarried and was by now Mrs Shand-Kydd. Even a decade before, such a situation would have presented a serious barrier to the marriage; it says something for Queen Elizabeth II's flexibility that by 1981 it was no longer an issue.

Added to the usual problems facing a royal bride-to-be was a contemporary one in its most devastating form: for months before and after the announcement of the engagement, on 24 February 1981, Lady Diana Spencer was hounded by the world's press. The fact that she lived a relatively ordinary life – sharing a flat with her three girlfriends, driving a Mini, working in a kindergarten – made her all the more accessible. On the whole, she handled this baptism of fire very well. The Queen, although coming close to losing her patience with the press on occasions, was heard to say, 'Well, she's going to have to learn to get used to this sort of thing. At least it's useful in that respect.'[41] The pre-wedding press, radio and television coverage was certainly unprecedented. By the dawn of the wedding day there could have been few people in the civilised world unaware of the background, career, tastes and temperament of this tall, good-looking girl with the thatch of blonde hair and the lowering, sideways glance.

It was sometimes wondered, at an early stage in the engagement, if the match had not been a somewhat calculated one. Prince Charles, at thirty-two, needed to be married. Lady Diana, at nineteen, seemed almost too perfect for the part. Pretty and pliable, she would liven up his somewhat staid image. She had even had gynaecological tests to prove that she could have children. To some, it seemed to smack of a marriage of convenience rather than a love match. The suspicion was strengthened by Prince Charles's blunt 'Whatever "in love" means'[42] when asked if he was in love with his future bride. If one is truly in love, one knows what it means.

But the couple's obvious devotion, in the weeks before, and during the wedding ceremony itself, dispelled any such thoughts. One had only to see them together – exchanging glances, clasping hands, sharing jokes, murmuring comments, whispering endearments – to realise that theirs was a deep relationship. Their kiss on the Palace balcony, in full view of the crowds below, was to set yet another royal precedent. Lady Diana obviously appreciated that she was gaining a husband of great kindness and sensitivity; he a wife with a great capacity for love.

And Prince Charles was gaining something else. He had fallen in love with a woman who would prove an invaluable asset in his public life. For already the new Princess of Wales has revealed traits that will give her, in time, a certain star quality. Her sparkling beauty, her unfeigned charm, her increasing assurance have heightened public interest in the monarchy. She has come to personify that renewal which manifests itself in each generation of the royal family. She is to the 1980s what Princess Margaret was to the 1950s or the Prince of Wales to the 1920s.

'A princely marriage is the brilliant edition of a universal fact,' wrote Bagehot, 'and as such it rivets mankind.'[43] The marriage of the Prince of Wales to Lady Diana Spencer in St Paul's Cathedral on 29 July 1981, certainly riveted mankind. If proof was needed of the enthusiasm, esteem and affection which the British royal family can arouse, not only in Britain but throughout the world, this royal wedding provided it. It was witnessed, through the medium of television, by an estimated 750 million people. Everything – the roaring crowds, the newly restored Cathedral, the illustrious guests, the swaggering carriage processions, the radiantly smiling royal family, the soaring music, the dashingly uniformed bridegroom, the beautiful bride in her opulent dress – ensured that the occasion was worthy of this worldwide attention.

But giving the marriage an even greater appeal was the fact that it was – in addition to being an international event of almost overwhelming magnificence – a family occasion: a brilliant version, as Bagehot has it, of an ordinary ceremony. 'You can't separate the private and public functions of the Queen,' a courtier once explained, 'that's the main difference between a monarchy and a republic. In a republic you know that the president's life is arranged by the state, and that eventually he'll retire back to his own home. What most impresses the visitors to Windsor . . . is the feeling that they're in a private home – that it's part of family life.'[44]

And this splendid public ceremony was very much part of family life. That Prince Charles was married in the presence of his parents, grandmother, sister, brothers, brother-in-law, aunt, great-aunt and cousins at various removes made the occasion all the more moving. To see the members of the royal family gathered under the great dome of St Paul's – the men so impressively uniformed, the women in their glowing colours – was to appreciate that the institution of monarchy had what the Archbishop of Canterbury had recently called 'a human face'; that for all the pomp and the glitter and the grandeur, the British monarchy was still very much a family affair.

In the year after the Prince of Wales's marriage, the Queen celebrated the thirtieth anniversary of her reign. By now she had been on the throne longer than any other twentieth-century British monarch. Still in her mid-fifties, there was every likelihood of her living to celebrate her Golden Jubilee in the year 2002, at which time she will be seventy-five, or even her Diamond Jubilee, at eighty-five. After all, the women of the dynasty are noted for their longevity. Queen Victoria, Queen Alexandra, Queen Mary and the Queen Mother all lived into their eighties. There is no reason why Queen Elizabeth II, with her strong constitution and healthy lifestyle, should not live an equally long time.

In many ways, her Silver Jubilee, five years before, had been something of a watershed. It happened to fall not long after her fiftieth birthday; a time of life at which most women have come to terms with themselves. By now they know their strengths and their limitations; they know how to make the best of what they have; their personalities, in short, are resolved. This was no less true of the Queen. She entered a new phase of her reign at the same time as she was entering a new phase of her life.

What had at one time been considered her failings have by now proved to be her strengths. Her much criticised reserve, which had been taken for gaucheness when she was younger, now comes across as dignity. It gives her an air of exclusiveness, of mystery, of being one-stage-removed from ordinary life. The conservatism of her clothes has become an advantage. She is recognised as having an understated, impeccable, particularly English style. She looks like many middle-aged Englishwomen would like to look. Maturity suits the Queen. As a princess and a young queen, she was thought to be too matronly; now that she is a matron, things seem to have fallen into place.

Gradually, the Queen has developed into a personality in her own right, with her own mannerisms, her own tastes, her own way of doing things. To come to full flower, she needed to feel accepted for what she is: an ordinary woman making a remarkable success of an extraordinary job. Her more relaxed attitude might well come from the realisation that her position, as a constitutional monarch, is currently held in very high esteem. 'At a time of social unrest,' writes Alan Hamilton in *The Times*, 'in an age when political leaders of all hues are tarred with the same brush of ineffectual mediocrity, when the decisions of judges show little understanding of reality, the monarchy is perceived as the only institution of state which is working as it was intended.'[45]

And Norman St John-Stevas MP, always an astute analyst of the parliamentary system, claims that 'the monarchy has become our only truly popular political institution at a time when the House of Commons has declined in public esteem, and the Lords is a matter of controversy. The monarchy is, in a real sense, underpinning the other two estates of the realm.'[46]

During Queen Elizabeth II's reign, the ideal of her great-great-grandfather, Prince Albert – that the monarchy should be a highly respected family institution, standing high above social and political faction – has been fully realised. This knowledge, together with the expertise that comes from doing the same tasks year in, year out, has given the Queen, not only greater self-confidence, but a stronger sense of vocation, a surer sense of majesty and a deeper sense of destiny. There can be little doubt that Queen Elizabeth II is standing on the threshold of her best years. She will make an awe-inspiring old Queen.

This is why it is unlikely that she will ever abdicate in favour of the Prince of Wales. Abdication is not a tradition in the British royal family; it smacks too much of dereliction of duty. Not only was the concept of abdication given a bad name by Edward VIII; it runs counter to the whole ideal of British monarchy. There are many reasons for the continuing popularity of the Crown: a national taste for tradition, an abhorrence of violent change, a lingering regard for class distinction, a reverence for something which represents virtue and excellence at the same time as providing colour, romance and human interest. Nor can the appeal of all the royal paraphernalia – the jewels, the orders, the sashes, the uniforms, the carriages, the caparisoned horses, the equerries, the footmen, the pages – be underrated. There is also a widespread admiration for the way in which this ancient institution has adapted itself to modern needs.

But perhaps, most of all, it is for its mystical element, its sense of dynastic continuity, its unbroken thread of succession, its 'lingering contemporary echo of the divine right of Kings'[47] that the British monarchy retains its hold on the imagination of the people. Queen Mary's celebrated gesture of turning from the deathbed of the old King, her husband, to make her obeisance to the new King, her son, was not just a piece of royal theatre: it was a reaffirmation of an age-old truth.

This is why the idea of abdication remains unacceptable. Sovereignty is not something that can be given up, like a pensionable job, at the age of sixty-five. Illogical and irrational as it might seem, sovereignty resides in the anointed monarch, even if that monarch be ill or mad, until death. It then passes to the heir.

It is this principle of hereditary monarchy, of family continuity, of one generation following another, that made the birth of the Prince of Wales's first child, Prince William, on 21 June 1982, such a dynastically significant event. Although the circumstances of the Prince's birth were very much in tune with contemporary custom – the Princess of Wales made no attempt to conceal her pregnancy, the Prince witnessed the birth – it was for its more traditional aspects that the event was so widely welcomed.

'Last year's princely marriage riveted the imagination of millions,' declared *The Times* on the day after the Prince's birth. 'This year's birth thus helps to perpetuate the pride of sovereignty as a *family* affair whose universality enhances its emotional as well as its symbolic connection with the people.'[48]

The christening, in the music room at Buckingham Palace on 4 August 1982, underlined this sense of dynastic progression. The ceremony took place on the eighty-second birthday of the baby's great-grandmother, the Queen Mother; behind the assembled relations and friends hung a portrait of a resplendently dressed Queen Alexandra; the baby wore the lace robe that had been worn by Edward VII as a baby in 1841 and by royal babies ever since.

'Such is our confidence in the stability of our institutions,' claimed one observer, that one was able to look ahead with conviction to the day when the baby would mount the throne as King William V. 'What other country can nowadays christen an infant knowing that it is likely to become its King in two generations' time?'[49]

Notes

PROLOGUE

1 Longford, *Victoria R.I.*, p 561
2 Ponsonby, *Recollections*, p 82
3 *Ibid*
4 Nicolson, *George V*, p 60
5 Ponsonby, *Recollections*, p 83
6 Coulter, *Queen Victoria*, p 223
7 Ponsonby, *Recollections*, p 89
8 *Ibid*
9 Longford, *Victoria R.I.*, p 562
10 Bennett, *Vicky*, pp 331–2
11 Pope-Hennessy, *Queen Mary*, p 353
12 St Aubyn, *Edward VII*, p 305

CHAPTER ONE

1 Longford, *Victoria R.I.*, p 512
2 Cust, *Edward VII*, pp 119–120
3 Brook-Shepherd, *Uncle of Europe*, p 111
4 Sampson, *Anatomy*, p 4
5 Ponsonby, *Henry Ponsonby*, p 109
6 Grey, *Twenty-five Years*, Vol II, p 15
7 Cust, *Edward VII*, p 91
8 *Times*, 23 Jan 1901
9 Ponsonby, *Henry Ponsonby*, p 109
10 Magnus, *Edward VII*, p 5
11 St Aubyn, *Edward VII*, p 199
12 Holden, *Charles*, p 257
13 Sampson, *Anatomy*, p 11
14 Magnus, *Edward VII*, p 117
15 Cust, *Edward VII*, p 259
16 St Aubyn, *Edward VII*, p 380
17 *Times*, 11 Nov 1859
18 Nicolson, *George V*, p 120
19 Bagehot, *Constitution*, p 28
20 *Times*, 11 Nov 1859
21 Ziegler, *Crown and People*, p 18
22 Bagehot, *Constitution*, p 38
23 *Ibid*, p 59
24 Pope-Hennessy, *Queen Mary*, p 301

25 St Aubyn, *Edward VII*, p 16
26 Victoria, Queen, *Dearest Mama*, p 142
27 Cust, *Edward VII*, pp 167–8
28 *Ibid*, p 91
29 *Ibid*, p 138
30 *Times*, 23 Jan 1901
31 Roby, *King, Press and People*, p 41
32 Windsor, *King's Story*, pp 45–6
33 St Aubyn, *Edward VII*, p 127
34 Nicholas II, *Letters*, p 173
35 Fisher, *Memories*, p 5
36 Ponsonby, *Recollections*, p 93
37 Mallet, *Life*, p 224
38 Portland, *Men, Women and Things*, p 316
39 Stamper, *What I Know*, p 86
40 Ponsonby, *Recollections*, p 272
41 Jullian, *Edward*, p 184
42 Ponsonby, *Recollections*, p 272
43 St Aubyn, *Edward VII*, p 130
44 *Reynolds*, 27 Jan 1901
45 *Times*, 23 Jan 1901
46 *Reynolds*, 29 June 1902
47 Windsor, *King's Story*, p 34
48 *Time*, 2 March 1959
49 Mallet, *Life*, p 225
50 Battiscombe, *Queen Alexandra*, p 206
51 *Ibid*, p 240
52 Ponsonby, *Recollections*, p 105
53 *Ibid*
54 St Aubyn, *Edward VII*, p 119
55 Battiscombe, *Queen Alexandra*, p 71
56 Nicolson, *George V*, pp 518–9n
57 Lee, *Edward VII*, Vol II, pp 4–5
58 St Aubyn, *Edward VII*, p 392
59 Esher, *Towers*, pp 173–4
60 St Aubyn, *Edward VII*, p 481
61 *Ibid*

CHAPTER TWO

1 Margaret Lane in *New Statesman*, 6 May 1953
2 Ziegler, *Crown and People*, p 21
3 Edward Shils and Michael Young in *Sociological Review*, Dec 1953
4 de Stoeckl, *Vanity*, p 98
5 Magnus, *Edward VII*, p 297
6 Nicolson, *George V*, p 80
7 Magnus, *Edward VII*, p 298
8 Windsor, *King's Story*, p 83
9 Esher, *Journals*, Vol I, p 318
10 Magnus, *Edward VII*, p 299
11 Esher, *Journals*, Vol I, p 345
12 Cust, *Edward VII*, pp 34–5
13 *Ibid*, p 11
14 *Ibid* p 16
15 *Ibid*, p 39
16 *Ibid*, p 13
17 Battiscombe, *Queen Alexandra*, p 219
18 Cust, *Edward VII*, p 11
19 Battiscombe, *Queen Alexandra*, p 124
20 Pope-Hennessy, *Queen Mary*, p 375
21 Cust, *Edward VII*, p 34
22 Nicholas II, *Letters*, p 221
23 Ponsonby, *Recollections*, p 151
24 Forbes, *Memories*, p 66
25 Ponsonby, *A Memoir*, p 5
26 Pope-Hennessy, *Queen Mary*, p 362
27 Windsor, *King's Story*, p 51
28 Ponsonby, *Recollections*, p 153
29 Lee, *Edward VII*, p 26
30 Nicolson, *George V*, p 32
31 Pope-Hennessy, *Queen Mary*, p 312
32 Nicolson, *George V*, p 64
33 *Ibid*, p 97
34 Pope-Hennessy, *Queen Mary*, p 357
35 Airlie, *Thatched*, p 106
36 Nicolson, *George V*, p 50
37 St Aubyn, *Edward VII*, p 278
38 Pope-Hennessy, *Queen Mary*, p 258
39 *Ibid*, p 262
40 *Ibid*, p 280
41 *Ibid*, p 372
42 Nicolson, *George V*, p 61
43 Pope-Hennessy, *Queen Mary*, p 366
44 Nicolson, *George V*, p 67
45 Pope-Hennessy, *Queen Mary*, p 367
46 *Ibid*, p 359

CHAPTER THREE

1 Lee, *Edward VII*, Vol II, p 235
2 *Ibid*, p 403
3 Hardinge, *Old Diplomacy*, p 157
4 Hibbert, *Edward VII*, p 273
5 Brook-Shepherd, *Uncle of Europe*, p 282
6 Ponsonby, *Recollections*, p 173
7 Young, *Balfour*, p 247
8 Pope-Hennessy, *Queen Mary*, p 328
9 *Ibid*
10 *Ibid*
11 *Ibid*, p 386
12 Gore, *George V*, p 211
13 Frankland, *Prince Henry*, p 32
14 Nicolson, *Diaries,* p 53
15 Windsor, *King's Story*, p 24
16 Pope-Hennessy, *Queen Mary*, p 258
17 *Ibid*, p 391
18 Wheeler-Bennett, *George VI*, p 13
19 Windsor, *King's Story*, p 26
20 *Ibid*, p 57
21 *Ibid*, p 42
22 *Ibid*, p 29
23 Queen Victoria, *Advice*, p 29
24 Holden, *Charles*, p 8
25 Kenneth Harris in *Observer*, 10 Aug 1980
26 Holden, *Charles*, p 181
27 Pope-Hennessy, *A Lonely Business*, p 231
28 Battiscombe, *Queen Alexandra*, p 121
29 Windsor, *King's Story*, p 15
30 Saunders, *Edward*, pp 17–18
31 Windsor, *King's Story*, p 47
32 *Ibid*, p 48
33 Hibbert, *Edward VII*, p 285
34 St Aubyn, *Edward VII*, p 392
35 Hibbert, *Edward VII*, p 210
36 Jullian, *Edward VII*, p 285
37 Ponsonby, *Recollections*, p 271
38 Hibbert, *Edward VII*, p 290
39 *Ibid*, p 291
40 Nicolson, *George V*, p 105

CHAPTER FOUR

1 Esher, *Journals*, Vol III, p 17
2 *Ibid*, p 49
3 *Ibid*, p 17
4 Gore, *George V*, p 248

5 *Ibid*, p 202
6 Pope-Hennessy, *Queen Mary*, p 423
7 *Ibid*, p 425
8 Gore, *George V*, p 259
9 Nicolson, *George V*, p 147
10 Windsor, *King's Story*, p 78
11 *Ibid*, p 57
12 Gore, *George V*, pp 247–8
13 Windsor, *King's Story*, p 62
14 Bolitho, *Edward VIII*, p 11
15 Wheeler-Bennett, *George VI*, p 41
16 *Times*, 18 Nov 1914
17 Esher, *Journals*, Vol III, pp 108–9
18 Windsor, *King's Story*, p 79
19 *Ibid*
20 Nicolson, *George V*, p 157
21 Esher, *Journals*, Vol III, p 65
22 Nicolson, *George V*, p 308
23 Ziegler, *Crown and People*, p 30
24 Longford, *Royal House*, p 73
25 Pope-Hennessy, *Queen Mary*, p 459
26 Nicolson, *George V*, p 172
27 Gore, *George V*, pp 263–4
28 Carey, *Princess Mary*, p 14
29 Airlie, *Thatched*, p 145
30 Carey, *Princess Mary*, p 29
31 Frankland, *Prince Henry*, p 13
32 *Ibid*, p 27
33 *Ibid*, p 33
34 Windsor, *King's Story*, p 82
35 Pope-Hennessy, *Queen Mary*, p 511
36 Esher, *Journals*, Vol III, p 207
37 Nicolson, *George V*, p 252
38 Windsor, *King's Story*, p 108
39 Esher, *Journals*, Vol III, p 266
40 Wheeler-Bennett, *George VI*, p 97
41 Nicolson, *George V*, p 250
42 *Ibid*, p 308
43 Pope-Hennessy, *Queen Mary*, p 509

CHAPTER FIVE

1 Wheeler-Bennett, *George VI*, p 159
2 *Ibid*, pp 159–60
3 *Ibid*, p 160
4 Nicolson, *George V*, p 341
5 Windsor, *King's Story*, p 83
6 *Ibid*, p 132
7 *Ibid*, p 136
8 Airlie, *Thatched*, p 145
9 Windsor, *King's Story*, p 160
10 *Ibid*, p 132

11 Conv. with Princess Alice
12 Battiscombe, *Queen Alexandra*, p 292
13 *Ibid*, p 286
14 *Ibid*, p 293
15 Windsor, *King's Story*, p 83
16 Battiscombe, *Queen Alexandra*, p 299
17 Ziegler, *Crown and People*, p 47
18 Airlie, *Thatched*, p 128
19 *Ibid*, p 162
20 Lyttelton Hart-Davis, *Letters*, Vol IV, p 161
21 Longford, *Royal House*, p 109
22 Bryan and Murphy, *Windsor Story*, p 118
23 Airlie, *Thatched*, p 129
24 Pope-Hennessy, *Queen Mary*, p 522
25 Hatch, *Mountbattens*, p 124
26 Airlie, *Thatched*, p 146
27 *Ibid*, p 145
28 Bryan and Murphy, *Windsor Story*, p 56
29 Kenneth Harris in *Observer*, 10 Aug 1980
30 St Aubyn, *William of Gloucester*, p 167
31 Wheeler-Bennett, *George VI*, p 147
32 *Ibid*, p 220
33 Airlie, *Thatched*, p 163
34 Longford, *Royal House*, p 78
35 Bryan and Murphy, *Windsor Story*, p 57
36 Airlie, *Thatched*, p 163
37 *Ibid*, p 146
38 Pope-Hennessy, *Queen Mary*, p 153
39 *Ibid*, p 514
40 Bryan and Murphy, *Windsor Story*, p 99
41 Carey, *Princess Mary*, p 113
42 *Ibid*, p 166
43 *Ibid*, p 179
44 Warwick, *Royal Weddings*, p 38
45 Pope-Hennessy, *Queen Mary*, p 520
46 Wheeler-Bennett, *George VI*, p 167
47 Conv. with the Queen Mother
48 *Ibid*, p 150
49 Airlie, *Thatched*, p 167
50 Wheeler-Bennett, *George VI*, p 150
51 *Ibid*, p 151
52 Donaldson, *George VI*, p 32
53 Wheeler-Bennett, *George VI*, p 151
54 Nicolson, *George V*, p 384
55 Clynes, *Memoirs*, pp 343–4

56 Airlie, *Thatched*, p 178
57 Nicolson, *George V*, p 418
58 Gore, *George V*, p 396
59 Wheeler-Bennett, *George VI*, p 216
60 Airlie, *Thatched*, p 180

CHAPTER SIX

1 Bruce-Lockhart, *Diaries*, Vol I, p 147
2 Pope-Hennessy, *Queen Mary*, p 517
3 Donaldson, *Edward VIII*, p 119
4 Windsor, *King's Story*, p 211
5 Windsor, *The Heart*, p 202
6 Vanderbilt, *Double Exposure*, p 246
7 Nicolson, *George V*, p 471
8 Gore, *George V*, p 403
9 Channon, *Chips*, p 50
10 Bryan and Murphy, *Windsor Story*, p 101
11 *Ibid*
12 Bruce-Lockhart, *Diaries*, Vol I, p 264
13 *Ibid*, p 215
14 Airlie, *Thatched*, p 195
15 *Ibid*, p 124
16 *Ibid*, p 200
17 Windsor, *The Heart*, p 211
18 Gore, *George V*, p 411
19 Bruce-Lockhart, *Diaries*, Vol I, p 190
20 Windsor, *King's Story*, p 183
21 Channon, *Chips*, p 32
22 Nicolson, *George V*, p 525
23 Frankland, *Prince Henry*, p 117
24 *Ibid*, p 118
25 *Ibid*
26 *Ibid*, p 121
27 *Ibid*
28 *Ibid*, p 125
29 *Ibid*
30 Gore, *George V*, p 435
31 Middlemas and Barnes, *Baldwin*, p 976
32 Airlie, *Thatched*, p 197
33 Nicolson, *George V*, p 531
34 Pope-Hennessy, *Queen Mary*, p 559
35 *Idem*, *A Lonely Business*, p 230
36 Donaldson, *Edward VIII*, p 181

CHAPTER SEVEN

1 Bryan and Murphy, *Windsor Story*, p 124
2 Nicolson, *Diaries 1930–39*, p 277
3 Channon, *Chips*, p 74

4 *Times*, 22 Jan 1936
5 Windsor, *King's Story*, p 278
6 Ziegler, *Crown and People*, p 200
7 Donaldson, *Edward VIII*, p 205
8 *Ibid*, p 184
9 Windsor, *The Heart*, p 225
10 *Ibid*, p 227
11 Windsor, *King's Story*, p 320
12 Donaldson, *Edward VIII*, p 220
13 Windsor, *King's Story*, p 258
14 Cooper, *Light*, p 73
15 Conv. with Queen Mother
16 Wheeler-Bennett, *George VI*, p 273
17 *Ibid*
18 *Ibid*, p 276
19 *Ibid*, p 277
20 Donaldson, *Edward VIII*, p 226
21 Middlemas and Barnes, *Baldwin*, p 995
22 *Ibid*, p 1007
23 *Ibid*
24 Pope-Hennessy, *Queen Mary*, p 578
25 *Ibid*, p 571
26 Airlie, *Thatched*, p 198
27 Windsor, *King's Story*, p 311
28 *Ibid*, p 334
29 Pope-Hennessy, *Queen Mary*, p 574
30 Donaldson, *Edward VIII*, p 274
31 Windsor, *King's Story*, p 334
32 Bryan and Murphy, *Windsor Story*, p 220
33 Airlie, *Thatched*, pp 198–201
34 Pope-Hennessy, *Queen Mary*, p 576
35 Airlie, *Thatched*, p 200
36 Donaldson, *Edward VIII*, p 250
37 Windsor, *King's Story*, p 335
38 *Ibid*
39 Wheeler-Bennett, *George VI*, p 284
40 Windsor, *King's Story*, p 335
41 Channon, *Chips*, p 91
42 Donaldson, *Edward VIII*, p 250
43 Wheeler-Bennett, *George VI*, p 284
44 Windsor, *King's Story*, p 365
45 Wheeler-Bennett, *George VI*, p 285
46 Windsor, *King's Story*, p 340
47 Windsor, *The Heart*, p 277
48 Donaldson, *Edward VIII*, p 289
49 Windsor, *King's Story*, p 404
50 Airlie, *Thatched*, p 201
51 Wheeler-Bennett, *George VI*, p 283
52 *Ibid*

53 Pope-Hennessy, *Queen Mary*, p 572
54 *Ibid*, p 579
55 Wheeler-Bennett, *George VI*, p 294
56 *Ibid*, p 286
57 Airlie, *Thatched*, p 200
58 Windsor, *King's Story*, p 410
59 Channon, *Chips*, p 103
60 Windsor, *King's Story*, p 414
61 Wheeler-Bennett, *George VI*, p 287

CHAPTER EIGHT

1 Airlie, *Thatched*, p 202
2 *Ibid*
3 Liversidge, *Queen Mother*, p 134
4 Wheeler-Bennett, *George VI*, p 310
5 Alice, Princess, *For My Grandchildren*, p 7
6 Channon, *Chips*, p 104
7 Wheeler-Bennett, *George VI*, p 297
8 *Ibid*
9 *Ibid*, p 296
10 Channon, *Chips*, p 126
11 *Ibid*, p 139
12 Wheeler-Bennett, *George VI*, p 311
13 *Ibid*, p 313
14 Nicolson, *Diaries 1930–39*, p 247
15 Donaldson, *Edward VIII*, p 295
16 *Ibid*, p 322
17 *Ibid*
18 Nicolson, *Diaries 1930–39*, p 405
19 Hartnell, *Silver and Gold*, p 94
20 Cooper, *Light*, p 193
21 Donaldson, *George VI*, p 105
22 Nicolson, *Diaries 1930–39*, p 405
23 *Ibid*, p 298
24 Liversidge, *Queen Mother*, p 99
25 Conv. with Princess Alice
26 Longford, *Queen Mother*, p 72
27 Wheeler-Bennett, *George VI*, p 319
28 *Ibid*, p 377
29 *Ibid*, p 380
30 Conv. with the Queen Mother
31 Wheeler-Bennett, *George VI*, p 380
32 *Ibid*, p 389
33 *Ibid*, p 385
34 *Ibid*, p 380
35 *Ibid*, p 393

CHAPTER NINE

1 Wheeler-Bennett, *George VI*, p 467
2 Ziegler, *Crown and People*, p 72

3 Longford, *Queen Mother*, p 80
4 *Ibid*
5 Wheeler-Bennett, *George VI*, p 479
6 *Ibid*, p 478
7 Longford, *Queen Mother*, p 86
8 Wheeler-Bennett, *George VI*, p 467
9 *Ibid*, p 470
10 Conv. with Queen Mother
11 *Ibid*
12 Wheeler-Bennett, *George VI*, p 552
13 *Ibid*, p 468
14 Shew, *Queen Elizabeth*, p 76
15 Wheeler-Bennett, *George VI*, p 447
16 *Ibid*, p 467
17 Pope-Hennessy, *Queen Mary*, p 596
18 *Ibid*, p 598
19 Alice, Princess, *For My Grandchildren*, p 260
20 *Ibid*, p 255
21 Frankland, *Prince Henry*, p 175
22 Pope-Hennessy, *Queen Mary*, p 609
23 Alice, Princess, *For My Grandchildren*, p 263
24 Sitwell, *Queen Mary*, p 28
25 Windsor, *The Heart*, p 329
26 Bryan and Murphy, *Windsor Story*, p 352
27 Nicolson, *Diaries 1930–39*, p 351–2
28 Wheeler-Bennett, *George VI*, p 417
29 Windsor, *The Heart*, p 355
30 *Ibid*, p 329
31 Bruce-Lockhart, *Diaries*, Vol I, p 413
32 Bryan and Murphy, *Windsor Story*, p 355
33 King, *Princess Marina*, p 151
34 Airlie, *Thatched*, p 195
35 King, *Princess Marina*, p 166
36 *Ibid*, p 158
37 Channon, *Chips*, p 329
38 Frankland, *Prince Henry*, p 161
39 King, *Princess Marina*, p 112
40 Wheeler-Bennett, *George VI*, p 548
41 King, *Princess Marina*, p 177
42 *Ibid*, p 170
43 Frankland, *Prince Henry*, p 174
44 *Ibid*, p 154
45 *Ibid*, p 155
46 *Ibid*, p 158
47 *Ibid*, p 163
48 Channon, *Chips*, p 334
49 *New Statesman*, 11 July 1942

50 Frankland, *Prince Henry*, p 160
51 *Ibid*, p 178
52 *Ibid*, p 175
53 *Ibid*, p 176
54 *Ibid*, p 177
55 *Ibid*, p 179
56 Wheeler-Bennett, *George VI*, p 553
57 *Ibid*, p 611
58 *Ibid*, p 570
59 Churchill, *Second World War*, Vol II, p 335
60 Wheeler-Bennett, *George VI*, p 558
61 *Times*, 18 May 1943
62 Wheeler-Bennett, *George VI*, p 606
63 *Ibid*, p 627

CHAPTER TEN

1 Wheeler-Bennett, *George VI*, p 650
2 *Ibid*, p 565
3 *Ibid*, p 654
4 *Ibid*, p 665
5 Longford, *Royal House*, p 196
6 Boothroyd, *Philip*, p 50
7 Hibbert, *Court of St James's*, p 211
8 Wheeler-Bennett, *George VI*, p 626
9 Airlie, *Thatched*, p 224
10 *Ibid*
11 *Ibid*, p 225
12 Conv. with Queen Mother
13 *Ibid*
14 Van der Byl, *Shadows*, p 123
15 *Cape Times*, 25 April 1947
16 Wheeler-Bennett, *George VI*, p 692
17 *Ibid*, p 691
18 King, *Princess Marina*, p 151
19 Frankland, *Prince Henry*, p 214
20 *Ibid*, p 182
21 *Ibid*, p 192
22 *Ibid*, p 214
23 Airlie, *Thatched*, p 230
24 Wheeler-Bennett, *George VI*, p 749
25 *Daily Express*, 11 July 1947
26 Ziegler, *Crown and People*, p 84
27 *Ibid*
28 Wheeler-Bennett, *George VI*, p 753
29 *Ibid*, p 755
30 Harewood, *Tongs and Bones*, p 27
31 *Ibid*, p 26
32 *Ibid*, p 18
33 *Ibid*, p 92
34 Wheeler-Bennett, *George VI*, p 379

35 *Ibid*, p 716
36 *Ibid*, p 726
37 *Ibid*, p 728
38 Private information
39 Morrah, *To Be a King*, p 21
40 Wheeler-Bennett, *George VI*, p 740
41 Longford, *Royal House*, p 198
42 Longford, *Queen Mother*, p 97
43 Van der Byl, *Shadows Lengthen*, p 137
44 Wheeler-Bennett, *George VI*, p 762
45 Channon, *Chips*, p 463
46 Boothroyd, *Philip*, p 148
47 Ziegler, *Crown and People*, p 86

CHAPTER ELEVEN

1 Longford, *Royal House*, p 205
2 Channon, *Chips*, p 463
3 *Ibid*, p 473
4 Sitwell, *Queen Mary*, p 40
5 Morley, *Gertrude Lawrence*, pp 178–9
6 Conv. with Prince Charles
7 Pope-Hennessy, *Queen Mary*, p 619
8 Channon, *Chips*, p 473
9 Sitwell, *Queen Mary*, p 60
10 Channon, *Chips*, p 439
11 *Times*, 24 Oct 1955
12 *Ibid*
13 King, *Princess Marina*, p 212
14 *National and English Review*, August 1957
15 Ziegler, *Crown and People*, p 132
16 Longford, *Royal House*, p 236
17 Nicolson, *Diaries, 1945–62*
18 Hibbert, *Court of St James's*, p 164
19 Boothroyd, *Philip*, p 226
20 Andrew Duncan in *Sunday Telegraph Magazine*, 7 June 1981
21 *Ibid*
22 Boothroyd, *Philip*, p 198
23 *Ibid*, 183
24 *Ibid*, 223
25 *Ibid*, p 47
26 *Ibid*, p 226
27 *Ibid*, p 46
28 Longford, *Royal House*, p 240
29 *Times*, 27 Feb 1960
30 *New Statesman*, 30 April 1960
31 Kenneth Harris in *Observer*, 10 Aug 1980

CHAPTER TWELVE

1 Holden, *Charles*, p 94
2 Holden, *Charles*, p 95
3 Howard, *British Monarchy*, p 128
4 Bagehot, *English Constitution*, p 53
5 Holden, *Charles*, p 134
6 *Ibid*, p 140
7 *Ibid*, p 143
8 *Ibid*, p 167
9 Private information
10 Talbot, *Royal Family*, p 169
11 King, *Princess Marina*, p 202
12 Clark, *Palace Diary*, p 143
13 Macmillan, *Pointing the Way*, p 472
14 Longford, *Royal House*, p 238
15 Howard, *British Monarchy*, p 65
16 Macmillan, *Pointing the Way*, p 472
17 *Ibid*
18 Howard, *British Monarchy*, p 64
19 *Cape Argus*, 28 July 1979
20 Frankland, *Prince Henry*, p 248
21 *Ibid*, p 262
22 Conv. with Sir Simon Bland
23 Conv. with Lord Napier
24 St Aubyn, *William of Gloucester*, p 175
25 *Ibid*, p 167
26 *Ibid*, p 186
27 *Ibid*, p 85
28 *Ibid*, p 128
29 *Ibid*, p 169
30 Conv. with Princess Alice
31 Windsor, *Family Album*, p 103
32 Windsor, *The Heart*, p 366
33 Sultzberger, *Age of Mediocrity*, p 581
34 Holden, *Charles*, p 33
35 Bryan and Murphy, *Windsor Story*, p 551
36 Kenneth Harris in *Observer*, 17 Aug 1980
37 *Ibid*
38 *Spectator*, 16 Oct 1982
39 *Times*, 23 Nov 1982
40 Select Committee 1971, XVII

CHAPTER THIRTEEN

1 Conv. with Princess Alice
2 Longford, *Queen Mother*, p 119
3 Conv. with the Queen Mother
4 Howard, *British Monarchy*, p 139
5 Nicolson, *Diaries 1945–62*, p 354
6 Conv. with the Queen Mother
7 Donaldson, *George VI*, p 115
8 Duncan, *Reality of Monarchy*, p 184
9 Private information
10 Conv. with the Queen Mother
11 Longford, *Queen Mother*, p 135
12 Talbot, *Queen Mother*, Foreword
13 Howard, *British Monarchy*, p 92
14 Harewood, *Tongs and Bones*, p 295
15 *Ibid*
16 Private information
17 Quoted in Hibbert, *Court of St James's*, p 226
18 *Times*, 1 Feb 1982
19 Hibbert, *Court of St James's*, p 109
20 *Times*, 7 Feb 1982
21 Private information
22 Conv. with Princess Alice
23 Howard, *British Monarchy*, p 108
24 Ziegler, *Crown and People*, p 183
25 Conv. with Prince Charles
26 *Ibid*
27 Holden, *Charles*, p 266
28 Conv. with Prince Charles
29 Kenneth Harris in *Observer*, 17 Aug 1980
30 Frankland, *Prince Henry*, p 127
31 Holden, *Their Royal Highnesses*, p 49
32 *Times*, 16 July 1980
33 Private information
34 *Express*, 4 Aug 1980
35 Townsend, *Time and Chance*, p 164
36 St Aubyn, *William of Gloucester*, p 169
37 Bryan and Murphy, *Windsor Story*, p 560
38 *Ibid*, p 568
39 *Ibid*
40 Holden, *Their Royal Highnesses*, p 41
41 *Ibid*, p 67
42 TV Interview, 24 Feb 1981
43 Bagehot, *English Constitution*, p 38
44 Sampson, *Changing Anatomy*, p 8
45 Alan Hamilton in *The Times*, 1 Feb 1982
46 *Ibid*
47 Holden, *Charles*, p 268
48 *Times*, 22 June 1982
49 *Express*, 5 August 1982

Bibliography

Airlie, Mabell, Countess of, *Thatched with Gold*, Hutchinson, London 1962
Alexandra of Yugoslavia, Queen, *Prince Philip: A Family Portrait*, Hodder & Stoughton, London, 1960
Alice, Countess of Athlone, Princess, *For My Grandchildren*, Evans, London, 1966
Alice, Duchess of Gloucester, Princess, *Memoirs*, Collins, London, 1983
Arthur, Sir George, *Queen Alexandra*, Chapman & Hall, London, 1934
Asquith, Lady Cynthia, *The Duchess of York*, Hutchinson, London, 1928
 – *The Married Life of the Duchess of York*, Hutchinson, London, 1933
 – *The Family Life of Queen Elizabeth*, Hutchinson, London, 1937
 – *The King's Daughters*, Hutchinson, London, 1937
Asquith, Margot, *Places and Persons*, Thornton Butterworth, London, 1925
Avon, The Earl of, *The Memoirs of the Rt Hon Sir Anthony Eden*, 3 vols., Cassell, London, 1960–1965

Bagehot, Walter, *The English Constitution*, Kegan Paul, London, 1898
Battiscombe, Georgina, *Queen Alexandra*, Constable, London, 1969
Beaton, Cecil, *Photobiography*, Odhams, London, 1951
 – *Diaries*, 3 vols., Weidenfeld & Nicolson, London, 1961–1978
Beaverbrook, Lord, *The Abdication of King Edward VIII*, Hamish Hamilton, London, 1966
Bennett, Daphne, *Vicky*, Collins, London, 1971
Benson, E.F., *King Edward VII*, Longman, London, 1933
Bloch, Michael, *The Duke of Windsor's War*, Weidenfeld & Nicolson, London 1982
Bolitho, Hector, *King Edward VIII*, Eyre & Spottiswoode, London, 1937
Boothroyd, Basil, *Philip: An Informal Biography*, Longman, London, 1971
Brook-Shepherd, Gordon, *Uncle of Europe*, Collins, London, 1975
Bruce-Lockhart, Sir Robert, *Diaries 1915–1938* (ed. Kenneth Young), Macmillan, London, 1973
Bryan III, J. and Murphy, J.V., *The Windsor Story*, Granada, London 1979
Burton, Aubrey, *The King in his Country*, Longman, London, 1955
Butler, R.A., *The Art of the Possible: Memoirs of Lord Butler*, Hamish Hamilton, London, 1971

Carey, M.C., *Princess Mary*, Nisbet & Company, London, 1922

Cathcart, Helen, *Her Majesty*, W.H. Allen, London, 1962
– *Prince Charles: The Biography*, W.H. Allen, London, 1976
Channon, Sir Henry, *Chips*, Weidenfeld & Nicolson, London, 1967
Churchill, Randolph S., *They Serve the Queen*, Hutchinson, London, 1953
Churchill, Winston S., *The Second World War*, 5 vols., Cassell, London,
    1948–54
Clark, Stanley, *Palace Diary*, Harrap, London, 1958
Clynes, J.R., *Memoirs 1924–1937*, Hutchinson, London, 1937
Colville, John, *The New Elizabethans, 1952–1977*, Collins, London, 1977
Connell, Brian, *Manifest Destiny*, Cassell, London, 1953
Cooper, Diana, *The Light of Common Day*, Hart-Davis, London, 1959
Cooper, Duff, *Old Men Forget*, Hart-Davis, London, 1953
Coulter, John (Editor), *Queen Victoria: Her Gracious Life and Glorious Reign*,
    World Publishers, Ontario, 1901
Cowles, Virginia, *Edward VII and his Circle*, Hamish Hamilton, London, 1956
Crawford, Marion, *The Little Princesses*, Cassell, London, 1950
Crossman, R.H., *The Diaries of a Cabinet Minister*, Jonathan Cape/Hamish
    Hamilton, London, 1975
Cust, Sir Lionel, *King Edward VII and his Court*, John Murray, London, 1930

Dean, John, *H.R.H. Prince Philip, Duke of Edinburgh: A Portrait by his Valet*,
    Robert Hale, London, 1954
Dempster, Nigel, *H.R.H. The Princess Margaret: A Life Unfulfilled*, Quartet
    Books, London, 1981
Dennis, Geoffrey, *Coronation Commentary*, Heinemann, London, 1937
Donaldson, Frances, *Edward VIII*, Weidenfeld & Nicolson, London, 1974
– *King George VI and Queen Elizabeth*, Weidenfeld & Nicolson, London,
    1977
Duncan, Andrew, *The Reality of Monarchy*, Heinemann, London, 1970

Esher, R.B.B., 2nd Viscount, *Cloud-capp'd Towers*, John Murray, London,
    1927
– *Journals and Letters*, 4 vols., I. Nicholson & Watson, London, 1934–8

Fisher, Graham and Heather, *The Queen's Life*, Robert Hale, London, 1976
Fisher, J.A.F., Baron, *Memories*, Hodder & Stoughton, London, 1919
Forbes, Lady Angela, *Memories and Base Details*, Hutchinson, London, 1921
Frankland, Noble, *Prince Henry, Duke of Gloucester*, Weidenfeld & Nicolson,
    London, 1980
Frere, J.A., *The British Monarchy at Home*, Gibbs & Phillips, London, 1963

Gore, John, *King George V: A Personal Memoir*, John Murray, London, 1941
Grey, Edward, 1st Viscount, *Twenty-Five Years, 1892–1916*, Hodder &
    Stoughton, London, 1925

Hamilton, Willie, *My Queen and I*, Quartet Books, London, 1975
Hancock, W.K., *Smuts*, 2 vols., Cambridge University Press, 1968

Hardie, Frank, *The Political Influence of the British Monarchy 1868–1952*, Batsford, London, 1970

Hardinge, Helen, *Loyal to Three Kings*, William Kimber, London, 1967

Hardinge, Lord, *Old Diplomacy*, John Murray, London, 1947

Harewood, Rt Hon the Earl of, *The Tongs and the Bones*, Weidenfeld & Nicolson, London, 1981

Harris, Leonard M., *Long to Reign over Us*, William Kimber, London, 1966

Hartnell, Norman, *Silver and Gold*, Evans Brothers, London, 1955
– *Royal Courts of Fashion*, Cassell, London, 1971

Hatch, Alden, *The Mountbattens*, Random House, New York, 1965

Hibbert, Christopher, *The Court at Windsor*, Longman, London, 1964
– *Edward VII: A Portrait*, Allen Lane, London, 1976
– *The Court of St James's*, Weidenfeld & Nicolson, London, 1979

Holden, Anthony, *Charles, Prince of Wales*, Weidenfeld & Nicolson, London, 1979
– *Their Royal Highnesses*, Weidenfeld & Nicolson, London, 1981

Howard, Philip, *The Royal Palaces*, Hamish Hamilton, London, 1970
– *The British Monarchy in the Twentieth Century*, Hamish Hamilton, London, 1977

Hyde, H. Montgomery, *Baldwin, the Unexpected Prime Minister*, Hart-Davis Macgibbon, London, 1973

Inglis, Brian, *Abdication*, Hodder & Stoughton, London, 1966

Judd, Denis, *Edward VII: A Pictorial Biography*, Macdonald & Jane, London, 1975
– *King George VI*, Michael Joseph, London, 1982

Jullian, Philippe, *Edward and the Edwardians*, Sidgwick & Jackson, London, 1967

Kidd, Charles and Montague-Smith, Patrick, *Royal Children*, Debrett, London, 1982

King, Stella, *Princess Marina: Her Life and Times*, Cassell, London, 1969

Lacey, Robert, *Majesty: Elizabeth II and the House of Windsor*, Hutchinson, London, 1977
– *Princess*, Hutchinson, London, 1982

Laird, Dorothy, *How the Queen Reigns*, Hodder & Stoughton, London, 1959
– *Queen Elizabeth the Queen Mother*, Hodder & Stoughton, London, 1966

Lawrence, Gertrude, *A Star Danced*, Doubleday, New York, 1945

Lee, Sir Sydney, *King Edward VII*, 2 vols., Macmillan, London, 1927

Leslie, Anita, *The Gilt and the Gingerbread*, Hutchinson, London, 1981

Liversidge, Douglas, *The Queen Mother*, Arthur Barker, London, 1977

Longford, Elizabeth, *Victoria R.I.*, Weidenfeld & Nicolson, London, 1964
– *The Royal House of Windsor*, Weidenfeld & Nicolson, London, 1974
– *The Queen Mother*, Weidenfeld & Nicolson, London, 1981

Lyttelton, G. and Hart-Davis, R., *The Lyttelton Hart-Davis Letters*, 6 vols., John Murray, London, 1978–84

Macmillan, Sir Harold, *Pointing the Way*, Macmillan, London, 1966–73
Macdonnaugh, Michael, *The English King: A Study of the Monarchy and the Royal Family*, Ernest Benn, London, 1929
Magnus, Sir Philip, *King Edward the Seventh*, John Murray, London, 1964
Mallet, Marie, *Life with Queen Victoria*, John Murray, London, 1968
Marie Louise, Princess, *My Memories of Six Reigns*, Evans, London, 1956
Marlborough, Laura, Duchess of, *Laughter from a Cloud*, Weidenfeld & Nicolson, London, 1980
Marples, Morris, *Princes in the Making: A Study of Royal Education*, Faber & Faber, London, 1965
Martin, Kingsley, *The Crown and the Establishment*, Hutchinson, London, 1962
Martin, Ralph G., *The Woman He Loved*, W.H. Allen, London, 1974
Masters, Brian, *Dreams about H.M. the Queen and other members of the Royal Family*, Blond & Briggs, London, 1972
Middlemas, K. and Barnes, J., *Baldwin*, Weidenfeld & Nicolson, London, 1969
Minney, R.J., *The Edwardian Age*, Cassell, London, 1964
Morley, Sheridan, *Gertrude Lawrence*, Weidenfeld & Nicolson, London, 1981
Morrah, Dermot, *The Royal Family in Africa*, Hutchinson, London, 1947
 – *The Work of the Queen*, William Kimber, London, 1958
 – *To Be a King*, Hutchinson, London, 1968
Murray-Brown, J. (Editor), *The Monarchy and its Future*, George Allen & Unwin, London, 1969

Nicholas II, Tsar of Russia, *The Letters of Tsar Nicholas and Empress Marie*, Ivor Nicholson & Watson, London, 1937
Nicolson, Harold, *King George the Fifth*, Constable, London, 1952
 – *Diaries and Letters*, 3 vols., Collins, London, 1966–68

Peacocke, Marguerite, *The Story of Buckingham Palace*, Odhams Press, London, 1951
Petrie, Sir Charles, *The Modern British Monarchy*, Eyre & Spottiswoode, London, 1961
Philip, H.R.H. Prince, *Selected Speeches*, Oxford University Press, 1957
 – *Prince Philip Speaks*, Collins, London, 1960
 – *A Question of Balance*, Michael Russell, London, 1982
Ponsonby, Arthur, *Henry Ponsonby: His Life from his Letters*, Macmillan, London, 1943
Ponsonby, Frederick, *Recollections of Three Reigns*, Eyre & Spottiswoode, London, 1951
Ponsonby, Mary, *A Memoir, Some Letters and a Journal*, John Murray, London, 1927

Pope-Hennessy, James, *Queen Mary 1867–1953*, George Allen & Unwin, London, 1959
Portland, William Cavendish-Bentinck, 6th Earl of, *Men, Women and Things*, Faber & Faber, London, 1937

Quennell, P. (Editor), *A Lonely Business*, Weidenfeld & Nicolson, London, 1981

Roby, Kinley, *The King, the Press and the People*, Barrie & Jenkins, London, 1975
Rose, Kenneth, *The Later Cecils*, Weidenfeld & Nicolson, London, 1945
Russell, Peter, *Butler Royal*, Hutchinson, London, 1982

St Aubyn, Giles (Editor), *William of Gloucester: Pioneer Prince*, Frederick Muller, London, 1977
– *Edward VII*, Collins, London, 1979
Sampson, Anthony, *The Changing Anatomy of Britain*, Hodder & Stoughton, London, 1982
Saunders, G. Ivy, *Edward, Prince of Wales*, Nisbet, London, 1921
Select Committee on the Civil List, 1971, Report, with Minutes of Evidence, HMSO 22 November 1971
Shew, Betty Spencer, *Queen Elizabeth, The Queen Mother*, Macdonald, London, 1955
Sitwell, Osbert, *Queen Mary and Others*, Michael Joseph, London, 1974
Stamper, C.W., *What I Know*, Mills & Boon, London, 1913
Stevas, Norman St John, *Walter Bagehot*, Eyre & Spottiswoode, London, 1959
Stoeckl, Agnes, Baroness de, *Not all Vanity*, John Murray, London, 1952
Sulzberger, C.L., *An Age of Mediocrity: Memoirs and Diaries*, Macmillan, New York, 1973

Talbot, Godfrey, *The Country Life Book of Queen Elizabeth the Queen Mother*, Country Life Books, Richmond, 1978
– *Royal Family*, Country Life Books, Richmond, 1980
Townsend, Peter, *The Last Emperor*, Weidenfeld & Nicolson, London, 1975
– *Time and Chance: An Autobiography*, Collins, London, 1978
Turner, E.S., *The Court of St James's*, Michael Joseph, London, 1959

Vanderbilt, Gloria, and Furness, Thelma, *Double Exposure*, Frederick Muller, London, 1959
Van der Byl, Piet, *The Shadows Lengthen*, Howard Timmins, Cape Town, 1973
Vickers, Hugo, *Debrett's Book of the Royal Wedding*, Debrett, London, 1981
Victoria, Queen, *Dearest Mama: Letters between Queen Victoria and the Crown Princess of Prussia*, (ed. Roger Fulford), Evans Brothers, London, 1968
– *Advice to a Grand-daughter*, Heinemann, London, 1975

Wakeford, Geoffrey, *The Heir Apparent*, Robert Hale, London, 1967
Warwick, Christopher, *Two Centuries of Royal Weddings*, Arthur Barker, London, 1980
– *Princess Margaret*, Weidenfeld & Nicolson, London, 1983
Warwick, Daisy, Countess of, *Afterthoughts*, Cassell, London, 1931
Wentworth Day, J., *H.R.H. Princess Marina, Duchess of Kent*, Robert Hale, London, 1962
Wheeler-Bennett, Sir John, *King George VI*, Macmillan, London, 1958
Windsor, H.R.H. The Duke of, *A King's Story*, Cassell, London, 1951
– *A Family Album*, Cassell, London, 1960
Windsor, Duchess of, *The Heart Has Its Reasons*, Michael Joseph, London, 1956

Young, Kenneth, *Arthur James Balfour*, Bell, London, 1963

Ziegler, Philip, *Crown and People*, Collins, London, 1978

Index